한국말 하시네요!

You Speak Korean!

First-year College Korean
Volume II

Second Edition

Library of Congress Cataloging-in-Publication Data

한국말 하시네요! / *You Speak Korean!*

First-year College Korean, Volume II (Second Edition)
Soohee Kim, Emily Curtis, Haewon Cho.

ISBN 0-9728356-5-2 (paperback)

1. Korean language – textbooks.
2. Korean language – grammar.

Clip art courtesy of *Microsoft Corporation.*

Additional clip art courtesy of the *Purdue Japanese Language Project*.

Cover Design by Dianne Gardner.

Printed by 동방 Bindery, Seong Dong Gu, Seoul, Republic of Korea.

www.ParadigmBusters.com

한국말 하시네요!

You Speak Korean!

First-year College Korean
Volume II
(Second Edition)

Soohee Kim
Emily Curtis
Haewon Cho

ACKNOWLEDGMENTS

We would like to acknowledge the Korea Foundation for their sponsorship and support in the form of a publisher's grant. The grant would not have been earned without the much-appreciated letter of review of Dr. Ross King of the University of British Columbia and Concordia Language Villages. Dr. King's review was exceptionally positive, thorough, thoughtful and fair. This edition has benefited enormously from his extensive comments and suggestions as well as his general review and linguistic analyses. We are thrilled to have such a colleague. We also thank Dr. Joe Ree of Florida State University for his letter of review, Nora Tums for editing and managing, Dianne Gardner for the cover design, and Jeehun Kim and Youngji Kim for their valuable feedback and volunteer work. Finally, we thank Microsoft Corporation and the Purdue University Japanese Language program for access to their clip art. Any errors remaining in the current edition are our own.

TABLE OF CONTENTS

INTRODUCTION TO THE TEXTBOOK

NOTE TO STUDENTS

This textbook was originally intended for a first-year classroom course for students with no background in the Korean language, but can be a fun and useful self-study book as well, especially with the help of a Korean-speaker friend or tutor. There are accompanying workbooks, and some online listening materials are available on the publisher's website. Students are encouraged to read the CONTENT and ORGANIZATION sections below. This particular volume is a continuation of **한국말 하시네요! / *You Speak Korean!* First Year College Korean Volume I.** It is intended that the two volumes together comprise the first year of a college-level course.

NOTE TO TEACHERS

This textbook is generally intended for a first-year classroom course for students with no background in the Korean language, although it can be a fun and useful self-study book as well.

The textbook can successfully be used in the classroom under the guidance of an experienced teacher, who will provide some supplementary activities for practice of the grammatical points and vocabulary introduced as well as basic reading, writing, speaking and listening practice.

The textbook exercises are generally intended to be oral, partner or group activities for classroom practice, though many can be used as homework (writing) exercises, even redundantly after classroom use. The accompanying workbook (Workbook to Accompany 한국말 하시네요! You Speak Korean!) provides more homework and listening activities. Audio material is also available on the publisher's website.

CONTENT

In determining the grammar and vocabulary to include, we have considered the conventions in many other textbooks – for Korean and other languages, -- and the linguistic structures of Korean and English, and we have tried to keep a balance between expressions and constructions English-speaking college students will want to know at an early learning stage as well as natural, frequently-occurring and useful expressions in Korean. We focus on the -어요 and -으세요 endings, as they are the most commonly used forms in spoken Korean. (-ㅂ니다 and the written -ㄴ다 forms are reserved for the second year course). Once students master the regular consonant- and vowel-ending verbs in the 어요 forms and with other connectors, the irregular verbs and adjectives (ㅂ-, 으-, ㅎ-, ㄹ-irregulars) are more readily learned. All forms and vocabulary are reinforced throughout the textbook, and at various points, summary charts and tables are included to help students to recall and categorize earlier grammar and vocabulary while incorporating new forms.

Vocabulary is introduced thematically and grammar by increasing difficulty or inversely by frequency of use. Both are introduced via natural, spoken dialogues. Grammar explanations are brief and as non-technical as possible, but examples and exercises are ample and carefully chosen to illustrate both usage and semantic nuance. (Explanation of the organization of the textbook is provided below.)

ORGANIZATION

The material in this textbook is intended to fill one academic year of a standard, non-intensive college-level introductory course (or a one-quarter, intensive course, where applicable). Earlier chapters are shorter and contain less difficult grammar lessons, so they are covered more quickly.

The **Preliminary** chapter is structured somewhat differently from the others to allow students to learn Han'gul, basic vocabulary and useful phrases before delving into grammar lessons. Having learned the preliminary material, students are prepared for an immersion classroom environment (where only Korean is used). Material in the Preliminary chapter is fundamental and should be taught before beginning Chapter 1. It will also be convenient for students to refer back to the lists and charts therein.

There are then six numbered **chapters** in the year-long course (Volumes 1 and 2). Each numbered chapter presents a unified theme or storyline, such as 'In the Classroom" or "Vacation." Each chapter has four **Lessons** that consist of a main **Vocabulary** lesson, a **Dialogue**[1], **Grammar** points and **Exercises** and finally, a **Checkpoint** that includes short readings including all the grammar points from the lesson. The vocabulary and main grammar point for each section are linked and exemplified in the dialogue. The grammar point is a useful structure, however, and vocabulary is complete along a theme (e.g. classroom items) so that students can go beyond the contents of the dialogue to discuss their own experiences and to understand the experiences of others, especially Koreans.

Vocabulary sections introduce basic, useful vocabulary *by theme*. For example, there are vocabulary sections on school subjects, clothing, food and everyday activities (verbs). Vocabulary sections are extensive to allow students to be conversant along a given theme regardless of the dialogue content or their own experiences. Vocabulary sections are thus lessons in their own right and should be covered before moving on to the dialogues. Vocabulary-learning exercises are provided in the textbook and in the workbook to help students to learn the vocabulary, which is essential for communication.

Introducing vocabulary by theme helps students to categorize new words and at times to see linguistic relationships, both of which help students to memorize and recall vocabulary. As much as possible, pictures are used alongside new vocabulary and as models for exercises in order to encourage students to associate Korean words with *concepts*, and not (only) with English words.

Vocabulary exercises are included to help students learn tactics for memorizing vocabulary, such as forming semantic categories, and for getting students to use the vocabulary right off the bat.

Dialogues make use of the preceding vocabulary from Vocabulary sections and preceding chapters, and they focus on a particular grammatical structure. Dialogues can be read for basic comprehension and as examples of vocabulary usage when the immediately preceding Vocabulary has been learned (passive/recognition stage). Dialogues can be re-examined as *examples* of the grammatical structures presented in the following Grammar section. And finally, the dialogues serve as a review once the Grammar section is completed. They may thus be practiced aloud several times or even memorized for classroom presentation.

Dialogues are generally written in the polite (요) form and focus on everyday conversational styles that learners of Korean may encounter and need to be familiar with. Vocabulary and grammar points also focus on spoken Korean and we are careful to point out differences in natural, spoken forms versus more formal, written forms, such as 봐요/보아요 or 그럼/그러면.

Where it arises, additional vocabulary necessary for understanding the dialogue is glossed in the right-hand margin of each dialogue.

[1] The dialogue may be a conversation, a monologue or a written passage, but it is labeled *dialogue* for simplicity.

Grammar sections are divided into one main point or **Focus** and smaller, numbered grammar points. A typical grammar **Focus** is a grammatical structure, such as a verb conjugation (e.g. the past tense, p-irregular verbs, etc.). Many times, the **Vocabulary** section consists of verbs and adjectives that should be conjugated according to the Grammar Focus. The **Dialogue** is intended to thoroughly exemplify the main grammar Focus. **Other Grammar Notes** are smaller lessons, such as new particles. These are also exemplified in the dialogue.

In the **Grammar** sections, care is taken to provide *brief* grammatical explanations that are clear and precise but not overly technical. Where confusion with other forms in Korean is common, a special note is made alongside a warning icon. Examples are provided of correct, and at times incorrect, usage of the grammar structures.

Exercises for all grammar points follow the Grammar section. Early exercises focus on one grammar point, while later exercises may combine grammar points. Each exercise has a title that should help to determine the intended focus. Instructions are provided in English for clarity and simplicity. Most exercises are readily used in the classroom as group or partner activities, and many can additionally be used as homework (written) practice.

At the end of each lesson is a **Checkpoint**; two or more readings that further exemplify and bring together the grammar points learned in the lesson. The idea is that if students can understand the **Checkpoint** materials, they are ready to move on.

Pronunciation, linguistic and cultural points and songs are added where relevant between main sections. Instructors may wish to spend class time further exemplifying or discussing these points.

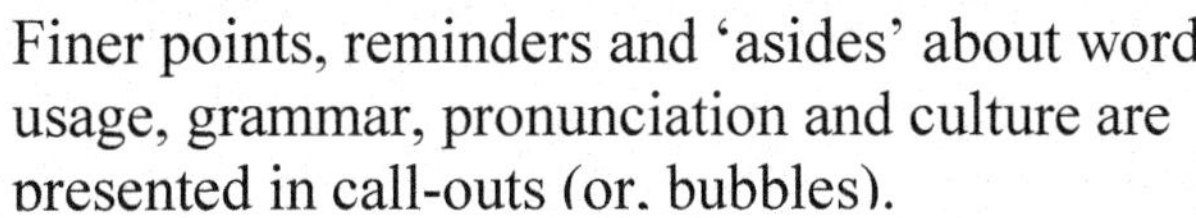

Finer points, reminders and 'asides' about word usage, grammar, pronunciation and culture are presented in call-outs (or, bubbles).

Finally, like some of the materials in the Preliminary Chapter, some topics are best learned as small, individual lessons – for example, telling time. These topics are presented in the **Let's Take a Break** lessons (Chapters 1.5, 2.5, etc.). The Break material is as relevant as the rest, and is integrated into the main text once it has been covered.

SECOND EDITION

The first edition having been used in several schools over three years (including manuscript form), a good number of comments and suggestions were gathered from students and instructors and have been integrated into this Second Edition. In addition to the correction of typos, translation errors and missing text or images, several grammar explanations were improved upon (notably the explanation of comparatives in Lesson 20), and exercises were added and reordered in some lessons.

Those who have the first edition may encounter confusion with the ordering of exercises and some repagination.

We will continue to collect and integrate users' comments in order to make the use of the textbook maximally successful. Please feel free to contact the publisher with your comments and suggestions (email to: paradigmbusters@comcast.net).

CHAPTER 4 뭐 먹을래요?

What do you wanna eat?

Preliminary Dialogue

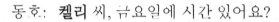

동호: **켈리** 씨, 금요일에 시간 있어요?

켈리: 한국어 수업 끝나고 시간 있어요. 왜요?

동호: 우리 엄마가 갈비를 만들 거에요[1]. 저녁에 우리 집에 오세요[2]!

켈리: 와! 갈비요? 좋아요! 나는 갈비를 아주 좋아해요!

동호: 그럼 한국어 수업 끝나고 나서, 학생회관 앞에서 만나요.

켈리: 네, 좋아요. 그 때[3] 봐요!

[1] is going to make

[2] Please come!

[3] then (at that time)

Dialogue practice

Practice the preliminary dialogue with a classmate.

Culture Point 많이 먹어요! (Eat a lot!)

Food and eating are very important in Korean culture. You will likely be invited to a Korean meal very early in your relationship with a Korean friend, so pay attention to this chapter! 많이 먹어요!

LESSON 13
갈비에는 뭐가 들어가요?

Lesson 13 Vocabulary  재료 *Ingredients*

채소 = 야채	Vegetables
1) 배추; 양배추	Napa cabbage; cabbage
2) 상추	lettuce
3) 파; 양파	scallion; onion
4) 무 = 무우	icicle radish
5) 당근 = 홍당무	carrot
6) 감자; 고구마	potato; sweet potato
7) 토마토	tomato
8) 오이	cucumber
9) 호박	squash (zucchini, pumpkin)
10) 버섯	mushroom
11) 시금치	spinach
12) 콩; 팥	(black) bean; red bean
13) 콩나물	bean sprouts
고기, 해물, 기타	**Meat, seafood, and others**
14) 소고기	beef
15) 닭고기	chicken
16) 돼지고기	pork
17) 생선	fish
18) 오징어	squid
19) 계란 = 달걀	eggs
20) 두부	tofu
21) 국수; 당면	noodles; clear noodles
22) 김	seaweed
23) 빵	bread
24) 쌀; 밥	uncooked rice; cooked rice, meal
	Cooking-related verbs and adjectives
25) 끓이다	boil (something)
26) 썰다	cut, chop
27) 들다	pick up; eat
28) 팔다	sell
29) 얼다	(something) freezes, is frozen
30) 갈다	grate (onions); sharpen (a knife)
31) 연하다	tender, weak (e.g., coffee, tea)
32) 질기다	tough, chewy
33) 진하다	strong (e.g., coffee, tea)
34) 중요하다	important
35) 오래 =오랫동안	(for) a long while

Another member in the 추 family is 상추, lettuce. Ask about 상추쌈, a delicious traditional lettuce wrap, when you visit a local restaurant!

It seems backwards, but *fish* that is alive in water are called 물고기!

"fried" eggs are called 계란 "후라이"!

In spoken Korean, concrete adjectives that can show *degree* are often **emphasized**:
진해요 → 찐해요 (quite strong)
질겨요 → 찔겨요 (quite tough and chewy)

Vocabulary Exercise 1. 어느 거 더 잘 먹어요? ***(which do you like more?)***
Circle your favorite among each set of foods – or list another in the same category.

1) 배추 시금치 콩나물
2) 오이 토마토 당근
3) 콩 두부 계란
4) 소고기 닭고기 돼지고기 생선
5) 빵 국수 감자

Vocabulary Exercise 2. How about you?
Answer the following questions.

1) _____씨는 샐러드에 무엇을 넣어요? 배추, 양배추, 파, 양파, 무, 당근, 홍당무, 토마토, 오이, 버섯, 시금치, 콩나물?
2) 프렌치 프라이는 뭐로 만들어요?
3) _____씨는 피자에 뭐 넣어요? 양파, 토마토, 버섯, 시금치, 소고기, 소세지, 치즈, 살라미?
4) _____씨는 버섯을 잘 먹어요?
5) _____씨는 오징어 먹어 봤어요 (tried eating)?
6) 보통 미국 식 아침밥이나 데니스 (Denny's) 아침밥에는 뭐가 있어요?
7) 라면, 스파게티하고 우동은 어떤 음식이에요? 고기, 국수, 채소 아니면 (or) 빵?
8) 무슨 채소를 좋아해요? / 무슨 채소를 싫어해요?
9) 무슨 고기를 좋아해요? / 무슨 고기를 싫어해요?
10) 무슨 과일을 좋아해요? / 무슨 과일을 싫어해요?

Vocabulary Exercise 3. Western Menu
Design several well-balanced meals (western-style) using the vocabulary.

Culture Point *Eat your veggies!*

Korean cuisine tends to have a lot of (healthy) vegetables, but mainly in cooked dishes or *kimchi*! So Korean kids just eat them right up!

노래하고 갑시다!

사과같은 내 얼굴

사과같은 내 얼굴.	My face, like an apple.
예쁘기도 하지요.	How pretty it is!
눈도 반짝 코도 반짝	My eyes twinkle, my nose shiny
입도 반짝 반짝	My lips also shiny
오이같은 내 얼굴.	My face, like a cucumber.
길기도 하지요.	How long it is!
눈도 길쭉 코도길쭉	My eyes longish, my nose longish
입도 길쭉 길쭉	My lips also longish
호박같은 내 얼굴.	My face, like a pumpkin.
밉기도 하지요.	How ugly it is!
눈도 삐뚤 코도 삐뚤	My eyes crooked, my nose crooked
입도 삐뚤 삐뚤	My lips also crooked

Lesson 13 Dialogue 갈비에는 뭐가 들어가요?

어머니: **동호**야, 오늘 저녁에 **켈리** 씨 몇 시에 오니[1]?

동호: 다섯 시나[2] 다섯 시 반쯤에 올 거에요[3].
엄마, **갈비**에는 뭐가 들어가요? **갈비**에 채소는 안 넣지요[4]?

어머니: 맞아. 근데[5], **갈비**를 만들기 전에 양파를 갈아서[6] 넣으면[7], **갈비**가 아주 연하지[8].

동호: 엄마, **갈비**하고 또 뭐 만들 거에요[3]?

어머니: **잡채**하고 **파전**.

1. come: *intimate-blunt* question
2. or
3. is going to
4. One doesn't put vegetables in 갈비, right?
5. but; and; by the way (short form for 그런데)
6. grind some onions and then
7. if you put in
3. surely tender

When parents call a child or when adults call to a bosom-buddy, the vocative ending –야 is used after the name. Use –아 instead, if the name ends in a consonant (**미경**아!). Use this ending *only* if the addressee is your intimate peer or a child!!

갈비 (ribs, typically beef, unless specified), 잡채 (boiled clear noodles fried with various steamed vegetables), and 파전 (Korean pancake made with scallions in flour) are three representative party foods made in Korean homes when (foreign or Korean) guests come over! Have you tried these before?

Lesson 13 Grammar

1. Focus　　Simple future　-(으)ㄹ 거에요

-(으)ㄹ 거에요	am/are/is going to

The ending -(으)ㄹ 거에요 expresses the simple future. The closest translation of this ending in English is "*am/are/is going to*". The -(으)ㄹ 거에요 sentences says something about *future* events, and they usually accompany time adverbs like 내일 (tomorrow), 이따가 (later (the same day)), 나중에 (some time later), 다음 주에 (next week), 오늘 밤에 (tonight), 이번 주말에 (this weekend) etc.

As is the case of English *be going to*, -(으)ㄹ 거에요 indicates the **intention** of the speaker more than probability, when the subject is *first* or *second person*:

저는 내일 도서관에 갈 거에요.　　I am going to go to the library tomorrow.

> The pronunciation of 거 in -(으)ㄹ 거에요 is always [꺼]!

All -(으) endings and suffixes, including the -(으)ㄹ 거에요 ending, are sensitive to whether the word they attach to ends in a vowel or a consonant. You have seen one example -(으)로, the tool marker:

펜<u>으로</u> 써요.　　We write with a pen.

버스<u>로</u> 가요.　　We go on a bus.

Thus -(으)ㄹ 거에요 will drop 으 after verbs that end in a vowel. The difference between -(으)로 and -(으)ㄹ 거에요 is that the latter is a sentence-ending (not a noun marker). Here are some examples of verbs that end in a consonant with -을 거에요 attached:

오늘은 점심을 안 <u>먹을 거에요</u>.　　I'm not going to have lunch today.

샐러드에 상추를 넣<u>을 거에요</u>.　　I'm going to put lettuce in the salad.

And here are examples of verbs that end in a vowel with -ㄹ 거에요 attached:

> A *very* sloppy pronunciation of (으)ㄹ 거에요 is [으꺼에요] or [으꼬에요]. You may hear these, but try to avoid saying these until you have gained fluency.

이따가 청소<u>할 거에요</u>.　　I'm going to clean the house later.

친구를 세 시까지 <u>기다릴 거에요</u>.　　I'm going to wait for my friend till 3:00.

물을 끓<u>일 거에요</u>.　　I'm going to boil the water.

 Verbs (and adjectives, as you will see later) that end in ㄹ in some special instances act like **vowel-ending verbs** by dropping the ㄹ. -(으)ㄹ 거에요 is one of those instances. (You will learn other instances are as they arise):

밖에서 놀 거에요.	I'm going to play outside.
한국에서 살 거에요.	I'm going to live in Korea.
양파를 썰 거에요.	I'm going to chop onions.
10 불에 사서 20 불에 팔 거에요.	I'll buy it for $10 and sell it for $20.
당근도 갈 거에요.	I will grate carrots also.

If you want to connect future sentences, get rid of the verb "이"!
(으)ㄹ 거고
(으)ㄹ 거지만
(으)ㄹ 거라서

내일은 올 거고 모레는 안 올 거에요. (I am coming tomorrow and not the day after tomorrow.)

The verb 넣다 ends in a consonant (ㅎ) that is not ㄹ, so it should be conjugated as 넣을 거에요 even though the consonant is silent!

A final note about the ending -(으)ㄹ 거에요 is that it is a composite expression. -(으)ㄹ has something to do with *future, uncertainty,* or *incompleteness*, 거 means *thing*, and 에요 is (a variant of) the polite form of the verb *be* (used after nouns ending in a vowel). Thus, you might see a form like -(으)ㄹ 것이에요, which sounds a little bookish and is found more often in writing, - (으)ㄹ 거지요, where the presumptive ending -지 is added (coming up in the next section!), -(으)ㄹ 거야, in which the *intimate-blunt* form of the verb *be* is used, or -(으)ㄹ 거니 where the *intimate-blunt* question ending -니 is used in place of -야.

You may see the future ending written as –(으)ㄹ 거예요, but as in the case of the verb *be*, -(으)ㄹ 거에요 is far more common in actual practice, which is adopted in this book.

2. Other Grammar Notes

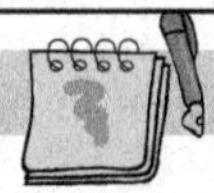

1. -지 *right? isn't it?; of course, surely, I think you(should/probably) know*

-지 is a sentence ending that indicates that the speaker presumes the listener has knowledge about what is being talked about. When used in a question, it makes the sentence very much like an English tag question, such as *isn't it?* or *don't you?* It is used often for *emphasis* more than for seeking confirmation (like tag questions with falling intonation in English). It comes after the verb or adjective stem (or past tense 었), and can be used with -요 for politeness.

계란 후라이도 만들지요? [만들지요]	We are frying eggs, too, right?
요즘 바쁘지요?	You are busy these days, eh?
우유가 없었지요?	(As we both know,) there wasn't any milk, eh?
이거 누구 거지요? [누구꺼지요]	Whose is this? (We should know.)
학교에 갈 거지요? [갈 꺼지요]	You will be going to school, won't you?

In fast speech, the ending 지요 is more frequently pronounced 죠 than 지요.

In statements, the ending -지 has a stronger implication that the information should be obvious to the listener. Be careful not to use -지 too much in statements or you will sound like a know-it-all:

당근은 된장찌개에 안 <u>들어가지</u>.	Carrots don't go in 된장찌개, of course.
양파를 넣으면 고기가 연하지.	If you put onions (in it), the meat is surely tender.

2. -어. -자. -어라! -니/-냐? *Intimate-blunt* speech style

You have learned that the sentence ending -요 shows social distance between the speaker and the listener, and expresses politeness or respect for the listener. In fact, all the verb and adjective conjugations you learned in -어/아요 forms are the -어/아 conjugation plus the -요 politeness marker. By taking the politeness marker out, you enter a realm of *intimate-blunt* speech. Usually parents use this type of speech to children, and young kids (and often adults) use it with their peers and friends. Just like -어요, the -어 ending (without 요) can express general facts and habitual actions, immediate plans and current activities. It can also ask a question as well as give a command:

너 지금 어디 가?	Where are you going?
집에 가.	I'm going home.
빨리 가!	Hurry and go!
나하고 같이 가!	Go with me! OR Wait up!

⚠ These endings should never be used to address someone who is older than you or whom you do not know well! (But it is always safe to use these endings toward children.) Also, never use 누구 "씨" when you are using the *familiar* endings! Nor should you use the 요 ending when you use the pronoun 너. They don't *agree* in politeness.

In speech, where you cannot see question marks or exclamation marks, however, using only this ending can be quite confusing, as you can imagine! It requires a mastery of delicate intonation patterns. Fortunately, there are other *intimate-blunt* endings you can use to mark invitations, commands, and questions, You should learn to recognize the following, which are *not* formed just by taking off -요. (You will learn these conjugations in second-year Korean.)

Invitation -자:

집에 같이 가자.	Let's go home together.
점심 먹자.	Let's have lunch.

Command -어라:

숙제 해라!	Do your homework!

밥 먹어라! (Come and) eat!

텔레비전 그만 봐라! Stop watching TV!

The -어라 ending has a strong sense of speaking down to the listener. Never use it to someone who is older than you. For a "softer" command, use –어.

Question -니/-냐:

너 집에 언제 오니? When are you coming home?

어제 어디 있었냐? Where were you yesterday?

내일 학교에 몇 시에 갈 거니? What time will you go to school tomorrow?

Questions ending in -니 sound friendlier and possibly feminine, whereas those ending in -냐 sound "tougher", blunt, and are often used by males, tomboys, and parents.

3. -(이)야 *it is* (*intimate-blunt* form)

The final bit of information that wraps up the *intimate-blunt* ending story is the verb BE. You have seen that the verb 이다 in –어/아 conjugation has a spelling quirk in modern Korean: 이에요 (not 이어요). There is a similar quirk in the *intimate-blunt* form; it is not formed by simply dropping the 요: it is not ~~이에~~. After a consonant-ending noun, it is 이야, and after a vowel-ending noun, it is 야.

여기가 우리 집이야. This is my house.

나는 내일 올 거야. I will come tomorrow.

이 사람은 우리 언니야. This (person) is my sister.

저건 우리 학교야. That is my school.

너는 누구야? Who are you? (This can be *very* rude)

Observe again how the future ending -(으)ㄹ 거에요 acts like a combination of many parts, (으)ㄹ + 거 + 이에요. The polite form of the verb *be* 이에요 is replaced with the *familiar* form (이)야.

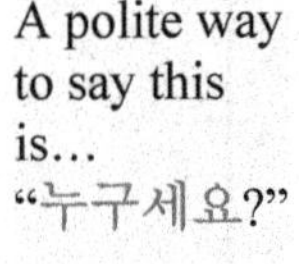

A polite way to say this is… "누구세요?"

Hey, you!

There are various second-person (*you*) pronouns in Korean whose usage is *very* limited and specific. Most often, pronouns (*I, you, he, she, they, it*, etc.) are not used.

너 is the *you*-pronoun to use in ***intimate-blunt*** speech, usually directed to a younger person or a bosom buddy whom you have known since childhood. Many modern folk songs and rock songs have been written in *intimate-blunt* speech, and you will hear 너 everywhere!

The forms are 너는, 너도, 너만, etc., 네가 (from 너+이, pronounced 니), and the possessive 네 (from 너+의, pronounced 니).

The plural is 니네 (니네는, 니네가, 니네만, 니네도, etc.). The same form is used for the possessive, e.g. 니네 고양이. Another plural form is 너희들 (or in colloquial speech [니:들] with a long "이" sound).

Never ever use these pronouns in polite speech (that is, when you end the sentence with 요)! Use the person's name + 씨 or their title (선생님, 아저씨) if you need to clarify who "you" is.

4. -(으)면 *if/when*

-(으)면 is a sentence connector meaning *if* or *when (the first clause happens).* Sentences with -(으)면 might be translated using *when* in some cases, but keep in mind that -(으)면 implies that the situation is hypothetical.

커피를 안 마시면 졸려요. If I don't drink coffee, I get sleepy. OR When I don't drink coffee, I get sleepy.

When used concerning future events, -(으)면 is better translated as English *when*:

집에 가면 나한테 전화해요 When you go home, call me.

It still carries a sense of a hypothetical situation here, since you might end up *not* going home.

To conjugate verbs and adjectives before -(으)면, drop 으 after vowels and ㄹ-ending verbs and adjectives:

시간 있으면 뭐 해요? When you have time, what do you do?

커피가 너무 진하면 물을 넣어요. If the coffee is too stong, put some water in it.

한국어가 중요하면 왜 공부 안 해요? If Korean is important, why do you not study?

⚠ The verb 이다 (usually) takes a special form when used with -으면: ~~이면~~ → (이)라면 . Also, drop the syllable -이 when the noun ends in a vowel.

커피라면 마실 거에요. If it's coffee, I'll drink some!

한국사람이라면 왜 김치를 잘 못 먹어요? If you're Korean, why can't you eat kimchi?

A cute use of this grammatical peculiarity is picked up by a Ramen advertising company: 라면이라면 **삼양**라면!

⚠ You learned clausal connectors (고, 지만, 어서, 으면.) As in English, the ordering of 고 and 지만 is naturally A and B / A but B. But the use of 어서 and 으면 is different. These adverbial phrases ALWAYS have to come before the main clause in Korean. If you want to say the adverbial clause alone, you can say them as a fragment, but no disordering is possible. So, ~~한국어로 써요, 한국어를 알면~~ is not a grammatically correct sentence in Korean!

Now you know *two* "이라" words: 이라서 and 이라면.

A LOT of people say -(으)믄, especially in fast speech, instead of –(으)면. Don't be surprised or baffled when you hear 먹으믄 or 가믄!

You were warned about the peculiar behavior of the ㄹ-ending verbs above. 으 of the -(으)면 connector disappears after ㄹ-ending verbs (and adjectives):

한국어를 알면 한국어로 써요.	If you know Korean, write in Korean.
양파를 갈면 눈물이 나요.	My eyes water when I grate onions.
채소가 얼면 맛이 없어요.	If the vegetables freeze, they don't taste good.

5. -(이)나 *or* for nouns

-(이)나 is a particle that means "or" and is used between *nouns*. The initial syllable "이" is dropped if the first noun to be connected ends in a vowel. This word for *or* implies that the choice is flexible, that not only one or the other option will suffice, that the nouns are suggestions or examples in a larger category of options.

동생이나 오빠가 할거에요.	My younger or older brother (or somebody) will do it.
엄마나 아버지한테 줘요.	Give it to Mom or Dad, either will do.
닭이나 돼지를 넣으세요.	Add chicken or pork (or some other meat).
김치는 무나 배추로 만들어요.	You make Kimchi of radish or cabbage, etc.

-(이)나 can even mark a single noun to mean *NOUN and forget about anything else.* In this usage the suggestion is more cursory, there seems to be no other relevant or interesting option. Commands with -(이)나 can sound very harsh and flippant:

영화나 볼 거에요.	(I have nothing else to do so), I'll just watch a movie…
빵이나 빨리 먹어요!	Hurry up and (just) eat your bread!

Then there is the other *or*… It is used in *either-or* questions. 지금 집에 갈 거에요 아니면 도서관에 갈 거에요? (Are you going home or to the library now?) Now that you have learned the suffix 으면, can you guess the make-up of the word 아니면?
(It literally means "if not", thus *OR*!)

Lesson 13 Exercises

Exercise 1. Dialogue practice I
Practice the dialogue in this lesson with a classmate. Try not to read from the textbook!

Exercise 2. Dialogue practice II
Practice the following dialogue. Replace the underlined nouns and verbs with other words. Be sure to use the *intimate-blunt* endings when you play the mother!

어머니: 정수야, 우유 좀 마시자.
정수: 우유가 없어요.
어머니: 냉장고[1] 위 쪽에 없니?
정수: 네, 없어요.
어머니: 그럼 오렌지 주스는 있지?
정수: 아니오, 오렌지 주스도 없어요.
어머니: 그럼 슈퍼에서 우유나 오렌지 주스 좀[2] 사 와라.

[1] fridge

[2] conversation softener

Exercise 3. -지요? Right?
Confirm what you (think you) know by converting the following to -지요 questions. Ask them of classmates who are relatively sure to know or fit the answers.

Example: 이번 학기에 바쁘지요? – 네, 바빠요.

1) 지금 몇시에요? (I think you know) – 12 시 25 분이에요.
2) (파트너 이름) 씨는 버섯을 좋아해요?
3) (파트너 이름) 씨는 국수를 잘 먹어요?
4) 집에 감자가 많아요?
5) (여학생 이름) 씨 예뻐요?
6) 대학 생활은 힘이 들어요? (힘이 들다 – tough, takes much energy)
7) 오늘이 무슨 요일이에요? (I think you know)
8) (영화 이름)은 괜찮았어요?

9) (식당 이름)이 싫어요?

10) 오징어는 질겨요? (질기다: chewy, tough)

Exercise 4. Use this or that…
Make up a sentence to suggest the two items to your partner to use/eat, etc. Use the correct form of the marker to connect the two words. Your partner will choose something and answer denoting his/her intentions.

Example: 피곤하면, 커피나 콜라를 마셔요. If you're tired, drink some coffee or cola.
네, 콜라 마실 거에요. Yeah, I'm going to have some pop.

1) 스낵으로 (as a snack): 홍당무, 오이

2) 피곤하면 점심으로: 고기, 생선

3) 편지 (letter) 쓰면: 펜, 연필

4) 어머니 생신이라면: 편지, 카드

5) 운동은: 농구, 배구 (volleyball)

6) 씨리얼 (cereal)이 없으면: 계란, 빵

7) 요리 (cooking)를 못 하면: 국수, 채소

Exercise 5. Where were you? Where are you going?
Your mom wants to know everything about your dorm/school life. Tell her what you did last week everyday and what you are doing this weekend. Some suggestions and an example are given below. You might choose to answer as if she knows – using –지요.

Example:

엄마: 지난 주에 어디 있었니? 왜 전화 안 받았니?

아들: 도서관에 있었어요. 그래서 전화 못 받았어요. OR

아들: 도서관에 있었지요. 그래서 전화 못 받았지요. ("Mom, you should know me" attitude)

1) On Friday night, who were you with? What were you doing?

2) Where are you going to be this Saturday?

3) Where are you going on Sunday?

4) When are you going to do your homework?

5) When are you going to study?

6) Why don't you ever call your brother? Are you going to call him this week? (ever 한 번도)

7) Why are your grades so bad? (grades 성적, so 그렇게)

If you want to yell out "Liar!" to your partner, you can say
거짓말! "That's a lie!"
or
거짓말 하지 마! "Don't lie!"

Exercise 6. What are you going to do tonight?
Talk to your partner about your plans.

1) 오늘 한국어 수업이 없으면, 뭐 할 거에요? 어디 갈 거에요?

2) 오늘 밤...

3) 다음 주...

4) 금요일 밤...

5) 토요일에 날씨(weather)가 좋으면... 날씨가 나쁘면...

6) 다음 (next) 방학...

7) 지금부터...

8) 졸업(graduation) 하면 ...

Exercise 7. When or if...
When or why do you/will you do the following? Supply the *if* clause according to the pictures.

Example: 엄마한테 전화해요.

→ 돈이 없으면 엄마한테 전화할 거에요.

1) 한국어 단어 (words)를  기억이 잘 나요. (기억이 나다: to remember)

2)  알 거에요.

3)  그냥 (just) 빵을 먹어요! (조리법: recipe, 모르다: to not know)

4)  잠을 못 자요. (잠을 자다 sleep)

5)  오늘 오후에 좀 사요. (좀 a little)

6)   새 스웨터를 입을 거에요. (새: new)

7) 저녁밥을  나도 줘!

Exercise 8. …and this week?
Talk to you partner about when you did the activities in each picture and when you plan to do them again – *use complete sentences.*

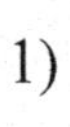

1) 

2) 

3) (먹다) 

4) 

5) (자전거) 

6) 

7) 코트 

8) 엄마한테 

9) 

10) 

11) 

12) 

Exercise 9. What are you going to do?
Explain what you (are going to) do in each situation.

Example:
Q: 여자친구/남자친구가 기분이 나쁘면 어떡할 거에요?
What are you gonna do when/if your girlfriend/boyfriend is in bad mood?

A: 여자친구/남자친구가 기분이 나쁘면… 내가 저녁을 할 거에요.
1) 엄마가 기분이 나쁘면, ________________________ (기분 mood)

2) 좋은 옷이 하나도 없으면, ________________________

3) 한국어 시험을 못 봤으면, ________________ (시험을 못 보다 do badly on the test)

4) 한국어 수업이 재미 없으면, ________________________

5) 블라인드 데이트가 못 생겼으면, ______________________________ (못생겼다 ugly)

6) *Make up your own!*

Exercise 10. 하자! 하니? 해라! 했니? 할 거니?
Circle the verb conjugation on the right that matches the sentence type/meaning on the left.

1) 저 하고 같이 TV를 봐요!	보자, 봐라, 보니, 봤니, 볼 거니
2) ___ 씨 방에 가요!	가자, 가라, 가니, 갔니, 갈 거니
3) 여기에서 같이 기다려요.	기다리자, 기다리니, 기다렸니, 기다릴 거니
4) 밖에서 놀아요!	놀자, 놀아라, 노니, 놀았니, 놀 거니
5) 당근 먹었어요?	먹자, 먹어라, 먹니, 먹었니, 먹을 거니
6) 여기 앉아요	앉자, 앉아라, 앉니, 앉았니, 앉을 거니
7) 오후에 집에 일찍 와요?	오자, 와라, 오니, 왔니, 올 거니 (일찍 early)
8) 시금치 먹어요!	먹자, 먹어라, 먹니, 먹었니, 먹을 거니
9) 나하고 같이 숙제를 끝내요.	끝내자, 끝내라, 끝내니, 끝냈니, 끝낼 거니
10) 그 시디 (CD) 사요!	사자, 사라, 사니, 샀니, 살 거니
11) 한국어 책 읽어요!	읽자, 읽어라, 읽니, 읽었니, 읽을 거니
12) 또 나갈 거에요?	나가자, 나가라, 나가니, 나갔니, 나갈 기니

Culture Point *Food suffixes*

When you go to a Korean restaurant, you will see recurrent parts of food names. Here are some tips that will make you Korean-cuisine savvy!

볶음, 볶기, 볶이	lightly stir-fried dish (오징어 볶음, 멸치 볶음, 떡볶이)
찌개	salty stew (김치 찌개, 된장 찌개)
-탕	soup based on meat broth (갈비탕, 설렁탕)
구이	broiled meat or fish (닭구이, 소금 구이)
-면	noodles (냉면, 라면, 짜장면)
-전	thin, savory Korean pancakes (파전, 해물전)
-밥	rice-based dish (비빔밥, 볶음밥)
불-	broiled or barbequed over open fire (불고기, 불갈비)

Lesson 13 Checkpoint

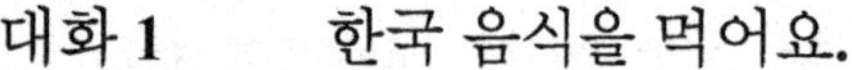

대화 1 한국 음식을 먹어요.

미미: **지미** 씨, 우리 점심으로 한국 음식을 먹어요.

지미: 비빔밥이 어때요?

미미: 비빔밥이 뭐에요? 비빔밥에는 뭐가 들어가요?

지미: 비빔밥에는 시금치, 무, 호박, 콩나물, 당근, 버섯, 소고기, 계란이 들어가요.

미미: 와[2], 재료가 여덟 가지[3]나 들어가요?

지미: 네, 재료가 많이 들어가서 맛있어요. 그런데 참, 미미씨는 당근 알레르기[4]가 있지요?

미미: 네, 그렇지만 다른 채소하고 같이 먹으면 괜찮아요.

지미: 그럼 몇 시에 점심을 먹을 거에요?

미미: 1 시 반이 어때요?

---

[2] Wow! (interjection)
[3] kind(s), type(s)
[4] allergy

대화 2 거기에 칼이 들어가요??

켈리: **동호** 씨, 왜 전화 안 해요? 이제[5] 내가 싫지요?

동호: 미안해요. 너무 바빠서 전화를 못 했어요.

켈리: 저는 이제 **동호** 씨랑[6] 안 만날 거에요! 전화도 안 기다릴 거에요!

동호: 정말로 미안해요. **윤희** 씨 내일 학교 안 가지요?

켈리: 네, 안 가요. 왜요?

동호: 내일 학교 안 가면 저하고 저녁에 칼국수 먹어요.

켈리: 칼국수가 뭐에요? 칼하고 국수? 거기에 칼 들어가요?

동호: 칼은 당연히[7] 안 들어가지요. 국수에 닭고기나 멸치[8]를 넣어요.

Language Point *The Story of 나 and 내 (or 너 and 네)*

Judging which spelling to use (나 or 내 or 네?) can be confusing. The bottom line is that 나 and 너 are **base** forms of the *intimate-blunt* pronouns "*I*" and "*you*". They come with almost all markers you have learned so far (나는, 나만, 나도, 나하고, 나부터, 나까지, 나의 and 너는, 너만, 너도, 너하고, 너부터, 너까지, 너의). When the possessive marker 의 is blended together with 나 and 너, you get 내 (나+의→내) and (너+의→네). 내 and 네, the possessive forms, are used far more frequently than 나의 and 너의 in spoken Korean.

One last crucial bit of information that will help you judge when to use 나 or 너 is the history of the Korean subject marker 이. Several hundred years ago, it was written with just the vowel ㅣ without the placeholder ㅇ after nouns ending in vowels. So the *intimate-blunt "I"* along with the subject marker would look like this: 나 ㅣ. In time, they were glued together to make 내. Years and years later, people started thinking this word was a word on its own that means "I" and that it needed a subject marker. By this time, a new subject marker 가 was being used. Naturally, 내, in need of a subject marker, started taking the subject marker 가, which is why modern Korean now uses 내가.

Can you figure out how 네가 and 제가 have come around? Any hypothesis about the history of *who* (누구도, 누구만, 누구하고 vs. 누가)?

[5] now (unlike before)
[6] with, together with (=하고)
[7] it goes without saying
[8] anchovy

노래하자!

원숭이 엉덩이

원숭이 엉덩이는 빨개
빨가면 사과
사과는 맛있어
맛있으면 바나나
바나나는 길어
길면 기차
기차는 빨라
빠르면 비행기
비행기는 높아
높으면 **백두산**

떴다 떴다 비행기

떴다 떴다 비행기
날아라 날아라
높이 높이 날아라
우리 비행기

학교종

학교종이 땡땡땡
어서 모이자
선생님이 우리를
기다리신다

산토끼

산토끼 토끼야!
어디를 가느냐?
깡총깡총 뛰면서
어디를 가느냐?

여우야 여우야, 뭐 하니? 잠 잔다!

여우야 여우야, 뭐 하니? → 잠 잔다!
잠꾸러기!
여우야 여우야, 뭐 하니? → 세수한다!
멋쟁이!
여우야 여우야, 뭐 하니? → 밥 먹는다!
무슨 반찬? → 개구리 반찬!
죽었니, 살았니? → 죽었다!/살았다!

Culture Point Setting the Korean table

When setting the Korean table, the food is always placed in the center. Main dishes are generally eaten from communally, or by putting small portions onto one's rice bowl.

The usual table consists of the following (you should learn these terms!):

밥	cooked rice (also means *meal*)
국	soup
찌개	Korean stew
반찬	side dishes (including…
김치	Kimchi)
나물	cooked vegetables

숟가락	spoon
젓가락	chopsticks
밥 그릇, 공기	bowl for rice
국그릇	bowl for soup

LESSON 14
시장에서

Lesson 14 Vocabulary  양념, 그리고 과일

양념	Seasonings
1. 소금; 깨소금	salt; sesame salt
2. 고춧가루; 고추장	red pepper (powder); paste
3. 후춧가루	black pepper (powder)
4. 설탕	sugar
5. 간장	soy sauce
6. 식초	vinegar
7. 참기름	sesame oil
8. 마늘	garlic
9. 생강	ginger
10. 멸치	anchovies
11. 버터 = 빠다	butter
과일	**Fruit**
12. 바나나	banana
13. 사과	apple/pear
14. 포도	grapes
15. 수박	watermelon
16. 딸기	strawberry
	Counters
17. 개	things (that can be held in the hand)
18. 단	bundle (of green onions, spinach, etc.)
19. 마리	animals
20. 명 (분 honorific)	people
	Other useful vocabulary
21. 휴지통; 쓰레기통	trash can; garbage can
22. 도마	cutting board
23. (가스) 레인지	(gas) stove
24. 냉장고/냉동실	fridge/freezer
25. 가게	store(s)
26. 시장	market
27. 두다	save/leave (for future use)
28. 꺼내다	pull out/take out
29. 길다	long
30. 달다	sweet
31. 이리/그리/저리	here/there/over there (used with motion verbs)
32. 조금, 좀 [쪼금, 쫌]	a little
33. 다	all, everything
34. 앞으로는 = 이제부터는	in the future, from now on
35. 그러니까	since that's the case

When it comes to counting for every-day business, Koreans enjoy rough numbers. Instead of 한 개 or 두 개, they would say 한두개. Instead of 두 개 or 세 개, they would say 두세 개. Can you guess what 세네 개, 네댓 개, 대여섯 개, 예닐곱 개, and 일고 여덟개 mean? How about 두어 개, 서너 개, 너댓 개? How about 두서너 개?

These are a shorter way to say 이쪽으로, 그쪽으로, and 저쪽으로!

Vocabulary Exercise 1. Pass the salt
What condiment (or seasoning) would you put on or in the following foods – *normally!*

Vocabulary Exercise 2. What fruit?
What fruit do you associate with each of the following pictures?

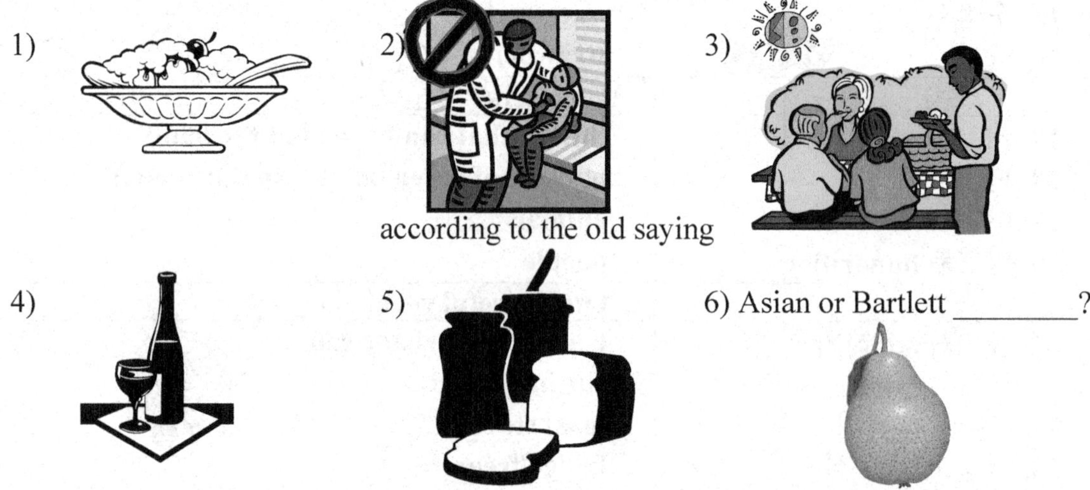

Culture Point *It's too sweet!*

Fruit acts as a dessert for Koreans – who eat much less cake and cookies (sugary sweets) than Westerners. Just a slice of watermelon or an orange-quarter tops of a Korean meal nicely! You will find that many Western-style sweets' names are borrowed words in Korean: 케이크, 초콜렛, 파이, 아이스크림. Also note that 과자 works for cookies and savory crackers.

Lesson 14 Dialogue 시장에서

어머니: 아저씨. 채소 좀 사러[1] 왔어요. 양파 서너 개하고 당근 두어 개만 주세요[2]. 참[3], 파전을 만들 거니까[4] 파도 한 단 주세요. 그리고, 오늘 오징어가 괜찮으면 오징어도 한 마리만 주세요.	1. (in order) to buy 2. Give, please 3 Oh yeah, (I just remembered) 4. I am going to make (잡채 and 파전) so
동호: 엄마, **켈리**는 오징어를 못 먹으니까[5] 오징어는 사지 마세요[6]. 해물은 잘 못 먹어요.	5. can't eat (squid) so 6. Don't buy
어머니: 오, 그래. 아저씨, 그럼 과일로[7] 주세요. **동호** 야, **켈리** 씨는 무슨 과일을 좋아하니?	7. (Let's make it) fruit.
동호: 아무 거나[8] 사세요. 과일은 다 좋아해요.	8. anything

좀 (shortened from 조금) literally means *a little*. In many cases, it is used as a conversational softener, comparable to English *sorta* and *kinda*. It is often pronounced as 쫌.

In the dialogue, 동호 might sound like a nag telling his mother what to do. However, he is playing a good son urging his mother not to buy too much for his sake (because Kelly is his friend). The key is in the intention and the intonation of the speaker, of course.

Lesson 14 Grammar

1. Focus Polite commands (positive) -(으)세요

-(으)세요	Do … please

The polite command form is made by adding -(으)세요 to verb stems that end in a consonant and -세요 to verb stems that end in a vowel.

Do you remember how to make a command in the *familiar* form? 방 청소해! or 방 청소해라!

여기 앉으세요. Please sit here.

방 청소하세요. Please clean (your room).

양배추 좀 주세요. Please give (me) a little bit of cabbage.

이름을 쓰세요. Please write your name.

⚠ -(으)세요 is yet another ending in front of which ㄹ-ending verbs drop the "ㄹ". After dropping 으, it now looks like a vowel-ending verb stem. Add -세요 as you would after other vowel-ending verbs:

여기에서 저하고 사세요. (살다) Live here with me, please.

운동장에서 노세요. (놀다) Play in the playground, please.

고기 좀 써세요. (썰다) Chop some meat, please.

Polite commands (negative) -지 마세요

-지 마세요	Do not…please

The polite negative command form (*don't do …*) is made by adding -지 마세요 to the verb stem.

테이블 위에 아무 것도 놓지 마세요. Don't put anything on the table.

여기에 들어 가지 마세요. Don't go in here, please.

밥을 더 만들지 마세요. Don't make more rice.

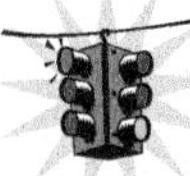

"마세요" is from the verb "말다 (*not do*)," which dropped its ㄹ when it was conjugating for the command form -(으)세요. When you want to make two commands such as "Don't do A but do B," the ㄹ comes alive before the connecting marker -고. Sometimes the first verb phrase -지 말고 is omitted and you get the structure N_1 말고 N_2, "not N_1 but N_2"! It only works with the object of the sentence!

놀지 말고 공부하세요!	Don't play, (but) *study*!
거기 가지 말고 여기 오세요.	Don't go there; come here!
찌개에 오징어 넣지 말고 새우 넣으세요.	Don't put squid (but) put shrimp in the stew.
찌개에 오징어 말고 새우 넣으세요.	Put shrimp not squid in the stew.
그 슈퍼에 가지 말고 저기 가세요.	Don't go to that grocery store but go there.
그 슈퍼에 말고 저기 가세요.	Go *there*, not to that grocery store.
그 슈퍼 말고 저기 가세요.	Go *there*, not that grocery store.

How would you make a negative command in the *familiar* form?
놀지 말고 공부해! or 놀지 말고 공부해라!

2. Other Grammar Notes

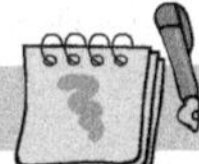

1. -(으)로 Selection marker

You already know the use of -(으)로 as a *tool* marker:

숟가락으로 밥하고 국을 먹어요.	One eats rice and soup with a spoon.
젓가락으로 반찬을 먹어요.	One eats side dishes with chopsticks.

-(으)로 also functions as a *selection* marker, which shows that the speaker has more than one choice and has decided on one thing:

오징어 말고 과일로 주세요.	(Well then), give me fruit, not squid.
휴가 때 하와이로 갈 거에요.	I'm going to go to Hawai'i (not Mexico or the Bahamas etc.) for vacation.

This *selectional* usage of -(으)로 reflects the sense of direction in the meaning of -(으)로, or, *toward.* "I've decided to go this way (fruit) and not that way (squid, etc.)." Since -(으)로 means *towards* or *in this direction*, it is seen as 'softer' than -에 when questioning others.

학교 끝나고 어디로 갈 거에요?	After school, where are you headed to? (where to, out of many different choices?)
학교 끝나고 어디에 갈 거에요?	Where are you going after school? - direct destination (can be taken as probing)
이쪽으로 앉으세요.	Sit over here, please.

The idiomatic expression "**noun**-으로 하다" means "I'll make it (noun)", or "I've decided on (noun)."

햄버거로 하세요.	Please make it a hamburger.
점심은 피자로 먹었어요.	For lunch, I went with pizza.

> when -(으)로 is used as a selectional marker, ㄹ sometimes doubles after 뭐 and 거 in colloquial speech.
> 오늘 점심은 뭘로 먹을 거에요?
> What are you going to "choose" for today's lunch?
> 이걸로 하세요!
> Make it this (one).

2. -(으)러 가다/오다 *(go/come) in order to…*

-(으)러 is a very useful ending to learn. To express the purpose or goal of a trip, the verb marker …-(으)러 can be used after the ***stem*** of the verb.

A: 어디 가요?	Where are you going?
B: 학생회관에 점심 먹으러 가요.	I am going to the Student Union to have lunch.

Just like all other -으 suffixes, use -으러 after verbs ending in a consonant and -러 after verbs ending in a vowel.

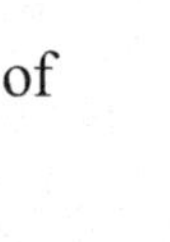

> You should only use the verbs 가요 and 와요 in this construction. You will learn how to express "goals" using other verbs.

토요일에 우리 집에 공부하러 와요.	Come to my house to study on Saturday.
친구하고 만나러 나가요.	I am going out to meet a friend.
슈퍼에 과일 사러 나갔어요.	(He/she) went out to get fruit at the store.

Again, about the peculiarity of the ㄹ-ending verbs: They require that the 으 of the -(으)러 ending disappear after ㄹ-ending verbs:

제임스는 한국에 살러 갔어요.	James went to Korea to live (there).
할머니는 시장에 고추 팔러 갔어요.	Grandma went to the market to sell peppers.
아빠는 옆집에 칼 갈러 갔어요.	Dad has gone to the neighbor's to sharpen his knife.

Be careful not to confuse -(으)러 with the -(으)로 ending. The ***purpose*** ending -(으)러 comes after a *verb*, and the ***tool/direction*** particle -(으)로 comes after a *noun*:

한국어로 얘기해요.	I speak *in* Korean.
숟가락으로 밥을 먹어요.	One eats rice *with* a spoon.

3. -(으)니까 *because*

-(으)니까 is used to mark the reasoning behind a command or a suggestion. When you give orders to someone, you have used your personal judgment about the way to go about things, whether the result of the order benefits you or the person who carries out the order. When you supply even a fact as the *reasoning* behind the order, you are still showing your judgment (in making the connection), no matter how "logical" you think you are being. You will always use the -(으)니까 connector before commands.

Verbs and adjectives before -(으)니까 conjugate as they would before -(으)세요 and -(으)ㄹ 거에요:

오징어는 안 먹으니까 사지 마세요.	Don't buy squid; (because) he doesn't eat it.
오늘은 바쁘니까 내일 만나요.	I'm busy today so let's meet tomorrow.
저 식당이 맛있으니까 거기서 먹어요.	That restaurant is good; let's eat there.
생강이 없으니까 생강 좀 사라.	We are out of ginger; buy some.

Verbs and adjectives ending in ㄹ drop ㄹ before -(으)니까 as they would before -(으)세요 and -(으)ㄹ 거에요:

파가 너무 <u>기니까</u> 좀 <u>써세요</u>.	The scallions are too long -- Cut (them) a little.
냉동실에 오래 두면 <u>어니까</u> 꺼내세요.	It will freeze if you leave it in the freezer for a long time -- Take it out, please.
커피가 너무 <u>다니까</u> 물을 넣으세요.	The coffee is too sweet -- Put some water in, please.

You can also use past tense stems and future marking -(으)ㄹ 거(에요) before -(으)니까:

엄마가 갈비를 만들 <u>거니까</u> 오세요. Mom's making 갈비, so come over!
(The less colloquial, full form of this would be 엄마가 갈비를 만들 <u>것이니까</u>...)

내가 못 했으니까 네가 해. I couldn't do it, so you do it.

It is ungrammatical to use -어서 to mark the reasoning behind a **command** because -어서 marks the **logical precursor** to the second action, with no personal judgment. In A 어서 B, B is the logical result of A. -어서 means *having done A* or *being as it is* or *so*.

~~그게 예뻐서 그거 사세요.~~ ~~That is pretty; buy that.~~

~~오늘 바빠서 내일 만나요!~~ ~~I'm busy today; let's meet tomorrow.~~
오늘 바쁘니까 내일 만나요. I'm busy today; let's meet tomorrow.

⚠ When you are stating factual background (not your judgment or personal circumstances), try to use the ending -어서/아서 instead of -(으)니까:

오늘 바빠서 그 사람하고 내일 만나요. Being busy today, I'm meeting him tomorrow.

어제 바빠서 그 사람을 못 만났어요. Since I was busy yesterday, I couldn't meet him.

그게 예뻐서 그거로 샀어요. Since it was pretty, I bought it.

Compare:

아침을 안 먹어서 배가 고파요. I didn't have breakfast so I'm hungry.
(simple statement of a fact with logical background)

A: 왜 배가 고파요?
B: 밥을 안 먹었으니까 배가 고프지요. I didn't eat, that is why I'm hungry, of course.
(which should be obvious! - supplying a reason when asked)

숙제 다 해서 놀 거에요. Having done all my homework, I'm going to play.

숙제 다 했으니까 놀 거에요. I'm going to play because I've done all my homework.
(most naturally the answer to a question – *why?)*

In Korean, ***always*** put the "reason" part in the beginning of the sentence.

Summary of the usage of -(으)니까

-(으)니까	"because"	• used when the main sentence is a command or a suggestion • used when indicating personal judgment or a justification	• 커피가 뜨거우<u>니까</u> 조금 이따가 마시세요. (command) The coffee is hot; drink it a while later. • 내일 휴일이<u>니까</u> 어디 놀러 갈래요? Tomorrow is a holiday; wanna go some place (to play)? • 내일 시험이 없<u>으니까</u> 놀지요. (As an answer to the question "Why am I playing?") I don't have a test tomorrow, that's why I am playing.

You can see there are some nuance differences between -(으)니까 and -어서 in some sentences but the bottom line is: as you do not have the native intuition yet,

Use only -(으)니까 with commands or suggestions.

4. Counters

Counting items in Korean requires a somewhat different structure from English. It is VERY important to adhere to this structure when you count items:

ITEM	NUMBER	COUNTER	
학생	한	명	one student
오징어	세	마리	three squid
포도	두	송이	a bunch of grapes
시금치	다섯	단	five bundles of spinach

For counting objects that are small and can be held by hand, you can use the general counter 개:

ITEM	NUMBER	COUNTER	
당근	세	개	three carrots
감자	두	개	two potatoes

 Never use direct translation from English. Saying 한 고양이 (for *one cat*), or 두 가방 (for *two bags*) is incorrect in Korean, and you won't be understood!

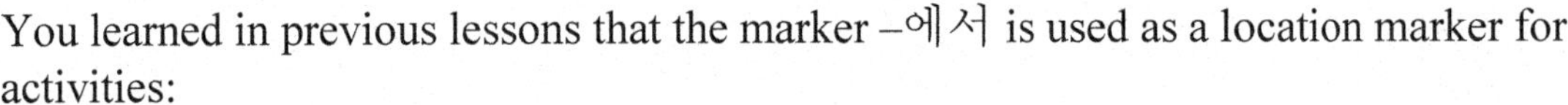

5. -에서 *from* Source marker

You learned in previous lessons that the marker –에서 is used as a location marker for activities:

도서관에서 공부해 보세요.	Try studying in the library.

-에서 is also used like *from* to mark a **source** as seen in the following examples:

어디에서 왔어요?	Where did you come from? / Where are you from?
서울에서 전화가 왔어요.	A phone call "came" from Seoul.
텔레비전 뉴스에서 들었어요.	I heard it on the T.V. news.
학교에서 집까지 걸어요.	I walk home from school.
그거 거기서 샀어요?	Did you buy it (from) there?
그거 어디서 났어요?	Where is that from? (Where did you get it?)
냉동실에서 고기 꺼내세요.	Take the meat out of the freezer, please.

Lesson 14 Exercises

Exercise 1. Dialogue practice
Practice the dialogue in this lesson with a classmate. When finished, replace the food nouns with new items and practice the dialogue again.

Exercise 2. 이거 하세요! 저거 하세요! Do this! Do that!
Make the following commands directly but politely, paying attention to the verb ending.

1) 공부를 해요
2) 숙제를 내요
3) 가방을 책상 위에 놓아요
4) 창문을 닫아요
5) 저하고 같이 시애틀에서 살아요
6) 매일 매일 한국어를 조금씩 읽어요 (조금씩: by small quantity)
7) 아침에 일찍 일어나요 (일찍: early)
8) 앞문을 열어요
9) 라운지에서 쉬어요
10) 자주 빨래해요
11) 용돈 좀 줘요 (용돈 [용똔] pocket money)

Exercise 3. Translation
Translate the following sentences.

1) Please come here (*this way*).
2) Look at the chalkboard.
3) Put (your) hand on the book. (hand: 손)
4) Eat three grapes.
5) Turn in today's homework only.
6) Give (me) a banana, please.
7) Eat some watermelon.
8) Wash this apple.
9) Put some more (더) sugar in my coffee.

Unless you are talking about the *inside* of something, do **not** use the word 안!

Exercise 4. 하지 마세요!
Make the following commands negative. Pay attention to the verb form and the ending.

1) 숙제를 많이 내줘요. (내주다: assign, give)

2) 옆 사람하고 말해요.

3) 공부 시간에 껌을 씹어요. (씹다: chew)

4) 그 물을 마셔요.

5) 칠판에 이름을 써요.

6) 텔레비전을 봐요.

7) 한국어 수업에 늦게 와요. (늦게: late)

8) 매일 친구하고 놀다.

9) **그린레이크**에서 수영해요. (수영하다: swim)

10) 장거리 전화를 너무 자주 해요 (장거리:long distance, 너무: excessively)

Exercise 5. Simon says 'now!'
Give your partner positive or negative commands. Your partner should at least mime each command but only if you first say 지금.

Example: 지금 칠판을 보세요.

If you say the command without 지금, and your partner follows your order, he/she is OUT!

Exercise 6. Counter practice
Request the following items, using a polite command.

1) 생선, 주세요 (2 fish)

2) 사과, 주세요 (5 apples)

3) 어머니, 이쪽으로 앉으세요 (4 mothers)

4) 오이, 주세요 (3 cucumbers)

5) 호박, 주세요 (1 zucchini)

6) 파, 주세요 (10 bundles of scallions)

7) 학생, 이리 오세요. (3 students)

Exercise 7. 시작하니까 문을 닫으세요... It's starting, so close the door, please...
Complete the following commands by conjugating the sentence-final verb and providing a reasoning for your command.

1) ...한국 신문을 사다 - negative

2) ...종이 좀 주다

3) ... 식탁 ((eating) table)을 닦다

4) ...이쪽으로 앉다 - negative

5) ...버스를 타다

6) ...사과를 씻다

7) ...과일이나 당근을 먹다

8) ...국수나 만들다

9) ...여기에서 기다리다 –negative

10) ...커피에다(into) 우유 (milk) 좀 넣다

Exercise 8. 그러니까
Based on the translation, complete the sentence with the correct connector -으니까 or -어서.

1) 피곤해 + 일찍 자라. (피곤하다 tired)
You are tired; go to bed early.

2) 오늘 바빠요 + 내일 만나요, 네?
Let's meet tomorrow, because I'm busy, O.K.?

3) 숙제가 많아요 + 오늘 친구들하고 영화 보지 마세요.
You have a lot of homework – Don't go to the movies with your friends today.

4) 배가 고파요 + 혼자 저녁 먹었어요. (배가 고프다 hungry)
I was hungry, so I had dinner by myself.

Exercise 9. 로/으로 Where are they headed to?
Choose the correct form of -로/-으로.

1) **은비**가 교실_____ 가요.

2) **경호**가 서점_____ 가요.

3) 선생님이 연구실_____ 가요.

4) **빌**이 기숙사_____ 가요.

5) **경수**가 은행_____ 가요.

6) **마돈나**가 체육관_____ 가요.

Exercise 10. 거기에 왜 가요?
Talk to your partner about why you go to each place (in order to do *what*).

Example: 서점
A: 서점에 왜 가요?
B: 책을 사러 가요.

1) 도서관	2) 친구 집	3) 슈퍼
4) 한국 식당	5) 우체국	6) 기숙사
7) 병원	8) 아버지 회사 (company)	9) 선생님 연구실
10) 체육관	11) 운동장	12) 서점

Exercise 11. Translation.

1) Please put sugar in the coffee.
2) I'm going to make bacon* and eggs, so you make some toast* or potatoes.
3) How many (people) are there (in your party)? -- There are three. (THINK: *honorific or not?)*
4) Friday night, I'm going to go out with my friends to drink (alcohol: 술).
5) We need three onions and two fish for this soup.
6) Don't put more salt on the meat!
7) The baby (아기) can't eat noodles, so don't give (him any).
8) I finished eating ("I ate all the rice"), so I'm resting now.
9) If you don't have chicken (if there is no chicken), then put in the beef (on the other hand).
10) Put some fruit on the table: apples and pears, etc.
11) Don't go to a café to study! Go to the library!
12) Tina has an allergy, so don't put ginger in the zucchini sitr-fry (볶음); make it garlic.
13) What (choice) are you going to have? – I'll make it spaghetti.
14) Where are you headed to? – I'm headed to the library.
15) If you are going to buy fruit, buy some grapes (choice).
16) (Because) these green onions are too long – chop them a little.
17) Take all the fruit out of the fridge – We'll make the salad last (마지막으로).
18) From now on, I am not going to eat garlic.
19) Don't go to that store to buy meat. I bought meat at that store, and it was too tough.

Lesson 14 Checkpoint

대화 1 바빠서 숙제를 못 했어요.

선생님: **사오정** 학생. 무슨 일이에요?
사오정: 선생님, 제가 어제 너무 바빠서 숙제를 못 했어요.
죄송해요. 내일까지 낼께요.[9]
선생님: 내일은 내가 어디를 가니까 학교에 없을 거에요. 모레 내세요.
사오정: 그렇지만 모레는 제가 **뉴욕**에 인터뷰하러 가요.
선생님: 그럼 이메일로 보내세요[10]. 그런데, **사오정** 학생, 주제[11]는 뭘로 했어요?
사오정: 네, 주제는 한국의 과일로 했어요.

대화 2 그 백화점은 너무 비싸니까 가지 마세요.

미리: **윤희** 씨, 크리스마스 선물 샀어요?
윤희: 아니오, 내일 사러 갈 거에요.
미리: **동호** 씨 선물은 뭘로 할 거에요?
윤희: 가방으로 할 거에요. **미리** 씨는 선물 다 샀어요?
미리: 네, 저는 지난 주에 쇼핑을 다 끝냈어요.
윤희: 백화점이라면 **미리** 씨가 잘 알지요? 어디로 가면 좋아요?
미리: **신세계** 백화점이 크니까 거기로 가세요.
윤희: **롯데** 백화점도 괜찮지요?
미리: 그 백화점은 너무 비싸니까[12] 가지 마세요.

The words in red are "focused", which is why they need the marker 이/가.

백화점이라면 미라 씨가 잘 알지요?
If it's a department store, it is you, 미라, who know it well.

신세계 백화점이 크니까 거기로 가세요.
It is 신세계 department store that is big, so go there.

---
[9] will submit (it), if that's OK with you
[10] send
[11] topic
[12] 비싸다 expensive

대화 3 미안해요. 귤은 없어요.

주희: 아줌마, 파 한 단하고 계란 한 줄[13] 주세요.

아줌마: 뭐를 만들 거에요?

주희: 계란찜[14]을 만들 거에요. 그리고 과일도 좀 주세요.

아줌마: 어떤 거요?

주희: 귤 5 개하고 사과 2 개 주세요.

아줌마: 미안해요. 귤은 없어요.

주희: 그럼 배로 5 개 주세요.

아줌마: 여기 있어요.

읽기 1 우리 집에 떡볶이 먹으러 놀러 오세요!

오늘은 일요일이에요. 그렇지만 나는 아침에 일찍[15] 일어났어요. 일찍 일어나니까 기분이 좋았어요. 우리 **해피**는 내가 일찍 일어나면 아주 기뻐해요.[16] 왜냐하면 일찍 일어나면 항상 **해피**하고 산책을 나가니까요. 아침을 먹기 전에 **해피**하고 공원에서 산책을 조금 하고 집으로 돌아왔어요. **해피**한테 밥을 주고 나도 아침밥을 먹었어요.

점심에 떡볶이가 먹고 싶었어요.[17] 그래서 떡볶이의 재료를 사러 11 시 쯤 시장에 갔어요. 당근 한 개, 양파 한 개, 어묵[18] 두 봉지[19], 고추장 한 병을 샀어요. 떡[20]은 집에 있어서 안 샀어요. 떡볶이는 너무 너무 맛있었어요. 그런데 너무 많이 먹어서 배가 조금 아팠어요. 여러분도 떡볶이 좋아하지요? 우리 집에 떡볶이 먹으러 놀러 오세요!

---

[13] (a) line (of eggs); a dozen
[14] non-sweet egg custard
[15] early
[16] 기뻐하다 to be happy about something
[17] wanted to eat
[18] fishcake
[19] (plastic) bag – (here, *two bags of fishcake*)
[20] ricecake

읽기 2 과일은 몸에 좋으니까 많이 먹으세요!

나는 과일을 별로 안 좋아하지만 한국 배는 좋아해요. 작년 여름[21]에는 한국 배를 마음껏[22] 먹으러 한국에 갔어요. 그런데 여름이라서 배가 없었어요. 배는 가을[23]에 나오니까 여름에는 없어요. 배가 없어서 나는 포도하고 수박을 먹었어요. 한국 과일은 미국 과일하고 많이 달랐어요[24]. 더[25] 작았지만 더 맛있었어요. 여러분도 한국 과일을 좋아하지요? 배를 좋아하면 한국에 여름에 가지 말고 가을이나 겨울[26]에 가세요. 과일은 몸[27]에 좋으니까 많이 많이 먹으세요!

노래할 거에요!

따르릉 따르릉 비켜나세요
자전거가 나갑니다 따르르르릉
저기 가는 저 노인 조심하세요
우물쭈물하다가는 큰 일 납니다

나는 콩!   나는 콩!   후라이팬에 들어갔었지.
아이 뜨거워! 아이 뜨거워!

나는 콩!   나는 콩!   냉장고에 들어갔었지.
아이 차가워! 아이 차가워!

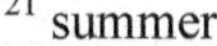

[21] summer
[22] to one's heart's content
[23] autumn
[24] different
[25] 더 expresses comparative degree: for example, *more, better*
[26] winter
[27] body

Culture Notes 시장

Modern Seoul still has many local open-air and street markets that sell everything from fruits and vegetables to rubber bands, to shoes, to pig heads (for rituals), to traditional celadon pottery and lackered boxes. At these markets, called 시장, it is customary to haggle and for the owners to cut prices for various customers. One famous 시장 is 남대문 시장 (South Gate Market), where many foreign tourists go to shop for cheap (sometimes fake) leather goods and imitation name brands. Except for 남대문 시장, local 시장 are slowly being replaced by 슈퍼, the equivalent of our local grocery stores (which may or may not be chains).

Korea doesn't have large domestic supermarket chains like those in the U.S. What might surprise you is that many 백화점 include a whole basement floor, supermarket-like grocery section.

You might also hear about 이태원, a district near an old U.S. army base, with many stores catering to Westerners. You can get tomato soup in a can and tubs of frosting there!

LESSON 15

잘 먹겠습니다!

Lesson 15 Vocabulary 음식, 그리고 맛

음식	Food
1. 갈비	barbecued beef ribs
2. 불고기	barbecued beef
3. 잡채	clear noodles with seasoned vegetables
4. (해물) 파전	(seafood) green onion pancake
5. 냉면	cold chewy noodles
6. 갈비탕	beef rib soup
7. 비빔밥	rice mixed with vegetables & 고추장
8. 된장 /된장찌개	soy bean paste (Korean *miso*) /stew
9. 김치찌개	Kimchi stew
10. 국	(clear) soup
주 반찬	**Main Side dishes**
11. 총각김치	icicle radish Kimchi
12. 배추김치	Kimchi made from Napa cabbage
13. 깍두기	sweetened Kimchi made of cubed icicle radish
맛/온도	**Taste/ Temperature**
14. 매워요 (맵다)	spicy
15. 짜요	salty
16. 써요 (쓰다)	bitter
17. 셔요 (시다)	sour
18. 맛있어요; 맛이 있어요	tasty
19. 맛없어요; 맛이 없어요	not tasty
20. 뜨거워요 (뜨겁다)	hot
21. 차가워요 (차갑다)	cold
22. 따뜻해요	warm
23. 시원해요	refreshing
24. 미지근해요	lukewarm
25. 싱거워요 (싱겁다)	bland; not salty or spicy
	Other cooking/food-related vocabulary
26. 구워요 (굽다)	broil, barbecue
27. 도와요 (돕다)	help
28. (상을) 차리다	set (the table)
29. 식어요 (식다)	cool down
30. 숟가락 = 숟갈	spoon
31. 젓가락 = 젓갈	chopsticks
32. 상	low, traditional eating table
33. 식탁	eating table
34. (Noun) 때	(at the) time (of Noun)
35. -(이)랑	and; with

The two temperature words 차갑다 (to be cold) and 뜨겁다 (to be hot) are only used for describing the temperature of physical things. They are *not* used to describe the weather or air temperature or one's overall sensation (of feeling cold, for example).

There is a shorter way to say 'a spoon and chopsticks' – 수저. Also, do you know how to say disposable chopsticks? Koreans' say 나무 젓가락, meaning wooden chopsticks (You can also say 일회용 젓가락 – one-time use chopsticks).

Vocabulary Exercise 1. Sugar is sweet
Think of an exemplary food for each vocabulary item.

1) 매워요	2) 달아요	3) 짜요	4) 써요
5) 셔요	6) 맛있어요	7) 맛없어요	8) 뜨거워요
9) 차가워요	10) 따뜻해요	11) 시원해요	12) 미지근해요
13) 싱거워요	14) 구워요		

Vocabulary Exercise 2. Try it!
Go to a Korean restaurant and try the dishes in the vocabulary list with some friends. Then come back and check off the foods you have tried. Organize them into *spicy* and *not spicy* or *dishes that you like* and *dishes that you don't like*.

Vocabulary Exercise 3. Menu
Using all the food terms you know and the names of Korean dishes, plan several tantalizing Korean meals. Then see what your Korean friends think of the meals – do the foods go together?

Vocabulary Exercise 4. Odd one out

1)	짜다	쓰다	달다	차갑다
2)	냉면	당근	라면	스파게티
3)	계란	빵	갈비	생선
4)	차갑다	시다	따뜻하다	뜨겁다
5)	불고기	비빔밥	파전	과자

6-10) Make your own and test your partner!

Food and culture 아, 고소하다!

There is a flavor word unique to Korean: 고소하다. Koreans tend to like things that have the "고소" flavor more than sweets. There is no equivalent word in English except perhaps "savory" in the British sense. Some things that have the "고소" flavor are: 과자, roasted 김, 땅콩 (peanuts), and roasted corn tea. But the quintessential 고소 flavor comes from 참기름 or slightly burnt rice (누룽지).

As an idiom, "아, 고소하다!" can also mean "It serves you (or *someone*) right" (i.e., "I am savoring this").

What other kinds of food do you think have the 고소 flavor?

노래하자!

너

낙엽지던 그 숲 속에
파란 바닷가에
떨리는 손 잡아 주던 너
별빛같은 눈망울로
영원을 약속하며
나를 위해 기도하던 너

웃음 지으며 눈 감은 너
네 곁을 떠난 뒤
외로운 짚시처럼
밤을 새워 버린
숱한 나날들
오늘도 추억 속에
맴돌다 지쳐 버린
창백한 나의 넋

Lesson 15 Dialogue 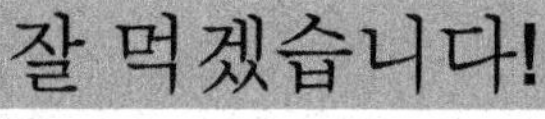 잘 먹겠습니다!

동호: **켈리** 씨, **갈비** 좀 먹어요. 소고기에요.

켈리: 매워요?

동호: 안 매워요. 어떤[1] 한국 음식은 맵고 어떤 한국 음식은 안 매워요.

켈리: (eating **잡채**) 이것도 안 맵네요.[2] 고소해요.

동호: 그건 **잡채**에요. 당면이랑[3] 채소가 들어갔어요.

켈리: (to herself) 매운 것[4]도 조금 먹자... **김치**...

동호: 한국 사람 다 됐네요![5]

1. some, certain
2. this isn't spicy either!
3. and
4. spicy thing (= something spicy)
5. Now you are really Korean! (*literally*, you have entirely become Korean)

The interaction between **켈리** and **동호**'s mother is very typical of a conversation between two people who just met over a meal (as a guest and a host at someone's house). The host customarily humbles herself and repeats "Sorry, I have prepared nothing," "The food turned out terrible!"

Also, the younger person of the two *always* invites the older one to *use* **반말** ("반말 하세요," "말씀 낮추세요.") after some rounds of conversation. The first reaction of the invitee is often resistance and hesitation, but the invitee smoothes into a lower register, as you can see in 동호's mom's use of 드세요 (the first time), and then 들어요 (after being asked to speak informally).

 Here is a conversation that might be typically heard between a Korean host and a foreign dinner guest. It is a little complex, but try to memorize it. It will come in handy!

켈리: 안녕하세요. 처음 뵙겠어요. **켈리 텀즈**에요.
어머니: 네, 어서 와요. 만나서 반가워요.
켈리: 와! 진수성찬이네요[1]!
어머니: 별 거 없어요.[2] 잡채 조금이랑[3] 갈비 조금 했어요[4]. 김치가 매우니까 조금씩[5] 들고, 갈비도 뜨거우니까 천천히[6] 들어요.
켈리: 아유[7], 어머니, 반말 하세요[8].
어머니: 그래도, 다 큰 아들[9] 친구한테 어떻게 반말을 해요. 자[10], 차린 건 없지만[11] 식기 전에 맛있게[12] 들어요.
켈리: 네, 잘 먹겠습니다[13]!

1. Wow, what a feast!
2. there is nothing special
3. and
4. made; prepared; cooked
5. little by little
6. taking it easy, slowly
7. Goodness!
8. Speak informally with me, please!
9. all grown-up son
10. here
11. There is nothing I have prepared, but
12. deliciously
13. Thank you for the food! (literally, I will eat well)

Lesson 15 Grammar

> Most ㅂ-irregular words you learn in this chapter are adjectives. This is true in general. There are far more ㅂ-irreguar *adjectives* than *verbs*. You learned two ㅂ-irregular verbs in this lesson: 굽다 and 돕다.

1. Focus ㅂ-irregular adjectives

ㅂ → 우	ㅂ다 → 워(요)

You know two verb stems that end in ㅂ: 입다, and 잡다. The -어/아 form of these verbs is 입어요 and 잡아요. However, some verbs and adjectives ending in ㅂ are ㅂ-irregular; they have irregular conjugations. ㅂ-irregular verbs and adjectives have two stem forms; in the "***consonantal***" stem form the ㅂ stays and conjugates like regular verbs and adjectives. The other stem form is the "vocalic" stem form, which drops ㅂ and replaces it with ㅜ in front of the -(으) and -어/아 ending. The choice of the consonantal or vocalic stem depends on the following ending or connector. Typically, ㅂ-irregular verbs and adjectives use the ***vocalic stem*** conjugation before endings and connectors that begin with a ***vowel*** (-어/아 and -으).

Citation form	Stem	Connectors & Endings	Conjugated form	Examples
맵다	맵 before consonant endings and connectors	-고	맵고	이건 맵고 짜요. This is spicy and salty.
		-지만	맵지만	이건 맵지만 안 짜요. This is spicy, but not salty.
		-지요	맵지요	그거 맵지요? That's spicy, isn't it?
		-네요	맵네요	이거 아주 맵네요. This is (unexpectedly) spicy.
	매우 before vowel endings and connectors	-(으)면	매우면	매우면 먹지 마세요. If it's spicy, don't eat it.
		-(으)니까	매우니까	매우니까 조금씩 드세요. It's spicy so take it little by little.
		-(으)ㄹ 거에요	매울 거에요	그 김치는 매울 거에요. That 김치 will be spicy.
		-어서	매워서	그거 너무 매워서 못 먹어요. It's too spicy so I can't eat it.
		-어요	매워요	김치가 아주 매워요. (This) 김치 is very spicy.
		-었어요	매웠어요	음식이 다 매웠어요. All the foods were spicy.

You may feel like the conjugated form of 매우 + -(으)니까 and 매우 + 어서 are different (매우니까 vs. 매워서), one having 우 and the other having 워 in the final shape. But if you think of the process of putting the 우 stem and the connectors together, you can see they are of the same sort:

매우 + (으)니까 → because the stem ends in a vowel, drop -으 → 매우니까
매우 + 어서 → the vowels 우 and 어 merge → 매워서

Make your own chart and fill in the blanks for 싱겁다, 차갑다, 뜨겁다, and 굽다!
-- 굽다 and 돕다 are the only ㅂ-irregular *verbs* you know now; they can also take the -(으)세요 ending: for example,구우세요 and 도우세요.

A final cautionary word about the ㅂ-irregular verbs/adjectives is that the two words 돕다 (to help) and 곱다 (to be refined, pretty) have yet another stem form. Before the -어/아 ending, ㅂ is replaced with ㅗ (instead of ㅜ), and of course then they use -아(요).

It would be easiest if you repeatedly say these forms out loud and memorize the sounds by heart.

Citation form	Stem	Connectors & Endings	Conjugated form	Examples
돕다	돕 consonantal stem	-고	돕고	엄마를 돕고 오세요. Help your mother and (then) come.
		-지만	돕지만	매일 돕지만 일이 많아요. I help daily, but there is much work.
		-지요	돕지요	그 사람이 많이 돕지요? She helps a lot, doesn't she?
		-네요	돕네요	그 사람이 많이 돕네요. He (unexpectedly) helps a lot.
	도우 vocalic stem 1	-(으)면	도우면	도우면 일이 곧 끝날 거에요. If we help, the matter will soon end.
		-(으)니까	도우니까	도우니까 곧 끝났어요. Because we helped (it) ended soon.
		-(으)ㄹ 거에요	도울 거에요	내일도 도울 거에요. They will help tomorrow too.
	도오 vocalic stem 2	-아서	**도와서**	우리가 도와서 일이 끝났어요. We helped so the matter ended.
		-아요	**도와요**	같이 도와요. Let's help together.
		-았어요	**도왔어요**	나도 도왔어요. I helped too.

You will learn about this ending on the next page!

Make your own chart and fill in the blanks for 곱다!

2. Other Grammar Notes

1. -네　　Particle for observing something *unexpected*

In English, different moods are often conveyed by varying intonations. In Korean, sentence endings are used for expressing the speaker's moods or attitudes. One ending you already know is the presumed knowledge suffix -지. -네 is another such ending; it expresses the speaker's emotional status, namely a **spontaneous (and short-lasting) reaction** to something unexpected or notable. (You can use an appropriate punctuation mark at the end of the sentence depending on the degree of emotionality intended.)

어, 비가 오네?	(I didn't realize it was) raining.
오늘은 숙제가 많네!	Wow, there is a lot of homework today!
한국음식을 잘 먹네요.	You can really eat Korean food (e.g., unlike my other foreign friends).
김치가 별로 안 맵네요.	김치 isn't all that spicy (unlike its fame).
그 사람이 아직도 안 왔네.	He is still not here yet. (How strange.)

Although this sentence is in the "past tense", the situation described here is spontaneous & current: *He has not come yet* (and not *He did not come yet.*)

ㄹ-verbs drop their "ㄹ" before this ending.

아이들이 점심도 안 먹고 노네.	Kids are playing even without having lunch.
한국어를 많이 아네요.	You surely know a lot of Korean!
이 반찬은 아주 다네요.	This side dish is very sweet.

You will be given a summary of this notorious conflict between ㄹ and ㄴ in Korean at the end of the chapter.

Here is a word of caution about the pronunciation of the ending –네: Remember the strong nose rule? Consonants like ㅂ, ㄱ, ㄷ (ㅅ, and ㅆ) become like the nasal sound that follows them. Practice saying these phrases aloud, CORRECTLY!

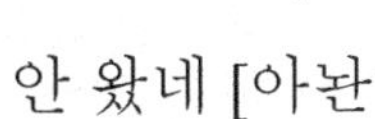

잘 먹네요 [잘 멍네요]	한국말 [항궁말]
안 왔네 [아놘네]	안 맵네요 [안 맴네요]

2. -게 *-ly*

-게 is a suffix that turns adjectives into adverbs, very much like English –ly (*happily, slowly*). It can attach to almost any adjective. Unlike English adverbs marked with *ly* that describe how the *verb* (or action) is done, Korean words marked with –게 add information about the *subject* or the *object*. Look carefully at the translation of the following sentences.

요즘 아주 바쁘게 살아요.	"I live very busily these days." I am living a busy life these days.
(음식을) 맛있게 드세요.	"Eat (the food) deliciously." Enjoy the meal.
그 책을 재미있게 읽었어요.	"I read that book interestingly." I enjoyed reading the book. (I read it and found it interesting.)
크게 말하세요.	"Speak big-ly." Speak loudly.

Translation of certain sentences works best if you use English adjectives:

종이에 이름을 작게 쓰세요.	"Write your name small on the paper."
걔는 나를 피곤하게 만들어요.	"He makes me tired."
예쁘게 그리세요.	"Draw (it) prettily." Draw (it) and make it pretty.

In general, -게 has the meaning of "in such-and-such way" or "so it becomes such-and-such ADJECTIVE". This is why the question word *how* (어떻게) has the marker -게 in it. Three other very useful manner adverb words are 이렇게 *like this*, 그렇게 *like that* 저렇게 *like that*:

이렇게 하세요!	Do (it) like this!
그렇게 하면 한국어 못 배워요.	If you do (it) like that, you can't learn Korean. (You can't learn Korean that way.)

3. -씩 *each; one by one*

-씩 is a noun marker that serves the function of the preposition *by* in English expressions such as *one by one*, *step by step*. It means *one at a time*, and it is attached to a noun or counter.

하나씩	one by one
한 과목씩	subject by subject; one subject at a time
한 사람씩 왔어요.	People came one by one.
조금씩 먹어.	Eat little by little, by small quantities

한 사람 앞에 하나씩 means *one per person.*

4. 때 *at the time of*

때 is used after a noun to mean *at the time of* (NOUN). Then the phrase sometimes substitutes for what might be a whole predicate (in English):

저녁 때	In the evening; at dinner time
초등학교 때	When I was in elementary school
크리스마스 때	At Christmas
휴가 때	During vacation

but not ~~아침 때~~!

Some more useful phrases are:

방학 때 during the school vacation
생일 때 on (one's) birthday
크리스마스 때
점심 때 in the afternoon
저녁 때 in the evening
그때 at that time; then

5. -(이)랑 *and, with*

-(이)랑 is exactly the same as -하고 in meaning and usage. It means *and* when it connects two nouns, and it means *with* when it comes after a noun and is used as a noun marker:

비빔밥에는 콩나물이랑 당근이랑 계란 후라이를 넣으면 맛있어요.
비빔밥 is good with (cooked) bean sprouts, carrots, and fried egg in it.

오늘 친구들이랑 같이 수영할 거에요. I'm going to swim with friends today.

Just like -하고, -(이)랑 is widely used in every-day spoken Korean. Use -랑 after nouns that end in a vowel, and -이랑 after nouns that end in a consonant:

A: 점심은 누구랑 먹을 거에요?	Who are you going to have lunch with?
B: **제이미**랑 **빌**이랑 먹을 거에요.	I'm going to eat with Jamie and Bill.
A: 뭘로 먹을 거에요?	What are you going to have?
B: 비빔밥이랑 감자국으로 먹을 거에요.	I'm going to have 비빔밥 and 감자국.

Language Point *"Endings"*

By now you should have a sense of three different kinds of suffixes in Korean. What we have called "markers" come after nouns. Some "endings" we have introduced attach to conjugated verbs and adjectives. Some of these endings can end a sentence, some of them can't. Can you figure out which of the following are markers, sentence connectors, or sentence endings? Do you know how the verb 맵다 would conjugate in front of each of them?

-고 -하고 -을 거에요 -지요 -이나 -어서 -어라 -으세요 -네 -자 -이랑

Lesson 15 Exercises

Exercise 1. Dialogue practice
Practice the dialogue in this lesson with a classmate.

Exercise 2. Conjugation
Conjugate the ㅂ-words according to the given endings, then pronounce them out loud.

	meaning of words	-지	-어/아서	-(으)면	-네
맵다					
싱겁다					
뜨겁다					
돕다					

Exercise 3. How does it taste?
Describe the following foods with *two* adjectives each.

1) 
2) 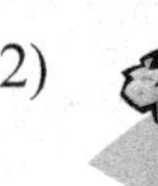 
3) 된장 찌개 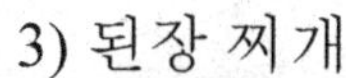 
4) 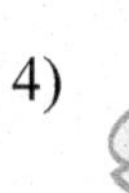 

5) 영국음식 (stereotypically)
6) 
7) 
8) 고추장 (ask a Korean)

Exercise 4. Pieces
Complete each sentence according to the pieces given.

1) 아이 (kids) // 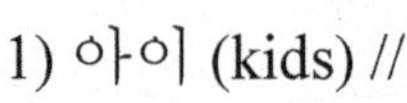  // 4 // 씩 // 주다 // (past tense)

2) 우리 //  // 3 // 씩 // 있다 // (present tense) 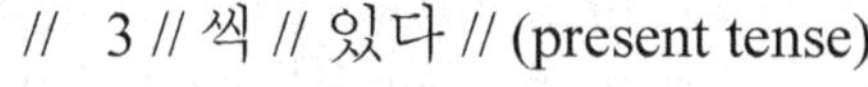

3) 우리 개 (dog) // 닭 //  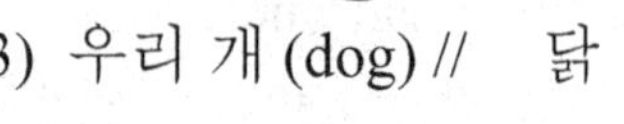  // 1 // 씩 // 먹다 // (past tense)

4) 야구 팀 // 9 // 있다

5) 식탁 (table)  // 5 // 씩 // 앉다 // (polite command)

Exercise 5. 이렇게 하세요. Do like this.
Translate the following sentences using ADJECTIVE+게 adverbs. They may sound odd in English, but they are very idiomatic in Korean!

1) Why do you act like it's no fun? (*Literally:* why do you do so no-fun-ly) Have fun studying Korean!
2) Mom made the cake really pretty. (cake: 케이크)
3) College students have a busy life.
4) Turn the TV down (*Literally:* do the TV more small-ly).
5) Because Grandma can't hear well, speak loudly. (hear: 들어요)
6) Why did you draw my face (얼굴) so* weirdly. (**so= like that*)
7) If there is no bread, how are you going to make sandwiches?
8) Don't speak badly of* the teacher (*OK with no "of" marker).
9) That person makes me tired!
10) Mom and Grandma make cabbage-Kimchi similarly.

Exercise 6. -네 practice
Express your surprise or bewilderment in the following situations.

1) 친구가 // 여기 // 살아요
2) 두부 피자 // 먹어요
3) 벌써 // 숙제 // 끝났어요
4) 동생 // 신문 // 읽어요
5) 배추 // 양배추 // 달라요 (달라요 different)
6) 고추장 // 맵다 // 달아요
7) 그 // 미국 사람 // 된장 찌개 // 잘 // 먹어요

Exercise 7. It's too hot!
You and a colleague are eating together, but the food is not quite right. Make a sentence pointing out (for your friend's confirmation) that each food has the wrong taste or temperature using -지요. Your "colleague" should respond agreeing with the shared knowledge, expressing a slight unexpectedness.

Example: 커피가 너무 싱겁지요? -- 네. 조금 싱겁네요.
This coffee is too bland, isn't it? – Yes, a little (although coffee is normally not so).

The following adverbs may be of use:
조금/좀 a little 아주 very 너무 too

1) 콜라 2) 사과 3) 국 4) 된장
5) 무 6) 맥주 7) 김치

Exercise 8. Association game
Take turns making associations, like this:

NOUN 1 는 ADJECTIVE 1	한국음식은? - 맛있어.
ADJECTIVE1 -으면 NOUN2	맛있으면? – 바나나
NOUN2 는 ADJECTIVE 2	바나나는? – 길어

Try keeping a beat and don't forget to conjugate the verbs and adjectives for -으면!

Exercise 10. Translation

1) 떡볶이 is hot and spicy.
2) This coffee is bland!
3) This soup is cold, isn't it?
4) Give me an apple and a pear, one each, please.
5) Don't put too much red pepper powder in your soup (국)! It's going to be spicy!
6) I put sugar in it, of course!
7) This is refreshing, but that is too cold (to my surprise).
8) That stew was bland and lukewarm.
9) If the noodles are bland, put some red pepper powder in them.

Lesson 15 Checkpoint

대화 1 **오늘 맛있게 먹고 재밌게 놀았어요.**

동호: **켈리** 씨, 제 칼국수가 어때요?
켈리: 맛있어요. 그런데 좀 짜네요.
동호: 짜요? 짜면 보리차[28]를 마시세요.
켈리: 앗, 뜨거워! 보리차가 너무 뜨거워요.

[28] Barley tea. The most common tea in Korea. People drink it like water.

동호: 그러면 조금씩 마시세요.

켈리: 김치가 너무 맛있어요. 이 것도 **동호** 씨가 만들었어요?

동호: 아니오, 우리 어머니가 만들었어요.

켈리: 잘 먹었어요. 오늘 맛있게 먹고 재밌게 놀았어요.

동호: 전화 안 해서 미안했어요. 내일부터 하루에 한 번 씩 전화할 거에요.

재밌게 = 재미있게
맛있게 = 맛이 있게

But don't use this *contracted* spelling in formal or official writing!

대화 2 한국 음식이 매워서 좋아요.

의사[29]: 또 왔네요. 또 배가 아파요[30]?

환자[31]: 네, 또 배가 아파요.

의사: 어제 뭘 먹었어요?

환자: 어제 떡볶이를 먹었어요. 왜 이렇게 배가 자주 아프지요, 의사 선생님?

의사: 저번에는 김치찌개를 너무 많이 먹어서 아팠지요? 한국 음식 좋아해요?

환자: 네, 한국 음식이 매워서 좋아요.

의사: 음식을 너무 맵게 먹지 마세요. 조금 싱겁게 드세요.

환자: 선생님, 그리고 목[32]도 아파요.

의사: 음... 감기[33]네요. 물을 따뜻하게 자주 마시세요.

환자: 그럼 저 이제 한국 음식을 못 먹어요?

의사: 아니에요. 조금만 싱겁게 먹으면 괜찮을 거에요. 간호사[34]한테 가서 약[35] 받고 가세요.

간호사: 여기 약 있어요. 아침, 점심, 저녁, 하루에 3 번씩 꼭[36] 드세요.

환자: 안녕히 계세요.

---

[29] doctor
[30] belly aches; stomach hurts
[31] patient
[32] throat
[33] cold
[34] nurse
[35] medicine
[36] definitely, without fail

Culture Point Got Kimchi?

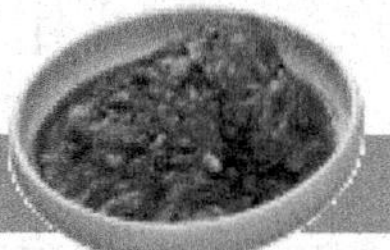

One bowl of rice and a dish of 김치 can make a complete meal to most Korean folks. Although 김치 is famous for its red-hot spice, it used to be made white in Korea. Red pepper was introduced into Korea in the 1600's and was not used as a main ingredient in 김치 until the 18th century! According to one of the many 김치 research institutes in Korea, there are almost 200 different kinds of 김치, which Koreans enjoy daily, including 25 different kinds of Napa cabbage-김치, 62 radish-김치, ten cucumber-김치, five seafood-based 김치, and 54 other kinds of 김치 made with various vegetables.

Each province has its own special 김치 recipes. 경상도 김치 is famous for its use of anchovy extract, 전라도's delicious 김치 uses a bounty of salted seafood, 충청도 김치 has a clean and refreshing aftertaste, and in North Korea, (e.g. 평안도, 함경도) red pepper or garlic is used sparingly.

Here are some of the names you can cite when you have an intellectual 김치 conversation: 배추 김치, 총각 김치, 깍뚜기, 동치미, 나박 김치, 오이 소배기.
Ask a friend or search the web for 여러가지 김치 (different kinds of 김치) to learn more about 김치!

Although the side dish 김치 is well-known for its spice, there are also plenty of spicy Korean *main* dishes. In general, anything red is spicy. Korean spice is usually based on 고추장 or 고춧가루, and it tends to last longer than Japanese *wasabi*. If you are up for spicy Korean dishes, try these!
떡볶이, 육개장, 매운탕, 김치찌개, and 비빔밥 (though for the last, some restaurants let you decide on the amount of 고추장 you use).

LESSON 16

뭐 먹을래요?

Lesson 16 Vocabulary  음식 expressions

르-불규칙 동사, 형용사	르-irregular verbs and adjectives
1. 몰라요 - 모르다 (르 -irr.)	to not know
2. 말라요 - 마르다 (르-irr.)	to be dry; skinny (person)
3. 불러요 - 부르다 (르-irr.)	to sing; call (out); (stomach) be full
4. 빨라요 - 빠르다 (르-irr.)	to be fast
5. 달라요 - 다르다 (르-irr.)	to be different; (다른: other, different)
다른 동사, 형용사	**Other verbs and adjectives**
6. 주문하다	to order (food), to place an order
7. 시키다	to order (food)
8. 취하다	to get drunk
9. (똑)같다	to be (exactly) the same
10. 비슷하다	to be similar
11. 느리다	to be slow
형용사	**Adjectives**
12. 새	new
13. 헌	old and worn out
	Nouns and Counters
14. 잔; 컵	coffee cup, liquor glass; cup, mug
15. 병	bottle
16. 그릇	bowl
17. 접시	plate, dish
18. 조각 [조각, 쪼각] = 쪽	piece
19. 주전자 (N)	kettle
20. 냄비 (N)	smallish pot with two short handles
음료수 [음뇨수]	**Beverages**
21. 물; 얼음물	water; iced water
22. 냉수	cold water
23. 보리/옥수수차	barley/corn tea (often called "물")
24. 우유	milk
25. 사이다	lemon-lime soda
26. 술	alcoholic beverages
27. 맥주	beer
28. 소주	rice vodka
29. 막걸리	unrefined rice wine
30. 인삼주/과일주	ginseng-based liquor/ fruit-made liquor
31. 안주	snack for beer and alcoholic beverages
32. 생선회	raw fish, "sashimi"
33. 육회	raw beef
34. 마른 오징어 채	shredded dried squid

Remember that with food, you can optionally ask for dishes without using counters: 떡볶이 하나 주세요.

Can you guess the meaning of these drinks? 커피, 코코아, 콜라, 주스

Supplementary Vocabulary

식당, 음식점	Restaurant
35. 배가 고파요. / 배고파요.	I am hungry.
36. 입이 궁금해요.	I feel munchy. (Literally, *my mouth is wondering about snacks).*
37. 입이 심심해요.	I feel munchy. (Literally, *my mouth is bored.*)
38. 배고파 죽겠어요.	I am starving (Literally, *I would die of hunger.*)
39. 배가 불러요. / 배불러요.	I am full.
40. 배(가)불러 죽겠어요.	I am stuffed. (Literally, *I would die of being full.*)
41. 목이 말라요. / 목말라요.	I am thirsty. (Literally, *My throat is dry.*)
42. 한 턱 내세요. [한텅 내세요]	Take (me) out. Treat us/me.
43. (뭐) 시킬래요? (used between customers) 44. (뭐) 주문하시겠어요? (used by waiter/waitress) – more polite	(What) would you like to order?
45. 잘/맛있게 먹겠습니다.	Thank you for the food. (*I will eat well/delicisouly.*)
46. 잘/맛있게 먹었습니다.	Thank you for the food. (*I ate well/deliciously.*)
47. 몇 분이세요? [며/메뿌니세요]	How many of you?
48. 저희 집은 냉면이 전문이에요.	Our specialty is 냉면.
49. 물 / 반찬 좀 더 주세요.	Give more water / side dishes, please.
50. 계산서 좀 주세요.	Please give (me/us) the check.
51. 어서 오세요!	Welcome! (Come on in!)
52. 잠시만/잠깐만 기다려 주세요.	Just a moment, please.
53. 또 오세요.	Please come again.
54. 종업원	waiter, waitress
55. 손님	customer, guest

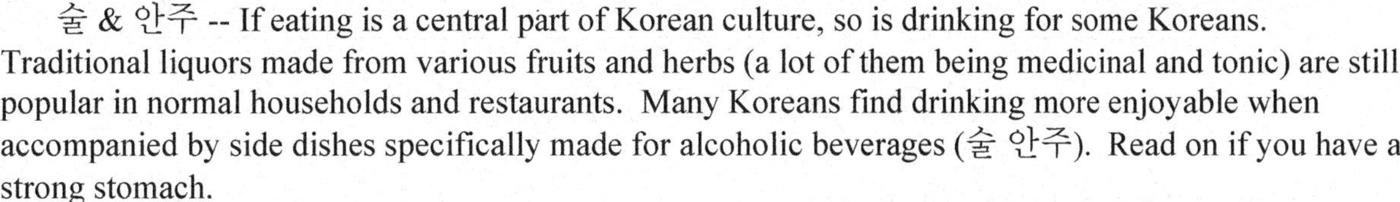

술 & 안주 -- If eating is a central part of Korean culture, so is drinking for some Koreans. Traditional liquors made from various fruits and herbs (a lot of them being medicinal and tonic) are still popular in normal households and restaurants. Many Koreans find drinking more enjoyable when accompanied by side dishes specifically made for alcoholic beverages (술 안주). Read on if you have a strong stomach.

돼지족발	pig feet	우족	cow feet
혀밑구이	cow tongue	마른 오징어 (채)	dried squid (shredded)
노가리	dried baby pollack	설렁탕	beef tripe soup
멸치볶음	salted, fried anchovies	골뱅이 무침	seasoned conch

Some enjoy raw vegetables like 오이 and 당무 in a 고추장 dip, and some even have fruit!

Vocabulary Exercise 1. What do you say?
Match each situation on the left with an appropriate prompt or response from the right.

1) "짠 팝콘을 많이 먹어서...	배가 고파요.
2) "제가 돈이 없으니까...	입이 심심해요.
3) 친구: "더 많이 먹어요!" YOU: "아니오 ...	계산서 주세요.
4) "아침을 안 먹어서...	배고파 죽겠어요.
5) "아침하고 점심을 둘 다 (both) 안 먹어서...	피곤해 죽겠어요.
6) 식당에 김치가 없어서, YOU: "여기요! ...	배불러 죽겠어요.
7) 피자 한 접시를 혼자 (by yourself) 먹고 나니까...	목이 말라요.
8) 식당에서 음식을 다 먹고 나서, YOU: "여기요! ...	반찬 좀 더 주세요.
9) 공부를 오랫동안 해서...	한 턱 내세요.
10) 종업원: ... YOU: "세 명이에요."	잠시만 기다려 주세요.
11) 식당에서 돈을 내고 나서: "...	잘 먹겠습니다.
14) 친구 엄마: "맛있게 먹어요." YOU: "...	잘 먹었습니다.
	또 오세요!

Vocabulary Exercise 2. A cup of coffee, please.
Make up food and beverage orders for your partner to complete, using the correct counter:

잔, 컵, 병, 그릇, 접시, 조각 (also use 개, 마리, 명, 분)

Example: 피자 → 피자 한 접시

Vocabulary Exercise 3. Milk and cookies
With a partner, come up with food-beverage combinations that sound good together.

물, 보리차/옥수수차,우유, 커피, 코코, 콜라/사이다, 술, 맥주, 과일주, (안주)

Example: 우유 → 우유 하고 초코 파이 (moon pies)

Vocabulary Exercise 4. Opposites
Write the word that has the opposite meaning, in -어/아요 form.

알아요 -- __________ 느려요 -- __________ 배가 고파요 -- ____________

Lesson 16 Dialogue 뭐 먹을래요?

시은: 아, 배 고파! 그리고 목도 말라. 오빠, 우리 빨리 어디 가서[1] 뭐 먹자!

동호: 한국 음식을 먹을래[2] 아니면,[3] 중국 음식을 먹을래?

시은: 나는 한국 음식. **켈리** 씨는 무슨 음식 먹을래요?[4]

켈리: 나도 한국 음식이 괜찮아요.

동호: 한국 음식이 좋으면, **신라** 식당에 갈래요?

시은: 거기는 김치에 미원[5]을 너무 많이 넣어서 맛이 없어.

동호: 그럼 학교 뒤의 **고려** 식당으로 갈래? 거기는 매운[6] 떡볶이하고 매운 오징어 볶음이 맛있어.

켈리: 좋아요. 난[7] 매운 음식을 좋아하니까 **고려** 식당으로 가요.

1. go and
2. want to, going to eat
3. if not, or
4. want to eat
5. MSG
6. spicy
7. spoken variant of 나는

Lesson 16 Grammar

1. Focus Immediate desire -(으)ㄹ래요

The ending for "immediate desire" is -(으)ㄹ래. You can add -요 to express politeness. We will refer to the ending as -(으)ㄹ래요.

-(으)ㄹ래요	I wanna

The ending -(으)ㄹ래요 indicates an immediate desire or intention. It can only be used with first or second person subjects (*I* or *you*). –ㄹ래요 attaches to vowel-final verb stems and -을래요 attaches to consonant-final stems. Note that there are two ㄹ letters and a doubly-long ㄹ sound:

뭐 시킬래요?	What do you wanna order (here & now)?
불고기로 먹을래요.	I wanna have 불고기.
막걸리 마실래요?	Do you wanna drink 막걸리 (here & now)?

Verbs that end in ㄹ again act like **vowel-ending verbs** before -(으)ㄹ래요 by dropping the ㄹ (으 naturally disappears because now the verb ends in a vowel):

저기에서 양파 좀 썰래요?	Do you wanna chop some onions over there?
졸업하고 어디 살래요?	Where do you wanna live after you graduate?

NOTE: -을 거에요, which you learned in a previous lesson, refers to plans for a more distant future whereas -을래요 is more emotionally-loaded and tied to the speakers' and the listeners' immediate intentions and desires.

오늘 몇 시에 점심 먹을 거에요?	What time are you going to eat lunch today?
오늘 몇 시에 점심 먹을래요?	What time do you wanna eat lunch today?

Because -(으)ㄹ래요 is so related to one's intentions and desires, it cannot be used with a third person subject – you can't speak for another's intentions and desires.

Also because -(으)래요 is so *immediate*, in phrases like 언제 점심 먹을래요? it is implied that the speaker is also going to be with the listener when the action takes place.

2. Other Grammar Notes

1. ADJ + (으)ㄴ　　Noun-modifier ending for adjectives

You already know that adjectives in Korean conjugate the same way as verbs do when they function as predicates and come at the end of the sentence. To use adjectives as noun modifiers, simply add -은 after *consonant*-ending adjective stems and -ㄴ after *vowel*-ending adjective stems:

Consonant-ending adjectives

많다	많은 돈	a lot of money
괜찮다	괜찮은 성적	an O.K. grade
작다	작은 사람	a small person
좋다	좋은 선생님	a good teacher
싫다	싫은 과목	a disfavored subject
똑같다	똑같은 얘기	the same exact story

Vowel-ending adjectives (including 하다-adjectives)

바쁘다	바쁜 학생	a busy student
예쁘다	예쁜 가방	a pretty bag
느리다	느린 컴퓨터	a slow computer
질기다	질긴 고기	tough meat
짜다	짠 국	salty soup
쓰다	쓴 맥주	bitter beer
시다	신 김치	sour 김치
크다	큰 소리	a loud voice, loud noise/sound
다르다	다른 음식	different food
필요하다	필요한 거	a needed thing (= thing that you need)
미지근하다	미지근한 차	lukewarm tea
진하다	진한 커피	strong coffee
중요하다	중요한 숙제	important homework
비슷하다	비슷한 맛	a similar taste

Because the noun-modifier ending begins with a vowel "으", the *vocalic* stem of the ㅂ-irregular adjectives is used before it. That is, use 차가우 and not 차갑 for the adjective *cold*:

차갑다	차가운 물	cold water
싱겁다	싱거운 거	something bland
맵다	매운 떡볶이	spicy 떡볶이

For adjectives ending in ㄹ, drop ㄹ from the stem (which will then "take" the ending ㄴ because the stem is now vowel-ending):

달다	**단 사탕**	sweet candy
헐다	**헌 가방**	old (worn out) bag

(헐다 means *to wear out.*)

There are of course words that are born as noun modifiers (like English *live* in "*a live squid*"). The word 새 (*new*) is an example.

The ㄴ-ㄹ battle in Korean is very interesting. Here is a brief summary of what you have seen so far:
If it is a conflict between ㄴ and ㄹ within or at the edge of a noun, ㄹ tends to win and ㄴ assimilates to (becomes) ㄹ in **pronunciation**: 칼날 → [칼랄] 신라 → [실라]

If it is across the boundary between a verb/adjective and an ending , ㄴ tends to win, chasing away ㄹ:
달 + 네 → 다네 달 + 니 → 다니? 달 + (으)ㄴ → 단 달 + (으)니까 → 다니까
In this interaction, it doesn't seem to matter whether the ending comes with the vowel 으.

Finally, for 있다 adjectives, add -는 instead of -은. This is because 있다 itself is a *verb*.

맛있다	맛있는	tasty
맛없다	맛없는	bland, unappetizing
재미있다	재미있는	interesting
재미없다	재미없는	un-interesting, boring

If you are a motivated/advanced student, learn this now: The ending "-은" can come after a verb as well, but in that case, the verb has to modify a noun with the sense of *completion* (past tense):
매일 거기에서 자는 사람은 내 동생이에요.
The person who **sleeps** there every day is my brother.
어제 거기에서 잔 사람은 내 동생이에요.
The person who **slept** there yesterday is my brother.
Don't say ~~맛있은~~ or ~~재미없은~~ ever! You'll learn how to make past modifying adjective forms in second year!

2. -어/아서 *go/come (and then and there) + activity*

The sentence connector -서 connects to the -어/아 form of the verb and means something close to the English *having done* ...or *since*:

시험 공부를 많이 해서, A를 받았어요.	Having studied a lot for the test, I got an A.
시간이 있어서 철수하고 만났어요	Since I had time, I met with 철수.

In this lesson, you learn the meaning of (*having come/gone...) and then and there*.
Generally, when the verb before -어서 expresses movement, the second clause expresses not so much a reason/result relationship but instead what happened at the movement's end or destination:

학교 가서 축구했어요. ← 학교에 갔어요. 거기에서 축구했어요.
Having gone to school, I played soccer. *or* I went to school, and played soccer there.

In fact, when the verb shows directional movement (가다, 오다, 떠나다, etc.) -어/아서 can *only* be used when there is an **immediate temporal and spatial connection** between going (or coming) to some place and the following action. If the place you go to is NOT the same place where you engage in an activity, you have to use the connector -고.

A: **미라** 씨, 오늘 뭐 해요?	What are you doing today, Mira?
B: 학교에 가서 공부해요.	I go to school and study (there)
B': 학교에 가고 공부해요.	I go to school, and (I also) study (somewhere else)

Clauses linked by -고 do not express any inherent connection between the events -- no ordering and no reason-result. This applies to a series of past events as well:

어제 학교에 갔고 축구를 했어요. I went to school and I played soccer (probably not at school).

⚠ As you see in a sentence like 저는 도서관에 가서 공부했어요, -어/아서 does **NOT** conjugate for the past tense. Remember this!

Be careful to pronounce a soft "s" sound in 가서 as compared to 갔어!

It is usually clear from the context whether -어/아서 means *so/since* or *and then and there*. If the verb with -어/아서 is physical and action-based (*go*, *come*, *sit*, *lie down*, for example), the translation tends to be *and then*.

와서 밥 먹어!	Come and eat!
가서 공부해라.	Go and study!
앉아서 좀 쉬세요.	Sit down and take a little break.
누워서 책을 읽었어요.	I read the book lying down.

If it is an adjective (or *stative verb*) that -어/아서 is attached to, or if the subject of the two clauses is not identical, the translation tends to be *so*.

배고파서 먼저 먹었어요.	I was hungry so I ate first.
그 사람이 떠나서 외로워요.	He left so I am lonely.

⚠ The verb 이다 (usually) takes a special form when used with -어/아서: 이어서 → 이라서 . Also, drop the syllable -이 when the noun ends in a vowel.

떡볶이는 매운 음식이라서 안 좋아해요. 떡볶이 is a spicy food, so I don't like it.

이건 소고기라서 안 먹어요. 저는 채식주의자에요.
Because this is beef, I am not eating (it). I am a vegetarian.

3. More counters

Some independent nouns can function as counters when it comes to food.

콜라 네 병	four bottles of cola
커피 한 잔	a cup of coffee
비빔밥 세 그릇	three bowls of 비빔밥
족발 한 접시	a plate of pig feet
우유 한 컵	a glass of milk
피자 한 조각	a piece of pizza
케잌 한 쪽	a piece of cake

In spoken Korean, 조각 is often pronounced as [쪼각].

4. 르-irregular verbs and adjectives

About ninety-nine percent of the verbs and adjectives that end in 르 conjugate irregularly. Unlike other types of irregular verbs and adjectives, however, 르-irregulars change ***only before the -어/아 ending***. Before –어/아 endings, -르 words drop the vowel 으 in the stem and add another ㄹ, so they end up with a double ㄹ (letter and pronunciation).

르-irregulars	Meaning	Consonantal ending	-어/아 ending	-으 ending
부르다	call out; sing: be full	부르고	불러요	부를래요
모르다	not know	모르지만	몰라서	모를 거에요
빠르다	be fast	빠르지요	빨라요	빠르니까
마르다	be dried	마르고	말라서	마르면
다르다	be different	다르고	달라요	다르면

우리 엄마는 노래를 잘 불러요.	My mom sings well.
기차는 빨라. 빠르면 비행기.	The train is fast; if it's fast, it's an airplane. (from a game)

Here are some more 르 words you will run into down the long but fun road of studying Korean. Can you fill in the blanks?

More 르-irregular words	어/아 form	Meaning
가르다		cut in half, divide
고르다		pick, choose
	굴러요	roll
기르다		raise (kids and animals)
나르다		carry
	눌러요	press down
두르다		wrap around
바르다		apply (e.g. ointment)
	올라요	climb
자르다		cut
흐르다		flow
	어질러요	make a mess (e.g. room)
엎지르다		knock over (liquid)
앞지르다		get ahead

5. N 같다

You learned 같다 to mean *the same* in this lesson, but you have seen this word in another form. Do you remember? 같이 was introduced earlier as an adverb that means *(together) with* in sentences like **제리**하고 같이 한국 음식을 만들었어요.

The meaning *together with* comes from the sense of *likeness*. Understanding this sense is very useful as you can see in the following examples:

그 사람은 우리 엄마 같아요.	She is like my mother.
저는 떡볶이같이 매운 음식은 못 먹어요.	I can't eat spicy food like 떡볶이.
나도 그 사람같이 한국어를 잘 할래요.	I'm gonna speak Korean well like her.
야채하고 채소는 같은 말이에요.	야채 and 채소 are the same thing ("word").

Memorizing these patterns may help you:

X-같이	*like X*
X 하고 같이	*with X*
X-같은 Y	*Y that's like X*
X 하고 Y 는 같다	*X is the same as Y (X is like Y)*

Lesson 16 Exercises

Exercise 1. Dialogue practice
Practice the dialogue in this lesson with a classmate.

Exercise 2. Conjugation
Conjugate the following adjectives for the noun-modifying form and provide a noun to follow each one.
Example: 크다 → 큰 코

1) 맵다
2) 작다
3) 달다
4) 좋다
5) 시끄럽다 (noisy)
6) 어렵다 (difficult)

Exercise 3. Descriptions
Describe what exists in each picture using an adjective-noun phrase.

Example: 뜨거운 물이 있어요. 

1) 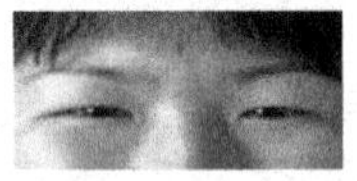 (눈)

2)  (개미)

3) 

4)  (코끼리)

5) 

6) 

Exercise 4. May I take your order?
Pretend that you are a waiter or a waitress at a Korean restaurant. Welcome the customers (동호, 시은, and 켈리) from the dialogue above), lead them to a seat, bring them water, ask what they want to order. Do the same for when the customers are done with their food.

Exercise 5. Go there and ~ / Come here and ~
Order your classmates around by making the following commands.

1) Come here and have lunch with me.
2) Go to the library and study (there).
3) Come here and meet me.
4) Go there and put your bag (down) on the table.
5) Come here and sit down.
6) *Make your own using words from this lesson!*

Exercise 6. I'm gonna/I wanna…
You are with a **very** admiring friend. Everywhere you go he/she asks you what you want to do (or what you are going to do next) by asking "뭐 할래?" so that he/she can do it with you. Answer using the "-(으)ㄹ 래" form, which means you are only expressing *your* immediate plan or desire not inviting your tag-along to join you in the activity! Your friend can answer with "나도 … -(으)ㄹ 래."

Example: (공원, 야구하다):
A: 뭐 할래? B: 공원에서 야구할래. A: 나도 할래!

1) 집, 텔레비전 보다
2) 공원, 친구하고 놀다
3) 한국 식당, 점심 먹다
4) 집, 저녁 만들다
5) 친구집, 한국어 숙제하다
6) 도서관 , 시험 공부하다
7) *Make your own using words from this lesson!*

Exercise 7. Adjective conversion
Change the sentence so you will have a modifying adjective in it.

Example: 음식이 짜요 → 짠 음식이에요.

1) 오렌지가 셔요. →

2) 영화가 재미있어요. →

3) 고추장이 아주 매워요. →

4) 수박이 너무 맛있어요. →

5) 선생님은 아주 바빠요. →

6) 사탕이 별로 안 달아요. →

7) 돼지 고기가 기름기가 많아요. (기름기 [기름끼]: fat) →

Exercise 8. What's your opinion?
Exchange opinions with your partner about the following topics. Come up with your own adjectives to describe each topic.

Example: 한국어, 과목

한국어는 재미없는 과목이에요. Korean is a boring subject.

네, 한국어는 정말 (really) 재미없는 과목이에요. Korean is really a boring subject. *or*

아니에요. 한국어는 재미있는 과목이에요! No, it's a fun subject!

1) 맥주, 술
2) 비빔밥, 음식
3) 김치, 반찬
4) 한국어 선생님, 분
5) 오렌지 주스, 음료수
6) 수박, 과일

Exercise 9. Fill in the blanks with appropriate 르 words.
Fill in the blanks with appropriate verbs and adjectives, conjugated for each context.

1) 배가 __________서 밥을 다 못 먹었어요.

2) 제가 내일 노래를 ________거에요.

3) 아, Ferrari 는 참 ________네요. (fast)

4) 내일 나하고 노래 _________러 노래방에 가요!

5) A: 시간이 ______지요? (fast)

B: 네, 참 ________요.

6) A: 브리트니 노래 잘 못 _________지요?

B: 네, 참 잘 ___________네요.

7) A: 저 남자 __________세요?

B: 네, __________아요.

Exercise 10. Translation

1) Hey, Mr. Tambourine man, sing a song for me!

2) If you don't know the answer, you didn't study.

3) If you are full, don't eat any more.

4) Take the inter-city bus. It's fast. (inter-city bus: 시외 버스)

5) I don't know that man.

6) Because I did badly on the test, I sang (a song) in class today.

7) Oh, I am so full!

8) I'm thirsty!

9) I like spicy side-dishes like 김치.

10) 당근 and 홍당무 are the same thing.

11) He is like a brother to me.

Here are some 보다 idioms.
Learn them!
영화를 보다 see a movie
책을 보다 read a book
손금을 보다 read the palm
관상을 보다 read the face (for fortune telling)
아기를 보다 baby-sit
집을 보다 house-sit
시험을 보다 (or 치다) take a test
손을 보다 fix, take care of something
알아보다 recognize (a face)
먹어보다 taste/try (food)

Exercise 11. -어/아서 versus -고

Read the following dialogue between 경아 and 민호. Try to get a sense of the different uses of -고 and -서.

경아: 오늘 뭐 했어요? 어디 갔어요?
민호: 네. 친구 집에 가서 친구하고 같이 공부했어요.
경아: 언제 갔어요?
민호: 점심 먹고 갔어요.
경아: 전화하고 갔어요, 그냥 갔어요? (그냥 just)
민호: 친한 친구라서 그냥 갔어요! (친한 close)

Exercise 12. Tell 'em why! (어서 as a background, review)

Come up with a reason for each situation below, and make a sentence expressing both the reason and the result, using -어서.

Example: You are not hungry. (Having eaten breakfast…)
→ 아침을 먹어서 배가 안 고파요.

1) You overslept.(*oversleep* 늦잠자다)

2) Your bag is heavy.(*heavy* 무겁다 – ㅂ-irregular)

3) You are lonely.(*lonely* 외롭다 – ㅂ-irregular)

4) Your soup is too bland.

5) You drank 5 bottles of beer.

6) You don't like _____ food.

Exercise 13. -고 or -어/아서?
Translate the sentences using either -고 or -어/아서.

1) This morning I took a shower and had breakfast. (this morning 오늘 아침)
2) Yesterday I went to a friend's house and did my Korean homework there.
3) Every day I go shopping, play soccer, and have ice cream.
4) My bag is heavy because there is a rock in it. (rock 돌 heavy 무거워요)
5) Since it is warm today, don't put on a sweater. (warm 따뜻해요 [따드태요])

Exercise 14. Counters.
Order the following items using appropriate counters.

어서 오세요. 뭐 주문하시겠어요?

1) Rour bottles of cola, please
2) Two bowls of noodles, please.
3) Three glasses of apple juice, please.
4) Two cups of tea and a cup of coffee, please.
5) A plate of 족발, please.

Exercise 15. 뭐 ...-(으)ㄹ래요? What are you gonna do if...?
Take turns asking and answering questions.

1) 이번 주말에 뭐 할래요?

날씨가 좋으면, ______________________ (if the weather is good)
날씨가 나쁘면, ______________________

2) 오늘 밤에 몇 시에 잘래요?

피곤하면 ______________________ (if I am tired)
안 피곤하면 ______________________

3) 내일 아침에 뭐 먹을래요?

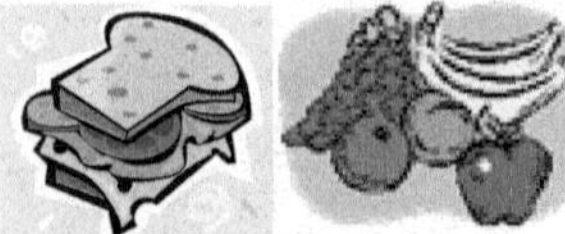

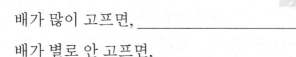

배가 많이 고프면, ______________________
배가 별로 안 고프면, ______________________

4) Make up your own!

Exercise 16. Reading and dialogue practice.

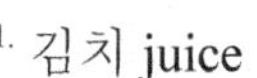

오빠: 그 김칫국물[1] 마시지 마! 매워.

영아: 마실래!

오빠: 아주 맵고 짜.

영아: 그럼, 커피 마실래.

오빠: 커피는 쓰고 맛도 없어. 게다가[2] 뜨거워.

영아: 그래도[3] 마실래. (drinks the coffee) 앗 뜨거![4]

오빠: 거 봐[5]. 뜨겁지? 자, 여기 콜라나 사이다 마셔. 시원하고 달아.

영아: (drinks coke) 매워!

오빠: 알았어[6]. 그럼 우유 마셔. 우유는 싱거워. 맛있지?

영아: 음~. 정말 맛있네!

1. 김치 juice
2. on top of that
3. even so, even if that's the case
4. Hotchacha! (exclamatory variant of 뜨거워)
5. See that? I told you (spoken variant of 그것 봐)
6. All right. OK. Gotcha.

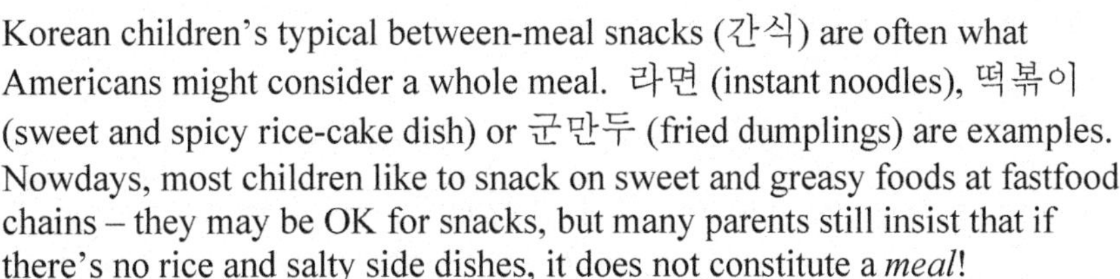

Korean children's typical between-meal snacks (간식) are often what Americans might consider a whole meal. 라면 (instant noodles), 떡볶이 (sweet and spicy rice-cake dish) or 군만두 (fried dumplings) are examples. Nowdays, most children like to snack on sweet and greasy foods at fastfood chains – they may be OK for snacks, but many parents still insist that if there's no rice and salty side dishes, it does not constitute a *meal*!

Fight of the century!! Tonight at the Key Arena!

vs.

Language Point *Food clichés*

Learn these cool clichés! Can you guess their meaning?

제 얼굴이 홍당무가 됐어요. — My face turned beet red!

검은 머리가 파뿌리 될 때까지... — Until death parts the two

어제 밤에 아주 파김치가 됐어요 — I was so exhausted last night!

버스가 콩나물 시루였어요. — Folks were packed like sardines on the bus!

왜 그렇게 뜻뜨미지근해요? — How come you are so wishy-washy?

Lesson 16 Checkpoint

대화 1 맛있게 드셨어요?

종업원: 손님, 뭐 주문하시겠어요?

손님: 여기는 뭐가 맛있어요?

종업원: 저희 집은 설렁탕 전문이에요.

손님: 그럼, 설렁탕 한 그릇하고 인삼주 한 병 주세요.

손님: 여기요! 계산서 주세요. 얼마지요?

종업원: 네, 만 천원입니다.

손님: 여기 있어요.

종업원: 설렁탕 어땠어요? 맛있게 드셨어요?

손님: 네, 아주 잘 먹었습니다.

종업원: 감사합니다. 또 오세요.

대화 2 오늘 술 마시러 갈래?

은영: 오늘 술 마시러 갈래?

원식: 좋아. **신광** 아니면 **해머**, 어디로 갈래?

은영: 학교 앞 **신광**으로 가자. 거기가 싸고[37] 맛있어.

원식: 맞아, **해머**는 맛없고 비싼[38] 안주만 팔아. 막걸리도 없어.

은영: 너 오늘 막걸리를 마실 거야?

원식: 응, 나는 **신광**의 따뜻한 막걸리가 좋아.

은영: 따뜻한 막걸리? 그런 것도 있었어?[39] 나는 차가운 막걸리 마실래.

원식: 우리 안주는 뭘 먹지?

은영: 가서 메뉴를 보고 시키자.

---

[37] cheap and
[38] expensive
[39] I've never heard of such a thing (*literally*, such a thing exists?)

읽기 1 앞으로는...

나는 음식을 맵게 먹으면 배가 아파요. 그제 떡볶이를 맵게 먹고 나서 배가 아팠어요. 고추장을 한 병이나 넣어서 아주 매웠어요. 그래서 병원에 가서 진찰[40]을 받았어요. 의사선생님이 약을 주었어요. 약은 하루에 세 번씩 먹어요. 어제는 침대에 누워서 좀 쉬었어요. 소파에 앉아서 텔레비전도 보고 신문도 읽었어요.

오늘은 화요일이에요. 매주 화요일에는 **미미**랑 놀러 나가요. 우리는 자주 노래방에 가서 놀아요. 그런데 목이 아파서 오늘은 노래방에 못 가요. 지금 목이 아파서 큰 소리로 말을 못 해요. 그래서 우리는 **녹색** 극장에 영화 보러 가요. 몸이 아프니까 마음껏[41] 못 놀아서 슬퍼요[42]. 이제부터는 음식을 싱겁게 먹을 거에요.

읽기 2 크리스마스 카드

오늘 공작 시간[43]에 크리스마스 카드를 만들었어요. 나는 종이 위에 **산타**[44]의 얼굴을 그렸어요. **산타**의 얼굴[45]만 크게 그렸어요. **산타** 옆에 **루돌프**[46]도 작게 그렸어요. 카드는 다섯 장[47]을 만들었어요. 카드 뒤하고 앞에 내 이름을 작게 썼어요. 학교가 끝나고 나서 문방구[48]에 갔어요. 예쁜 봉투[49] 다섯 장을 샀어요. 봉투에 내 이름은 작게 쓰고 친구들 이름은 크고 예쁘게 썼어요. 봉투에 카드를 한 장 씩 넣었어요. 그리고 우체국에 카드를 부치러[50] 갔어요. 많은 사람들이 크리스마스 카드를 부치러 왔어요. 그래서 오랫동안 기다렸어요. 카드를 만들어서 보내니까 기분이 좋네요.

---

40 medical examination
41 to one's heart's content
42 bored
43 Shop class
44 Santa
45 face
46 Rudolf
47 sheet(s) - counter
48 stationary; school supply store
49 envelope
50 to send by mail

노래할래요!

귀여운 꼬마	이슬비
귀여운 꼬마가 닭장에 가서 암탉을 잡으려다 놓쳤다네 닭장 밖에 있던 배 고픈 여우 옳거니 하면서 물고 갔다네 꼬꼬댁 암탉 소리를 쳤네 꼬꼬댁 암탉 소리를 쳤네 귀여운 꼬마가 그 꼴을 보고 웃을까 울까 망설였다네	이슬비 내리는 이른 아침에 우산 셋이 나란히 걸어갑니다 빨간 우산 파란 우산 찢어진 우산 좁다란 학교 길에 우산 세 개가 이마를 마주 대고 걸어갑니다. 

Language Point *Excuse me!*

As you know, second person pronouns (*you*) in Korean are rarely used in polite speech. What should you do if you want to get somebody's attention in a store, for example? Here are some useful titles you can use depending on the person's gender and estimated age: 할머니 (grandma), 할아버지 (grandma) -- for older people, 아줌마 or 아주머니 and 아저씨 -- for (married) people in their 30's-50's, and 아가씨 ("miss", "lady") for unmarried young women.

At a restaurant, you can use this attention getter, without being rude: 여기요! Typical Korean restaurants hire waitresses more often than waiters. To youngish servers, you can use 언니 (if you are younger than the server, or 아가씨 (if you are older). For the rare waiter, you might hear 아저씨 (or women can say 오빠). Since it is not always easy to figure out everyone's respective ages, people often avoid the confusion and just call out 여기요!

실례합니다 is used to mean "Excuse me" only when you are interrupting something or being intrusive. To catch someone's attention, people usually start with 저....

쉬어갑시다!

LET'S TAKE A BREAK!

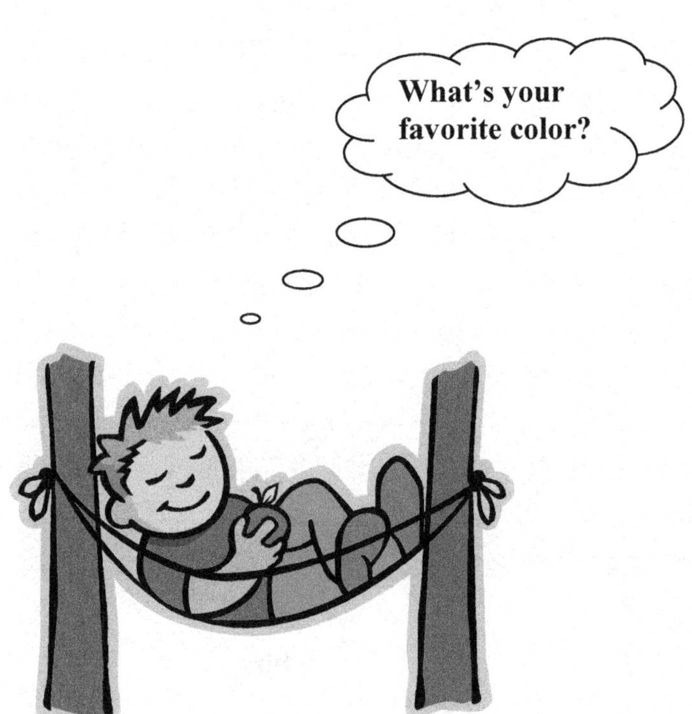
What's your
favorite color?

CHAPTER 4.5 무슨 색을 제일 좋아해요?

What is your favorite color?

1. Vocabulary

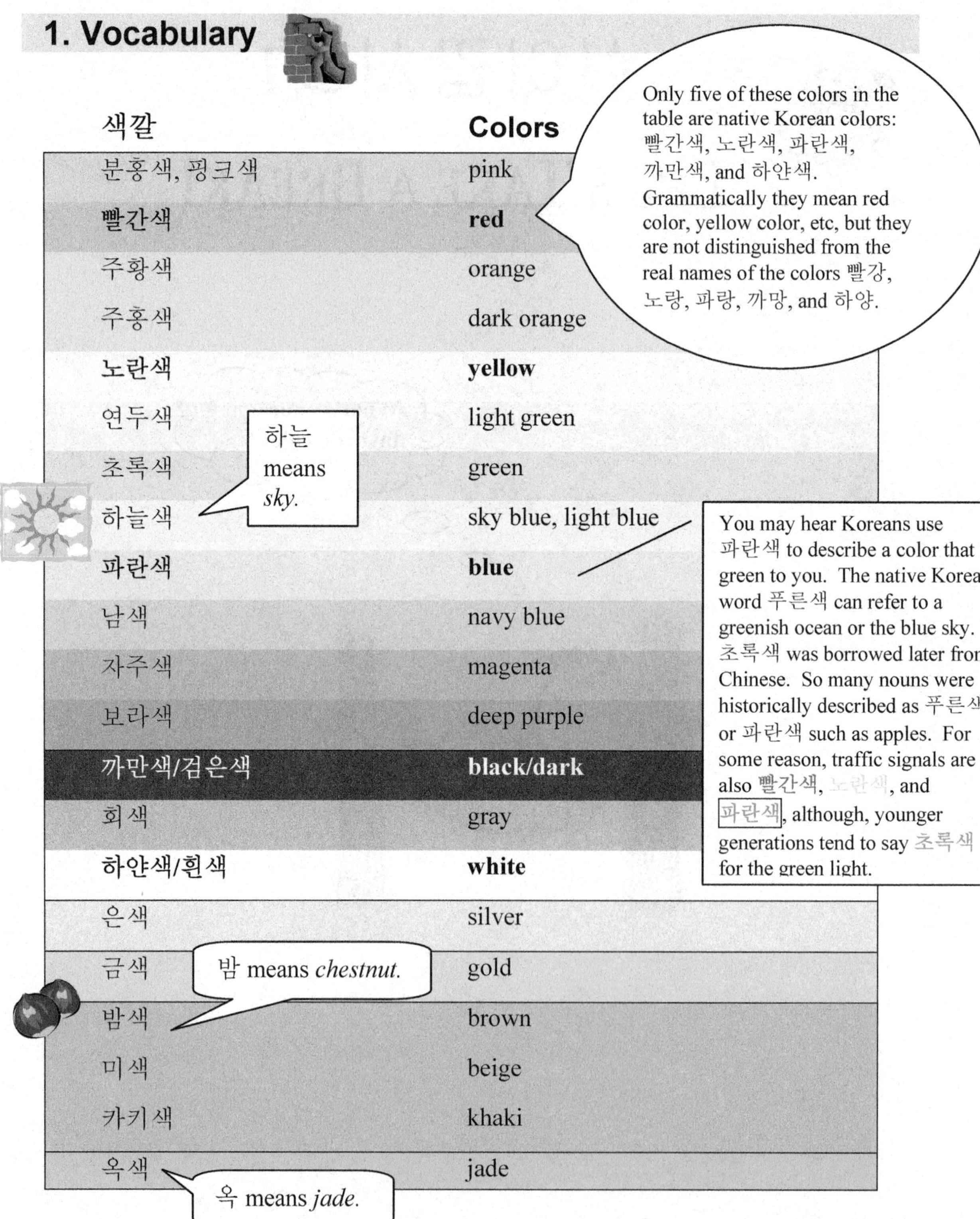

색깔	Colors
분홍색, 핑크색	pink
빨간색	**red**
주황색	orange
주홍색	dark orange
노란색	**yellow**
연두색	light green
초록색	green
하늘색	sky blue, light blue
파란색	**blue**
남색	navy blue
자주색	magenta
보라색	deep purple
까만색/검은색	**black/dark**
회색	gray
하얀색/흰색	**white**
은색	silver
금색	gold
밤색	brown
미색	beige
카키색	khaki
옥색	jade

Only five of these colors in the table are native Korean colors: 빨간색, 노란색, 파란색, 까만색, and 하얀색. Grammatically they mean red color, yellow color, etc, but they are not distinguished from the real names of the colors 빨강, 노랑, 파랑, 까망, and 하양.

하늘 means *sky.*

You may hear Koreans use 파란색 to describe a color that is green to you. The native Korean word 푸른색 can refer to a greenish ocean or the blue sky. 초록색 was borrowed later from Chinese. So many nouns were historically described as 푸른색 or 파란색 such as apples. For some reason, traffic signals are also 빨간색, 노란색, and 파란색, although, younger generations tend to say 초록색 for the green light.

밤 means *chestnut.*

옥 means *jade.*

2. Grammar Notes

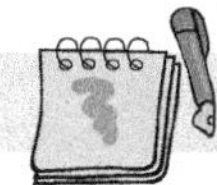

1. 무슨 색을 제일 좋아해요? **What is your favorite color?**
제일: most, best

2. Color terms and conjugation
There are two types of color terms in Korean. One is native, and the other borrowed from Chinese. Native color terms are the 5 core color terms, red, yellow, blue, white, and black (in bold on the chart) that are ***adjectives***, so they behave like any other adjectives. They conjugate in 어/아요 form when they are used as a predicate, and they conjugate in 은/ㄴ form when they come before a noun to modify it.

Outside the 5 core color words, most other color terms (borrowed from Chinese) are ***nouns*** and they (always) end in the word 색, which means *color*. Since these are *nouns*, you cannot conjugate them, of course. To describe an item using these color terms in a predicate, you will need to use the verb 이다:

선생님 눈은 밤색이에요. 그리고 선생님 신발도 밤색이에요.

If you want to modify a noun to describe the color of the item (e.g. *brown shoes*), you can simply put the color noun in front of the noun you are trying to describe:

밤색 신발 밤색 머리 초록색 지우개 주황색 모자 보라색 의자

The native Korean color terms can act like color *nouns* when they are used with the noun 색:

노란색 신발 (신발 shoes) 빨간색 구두 (구두 dress shoes) 하얀색/흰색 종이 까만색/검은색 가방

You may hear Koreans drop the word 색 a lot especially after the five native colors 빨간, 노란, 파란, 하얀/흰, and 까만/검은.

3. Exercises

Exercise 1. Find out the following information and report to the class!

1) 선생님 가방은 무슨 색이에요?

2) _____ 씨 머리는 무슨 색이에요? (머리: hair)

3) _____ 씨 지갑은 무슨 색이에요?

4) _____ 씨 신발*은 무슨 색이에요? (신발: shoes)

5) _____ 씨 펜은 무슨 색이에요?

신호등은 무슨 색이에요?

신호등을지킵시다

Exercise 2. 무지개는 무슨 색이에요?

What colors are there in a rainbow (무지개)? Do you know how Koreans abbreviate the color names in a rainbow?

Exercise 3. What color are they?

1) 사과는 무슨 색이에요?

2) 바나나는 무슨 색이에요?

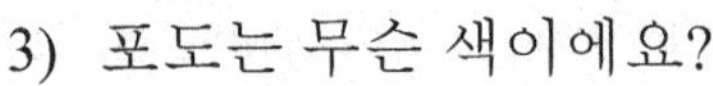

3) 포도는 무슨 색이에요?

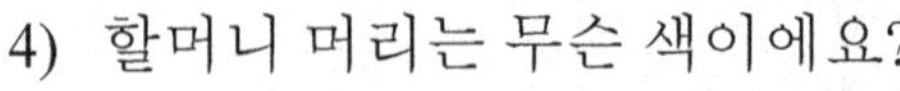

4) 할머니 머리는 무슨 색이에요?

5) 미국 성조기는 무슨 색이에요? (성조기: Stars and Stripes)

6) 태극기는 무슨 색이에요? (태극기: Korean flag)

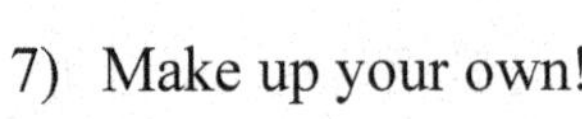

7) Make up your own!

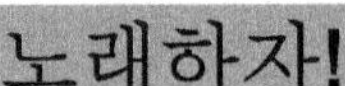

노래하자!

빨간 꽃, 파란 새

빨간 빨간 종이론 무얼 접을까?
파란 파란 종이론 무얼 접을까?

빨간 꽃들 피어라! 푸른 벌판에!
파란 새들 날아라! 푸른 하늘에!

CHAPTER 5 추운데...문을 닫아도 돼요?

It's cold... May I close the door?

Preliminary Dialogue

병곤: 히터가[1] 너무 뜨거워서 머리가[2] 아파요[3].	1. heater
수진: 그럼, 창문을 여세요.	2. head
병곤: 그래요. (opening the door) 문도 열래요.	3. hurts
수진: 어, 글쎄요[4]... 문을 열면 너무 추운데[5]...	4. I'm not sure... let's see... 5. It is cold so/but...

This word usually follows a long noise inhaled through teeth (like the *s* sound, only breathed in), to indicate the speaker's hesitation!

Dialogue practice

Practice the preliminary dialogue with a classmate.

LESSON 17
코가 높은 남자

Lesson 17 Vocabulary 우리의 몸

얼굴	Face
1. 이마	forehead
2. 턱	chin, jaws
3. 눈; 눈썹; 속눈썹	eyes; eye brows; eyelashes
4. 코; 콧구멍	nose; nostrils
5. 입; 입술	mouth; lips
6. 혀=혓바닥	tongue
7. 귀	ears
8. 수염; 콧수염	beard; mustache
9. 머리; 흰 머리; 금발	head, hair; "gray" hair; blond
10. 머리카락	hair strands
몸	Body
11. 손; 손가락; 손톱	hands; fingers; fingernails
12. 발; 발가락; 발톱	feet; toes; toenails
13. 목; 손목; 발목	neck; wrist; ankle
14. 어깨	shoulders
15. 팔	arms
16. 다리	legs
17. 등; 손등; 발등	back; back of the hand; top of the foot
18. 배	belly
19. 허리	waist, lower back
20. 엉덩이	hips, buttocks
21. 꼬리	tail
22. 피부	skin
23. 길어요	long
24. 짧아요	short
25. 높아요	high
26. 낮아요	low
27. 넓어요	wide
28. 좁아요	crowded (room), narrow (road)
29. 굵어요	thick (for circumference or girth of something)
30. 가늘어요	thin (for circumference or girth of something)
31. 두꺼워요 (두껍다)	thick (for layers or flat items)
32. 얇아요	thin (for layers or flat items)
33. 깊어요	deep
34. 얕아요	shallow
35. 키가 커요; 키가 작아요	tall; short
36. 됐어요 (되다)	that's enough; that's O.K.
37. 그런데 ; 근데	it is so, but; but then; but, if that's the case; yeah, but

혓바닥 is more colloquial than 혀, so use 혀 in polite company.

Nail-clippers are called 손톱깎이 in Korean!

The palm is called 손바닥, and the sole of the foot is called 발바닥. You saw 바닥 in 혓바닥. Guess what 바닥 means.... In fact, it means *floor* (or a similar *flat surface*)!

The expression "피부로 느껴요." means *I can really feel it* (something abstract).

Because 됐어(요) means *That's fine* or *It's good enough*, it can be used idiomatically to mean something like *Give me a break*, *Whatever*, or *Yeah, yeah. Drop it already*.

When you describe someone's looks, make sure you make the description the predicate of the sentence. A direct translation of *He has blue eyes*, for example sounds unnatural in Korean!

그 사람은 눈이 파래요. ~~그 사람은 파란 눈 있어요.~~	He has blue eyes.
그 친구는 머리가 길어요. ~~그 친구는 긴 머리 있어요.~~	He has long hair.
내 동생은 키가 커요. ~~내 동생은 큰 키 있어요.~~	My sister is tall.

Vocabulary Exercise 1. Odd one out

Circle the word that does not fit with the others.

1) 이마	등	눈	코
2) 팔	손	손가락	발
3) 허리	엉덩이	배	꼬리
4) 다리	발가락	목	발

Vocabulary Exercise 2. Head and Shoulders, Knees and Toes

Sing the *head and shoulders* song in Korean!

머리 어깨 무릎 발 무릎 발

머리 어깨 무릎 발 무릎 바~ㄹ

머리 어깨 바-ㄹ 무릎 발

머리 어깨 무릎 귀 코 귀 (무릎: knees)

Vocabulary Exercise 3. Singer-songwriter

Continue the following song with your own words.

리 리 리자로 끝나는 말은?	리, 리, 리, What word ends in 리?
고리, 소리, 자리, 마리	chain, sound, seat, animal (counter), and
유리 항아리!	a glass jar!

Vocabulary Exercise 4. Label the picture

Vocabulary Exercise 5. Odd one out

Using adjectives from the new vocabulary, make up a sentence grouping some of the items listed and differentiating one of them.

> *Example*: 뒷골목 (back alley), 고속도로(freeway), 기찻길 (train tracks)
> → 뒷골목이랑 고속도로는 넓고 기찻길은 좁아요.

1) 엠파이어 스테이트 빌딩, 내 성적 (grades), 에펠탑(Eiffel Tower), 백두산
2) 기차 (train), 바나나, 코끼리 (elephant) 코, 미니스커트
3) 수영장, 바다, 에베레스트 산 위의 눈 (snow), 물 웅덩이 (puddle)
4) 스웨터, 사전, 일요 신문, 김
5) 강당 (concert hall), 한국어 교실, 기숙사 방, 지하철(subway car)

Vocabulary Exercise 6. Opposites

Come up with a real-life celebrity example for each trait. All in Korean, of course!

1) have long/short hair
2) have a big, high nose/flat nose
3) have a wide/short forehead
4) have fat/thin fingers
5) have a thick/thin neck
6) tall/short

Language Point　*Is your nose high?*

There are many idiomatic phrases in Korean that developed out of body + adjective metaphors. These idioms are used quite frequently in daily conversations. Can you guess the meaning?

눈이 높다	*eyes are high*
코가 높다	*nose is high*
손이 맵다	*hand is spicy*
손이 크다	*hand is big*
발이 넓다	*feet are wide*
귀가 얇다	*ears are thin*
얼굴이 두껍다 (ㅂ-irregular)	*face is thick*
입이 짧다	*mouth is short*
머리가 좋다	*head is good*

Learn some more idiomatic expressions. Can you guess the meaning of these?
속이 깊다 one's inside is deep.
귀가 얇다 one's ears are thin.

속이 깊다 means one is thoughtful, and 귀가 얇다 means one has no opinion or direction of his/her own as he/she listens to other people and changes his/her mind frequently.

you have high standards; you are snobbish; your slap stings or you hit too hard
you go overboard or are generous (in giving or estimating); you have a lot of
connections; you follow everyone's advice; you are brazen or you have no shame;
you like to graze and eat snack foods often; you are smart

Language Point Exercise 1.
Complete the idioms and translate the missing words into English.

눈이 높다	eyes are high; you have high standards
______ 높다	you are snobbish
손이______	your slap stings, you hit too hard
손이______	you go overboard (in giving or estimating)
______ 넓다	you have a lot of connections
귀가 얇다	ears are thin; you follow everyone's advice
______ 두껍다	you are brazen, you have no shame
입이 짧다	mouth is short; you like to graze, eat snacky foods often

Language Point Exercise 2. Whose ears are thin?

Using the expressions in the language note, describe your family members or close friends. Don't forget to add a sentence to explain what you mean.

e.g. 제 동생은 입이 짧아요. 밥은 잘 안 먹고 초콜렛을 많이 먹어요. (or, 군것질을 많이 해요- he snacks a lot).

가락 means a long, thin strand (like 숟가락, 젓가락, and 국수 가락). 손가락, 발가락 came from 손+가락, and 발+가락. How about 머리카락?

맨손으로 and 맨발로 means 'with bare hands' and 'bare foot', respectively.

발가벗었어요 or 빨가벗었어요 means 'absolutely naked!'

노래하고 갑시다!

바닷가 모래밭에 손가락으로

그림을 그립니다 당신을 그립니다

코와 입 그리고 눈과 귀 턱 밑에 점 하나

입가에 미소까지 그렸지마는 마지막 한 가지 못 그린 것은

지금도 알 수 없는 당신의 마음

Or, some folks would spell this "그렸지만은"...

Lesson 17 Dialogue 코가 높은 남자

시은: **켈리** 씨, 내가 멋있는[1] 남자를 아는데[2], 만날래요?

켈리: 어떻게 생겼는데요[3]?

시은: 잘 생겼어요[4]. 머리는 금발이고, 눈이 파래요. 키도 크고 다리도 길고, 코도아주 높아요.

켈리: 코가 높아요? 나는 높은 코는 싫은데[5]...

시은: 어머, 왜요? 한국 사람들은 크고 높은 코를 좋아하는데[6].

켈리: 미국 사람들은 아무도[7] 큰 코 안 좋아해요.

시은: 그럼 어떤 코를 좋아하는데요[8]?

켈리: (pointing to her own nose) 이런[9] 코를 좋아해요.

시은: 됐어요[10]. 차나 마십시다[11]!

1. cool (stylish)
2. I know..., so
3. What does he look like?
4. (He is) good-looking
5. I don't like big noses...
6. Koreans like (high noses)...(what's the matter?)
7. No Americans
8. Then what kinds of nose do they like (tell me)?
9. (a nose) like this
10. Enough already. What-ever.
11. Let's just drink tea.

English *what* often translates as *how* in Korean. In phrases such as "What does he look like?" 어떻게 생겼어요?

"What do you think?" 어떻게 생각하세요?

"What are you going to do?" 어떻게 할 거에요?

Korean uses 어떻게 and not 무엇!

The interjection for slight surprise "어머" (sometimes 어머나) is used only by female speakers. Male speakers tend to use "어?" For a startled or jolted scare, both genders use "엄마!", for unexpected surprise "엇!" or "앗!"

Lesson 17 Grammar

1. Focus so…, but…, and…

-(으)ㄴ데/-는데	so…, but…, and…

To avoid being blunt or rude, be sure to use either -요 or a second clause after -(으)데/는데.

The -(으)ㄴ데/는데 ending is very useful in Korean. It is used as a sentence connector indicating the **background** for the second clause. It translates as something like *and*, *so*, *but*, ellipses (…), or *semicolon* (;).

배 고픈데 뭐 먹읍시다. I'm hungry; let's eat something.

지금 시간 없는데 내일 만납시다. I don't have time now so/but let's meet tomorrow.

You can end the sentence with -(으)ㄴ데/는데 with the politeness ending 요. It has the same indication, that your statement is the **background** for some further consideration which may or may not be stated.

지금 여기 없는데요. He is not here now, … *implied*: (so/but) can I take a message?

-(으)ㄴ데/는데(요) is a good way to end a sentence (with a dying down voice) when you want to avoid confrontation, turn down a proposal, or to show reservation about something.

A: 내일 같이 점심 먹을래요? Want to have lunch with me tomorrow?
B: 내일은 좀 바쁜데요… I'm kind of busy tomorrow…

So far, you have seen that verbs and adjectives act almost the same. There are some differences, however. There is an important difference when you use the *background* ending:

To conjugate verbs, add -는데 regardless of the last sound in the stem:

A: 수업 후에 뭐 해요? What are you doing after class?
B: 집에 가는데요. I'm going home (why?)

To conjugate adjectives add -은데 to consonant-ending stems, and -ㄴ데 to vowel-ending stems. Here are some examples:

A: 한국어 수업 어때요? How is your Korean class?
B: 선생님은 좋은데, 숙제가 많아요! The teacher is good, but there is a lot of homework!

 Since 있다 and 없다 are verbs, "adjectives" that use them take the -는데 ending like verbs: 맛이 있는데.

> For the most part, the English part of speech corresponds to the Korean one, but note, 필요하다 *to be needed* is an adjective (even though the most natural English translations use the verb *to need*).

Also remember that there are 하다 *verbs* as well as 하다 *adjectives* – they will conjugate differently for this ending (-는데 for verbs and -은 for adjectives):

공부하는데 vs. 심심한데

For all verbs and adjectives in the <u>past tense</u>, you can simply add -는데.

아까 선생님 사무실에 갔는데 선생님을 못 만났어요.
I went to the teacher's office a while ago, but I couldn't meet with her.

내 동생은 작년에 키가 작았는데 지금은 아주 커요.
My brother was short last year, but now he's really tall!

Examples

Verbs:

(공부)하다	하는데	공부 하는데	I'm studying…
가다	가는데	서울에 가는데	He's going to Seoul…
먹다	먹었는데	아침을 안 먹었는데	I didn't have breakfast;
있다	있는데	학교에 있는데	She's at school…
살다	사는데	서울에 사는데	They are living in Seoul…

Adjectives:

예쁘다	예쁜데	얼굴이 예쁜데	Her face is pretty, but…
높다	높은데	코가 높은데	His nose is "high", but…
길다	긴데	머리가 긴데	His hair is long…
뜨겁다	뜨거운데	국이 뜨거운데	The soup is hot …
작았다	작았는데	키가 작았는데	She was short, but…
이상하다	이상한데	맛이 이상한데	It tastes weird…
이다	인데	선생님인데	He's a teacher…
이다*	ㄴ데	아인데	He's a child…

이다*: The 이 of 인데 is deleted when the preceding noun ends in a vowel.

2. Other Grammar Notes

1. 되다 *become, be suitable, be satisfactory, be sufficient, 'will do,' be allowed*

If you asked native Korean speakers what the word "되다" means in Korean, they would say, without hesitation, that it means "to become". The written conjugation form of 되다 is 되어요, but you will see the contracted form 돼요 (just like the first syllable of the word *pig* 돼지), and no one says 되어요 in spoken Korean.

The verb 되다, when it means *become* (in the sense of *turn into*), is typically used in the "formula" X (has) become Y. How you say this in Korean is very interesting:

X 이/가	**Y 이/가**	**돼요/됐어요.**

물이 얼음이 되었어요. Water has turned into ice.

Since the first noun is usually a topic one discusses, what you will see more often is the first noun with topic marker 은/는:

(X 은/는)	**Y 이/가**	**돼요/됐어요.**

이번 학기에 저는 3 학년이 됐어요. I have become a junior this quarter.

너는 커서 뭐가 될래? What do you want to be when you grow up?

그 아이는 어른이 되었어요. The child has turned into an adult.

Or, when the first noun would be an "empty" *it* in English, the whole noun is omitted:

점심 시간이 되었어요. It's become lunchtime.

벌써 3 시나 됐어요. It's 3 already.

You will see ***idiomatic*** uses of 되다 far more frequently during your Korean learning career:

안돼요! No way! No can do! You shouldn't!

이거 안 돼요! This isn't working. I can't get it to work.

다 됐어요. It's all done/finished.

거의 다 돼 가요. It's getting there. Almost finished.

한국 사람 다 됐네요. You are so Koreanized! (very Korean!)

마침 잘 됐어요. It hits the spot. Just in time.

아직 때가 안 됐어요. It's not time yet.

그 사람, 몇 살이나 됐어요? How old is he?

요즘은 되는 일이 없어요. Everything is going wrong these days.

Often, English idioms with "go", "do", or "make" can translate using 되다:

A: 공부 잘 돼요? (or, 공부 잘 돼 가요?) Is your study going well?
B: 아니오, 오늘은 공부가 잘 안 돼요. No, it is not going well today.

A: 장사 잘 돼요? Is your business doing well?
B: 네, 잘 돼요. Yes, it is.

그건 말이 안 돼요. That doesn't make any sense.
(Literally, that doesn't make a word.)

그 사람하고 얘기가 잘 됐어요? Did you reach an agreement with him?
(How did your talk go with him?)

새 한국 친구가 한국어 공부에 도움이 많이 돼요.
Having this new Korean friend is beneficial for my Korean studies.
(Literally, "The new Korean friend *becomes* much help toward my Korean studies.")

"도움" is a nominalized form of the verb 돕다. It means *help* (N.)

Remember! 되다 becomes 돼 (fat like 돼지) *only* when you conjugate it in the -어/아 form and contract it. Before all ther connectors and endings that begin with a consonant like -지 or -고, or the 으 kind like -(으)ㄹ래요 or -(으)세요, use 되.

	Stem requiring suffixes	-어 form suffixes	
		Full form	Contracted form
되다	되고	되어서	돼서
	되지만	되어요	돼요
	되면	되어도	돼도
	되는데	되었어요	됐어요
	될 거에요		
	되지요		

You will learn later how to make the Korean equivalent of **become + ADJECTIVE** such as become cold, get prettier, etc. **Use -이/가 되다 only after a noun!**

2. *let's/let's not* -(으)ㅂ시다! / -지 맙시다!

You know you can invite someone to do something together if you use the -어요 ending with 우리(하고 같이):

우리 공원에 가요. Let's go to the park.

This sentence can be quite confusing, as you can imagine. Is it a statement, a question, or a command? The ending -(으)ㅂ시다 is used specifically for making an invitation in a polite setting:

우리 공원에 갑시다.	Let's go to the park.

Remember how to say *Please do* and *Please don't*? You learned these grammar constructions in the last chapter, and they were: -(으)세요, and -지 마세요. Quite similarly, the expression -지 맙시다 *Let's not* forms a parallel pair to *Let's*:

우리 공원에 가지 맙시다.	Let's not go to the park.
이번 학기에 수학을 듣지 맙시다.	Let's not take math this quarter.
은비 씨를 기다리지 맙시다.	Let's not wait for **은비**.
숙제를 내지 맙시다.	Let's not turn in our homework.
이번 주말에 술 마시지 맙시다.	Let's not drink this weekend.
버스를 타지 맙시다.	Let's not ride the bus.

Don't forget the *familiar* ending -자 that you would use to talk to your own children, a younger sibling or a bosom buddy!
우리 공원에 가자. (You can't add 요 to this ending!)

Though -(으)ㅂ시다 is more formal than -자, it still sounds too direct and too forward when used toward one's elders or superiors. There you need to use more complex, indirect paraphrases.

3. -(이)나 *or something like that*

-(이)나 has already been introduced twice in this textbook-- once as a marker that means *as many as* or *up to* (Chapter 3 lesson 12), and the second time as a noun connector that means *or* (Chapter 4, lesson 13):

오늘은 세수를 네 번이나 했어요.	I washed my face (as many as) four times today. (That many times!)
숟가락이나 젓가락 좀 주세요.	Give me (either) a spoon or chopsticks, please.

Remember. -이나 is a ***noun*** connector!

There is a third meaning (or usage): -(이)나 means *or something (like that)*, where -(이)나 lessens the importance of the noun it is attached to:

A: 이번 일요일에 뭐 할 거에요?	What are you doing this Sunday?
B: 집에서 잠이나 잘 거에요.	I'm just going to sleep or something.
A: 영화보러 갑시다.	Let's go watch a movie.
B: 집에서 설거지나 합시다.	Let's just wash dishes (which is admittedly a drag).

When -(이)나 means *or something (insignificant of that sort)*, it is the **OBJECT** of the sentence that is talked down. Thus -(이)나 is used instead of the object marker -을/를.

-(이)나 can be rude if used in a command. Use it sparingly. Here are some more examples.

A: 이거 먹을래?	Y'want this?
B: 맛 없어. 개한테나 줘.	It's no good. Give it to the dog.
A: 아, 목 너무 말라! 맛있는 거 없어?	Ugh, I'm so thirsty. You got anything good?
B: 맛있는 게 어딨어! 물이나 마셔!	What do you mean *good*? How about water!

4. -도 *even*

You learned -도 as a marker with the meaning "also" or "too". It is sometimes interpreted as *even* with an emphatic meaning. That is, the interpretation of the marker -도 is. If you, as a hearer, judge that it is *neutrally* adding another entity, it means contextual *also* (usually in a sentence stating a fact). When you sense negative emotion, exasperation or surprise, -도 is used to mean *even*:

돈이 있어요. 크레딧 카드도 있어요. I have money. I *also* have a credit card.

우리 아빠는 매일 일해요. 주말에도 사무실에 가요.
My dad works every day. He *even* goes to his office on weekends.

Thus the following sentence from the dialogue may be interpreted either as *also* or as *even*:

키가 크고 다리도 길어요. 코도 아주 높아요. 어떻게 생각해요?
He is tall and has long legs. He also has a "high" nose. (The speaker is merely listing facts.)

OR He is tall and has long legs. He even has a "high" nose. (The speaker is trying to talk the listener into going on a blind date, emphasizing the fact that this guy is *really* handsome.)

5. 아무 *any, no*

아무 corresponds more or less to *any* in English, but its usage is limited. When it comes with -이나, it means *any*, and when it comes with -도, it means *no* and ALWAYS comes with negative verbs.

아무나	***anyone***
아무거나 (or 아무것이나)	***anything***
아무도 (+ negative verb)	***no one***
아무것도 (+ negative verb)	***nothing***

Korean doesn't have a word for *either*. Use 아무나 and 아무거나 for *either (one)* and *either (thing)*.

A: 이거 먹을래, 저거 먹을래? Which one do you want (to eat)?
B: 아무거나. Either/whatever/whichever/anything.

집에 아무도 없어요? Is anyone home? (*Literally*, Is no one home?)

내일은 집에 아무도 없으니까 모레 올래요?
No one is home tomorrow – do you want to come by the day after tomorrow?

벌써 세 신데 아직까지 아무것도 안 먹었어요? 배 안 고파요?
It's already 3; you haven't had anything yet? Aren't you hungry?

A: 잘생긴 남자가 좋아요, 아니면 머리가 좋은 남자가 좋아요?
B: 아무나 다 좋아요. 저는 남자친구가 없으니까요. ☺
Do you like a handsome man or a smart man?
Either one (I'll take anybody) , 'cause I don't have a boyfriend. ☺

잘생긴 means "well made", and it means *good-looking!* "Good head" means *smart!*

When modifying a noun (as in *no Americans would...*), you need to put a topic phrase first:

미국 사람은 아무도 큰 코를 안 좋아해요. No Americans like big noses.

저는 단 음식은 아무거나 다 좋아해요. I like any sweet food/anything sweet.

저는 이 동네에 지난 주에 와서, 동네 사람을 아무도 몰라요.
I got to this town last week – I don't know any neighbors.

요즘 좋은 영화를 아무 것도 못 봤는데, 뭐 재미있는 거 있어요?
I haven't seen any good movies lately – Is there anything fun out?

⚠ You will not be understood if you say ~~아무 미국 사람~~ or ~~아무 단 음식~~!

6. ㄹ- Type Conjugation Review

The following is a summary of all the endings that act "weirdly" after ㄹ-ending verbs and adjectives. Study the shaded parts carefully. The best way to learn them is to repeat them to yourself out loud until they sound natural to you. As you are saying them out loud, you should think of their meanings as well. Better yet, once you are done getting used to the sounds, make a simple sentence using these endings and connectors and memorize them. When you feel comfortable with them, move on to an adjective (달다, for example). Draw out your chart, and repeat the same exercise.

	Consonantal endings & -어 endings	-(으) endings			Endings that begin with -ㄴ
ㄹ behavior	ㄹ stays	ㄹ stays and 으 of the ending disappears	ㄹ drops out and 으 of the ending disappears	ㄹ drops out and 으 of the ending disappears	ㄹ drops out
Is ㄹ "there"?	ㄹ is there	ㄹ is there	ㄹ looks like it is there because the verb ending contains ㄹ	ㄹ is not there	ㄹ is not there
Examples	살다	살면	살 거야*	사세요	사네(요)
	살지(요)	살러*	살 거에요*	사니까	사니?
	살고		살래(요)*	삽시다	사는**
	살지만			(달다: 단)**	
	살아서				
	살아요				

* Adjectives do not ever come with these asterisked endings as they express intention.
** The noun-modifying **verb** ending is 는, and the noun-modifying **adjective** ending is (으)ㄴ.

Lesson 17 Exercises

Exercise 1. Dialogue practice
Practice the dialogue in this lesson with a classmate.

Exercise 2. Even you, Brutus?
Challenge your partner's statement by raising a question "even…?" (To make it more interesting, replace the people with someone you know!)

Example:
A: 제 동생은 매일 도서관에서 공부해요. (주말)
B: 매일 공부해요? 주말에도 도서관에서 공부해요?
A: 네, 주말에도 도서관에 가요. (or) 아니오... 주말에는 도서관에 안 가요.

1) 그 사람은 항상 반바지만 입어요. (반바지 half pants = shorts 겨울 winter)

2) 한국 음식은 다 매워요. (불고기)

3) 그 사람은 음악은 다 좋아해요. (랩)

4) 제 동생은 아침을 전혀 안 먹어요. (아무것도)

5) Make up your own!

Exercise 3. Conjugation practice

Conjugate the underlined verbs and adjectives in -는데요 or - (으)ㄴ데요 form and connect the conjugated sentence with 어떻게 하지요? *What should I do?* Your partner (B) will give you a suggestion.

> You can cheat and pronounce this word 어트게 or 어터게.

Example:
A: 배가 <u>고프다</u> → 배가 고픈데 어떻게 하지요? B: 뭐 좀 먹으세요.

1) A: 주스가 너무 <u>시다</u> B: 설탕을 좀 넣으세요.
2) A: 머리가 너무 <u>길다</u> B: 괜찮아요. 예뻐요.
3) A: 숙제가 너무 <u>어렵다</u> (어렵다 difficult) B: 나하고 같이 합시다. 내일 시간 있어요?
4) A: 내일 할머니 생신이다. 할머니는 서울에 <u>살다</u> (생신: *honorific* birthday) B: 할머니한테 전화하세요.
5) A: 학생들이 공부를 안 <u>하다</u> B: 시험을 어렵게 만드세요! (어렵게: difficult)

Exercise 4. Turn them down politely

Ask your partner whether he/she has time. Invite him/her to do various things. Take turns turning the proposals down! Practice using the expressions "같이 ... -(으)ㄹ래요?" or "같이 -(으)ㅂ시다!" when you are inviting your partner. If you are turning the invitation down, don't forget to use "-(으)ㄴ데요/-는데요..."

Exercise 5. 안돼요!

Guess the meaning of these sentences with 되다 in them.

시은: 그 일 어떻게 됐어요?	(What has become of that business? → How did it turn/work out?)
제프: 잘 안 됐어요.	(It didn't work out.)
제프: 그 사람 참 못됐어요.	(He doesn't meet the qualifications of a decent human being → He is so mean.)
시은: 사람이 없는데 말하면 안돼요.	(If you talk when he is not there, it won't do → You shouldn't.)

Exercise 6. 뭐가 돼요? 어떻게 돼요?

Guess the result of each concoction and complete the sentence with *become*.

1) 빨간색 물감에 파란색 물감을 넣으면 ___________이 돼요. (물감 [물깜]: water color)
2) 계란하고 치즈를 섞으면 ___________. (섞다: mix)
3) 보드카에 오렌지 주스를 넣으면 ___________.
4) 빵에 고기하고 치즈하고 상추를 넣으면 ___________.
5) 밥에 고추장하고 여러가지 채소를 넣으면___________. (여러가지: several)

Exercise 7. 아무것도, 아무도

Ask the following questions in Korean and your partner will answer with absolute negatives!

1) Who is at home?
2) What's in your bag?
3) What did you eat today?
4) Who did you meet yesterday?
5) What are you doing this afternoon?
6) *make your own*

Exercise 8. 아무거나, 아무나

Ask your partner which of the two choices they like (prefer). Your partner figures "anything goes".

1) a thick sweater or a thin sweater?
2) coffee or tea?
3) a high car or a low car?
4) a big room or a small room?
5) long haired man/woman or short haired man/woman?

Exercise 9. Let's do! -- Let's not! (heh heh heh)

Make a suggestion to your partner. He or she will disagree and suggest the opposite – even if it's naughty!

Example: 점심에 외식합시다. – 안돼요! 돈이 없어요. 집에 가서 먹읍시다.

1) 숙제
2) 술 + 운전
3) 시험 공부
4) 언니/형 옷
5) 신발, 집 안 (shoes, inside the house)
6) 아침(밥)

Exercise 10. -이나 ...

Your younger sibling has come to visit, but don't have time to entertain him/her. For every need your brother or sister expresses, make an off-handed suggestion using -이나.

Example: 배고파! → 빵이나 먹어!

1) I'm cold. (추워!)
2) I'm bored. (심심해!)
3) Let's go out and eat.
4) All the bowls are dirty.
5) I'm hot. (더워!)
6) I'm thirsty.
7) Let's go out and play basketball.
8) I can't find my shorts. (반바지)
9) Your apartment is messy. (지저분해!)
10) Let's go to the barbers.

Exercise 11. But, and, so ...

Complete the following sentences with an appropriate continuation of the sentence. Have a conversation!

1) 돈이 없는데...
2) 배가 고픈데...
3) 남자 친구가 키가 너무 작은데...
4) 숙제가 많은데...
5) 머리가 너무 긴데...
6) 시험이 너무 어려운데... (어렵다: difficult)

Lesson 17 Checkpoint

대화 1 열 한 시에 전화하면 너무 늦지요?

철수: 여보세요, 거기 **김민수** 씨 댁[51]이지요? **김민수** 씨 계세요?

시은: 네, 맞는데요, **민수** 오빠는 지금 집에 없는데요. 학교에 갔어요.

철수: 일요일인데 학교에 갔어요?

시은: 네, 오빠는 일요일도 학교에 공부하러 가요.

철수: 그래요? 그럼 언제 다시 전화하면 돼요?

시은: 8 시 쯤 다시 전화주세요.

철수: 8 시에는 제가 누구하고 약속[52]이 좀 있는데요. 11 시에 전화하면 너무 늦지요[53]?

시은: 괜찮아요. 12 시까지는 아무도 안 자니까요.

대화 2 뭐 좀 먹고 올께요.

철수: 배 고픈데 뭐 밥 먹고 합시다!

민수: 아직 11 시인데 벌써 배가 고파요?

순희: **철수** 씨 아침 안 먹었지요? 아침을 안 먹으니까 벌써 배가 고프지요.

민수: **철수** 씨 아침에 아무것도 안 먹어요?

철수: 아침에는 너무 바빠서요.

민수: 아침을 거르면[54] 안 돼요. 건강에 안 좋아요.

순희: 맞아요. 우유[55]라도 마시세요.

철수: 네, 알았습니다. 그건 그렇고[56] 정말[57] 뭐 안 먹을래요?

순희: 우리는 별로 배 안 고픈데요.

철수: 그럼 저 잠깐 뭐 좀 잠깐 먹고 올께요.[58]

> Guess why **시은** used (으)니까요 and **철수** used 어서...
> **시은** is giving her ***reasoning*** for her previous command/suggestion (전화주세요). **철수**, on the other hand, is just stating a ***reason*** why he skps breakfast.

---

[51] honorific form of 집
[52] appointment
[53] late (늦다)
[54] skip (a meal – 거르다, 거르니까, 거르면, 걸러서, 걸러도)
[55] milk
[56] Well, anyway
[57] really
[58] I'll be back

LESSON 18

엄마 스타킹 신을께.

Lesson 18 Vocabulary 옷, 그리고 기타 단어

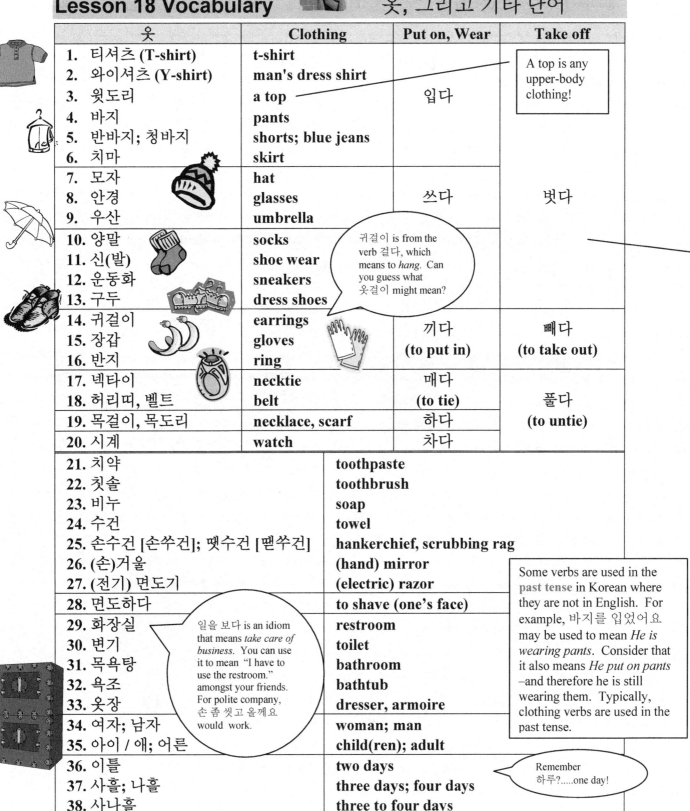

옷	Clothing	Put on, Wear	Take off
1. 티셔츠 (T-shirt) 2. 와이셔츠 (Y-shirt) 3. 윗도리 4. 바지 5. 반바지; 청바지 6. 치마	t-shirt man's dress shirt a top pants shorts; blue jeans skirt	입다	벗다
7. 모자 8. 안경 9. 우산	hat glasses umbrella	쓰다	
10. 양말 11. 신(발) 12. 운동화 13. 구두	socks shoe wear sneakers dress shoes		
14. 귀걸이 15. 장갑 16. 반지	earrings gloves ring	끼다 (to put in)	빼다 (to take out)
17. 넥타이 18. 허리띠, 벨트	necktie belt	매다 (to tie)	풀다 (to untie)
19. 목걸이, 목도리	necklace, scarf	하다	
20. 시계	watch	차다	

A top is any upper-body clothing!

귀걸이 is from the verb 걸다, which means to *hang*. Can you guess what 옷걸이 might mean?

21. 치약 22. 칫솔 23. 비누 24. 수건 25. 손수건 [손쑤건]; 땟수건 [땐쑤건] 26. (손)거울 27. (전기) 면도기	toothpaste toothbrush soap towel hankerchief, scrubbing rag (hand) mirror (electric) razor
28. 면도하다	to shave (one's face)
29. 화장실 30. 변기 31. 목욕탕 32. 욕조 33. 옷장	restroom toilet bathroom bathtub dresser, armoire
34. 여자; 남자 35. 아이 / 애; 어른	woman; man child(ren); adult
36. 이틀 37. 사흘; 나흘 38. 사나흘 39. (TIME) 동안	two days three days; four days three to four days during (TIME), for the period of (TIME)

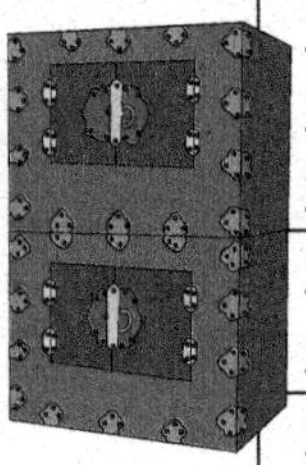

일을 보다 is an idiom that means *take care of business*. You can use it to mean "I have to use the restroom." amongst your friends. For polite company, 손 좀 씻고 올께요 would work.

Some verbs are used in the past tense in Korean where they are not in English. For example, 바지를 입었어요 may be used to mean *He is wearing pants*. Consider that it also means *He put on pants* –and therefore he is still wearing them. Typically, clothing verbs are used in the past tense.

Remember 하루?.....one day!

Language Point *Clothing vocabulary*

Here are some more clothing terms borrowed from English. Can you guess their meaning?

스웨터 벨트 파자마 부츠 썬글래스

레인코트 = 비옷 = 우비 (rain coat) 유니폼 웨딩드레스

The following words are a little more difficult to guess. They are given with their meaning:

재키트 = 자켓 (sport coat) 점퍼/잠바 (casual jacket with elastic waist)

원피스 (dress) 투피스 (lady's suit)

노래하고 갑시다!

샤쓰 is an older pronunciation of the word *shirt* borrowed from English. Although 셔츠 is the standard pronunciation of the word nowdays, 샤쓰 is also widely used especially among folks from an older generation.

노란 샤쓰

노란 샤쓰 입은 말없는 그 사람이
어쩐지 나는 좋아 어쩐지 맘에 들어.

미남은 아니지만 씩씩한 생김생김
그 이가 나는 좋아 어쩐지 맘에 끌려.

아아 야릇한 마음 처음 느껴본 심정
아아 그 이도 나를 좋아하고 계실까?

노란 샤쓰 입은 말없는 그 사람이
어쩐지 나는 좋아 어쩐지 맘에 들어.

Summary

쓰다 - By now you know at least three meanings of this word. Can you think of all of them? (*to write*, *to be bitter*, and *to put on a hat/glasses* or *open an umbrella.*) There is one more useful meaning – *to use.*
제 책상을 쓰세요. *Use my desk.*

끼다 and 빼다 mean *to put on* (or *in*) or *take off* (or *out*) when the action is *difficult* to do. Putting on or taking off a ring or gloves requires hand-to-eye coordination and force. For this reason, the words 끼다 and 빼다 can also be used for glasses. What do you picture, reading the following sentence?
책꽂이에 책을 꼈어요.
책꽂이에서 책을 뺐어요.
(책꽂이: bookshelf)

쓰다

For 안경, you can also use 끼다, considering the "difficulty" of the action or "coordination" required to put on gloves (끼다 is usually used for what you might consider challenging coordination for children such as putting on 귀걸이 or 장갑).

입다

You can also use 들다 for umbrellas. 들다 means *pick up* and *hold*, and you saw it in the previous chapter as a word that means *eat.* The meaning *eat* probably comes from the fact that you have to *pick up your spoon* and start eating. More polite to say 들어요 than 먹어요. To a person you shoud really be polite towards, you should of course say 드세요.

신다

You learned 풀다 as a word that means *to untie*. The word is much more useful, however:

신발 끈을 풀다	untie one's shoe strings
문제를, 퍼즐을 풀다	solve a problem, puzzle
스트레스를 풀다	relieve stress
선물을 풀다	unwrap a present
코를 풀다	blow one's nose
매듭을 풀다	untangle a knot
물에 세제를 풀다	dissolve detergent in water

Can you see what is common to all these expressions?

Vocabulary Exercise 1. What's Santa wearing?
What's Santa wearing? Can you name each item? What verbs would you use to put them on or take them off?

Vocabulary Exercise 2. To wear
Write the correct verb for each clothing item.

1) 옷을 __________ 5) 치마를 __________

2) 청바지를__________ 6) 모자를__________

3) 안경을__________ 7) 반지를__________

4) 신발을__________ 8) 넥타이를__________

Vocabulary Exercise 3. A purple hat
Describe the following person. Say the color and the length of the clothing items.

이 사람은 ____

____

____

____

Vocabulary Exercise 4. Verbs
1) Which of the following clothing items would you use the verb "빼요" with?

청바지, 양말, 속옷, 구두, 귀걸이, 치마, 와이셔츠, 반지

2) Which of the following would you NOT use the verb "풀어요" with?

넥타이, 허리띠, 치마, 시계, 모자, 스트레스, 코

Vocabulary Exercise 5. Picasso?
In the picture below, color in each body part with a different color. Then on a separate sheet of paper, write an explanation of your artwork using colors and body terms.

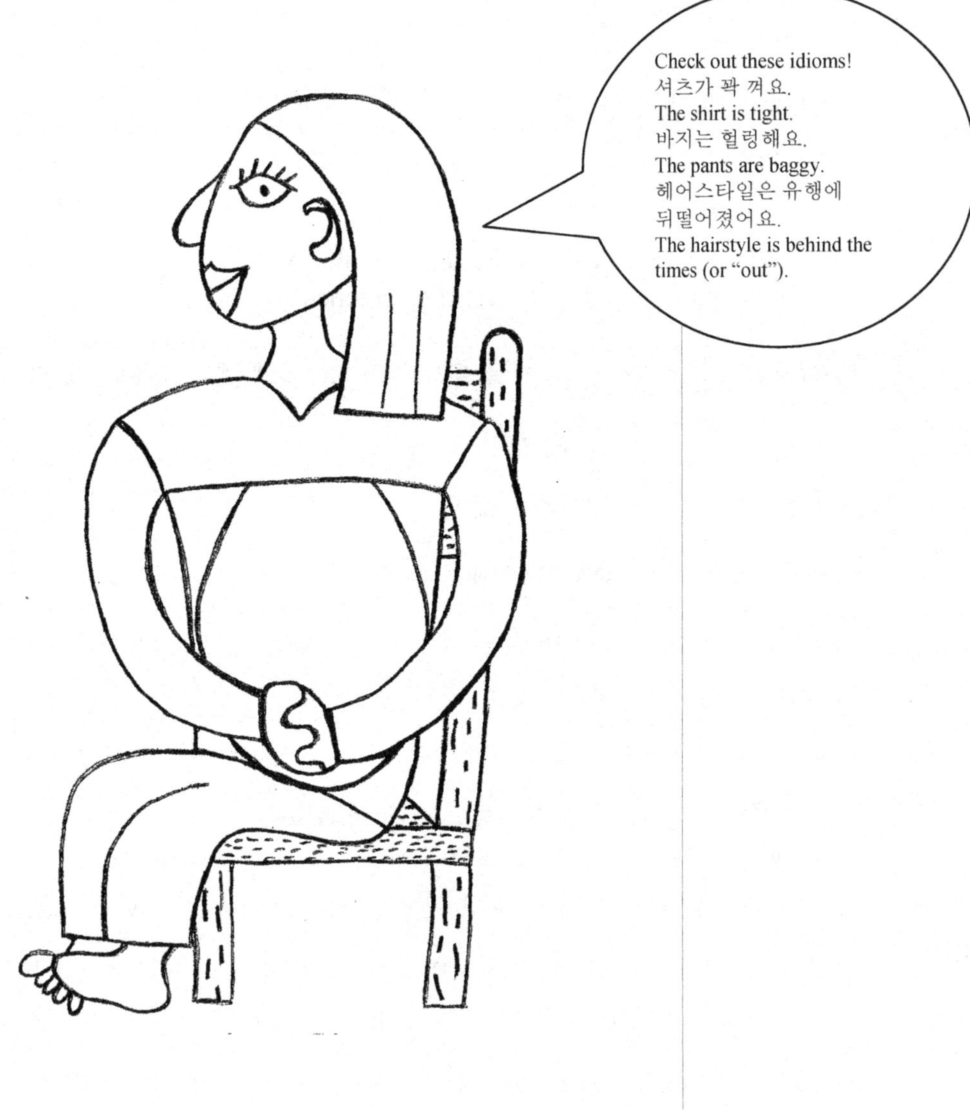

Check out these idioms!
셔츠가 꽉 껴요.
The shirt is tight.
바지는 헐렁해요.
The pants are baggy.
헤어스타일은 유행에 뒤떨어졌어요.
The hairstyle is behind the times (or "out").

Vocabulary Exercise 6. Picasso Bingo
Your instructor will arbitrarily call off names of body parts of different colors (머리가 파래요). If she calls out a color-body part pair that matches your picture: "you get the square" as in bingo. That is, put a marker on that body part. When you get 5 parts marked, call out "피카소!" You have won.

Vocabulary Exercise 7.
Fill in the blanks with a clothing item and then <u>*translate*</u> the sentence.

1) 오늘은 추워요. 짧은 치마 말고 __________를 입고 가세요.
translation:

2) 인터뷰가 있으면 ________를 _____세요. 그리고 _______를 _________세요.
translation:

Vocabulary Exercise 8. Sentence completion
Follow the pattern and complete the sentences.

Example: 나는 빨간 모자를 좋아해서… → 빨간 모자를 세 개나 샀어요.

1) 나는 노란 스웨터를 좋아해서…
2) 나는 파란 양말을 좋아해서…
3) 나는 까만 장갑을 좋아해서…
4) 나는 하얀 셔츠를 좋아해서…
5) 나는 초록색 가방을 좋아해서…

Vocabulary Exercise 9. Sentence completion
Ask and answer the following questions.

1) If you are traveling for one day, what would you take with you?
2) If you are traveling for four days, what would you take with you?
3) What do you find in the 화장실 at home? (Use the verb 있어요)
4) What do you have in your 옷장?
5) How many clothing items could you wear at one time? Use the verbs with 고 in present present tense.

The traditional costumes for men and women are called 한복. Women's wear is called 치마저고리, and men's wear is called 바지저고리 (저고리 is the traditional upper-wear). The ribbon on my 저고리 is called 고름, and the traditional "socks" are called 버선. The traditional footwear is called 고무신 because it is made of 고무 (French *gomme*). Before 고무 was introduced, high officials had leather shoes for visiting the court, and otherwise everyone had wooden (나막신) or woven straw shoes (짚신). Apart from the 함지박 I am holding on my head, I am also wearing an 앞치마.

Lesson 18 Dialogue 엄마 스타킹 신을께.

엄마: **은비**야, 옷 입자! 여기 스웨터하고 바지 있어.

은비: 엄마, 나 오늘 바지 말고, 치마 입을께[1].

엄마: 안돼[2]. 오늘은 아주 추워[3].

은비: 그래도 치마 입고 싶어[5].

엄마: 엄마도 오늘 추워서 치마 안 입었어. 그치[5]?
파란 바지가 싫으면 노란 바지 입을래?

은비: 아니, 노란 바지는 이번 주에 이틀이나 입었어.
오늘은 치마 입고 스타킹 신을께[6], 엄마, 응?

엄마: 집에 작은 스타킹이 없어. 엄마 스타킹만 있어.

은비: 그럼, 엄마 스타킹 신을께[7]. 큰 거 신으면 안 춥지?

1. I am going to wear a skirt, O.K.?
2. Can't do.
3. cold (weather)
4. [입꼬시퍼]
I *want to* wear
5. Right? Isn't it so?

6. I am going to wear a skirt and pantyhose, OK, mom?
7. Then I am going to wear your pantyhose, OK?

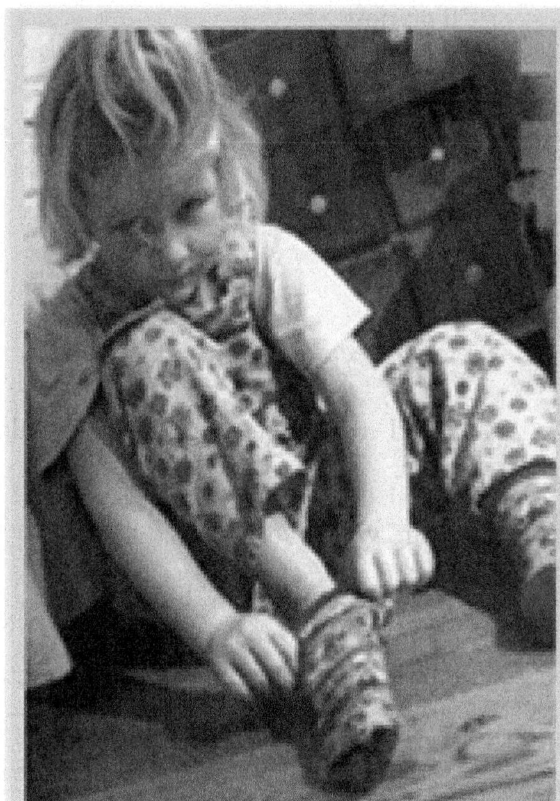

Remember how to conjugate a ㅂ-irregular word?
차갑다: be cold (thing)
차갑고: cold and
차갑네: ho… it's cold
차갑지만: cold but
차가운데: cold so…
차가우니까: cold-because
차가워서: cold-so
차가워도: cold-though

Do you know how to say *pitch black* or *bright red*?
새까만, 새빨간, 샛노란,
새하얀, 새파란!

Lesson 18 Grammar

1. Focus Promissory future -(으)ㄹ께요

-(으)ㄹ께요	will, OK?

The sentence ending -(으)ㄹ께요 corresponds to the English "I will VERB," but has a strong ***promissory sense*** to it along with the indication of a future action. For example, 할께요 *I'll do it* indicates a ***promise*** or an ***offer*** or seeks the ***listener's approval*** in some way. Therefore it cannot be used to talk about someone else's actions (you can't promise for them) or about inanimate subjects such as the weather or falling objects!

The ending for "promissory future" is -(으)ㄹ께. You can add -요 to express politeness. We will refer to the ending as -(으)ㄹ께요.

Here are some illustrative examples:

엄마: 애, 빨리 방 청소해!	Hey you, hurry and clean your room!
아이: 조금 이따 할께요.	I'll do it in a bit.
할머니: 슈퍼에가서, 배추 사 와.	Go get (me) cabbage at the grocery store.
손자: 지금 갈께요.	I'll go now.
은비: 아, 설거지가 너무 많아요.	There are too many dishes to do!
엄마: 지금 하지 마. 아침에 내가 할께.	Don't do it now. I will do it in the morning.

A:   B: 아! 제가 문을 열께요. Oh, I'll get the door.

You can also use -(으)ㄹ께 when you are seeking ***agreement*** on your plan.

엄마, 나 오늘 치마 입을께.	Mom, I'm going to wear this skirt today, O.K.?
은비: 엄마, 저, 친구 집에 갈께요.	Mom, I'm going to my friend's house, O.K.?
엄마: 그래? 너무 늦게 오지 마!	Oh, are you? Don't be too late!

One mnemonic for this ending is to think of it as "I'***ll*** (do it), **o*kay***" for -(으)ㄹ께.

Verbs before the ending -(으)ㄹ께요 conjugate like they normally would before other -(으) endings:

가다 → 갈께요　　먹다 → 먹을께요

돕다 → 도울께요　　살다 → 살께요

You might see the *promissory* ending written with one 기역 (ㄱ) as in -(으)ㄹ게, especially in books. Some people consider this standard, but it doesn't reflect the current usage.

-(으)ㄹ께 vs. -(으)ㄹ래

When you use -(으)ㄹ께(요), you are in the mood of promising, volunteering, or seeking agreement on your plans:

미진: 누가 이번 주말에 청소할래? **은이**, 너, 지난 주말에 청소 안 했지?

은이: 알았어. 이번 주말에는 내가 청소할께.

When you are using -(으)ㄹ래(요), you are in the mood of asserting what your immediate desire is:

현진: 피자가 한 조각이 있는데 누가 먹을래?

찬진: 내가 먹을래!

In a statement, both -(으)ㄹ께(요) and -(으)ㄹ래(요) are used with a **first** person subject. You may use "-(으)ㄹ래(요)?" to ask about the listener's desire but can *never* use -(으)ㄹ께(요) in a question.

Although you are trying to get agreement from the listener, you are still expressing willfulness when you use the ending -(으)ㄹ께요, which is why it is rather odd to say things like 주말에 취할께요. 취하다 is supposedly non-voluntary.

이거 먹을래요?	Do you wanna eat this?
네, 먹을래요.	Sure, I will (for *my* benefit).
네, 먹을께요.	Sure, if it makes you happy (it doesn't matter to me, either way).

Punctuation-wise, you should NOT use -(으)ㄹ께(요) with a question, although it seeks for the listener's agreement. To express "*I'm going to eat this, OK?*" you should write "이거 내가 먹을께." and not "~~이거 내가 먹을께?~~". Use a rising intonation at the end of the long 께 perhaps like a warning in English. (Of course, if the sentence is polite, the rising intonation is put on the extended 요.)

2. Other Grammar Notes

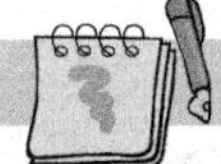

1. -고 싶다/ -고 싶어하다 *want to*

You know -고 as a sentence connector meaning *and*, and you know how to conjugate verbs and adjectives to attach -고. In this lesson, you will learn to use it as a grammatical connector, where -고 connects a main verb to a helping verb to mean *want to VERB.*

저는 오늘 빨간 허리띠를 매고 싶어요.　　I want to wear a red belt today.

저는 그 예쁜 귀걸이를 끼고 싶어요. I want to put on those pretty earrings.

But! You can only do this when you talk about **yourself!**
~~형은 오늘 노란 넥타이가 매고 싶어해요.~~

Odd but true!
The following sentences are used interchangeably:
저는 오늘 빨간 허리띠를 매고 싶어요.
저는 오늘 빨간 허리띠가 매고 싶어요.
Usually, you can replace 를 with 가 when you want to emphasize that it is **빨간 허리띠** that you want to put on today. Very much like when you would use the subject marker 이/가 – Make it your *focus*.!

-고 싶어요 expresses a long-standing desire, wish or hope. On the other hand, the expression -(으)ㄹ래요 expresses an immediate desire, almost an intention. You might think of -고 싶어요 as *I would like to* or *I want to* and 할래요 as *I wanna / I'm gonna.* At the point you say 공부할래요, for example, you have already made up your mind and are *going to* study now or very soon.

Consider another situation that highlights the difference between the two expressions: In the morning you might decide 오늘은 한국 음식을 먹고 싶어요 (*I feel like* or *I would like to have Korean food today*), but just as you order, you would say to your friend 비빔밥 먹을래요 (I'm going to have 비빔밥.)

In the Korean language, talking about someone else's feelings or desire is NOT possible. **To describe someone else's desire, another phrase (-고 싶어하다) should be used instead of -고 싶다.**

언니가 집에 가고 싶어해요. My sister wants to go home.

The obvious negative form 언니가 집에 안 가고 싶어해요 sounds childish. You will learn another way to express negative wishes in a later chapter. Also, the expression -고 싶다 cannot be used to mean *I want a NOUN*; for this you must use 원하다 (*to want* (a NOUN)), or 갖다 (가지다) plus -고 싶다 (갖고 싶다: *to want to have*).

If you are an advanced student who wants to say "I wish the class would end soon." second-year material, here it is:
수업이 빨리 끝났으면 좋겠다...

How would you say "I would like to become a teacher." in Korean?
How about, "My sister wants to become a doctor (의사)."?

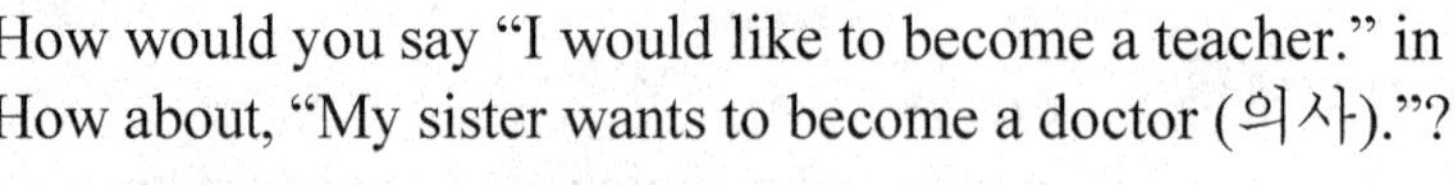
저는 선생님이 되고 싶어요.
저희 누나는 의사가 되고 싶어해요.

If you "miss" someone, all you have to say is 보고 싶어요... Another part of gaining fluency in Korean is to learn **idioms**!

Can you say the following sentence fast (knowing what it means)?
나오미 씨는 이번 주말에 숙제는 하고 싶어하지만 공부는 안 하고 싶어해요.

Part of gaining fluency in Korean is to be able to conjugate verbs freely on command!

2. ㅎ-irregular adjectives (and verbs)

Some adjectives that end in ㅎ are irregular, and they conjugate irregularly in the -어/아 form and also in the noun modifying form. All ㅎ-irregular words are adjectives, and there is a limited number of them. One type is native color terms (하얗다, 빨갛다, 노랗다, 파랗다, 까맣다), and another is the determiner terms 이렇다, 저렇다, 그렇다. Finally, the word *how* (어떻다) belongs to this category, too.

For suffixes that begin with consonants (① below), no change to the stem is necessary. For suffixes that begin with -으 (②), the final consonant ㅎ drops out. Finally, for suffixes that begin with -어/아 (③), the vowel changes to ㅐ (or ㅒ, for *white*), and the final consonant ㅎ disappears. Try filling in the rest of the blanks below!

citation form	meaning	① before consonant-beginning suffixes	② before -으 type suffixes	③ before -어/아 type suffixes
Examples		-고, -지(요), -네(요)	-은, -은데, -으면 -을 거예(요)	-어서, -어도, -어(요), -었어(요)
1) 하얗다	white	하얗고 [하야코]	하얀	(손이) 하얘요
2) 까맣다	black	까맣고 [까마코]		(머리가) 까매요
3) 노랗다	yellow	노랗고 [노라코]		(바나나가) 노래요
4) 빨갛다	red		빨간	(사과가) 빨개요
5) 파랗다	blue			(눈이) 파래요
6) 어떻다	be how	어떻지요 [어떠치요]	어떤 (성격) what kind of personality	
7) 이렇다	be this way, kind, sort		이런 (사람) this kind of person	이래요
8) 그렇다	be that way, kind, sort	그렇지요 [그러치요]	그런 (얘기) that kind of story	그래요
9) 저렇다	be that way, kind, sort (distant)		저런 (일) that kind of happening (distant)	

Some adjectives come with the vowel 어 and others 아 in the stem. Keep the stem vowels in all -으 conjugations, for example, 빨가면!

Other than the irregular adjectives introduced above, most other ㅎ-words are regular!
좋다, 놓다, 넣다..., etc.
Also, words that end in complex final consonants containing ㅎ are always regular!
많다, 잃다, 끊다...

The adjectives 이렇다, 그렇다, and 저렇다 have a related VERB form (이러다, 그러다, and 저러다). These are not ㅎ-irregular words (they don't contain ㅎ in the dictionary form), but they conjugate just like their adjective counter parts. It will be very useful to learn the verbs along with the adjectives. Can you fill in the blanks?

citation form	meaning	before consonant-beginning suffixes	before -으 type suffixes	before -어/ 아 type suffixes
10) 이러다	do, act, behave like this	이러지요 이러네요	이럴 거에요? Are you going to act (be) this way	
11) 그러다	do, act, behave like that		그럴께요 I'll do that, OK?	그래요
12) 저러다	do, act, behave like that (distant)	저러지요 저러네요	저럴 거에요 (He) will act that way.	

In most cases, the verbs and the adjectives are interchangeable in meaning, more or less like "be this way", or "be so". The conjugation is also very similar. What is notably different is shaded.

3. -어도 Concession connector *Even if, even though*

In the last section, you saw how the marker –도 can be used to mean *even*, depending on the context or interpretation.

오빠<u>도</u> 스웨터 입었는데 너는 왜 그래?
Even your brother is wearing a sweater. Why are you doing this?

엄마<u>도</u> 오늘 추워서 치마 안 입었어.
Even Mom is not wearing a skirt because it's cold today.

The marker -어/아도 (which is -어/아 + 도) means *even if* or *even though*. The word 그래도 (*even so*) comes from the combination of 그렇 in its -어/아 form plus the ending -어/아도:

Korean makes no distinction between whether the event happened in the past (*even though)* or whether it is a hypothetical situation (*even if)*. The interpretation depends on the context.

김치는 매워도 맛있어요.	Although 김치 is spicy, it is yummy.
재미가 없었어요 끝까지 봤어요.	Even though it wasn't good, we watched it till the end.

For the verb *to be*, a somewhat changed ending -(이)라도 is used more often than -이어도.

난 보통 분홍색 옷을 싫어하지만, 이 치마는 분홍색이라도 예뻐요.
I don't usually like pink clothes, but this skirt is pretty despite the (pink) color.

Odd but true!
The command "운동화라도 신어라." literally translates as *Even if (it's) sneakers, wear them*, but in actuality, it is used to mean *Wear the sneakers, at least (if you have nothing else).*

4. 그렇지(요?), 그쵸? 그치(요)? *Isn't it so? Isn't it right?*

그렇지요 is a combination of many small parts: 그렇(to be that way) + 지(right?)+ 요(politeness). It often gets reduced to 그쵸 or 그죠 in everyday speech. If there is no need to use the politeness marker 요, the pronunciation becomes [그치] or [그지].

으 and 이 are the weakest vowels in Korean, and ㅎ and ㄹ are the weakest consonants in pronunciation!

Language Point *"Past tense"*

었/았/ㅆ is not really for "past tense"… but for "completion of events"!

Some verbs are used in the "past tense" in Korean where they are not in English. For example, 바지를 입었어요 may be used to mean *He is wearing pants*. Consider that it also means *He put on pants* –and therefore he is still wearing them. Typically, clothing verbs are used in the past tense because the "past tense" ㅆ어요 in Korean expresses the ***completion*** of an event more so than an activity that took place in the past. When verbs are used like adjectives to describe *states*, they tend to be marked in the past tense. Here are some examples. You will learn more about verbs in the past tense in later chapters.

우리 할머니는 늙었어요. — My grandmother is old.
(늙다: to age, 늙었다: to be old)

오늘은 구름이 꼈어요. — Today is cloudy.
(구름이 끼다: to cloud up; 구름이 꼈다: be cloudy)

살이 많이 쪘어요. — I gained a lot of weight.
(살이 찌다: to get plump; 살이 쪘다: be fat)

Lesson 18 Exercises

Exercise 1. Dialogue practice
Practice the dialogue in this lesson with a classmate.

Exercise 2. 뭐 입었어요?
Describe what each person is wearing. Use the correct clothing verbs and put them in the past tense!

Exercise 3. ㅎ-irregular conjugation practice

1) 하늘이 ________________요. (blue) (하늘 sky)

2) 이 __________ 연필은 누구 거에요? (yellow).

3) 이빨을 매일 닦아서 이빨이 ____________요. (white)

4) HUB 음식이 ______________요? (how)

5) 나는 _________ 색은 좋아하지만 ________색은 싫어해요. (red, black)

6) 나는 ________ 사람은 싫어해요. (this kind of)

7) 김치는 색깔이 ____________지요? (red)

Exercise 4. More ㅎ-conjugation practice
Fill in the blanks with an appropriately conjugated ㅎ-adjective.

1) 그 사람은 ________ 사람이에요? (어떻다)
What kind of a person is he?

2) 저는 _________ 색을 좋아해요. (빨갛다)

3) "백수"는 일을 안 하는 사람이에요. Literally, "________ 손"의 뜻이에요.
"백수" is a person who doesn't work. Literally, "white hand" it means.

4) Stars and Stripes 에는 _________ 색, _________색, 그리고 _________이 들어가요.

5) 저는 _______ 사람하고는 자주 만나지만 ______ 사람하고는 한 번만 만나요.
I meet with people that I like often, but meet with those that I do not like only once.

6) 파는 무슨 색이에요? (What color is 파?) -- 파는 _______ 색이에요.

7) 요즘에 무슨 영화가 _______? (괜찮다)
What movies are relatively good these days?

8) 매운 한국 음식은 보통 ___________, 싱거운 음식은 보통 __________.
Spicy Korean food is usually red and bland food is usually white.

9) 한국어 _________? – 지난 학기에는 재미있었는데 이번 학기에는 지겨워요!
How is Korean? – It was fun last quarter but this quarter it is a drag!

10) 저는 _________ 학생을 좋아해요: 매일 수업에 오는 학생 + 숙제를 내는 학생.
I like this kind of student: a student who comes to class every day + a student who turns in hw.

11) 딸기는 ______고, 바나나는 ______고 포도는 _______색이에요.
Strawberries are red, and bananas are yellow, and grapes are green.

Exercise 5. Promises, promises.
Pretend the following people are in front of you (or you can write a brief note to them), and *promise* them you will do something.

1) 선생님

2) 남자/여자 친구

3) 엄마

4) To your best friend (친한 친구)

5) 언니/오빠/형/누나/동생

Exercise 6. 누구일까요? (Who could it be?)
1) Write a description of one of your classmates in as much detail as possible. (Is their hair long? What clothes and shoes are they wearing and what color are they? Any accessories?)

____

____

2) Read your description to your partner and see if he/she can guess who the person is! (When you are giving tips, try not to make it too obvious. Reserve obvious clues such as eye glasses and nose rings till the last moment, so your partner will have to keep guessing; it will be more fun!)

3) *Alternately*, have your partner ask *you* Yes/No questions to try and guess. You can only answer *yes* or *no*. You get to pick a different person in your mind when your partner names a wrong person (a warning to the guesser: Start with general questions like '바지를 입었어요?', and wait till the moment you are sure who the person is before you blurt out the name. Remember! Your partner has the right to change the person in his/her mind and start all over when you say the wrong name!)

Exercise 7. 우리 가족

Bring a family picture. Describe your family in the picture, talking about their appearances and clothing. Say where they are with respect to other family members. You can also add other information about where they live and what they do.

Exercise 8. Reading practice

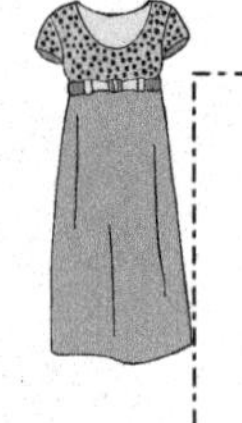

이번 주말에 데이트가 있어서 예쁜 옷을 입고 싶은데 좋은 옷이 없어요. 원피스는 너무 긴데 투피스는 너무 짧아요. 이 반바지는 너무 작고 저 치마는 너무 커요. 또, 구두가 있어도 좋은 구두는 없어요. 이 구두는 너무 높고 저 구두는 너무 빨개요. 좋은 옷하고 구두가 하나도 없어요! 오늘 오후에 백화점에 가서 쇼핑할래요. 예쁜 티셔츠랑 로우 컷 청바지를 살래요. 연두색 신발도 살래요. 주말에는 티셔츠하고 청바지를 입고 노란 신발을 신고 싶어요. 귀걸이도 끼고 목걸이도 하고 싶어요. 예쁘게 보이고 싶어요[1].

[1] want to look pretty

Exercise 9. Translate the following "although" sentences.

1) Although there is soap, wash your hands.

2) Although I am travelling for two days, I am not taking a razor. (travel 여행하다 take 가져가다)

3) Although it is a casual party, I am going to wear a dress shirt. (casual 캐주얼)

4) Even though the girlfriend's mother was there, he undid his necktie.

5) Even though he has a new watch, he is always late for class (late for ~에 늦다)

6) Although she looked in the mirror, she didn't want to see gray hair.

7) Even though he is tall, his legs are short.

8) Although I studied 5 hours last night, I still did badly on the test. (still 그래도)

9) Although he is 14 (years old), he has a mustache.

10) Even though she had two glasses of beer, she got drunk.

Exercise 10. -고 싶어해요 vs. -고 싶어요
Melinda is daydreaming about things she would like to do. Make up sentences expressing *her* wants and then compare yours.

Example: 멜린다 씨는 하와이에 가고 싶어해요. 나도 하와이에 가고 싶어요.
or 멜린다 씨는 하와이에 가고 싶어해요. 나는 하와이에 안 가고 싶어요.

Exercise 11. Reading practice
Make your own story by replacing the underlined words.

<u>다음 주</u>에 데이트가 있는데 좋은 옷이 없어요. 이 <u>청바지</u>는 너무 <u>짧은데</u>, 저 <u>청바지</u>는 또 너무 <u>길어요</u>. 이 <u>와이셔츠</u>는 너무 <u>노래요</u>. 저 <u>구두</u>는 너무 <u>커요</u>. <u>운동화</u>는 너무 <u>작아요</u>. 좋은 옷도 하나도 없고 좋은 신발도 하나도 없어요. <u>이번 주말에</u> <u>백화점</u>에 가서 옷을 사고 싶어요. <u>다음 주</u>에 <u>멋있게</u> 보이고 싶어요. <u>멋있는</u> <u>청바지</u>하고 <u>까만 구두</u>를 사고 싶어요. ____씨, 나하고 백화점에 같이 갈래요?

Exercise 12. Reading Practice

Read the following passage and answer the questions about 랜덤맨.

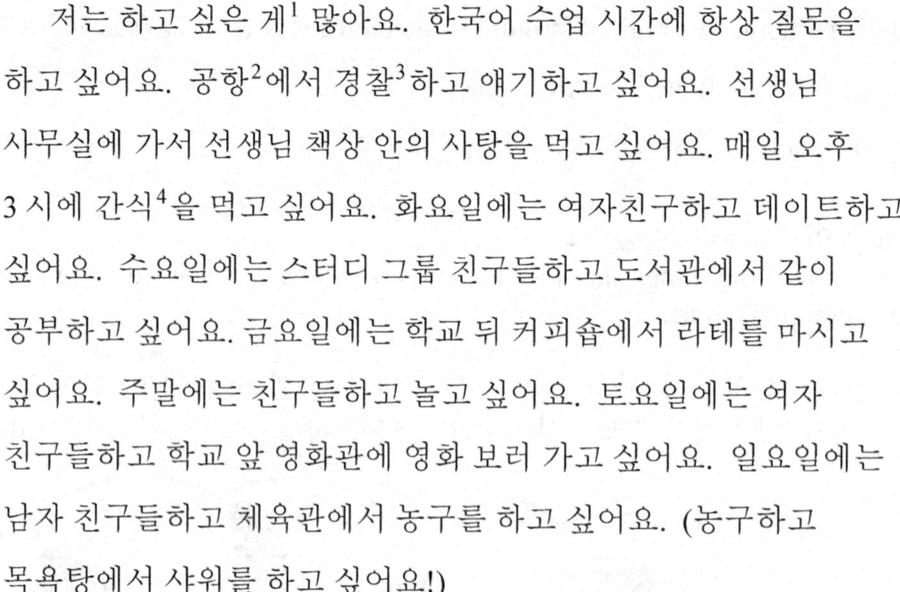

Random-Man

저는 하고 싶은 게[1] 많아요. 한국어 수업 시간에 항상 질문을 하고 싶어요. 공항[2]에서 경찰[3]하고 얘기하고 싶어요. 선생님 사무실에 가서 선생님 책상 안의 사탕을 먹고 싶어요. 매일 오후 3 시에 간식[4]을 먹고 싶어요. 화요일에는 여자친구하고 데이트하고 싶어요. 수요일에는 스터디 그룹 친구들하고 도서관에서 같이 공부하고 싶어요. 금요일에는 학교 뒤 커피숍에서 라테를 마시고 싶어요. 주말에는 친구들하고 놀고 싶어요. 토요일에는 여자 친구들하고 학교 앞 영화관에 영화 보러 가고 싶어요. 일요일에는 남자 친구들하고 체육관에서 농구를 하고 싶어요. (농구하고 목욕탕에서 샤워를 하고 싶어요!)

그렇지만! 저는 청소는 안 하고 싶어요. 빨래도 안 하고 싶어요. 아르바이트도 안 하고 싶어요. 숙제도 안 하고 싶어요. (제 전공은 컴퓨터 공학이에요. 그래서 선생님들이 숙제를 매일 많이 내줘요!) 시험도 안 보고 싶어요! 놀고만 싶어요. 주말에는 또, 집에 전화해서 형하고 엄마를 만나고 싶어요. 엄마는 한국사람인데 한국음식을 아주 맛있게 만들어요. 저는 엄마가 만드는 불고기를 특히[5] 좋아해요. 엄마는 떡볶이도 잘 만들지만 떡볶이는 너무 매워서 별로 안 먹고 싶어요. 아! 그리고 저는 평일에 멋있게 보이고[6] 싶어요. 새[7] 청바지를 입고 멋있는 구두를 신고 싶어요. 이번 주말에 엄마 집에 가서 엄마하고 옷을 사러 가고 싶어요. 하지만[8] 돈은 안 내고 싶어요!

1. things that I want to do
2. airport
3. police officer
4. snack
5. especially
6. look cool
7. new
8. but (a spoken variant of 그렇지만)

1) Random-Man 은 무엇을 하고 싶어해요?

2) Random-Man 은 무엇을 안 하고 싶어해요?

Lesson 18 Checkpoint

대화 1 사람이 많아도 금방 찾을 수 있을 거에요.

철수: **영희** 씨, 이번 주말에 춘천에 놀러 갈래요?
영희: 좋아요. 주말에는 길이 막히니까[59] 기차로 가요.
철수: 그럼, 일요일 아침 8 시에 서울역[60]에서 만나요.
영희: 서울역에는 사람이 많은데 어떻게 **철수** 씨를 알아보지요[61]?
철수: 제가 빨간 모자를 쓸께요. 빨간 모자라면 사람이 많아도 금방 찾을 거에요.
영희: 그럼 저는 노란 잠바[62]를 입을께요.
철수: 춘천에 가서 뭘 할래요?
영희: 춘천호[63]에도 가고 싶고 춘천 닭갈비[64]도 먹고 싶어요.

대화 2 옷장 앞에서 뭐 해요?

수미: **경미** 씨, 옷장 앞에서 뭐 해요?
경미: 내일 소개팅이 있는데 뭘 입으면 좋을까요[65]?
수미: **경미** 씨는 다리가 길고 예쁘니까 치마를 입으세요.
경미: 요새[66] 날씨가 추운데요[67].
수미: 추워도 입어요. 어차피[68] 밖에서 안 만나지요?
경미: 네, 커피숍에서 만나서 차 마실 거에요. 이 빨간 스웨터를 입고 싶은데...
수미: 그 스웨터는 너무 빨개요. 다른 색깔 없어요?
경미: 분홍색이 있는데 조금 커서요.
수미: 조금 커도 분홍색이 더 예뻐요.

---

[59] 길이 막히다 there is bad traffic; traffic is bad, backed up
[60] Seoul station
[61] recognize
[62] jacket with elastic waist
[63] Chuncheon Lake
[64] Korean chicken barbecue
[65] what do you suggest I wear?
[66] these days 요즘
[67] it's cold ("weather" is cold)
[68] in any case, anyway

읽기 1 어제 하루

어제는 **철수** 씨랑 같이 춘천에 놀러 갔어요. 아침에 서울역에서 만났어요. **철수** 씨가 빨간 모자를 써서 쉽게[69] 알아보았어요.[70] **철수** 씨는 장갑을 끼고 운동화를 신었어요. 저는 노란 잠바를 입고 하얀 모자를 썼어요. 춘천에 도착하고[71] 나서 갑자기[72] 비[73]가 와서 추웠어요[74]. 우리는 먼저[75] 춘천호에 갔는데 비 때문에[76] 아무 것도 안 보였어요[77]. 멋진 경치[78]를 구경하고[79] 싶었는데 아쉬웠어요[80]. 그리고 나서 춘천 시내[81]에 닭갈비를 먹으러 갔어요. 닭갈비는 제가 제일[82] 좋아하는 음식이에요. 저는 매운 음식을 별로 안 좋아하지만 닭갈비는 매워도 잘 먹어요. 이번 겨울 방학[83]에는 부산에 같이 놀러 가기로[84] 했어요. 빨리 부산의 겨울바다[85]가 보고 싶어요.

읽기 2 저는 한국어가 정말 좋아요.

저는 다음 달에 한국에 가요. 그래서 요새[86]는 한국어 공부를 더 열심히 해요. 하루에 5 시간씩 도서관에서 공부해요. 한국에 가면 한국 음식을 매일 매일 먹고 싶어요. 고궁[87]에도 가고 싶고 서울 타워[88]에도 가고 싶고 쇼핑도 하고 싶어요. 그리고 물론[89] 한국어도 많이 연습하고[90] 싶어요. 한국에서 하고 싶은 일은 많은데 새 학년이 곧 시작돼서 한국에 이 주일밖에 못 있어요. 한국에서 돌아와도 한국어 공부를 열심히 할 거에요. 저는 한국어가 정말 좋아요.

---

[69] easily
[70] 알아보다 recognize
[71] 도착하다 arrive
[72] suddenly
[73] rain
[74] 춥다 cold (weather)
[75] first, before other things
[76] due to, because of
[77] 보이다 is visible, can be seen
[78] scenery
[79] 구경하다 look around
[80] What a shame, (we were/it was) so close, what a bummer
[81] downtown
[82] most
[83] winter break (school)
[84] (놀러 가)기로 하다 decide to (go play, hang out)
[85] winter sea
[86] these days 요즘
[87] old palace
[88] Seoul Tower
[89] of course
[90] 연습하다 practice

노래하고 갑시다!

토요일 밤

긴 머리
짧은 치마
아름다운
그녀를 보면
무슨 말을
해야할까?
오! 토요일 밤에
토요일 밤
토요일 밤에
나 그대를 만나리
토요일 밤
토요일 밤에
나 그대를 만나리라

LESSON 19
두 얼굴의 사나이

Lesson 19 Vocabulary 기분, 성격 그리고 외모

기분	Mood
1. 심심하다	bored
2. 답답하다	frustrated, stir-crazy, trapped
3. 재미있다	interested
4. 재미없다	disinterested
5. 기분이 좋다	in a good mood
6. 기분이 나쁘다	in a bad mood
성격	**Personality**
7. 착하다	good (well-behaved; a good person)
8. 말이 많다	talkative
9. 말이 없다, 말이 적다	doesn't talk much, quiet
10. 털털하다	not picky, easy-going
11. 똑똑하다	smart
12. 멍청하다	not so sharp, dumb
13. 꼼꼼하다	meticulous (*positive implication*)
14. 깐깐하다 = 까다롭다 (ㅂ irr.)	picky, difficult (*negative implication*)
15. 친절하다	friendly, kind
16. 불친절하다	unfriendly, rude
17. 새침하다	aloof and reserved
18. 이기적이다	selfish
19. 고집이 세다	stubborn
20. 터프하다	macho
외모	**Appearance**
21. 뚱뚱하다	fat, plump
22. (빼빼) 마르다 (르 irr.)	skinny
23. 날씬하다	slim
24. 잘 생겼다 (잘 생기다)	good-looking (man)
25. 못 생겼다 (못 생기다)	ugly
26. 귀엽다 (ㅂ-irregular)	cute
27. 멋있다	stylish, be cool
28. 섹시하다	sexy
29. (얼굴이) 창백하다	pale
30. 살이 쪘다 (살이 찌다)	fat (gain weight)
31. 살이 빠졌다 (살이 빠지다)	has lost weight (lose weight)
32. 살을 빼다	(try to) lose wait
33. 다이어트하다	go on a diet (to lose weight)
34. (누구를, 누구하고) 사귀다	make friends with, go out with
35. 그런데도	inspite of that, even so

It seems a little politically incorrect to talk about someone being "fat" or "slim", but in Korea you will hear the words used quite often across gender and age. This is true of many physical attributes—such as noses and eyes.

Vocabulary Exercise 1. Opposites
Give the opposite moods or appearances.

1) 기분이 좋아요 ________________ 2) 예뻐요 ________________

3) 날씬해요 ________________ 4) 친절해요 ________________

5) 멍청해요 ________________

Vocabulary Exercise 2. Word Search
Circle all the 성격, 기분, and 외모 words you see!

뚱	뚱	쁘	양	이
재	고	치	재	상
멍	집	친	물	미
예	청	엾	절	불
날	씬	귀	기	심
답	털	분	엽	심
상	털	똑	착	다

Vocabulary Exercise 3. What's she like?
Complete the sentence with 성격 or 외모 words.

1) 브리트니 스피어즈는__________. 2) 탐 크루즈는________________.

3) South Park 의 카트맨은__________. 4) 할리 베리는________________.

5) 벅스 버니는________________. 6) 믹 재거는________________.

7) 아놀드 슈워츠네거는____________. 8) 덴젤 워싱턴은________________.

9) 알버트 아인슈타인은____________.

Vocabulary Exercise 4. Conjugation
Complete the following words in 어/아 form and write their meaning.

1) 털______ (   ) 2) 똑______ (   )

3) 이______ (   ) 4) 착______ (   )

5) 심______ (   )

Vocabulary Exercise 5. Idioms
What do you have? Complete the idioms.

1) cool, stylish: _________ 있다 2) fun: _________ 있다

3) talkative: _________ 많다

Vocabulary Exercise 6. How do you think they feel?
Describe how the people in each picture are feeling.

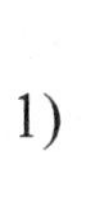
1) 

2) 

3) 

4) 

5) 

6) 

Lesson 19 Dialogue 두 얼굴의 사나이

리사: 아, 심심하다! (Calls her friend)
은이 씨! 나 **리산**데요, 뭐 하고 있었어요?[1]
은이: 아무것도 안 하고 있었어요.[1]
리사: 나하고 같이 **피터** 씨네[2] 갈래요?
리사: **피터** 씨네요?! **피터** 씨 아주 불친절한 사람이에요.
피터 씨하고 사귀면 안돼요[3]!!
은이: 어머, **리사** 씨 진정하세요[4]. **피터** 씨네[2] 안 가고 싶으면 안 가도 돼요[5]. **피터** 씨 아주 재미있고 친절한 사람인데.
리사: 참 이상하네요. **피터** 씨 두 얼굴의 사나이[6]에요?

1. was/were doing
2. Peter's place
3. shouldn't , won't do, not good
4. Calm down!
5. you don't have to go
6. man, guy

<나 **리산**데요>
Unless you are adding specific meaning elements, 나 (or 저) and 너 are more often used without a marker than with one, in spoken Korean. Note the meaning difference below:

나 피곤한데 I'm tired so/but…
난 피곤한데 _I_ am tired so/but (I don't know about _you_)…
내가 피곤한데 It is me who is tired…
나도 피곤한데 I am also tired…

Markers are frequently dropped in everyday speech with other subjects as well. Observe:

피터 씨 아주 불친절한 사람이에요.
피터 씨 아주 재미있고 친절한 사람인데.
피터 씨 두얼굴의 사나이에요?

Lesson 19 Grammar

1. Focus a. Permission -어도 돼요

-어도 돼요?	Is it all right to/if...? (May I? Can you?)

Remember the idiomatic phrases you learned that use the verb 되다? The same verb is used in a phrase to mean *may/can/it is OK to* (do something). The phrase -도 되다 is added to the -어/아 form of the verb and 되다 is usually conjugated for the (polite) present tense. A literal translation of the expression is *even if I do that, is that O.K.?*

언니, 언니 청바지 입어도 돼?	Sis, can I wear your jeans?
학교에 미니스커트 입고 가도 돼요?	Is it O.K. to wear a miniskirt to school?
아빠한테 다음 주에 전화해도 돼요?	May I call Dad next week?

If the answer to "may I" or "can I" is a *yes*, you can simply use the same construction:

A: 언니, 언니 청바지 입어도 돼?	Sis, can I wear your jeans?
B: 응, 입어도 돼.	Yes, you may.

If the answer is negative, you will need to say, *if you do that, it's not good* (See the next section).

Focus b. Denying permission -(으)면 안돼요

-(으)면 안돼요!	It is not OK to/if... (may not, cannot, should not, must not)

To deny permission (*you may not, it's not OK to...*), an -(으)면 clause is used with 안 되다 (*if you do that, it's not OK.*) Note that Korean does not make a distinction between *may not*, *should not*, and *must not*.

오늘 내 청바지 입으면 안돼.	You may not wear my jeans today.
학교에 미니스커트 입고 가면 안돼요.	It is not O.K. to wear a miniskirt to school.
아빠한테 내일 전화하면 안돼. 지금해.	You shouldn't call Dad tomorrow. Call him now.

2. Other Grammar Notes

1. -고 있다 *am/is/are doing*

Another common use of -고 is to connect a main verb to the helping verb 있어요 to express an action in progress.

동생은 신발을 신고 있어요.	My younger brother is putting on his shoes.
언니는 자고 있어요.	My older sister is sleeping.

While the -어요/아요 ending can be used to express the present tense in general, -고 있어요 emphasizes the action in progress.

지금 뭐 해요?	What are you doing now? (no particular action in progress is assumed)
지금 뭐 하고 있어요?	(I see you doing something) What are you doing now?

Use -고 **있었어요** for an action that was in progress in the past:

동생은 신발을 신고 있었어요. My younger brother was putting on his shoes.

Now, can you guess the meaning of the following sentences?

A: 내일 세 시에 어디에서 뭐 하고 있을 거에요?
Tomorrow at 3:00, what are you going to be doing and where are you going to be?

B: 집에서 전화 기다리**고** 있을께요. I will be waiting for your call at home, OK?

or B: 집에서 잠이나 자**고** 있을래요. I am just gonna sleep at home or something.

or B': 친구 집에 가**고** 있을 거에요. I will be on my way to my friend's house.

You know the difference between 잘 있어! (*Good bye!* Literally, *Stay well*) and 안녕히 계세요 (same meaning, honoring the subject). The same is true for the progressive expression -고 있어요. When you wish to express respect for the subject, you have to use -고 계세요 in place of -고 있어요.

지금 뭐 하고 계세요?	(I see you doing something) What are you doing now?
할머니 지금 뭐 하고 계세요?	What is Grandmother doing now?

> You saw 계세요 in expressions like 안녕히 계세요, which means *Stay in peace* or *Stay well* (intimate-blunt version is 잘 있어). 계세요 is a conjugated form of 계시다, and the past and the future forms are 계셨어요 and 계실 거에요, respectively.

2. TIME 내내 *all TIME; the whole TIME*

내내 can be added after time-duration expressions to mean *all*… or *the whole*…. The first 내 is pronounced longer than usual.

세 시간 내내 for three whole hours
아침 내내 all morning (long)
오후 내내 all afternoon
저녁 내내 all evening
일주일 내내 all week
한 달 내내 the whole month long
일 년 내내 for a whole year/ all year long

Only 하루 종일 is different, meaning *all day long*.

3. Adjectives in self-talk (for no targeted audience)

Adjectives can be used *without* being conjugated! When they are, the speaker is talking to him/herself, with no particular listener. Such phrases often follow an exclamation.

아, 배고프다! Boy, am I hungry!
아, 심심하다! I'm so bored!
아, 바쁘다! Darn, am I so busy!
야, 저 옷 참 예쁘다! Hey, that outfit is really pretty!
와, 한국어 너무 어렵다!! Man, isn't Korean hard!

(These might be considered to be conjugated for 'self-talk', as opposed to *unconjugated*, but in any case, the self-talk form of adjectives looks just like the "unconjugated" citation form.)

4. Adjective-어 죽겠다 and Verb-고 싶어 죽겠다 *dying of* and *dying to*

You already learned two phrases with the *dying of* sense: 배고파 죽겠다 and 배불러 죽겠다. The *dying of* phrase is very productive in Korean. You can add 죽겠다 (*I would die*) after the 어/아 form of many adjectives to mean *dying from ADJECTIVE:*

더워 죽겠어요! It's so hot, I'm dying.
힘들어 죽겠다! This is so hard to do that I'm dying!
매워 죽겠죠? It's so spicy, you are dying, eh?

With "있다" and "없다" words,
use "-어 죽겠다"
맛있어 죽겠어요
재미없어 죽겠어요

If you add 죽겠다 after *VER-고 싶어*, then you get the sense *dying to* (*dying from wanting to*):

파티에 가고 싶어 죽겠다. I am dying to go to the party.

한국 음식 먹고 싶어 죽겠어요. I am dying to have some Korean food!

5. ADJ-어 하다 describing someone else's feelings

Just like 좋아하다 and -고 싶어하다, when talking about others' feelings and thoughts (when the subject is in the third person) adjectives are also conjugated to use 하다 as a helping verb. The main adjective conjugates in the -아/어 form.

그 여자는 기분 나빠해요. She is ticked off.

그 사람 지금 심심해하고 있어요. He's bored now.

If the adjective does not express emotion or feelings, you should not insert an extra -어 해요: ~~똑똑해 해요~~

This construction is a way of avoiding talking (as if you *know*) about someone else's feelings.

노래해도 돼요?

어린 송아지가 굴뚝 위에 앉아 울고 있어요.

엄마! 엄마! 엉덩이가 뜨거워!

Lesson 19 Exercises

Exercise 1. Dialogue practice

Practice the dialogue in this lesson with a classmate.

Exercise 2. May I?

Given the situation (use either -(으)ㄴ데, or -(으)니까), ask for permission.

1) 한국어 숙제가 너무 많다 – turn in late 2) 국이 너무 짜다 -add water

3) 커피가 쓰다 - put sugar in

4) 배가 고프다 - eat the chicken

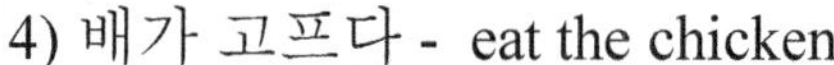

5) 쌍둥이 형이 토가를 입다 –wear a toga
(쌍둥이: twin)

6) 토마토가 있다 - make spaghetti

7) 심심하다 - play with a friend

8) 답답하다 - open the window

Exercise 3. Complain, complain, complain.
Complain about how long each activity took.

Example: **하루 종일** 집 청소를 했어요. 피곤해 죽겠어요.

1) homework – 3 hours
2) father, bad mood – 1 week
3) younger brother, sleep – all day
4) I, wait for a phone call – 1 week
5) do the dishes – all evening (tough 힘들다)
6) neighbor, playing guitar – all day (neighbor 옆집 사람, noisy 시끄럽다)

Exercise 4. 뭐 하고 있어요? 뭐 하고 있었어요? 뭐 하고 있을 거예요?
Describe what the people in each picture are/were or will be doing at the time indicated. Then tell your partner what you are/were or will be doing. For future, you can use -(으)ㄹ래요 and -(으)ㄹ게요 as well.

1) 어제 오후

2) 학교 끝나고 집에 가서

3) 지금

4) 그저께 3 시에

5) 오늘 아침

6) 아까 (just a while ago)

7) 이번 주 토요일

8) 다음 주 금요일

Exercise 5. -고 있어요 vs. -고 계세요

Part I. Describe what the following people are doing. Be careful to use the correct form according to the subject (honorific or not?).

1) 친구

2) **페페 르퓨** 부인 (wife)

3) 할머니

4) 형/오빠

5) 언니/누나의 남자 친구

6) 우리 할머니

7) 동생

8) 직장 상사 (your boss)

9) 이 할아버지

10) 친구 아빠

smoke (담배를 피우다)

Part II. This time, tell your partner what the people in each picture were doing yesterday, 10 minutes ago, a week ago, etc.

Part III. Now, tell your partner what the people in each picture will be doing 10:00 p.m. tonight, tomorrow, this weekend, next Wednesday, next week, etc., etc.

Exercise 6. Detective

Your best pen is missing from your bag! You last saw it there yesterday at 6pm. Find out who in your class might have *taken it* by asking them what they were doing at different times last night and this morning, and who they were with. If they do not have an alibi, put them on your list of suspects.

Exercise 7. No, you may not!

Ask for permission to do the following; your partner will deny permission every time!

Example: 국에, 소금, 넣다

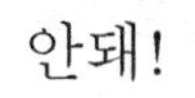

A: 국에 소금 넣어도 돼요?
B: 국에 소금을 넣으면 국이 짤 거에요. 소금 넣으면 안돼요.

1) 점심, 안 먹다

2) 숙제, 내일, 내다

3) 점심에, 외식하다

4) 술 마시다, 운전하다

5) 파티에, 빨간 가죽 치마, 입고 가다 (가죽 leather)

Exercise 8. I'm dying to ...
Talk to your partner about things you are dying to do, places you want to go, etc. Ask why. Have a conversation!

읽다, 먹다, (어떤 어떤 옷을-some certain kind of clothing) 입다, 자다, 다이어트를 하다, 알다, 마시다, 보다, 가다, 살을 빼다, 면도하다 배우다, 만나다, 사다, 만들다, (누구하고) 사귀다, 졸업하다

Exercise 9. Reading practice 우리 가족
Read the following descriptions about "나" and her family. Is your family much like hers or very different? Talk with your classmates about how *your* family is.

나는 우리 가족에 불만[1]이 많아요. 아빠는 항상 기분이 나쁘고 말이 너무 많아요. 고집도 세고 불친절해요. (내 친구들은 우리 아빠를 이상하다고 생각해요[2]). 엄마는 항상 청소하고 빨래를 해요. 집안 일만 해서 힘들어하고 심심해하고 답답해해요. 우리 언니는 키가 크고 다리가 길고 얼굴이 예쁘고 날씬해요. 옷도 잘 입어요[3]. 똑똑하고 친절해서 친구가 많아요. 우리 오빠는 말이 없고 조금 못 생겼어요. 나는...?

내 이상적인[4] 가족은 다음과 같아요[5].

아빠는 털털하고 항상 기분이 좋아요. 용돈[6]도 많이 줘요. 엄마는 친절하고 재미있어요. 재미있는 농담[7]도 많이 해요. 언니는 뚱뚱하고 못 생겼지만 똑똑하고 착해요. 오빠는 멋있고 섹시해요. (멋있는 오빠 친구들이 언니말고 나를 좋아해요!) 나는 귀엽고, 날씬하고, 똑똑하고 재미있어요. 남자 친구도 많고, 재미있는 파티에 많이 초대[8]를 받아서 가는데, 한국어 시험은 잘 봐서 항상 A를 받아요. ☺

1. discontent
2. think that
3. has a good sense of fashion
4. ideal
5. as follows (literally, 'same as next')
6. [용똔] pocket money
7. joke
8. invitation

Exercise 10. Reading practice. 미셸하고 롤디

미셸: 아! 답답하다! 아! 심심하다!

(전화 소리: 때르릉~ 때르릉)

롤디: 여보세요.

미셸: 아, **롤디** 씨! 지금 뭐 하고 있어요?

롤디: 아무 것도 안 하고 있었어요. 토요일인데 심심하게 집에만 있어요. **미셸** 씨, 뭐, 재미있는 일 없어요?

미셸: 나도 심심해서 전화 했어요. **롤디** 씨, 점심 먹었어요?

롤디: 아니오. 왜, 같이 먹으러 갈래요?

미셸: 네. 나가서 밥을 사 먹고 싶은데 돈이 별로 없어요.

롤디: 음... 그럼, 우리 다운타운 **팔로미노**에 갈래요? 거기서 지미 씨가 아르바이트를 해요.

미셸: 돈이 없는데 가면 뭐 해요?

롤디: 우리, 점심을 시켜서 먹고 그냥 옵시다.

미셸: 돈은 안 내요?

롤디: **지미** 씨는 착하고 친절한 사람이라서 괜찮아요.

미셸: **롤디** 씨, 정말 이상한 사람이네요. 얼굴이 잘 생겨서 좋아했는데, 내가 바보 같았어요. 그 식당에 가고 싶으면 **롤디** 씨 혼자 가세요. 나는 집에서 텔레비전이나 볼래요.

롤디: 아, **미셸** 씨! 농담이었어요. **미셸** 씨, 그런데 정말 내가 잘 생겼다고 생각해요?

미셸: 정말 농담이었죠? 음... 네. 난 **롤디** 씨가 섹시하고 터프하다고 생각해요. 성격도 좋고 얼굴도 잘 생겼다고 생각해요. 근데 **롤디** 씨, 돈 많아요? 나, **팔로미노**에서 점심 사 줄래요?

재미 있는 일: fun stuff
그냥 옵시다: let's just come back
농담이었어요: it was a joke
-고 생각하다: think that...
친절한 사람이라서: he is a kind person so...

Lesson 19 Checkpoint

대화 1 켈리 씨는 너무 까다로워요!

수미: 저, **켈리** 씨 **동호** 씨를 어떻게 생각해요[91]?

켈리: **동호** 씨하고 같이 있으면 심심하고 재미없어요.

수미: 그럼 **타미** 씨는 어때요?

켈리: **타미** 씨는 똑똑하지만 너무 말이 많아요.

수미: 그럼 **철수** 씨는요?

켈리: **철수** 씨는 잘 생겼고 멋있지만 너무 고집이 세요.

수미: 그럼 **상인** 씨는요?

켈리: **상인** 씨는 터프하고 섹시하지만 좀 멍청해요.

수미: **켈리** 씨는 너무 까다로워요!

대화 2 힘들면 우리 같이 숙제합시다.

미미: **창수** 씨 지금 뭐 해요? 바빠요?

창수: 네, 저 한국어 작문[92] 숙제 하고 있어요.

미미: 네? 아직도 하고 있어요? 일주일 내내 했는데 아직도 못 끝냈어요?

창수: 네, 힘들어 죽겠어요. 그런데 **미미** 씨는 이렇게 놀아도 돼요? 숙제 다 했어요?

미미: 아니오. 어제 하루 종일 했는데 아직 못 끝냈어요.

창수: 그러면 안 돼요, **미미** 씨. 힘들면 우리 같이 숙제해요.

미미: 그래도 돼요?

창수: 그럼요.

[91] what do you think of...
[92] composition

Vocabulary Power!

You have seen some descriptive adjectives that involve repeating syllables such as 똑똑하다 and 심심하다. This kind of *reduplicative* adjectives is quite common in the native* Korean vocabulary. Here are some more common adjectives that repeat syllables.

싹싹하다	tactful, tending others' comfort well
통통하다	plump
튼튼하다	strong, sturdy, healthy
씩씩하다	energetic, outgoing, keen
팔팔하다	energetic
도도하다	arrogant
무뚝뚝하다	blunt, curt, not sociable
칠칠맞다 (some reduplicative words are used with other endings than 하다)	sloppy

Learn these words and impress your Korean friends with your powerful ***native**** vocabulary!

*native: not borrowed from Chinese, Japanese, or English, etc.

LESSON 20
까만 머리가 더 좋아요.

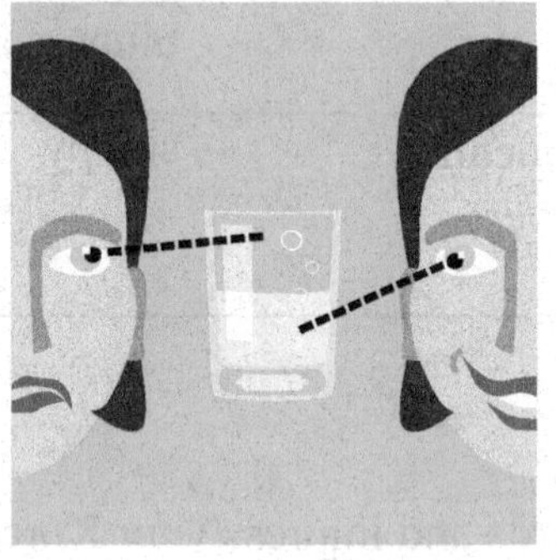

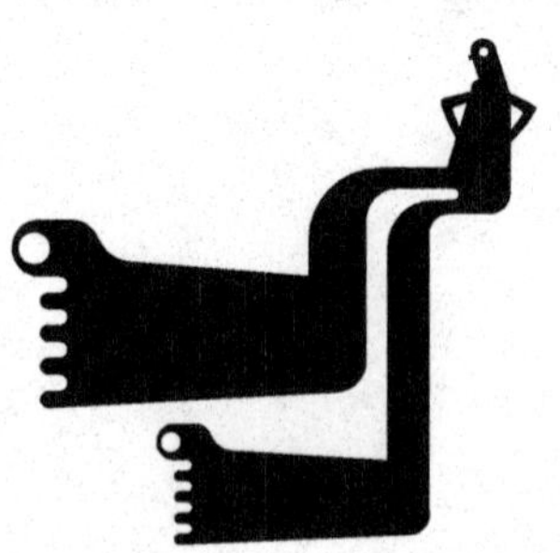

Lesson 20 Vocabulary  *Important Miscellany*

nouns, adverbs, and markers	
1. 자기	oneself
2. 남	others
3. 얘, 걔, 쟤 (+네)	she, he (*intimate-blunt* form) (+네=they)
4. N_1하고 N_2 사이; $N_{category}$ 사이	between N_1 and N_2; among N's
5. 최고 (N) = 제일 (ADV)	the best (one)
6. 먼저	first
7. 나중에	later
8. 조금 전에, 좀 전에	a minute a go
9. 아까	a while ago
10. 전에	before
11. 옛날에, 예전에	long time ago, in the olden days
12. 최근에	recently
13. 이따가	later
14. 일찍	early
15. 늦게	late (not on time)
16. 빨리	quickly
17. 천천히	slowly
18. 동안	during; for TIME
19. 제일	best, most
20. 처음으로; 처음에	for the first time; at first
21. 마지막으로; 마지막에	for the last time; at the end
22. 중에(서)	among (in comparison)
23. -보다	(rather) than
24. 더; 덜	more; less
25. 훨씬	far, much, way (more, better, etc.)
26. -같이 = -처럼	like (something, someone)

나중에 means some undefined "later" in time. 이따가 usually means "later (the same day)".

More personality-related verbs and adjectives	
27. 잘난 체하다, 잘난 척하다	act like one is so great
28. 아는 체하다, 아는 척하다	act like a know-it-all
29. 말을 걸다	start a conversation
30. 도와주다	help (out)
31. 사교성이 좋다	have good social skills, make many friends
32. 발이 넓다	know many people (*literally* wide-footed)
33. 서먹서먹하다	be awkward (for not knowing someone well)
34. 겸손하다	be humble
35. (누구하고) 사이가 좋다	get along well with, be on good terms
36. (누구하고) 친하다	be good friends with, close
37. (친구들한테/사이에) 인기가 좋다, 많다	be popular (among friends)

These are verbs, so they need the -는 suffix to modify a noun.

These are adjectives, so they need the -은 suffix to modify a noun.

Vocabulary Exercise 1. In real life
Think of a real life example for each of the following vocabulary phrases.

1) ____________ 는 **잘난 체해요**.

1) ____________는 항상 **아는 체해요.**

2) __________한테 한 번 **말을 걸고** 싶어요.

3) ___________는 나를 항상 **도와줘요**.

4) ___________는 **사교성이 좋아요.**

5) ___________는 **발이 넓어요.**

6) ___________하고는 아주 **서먹서먹해요.**

7) __________는 아주 **겸손해요**.

8) ___________하고 **사이가 좋아요.**

9) ____________하고 **친해요**.

10) ____________는 ____________사이에 **인기가 좋아요**.

Vocabulary Exercise 2.
Fill in the blanks with an appropriate vocabulary item from the choices. Use each word only once.

사이　마지막으로　나중에　동안　마지막에　같이 (or 처럼) 제일　먼저　자기　최고　처음에　남　처음으로

1) 기숙사는 도서관하고 체육관 ________에 있어요.

2) 청바지는 리바이스가________에요.

3) ________의 의자말고________ 의자에 앉으세요!

4) 나가서 놀지 말고 숙제 ________ 해!

5) 너는 왜 원숭이________ 웃니? (원숭이 monkey, 웃다 laugh)

6) 지금 바쁘니까 ________ 만납시다.

7) 청바지 중에는 리바이스가 ________ 좋아요.

8) ________는 한국어 반 친구들의 이름을 몰랐어요. (반 class)

9) ________ 이 질문에 대답하세요.　(대답 answer)

10) 저는 1 년________ 한국어 수업을 들었어요. (수업을 듣다: take a class)

Lesson 20 Dialogue 까만 머리가 더 좋아요

훈: **윌** 씨는 어떤[1] 여자가 제일 좋아요?

윌: 나는 예쁘고 멍청한 여자보다는 똑똑하고 친절한 여자가 좋아요.

훈: 그럼, **루시 루**하고 **위노나 라이더**하고 **드루 베리모어** 중에 어떤 영화배우[2]가 제일 좋아요?

윌: 난 금발보다 까만 머리가 더 좋아요. **위노나 라이더**는 내 여자 친구처럼 눈이 크고 예쁘죠.

훈: 우리 한국어 반[3]에서는 누가 제일 예쁜 것 같아요[4]?

윌: **제시카가** 예쁘지만 좀 잘난 체를 하는 것 같아요[4].

훈: 그럼, **제시카**하고 사귀고 싶어요?

윌: 네. 친해지고 싶어요[4].

1. what sort, what type
2. actors, actresses
3. in our Korean class
4. seems
5. want to get close (to someone)

go out with in the sense of *dating* = (person 하고) 사귀다 / 데이트하다.

나가다 only means *go out of* some physical space.

Lesson 20 Grammar

1. Focus Smoothing out one's opinions -(으)ㄴ/는 것 같아요

-(으)ㄴ/ -는 것 같아요	seem, seems

-(으)ㄴ/는 것 같아요 is an idiomatic ending that means *it seems that* + sentence (literally, *it is like* + sentence).

개는 발이 넓은 것 같아. She seems to know tons of people.

개네 둘은 친한 것 같아. They (the two) seem to be close.

재는 너무 잘난 척을 하는 것 같아. He seems to think he is so great.

g.o.d. 는 동양 젊은이들 사이에 인기가 좋은 것 같아요.
g.o.d. seems to be popular among the Asian youth.

Other more colloquial pronunciations of 은/는 것 같아요 are 은/는 거 같아요 and 은/는 거 같애요. Practice them all!

Use -(으)ㄴ것 같아요 after **adjectives** and -는 것 같아요 after **verbs**. And, remember that there are both 하다 *verbs* and 하다 *adjectives* that conjugate differently, and that "있다/없다 adjectives" act as verbs.

그 사람은 아주 친절한 것 같아. He seems really (kind and) nice.

개네는 항상 다이어트를 하는 것 같아. They always seem to be on a diet.

Can you predict how ㅂ-ending and ㄹ-ending words are conjugated?

Citation form	Verb	Adjective
돕다		
굽다		
입다		
춥다		
덥다		
살다		
알다		
길다		

2. Other Grammar Notes

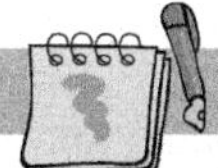

1. -(으)ㄹ 수 있다, -(으)ㄹ 수 없다 *is/isn't possible*

-(으)ㄹ 수 있어요 means *it is possible to/that...* and -(으)ㄹ 수 없어요 means *it is not possible to....* While 못 해요 focuses more on the individual's inability, -(으)ㄹ 수 있다/없다 literally addresses whether the action is possible (at all). But both are used to express a person's abilities, especially since there is no positive counterpart to 못 하다. Of course, you drop 으 when the verb ends in a vowel.

여기서 수영 할 수 없어요.	One/we can't swim here.
걔는 밥을 세 그릇이나 먹을 수 있어요.	He can eat up to three servings of rice.

Because 수 is a noun, it can be marked with -는, -가, or -도:

> 오늘 집에 아무도 없어요. 그래서 우리 집에서 공부 할 수가 있어요 놀고 싶으면 놀 수도 있어요. 파티를 할 수는 없지만...
>
> Nobody is home today, so we can study at our place. If you want to play, we can also play (at our place). We *can't* have a party, though…

2. 얘, 걔, 쟤(네) *he, she, they (literally, this, that, that child over there)*

Korean does not really have a set of third person pronouns (*he/she/they*), so phrases like *this person* are used instead. You might already have heard the following being used: 그 사람, 그 남자, 그 여자, 그 학생. You can figure out 그 아이 (아이=child) and 그 분. You can add -들 to any of these to make a plural, and 그 can be replaced by 이 and 저, of course.

> The *pronunciation* of the words 걔 and 쟤 is usually simplified to 개, and 재…

> In written Korean, you will also see 그 to mean *he* or *she* and 그녀 to mean *she*.

이 아이, 그 아이 and 저 아이 are commonly used in casual conversation, shortened to 얘, 걔, 쟤 (after 아이 has been shortened to [애]). Then an alternative plural marker is 네: 걔네, etc.

⚠ This generalized use of 아이 is only to refer to people you grew up with or those who are younger than you! Use 사람, if you want to talk about someone you do not know well. Use 분 if you are describing someone who is far older than you or someone you need to respect (teachers, grandparents, parents' friends, etc.)

> Did you know that Koreans sometimes use the word '것 (거)' to talk about human beings? When grandparents or parents express their adoration to an infant, they may say '에이구, 귀여운 것"(*cute little thing*) . "이게!" is also used in fights or threats.

3. -보다 …(더/덜) *more/less … than*

Making comparative sentences in Korean is simple. Just attach the particle –보다 (*than*) to the noun that is being compared. Adding 더 in front of the predicate *emphasizes* the comparison, but there are no comparative adjectives (e.g. bigg*er*) and adverbs (e.g. often*er*) to learn.

나는 커요. → 나는 미미보다 커요. or 나는 미미보다 더 커요.
I am tall. → I am taller than **Mimi**.

It is also possible to make comparatives using 덜 (*less*) -- you get something like X is not as ADJECTIVE as Y. "More than" comparisons are more common than "less than" comparisons, and note that, unlike 더, you cannot leave out 덜 or you get the opposite meaning.

미미는 나보다 덜 커요.
Mimi is less tall than I am. (*sounds odd*)

미미는 나보다 ~~덜~~ 커요.
Mimi is ~~less~~ taller than I am. (*different meaning!*)

Notice in the next three examples that the same rule works for non-adjective comparisons: **add -보다 to the noun being compared** -- whether it is a Subject or an Object – and **add the 보다 phrase into an otherwise regular sentence**:

나는 바지를 자주 입어요. → 나는 치마보다 바지를 (더) 자주 입어요.
I wear pants often. → I wear pants more often than skirts.

나는 테니스를 잘 쳐요. → 나는 야구보다 테니스를 잘 쳐요.
I play tennis well. → I play tennis better than baseball.

나는 테니스를 잘 쳐요. → 나는 동현이보다 테니스를 잘 쳐요.
I play tennis well. → I play tennis better than 동현 (does).

In English, one might say "I play tennis better than 동현 does" and "I play tennis better than I play baseball," but in Korean, it is not necessary to differentiate subjects and objects in comparisons and not possible to compare whole sentences or phrases. Be sure to compare two ***nouns*** and attach –보다 to the "loser."

A: **윌리엄스** 자매 (sisters) 중에 (among) 누가 테니스를 더 잘 쳐?
B: **세리나 윌리엄스**가 더 잘 쳐.

A: 누가 **세리나**보다 테니스를 잘 쳐?
B: 내가 **세리나보다** 테니스를 잘 쳐.
I play tennis better than **Serena** (does).

A: 너는 누구보다 테니스를 잘 쳐?
B: 나는 **세리나**보다 테니스를 잘 쳐.

Remember that the grammar you learned for regular sentences holds for comparative sentences. This includes particles, and selection of 은/는 or 이/가. All you have to do is add a 보다 phrase to make a comparative sentence.

훨씬 means 'far more/less':
파란 사과보다 빨간 사과가 훨씬 (더) 달아요.
Red apples are much/far sweeter than green apples.

4. MEMBERS 중에(서)/PLACE-에서 ...제일 *among MEMBERS/in CATEGORY, the most ...*

When comparing more than two things, use 제일 (*most*) instead of 더 (*more*). After category-naming nouns or when you are listing three or more individuals, use 중에 (*among*). Use –에서 to mark phrases like *in the world, in our class*, etc.

우리는 외국음식 중에서 중국음식을 제일 많이 먹어요.
We eat Chinese food most among ethnic foods.

When something is (metaphorically) "the best ever," (or "the bomb") it is "최고."

세 언니 중에 나는 둘째 언니하고 제일 친해요.
Of my three sisters, I am closest with the second oldest sister.

거울아, 거울아, 이 세상에서 누가 제일 예쁘니?
Mirror, mirror, who is the fairest in the world?

이 세 옷 중에 어느 옷이 제일 비싸요?
Among these three clothes (items), which is the most expensive?

5. -한테 *to* or *for* (a person)

(Indirect Object Person Marker) The marker -한테, which means *to* or *for*, is added to an *animate* noun. English indirect objects are not always marked with *to* or *for*, so you will have to be careful to mark the indirect object in Korean.

Even when *to* and *for* are not used in English, the *indirect object* is the goal/**destination** or **beneficiary** of the *direct object* in a kind of transfer denoted by the verb.

That is, the **direct object** goes from the **subject** to the **indirect object**: I gave **food** to the **dog**. (=I gave the **dog food**.)

엄마한테 전화했어요.	I called Mom. (I gave a call to Mom.)
친구한테 생일 선물을 줬어요.	I gave my friend a birthday present.
고양이한테 물 좀 주세요.	Give the cat some water, please.
할머니가 저한테 용돈을 줬어요.	Grandmother gave me pocket money.
강아지한테 밥을 줬어요.	(I) gave the dog food.
토요일에 친구한테 전화할 거에요.	I am planning to call my friend on Saturday.
나한테 자꾸 그런 부탁하지 마세요!	Don't ask me such favors over and over!
우리 언니한테 인사하세요.	Say hello to my older sister.
질문 있으면 선생님한테 물어 보세요	If you have a question, try asking the teacher.

In written and for more formal usage, use -에게 where you would use -한테. Thus as an opening sentence in a letter, you might write:

> 보고 싶은 친구 은비에게:
>
> 은비야 잘 있었니? 나도 잘 있어. 여기 시애틀에도 봄이 왔어…

Also don't forget to use -에 when the destination or is a *place* or a *thing*:

일요일인데도 학교에 갔어요.	Although it was Sunday, I went to school.
어제는 한국에 전화했어요.	I called Korea yesterday.
꽃에 물을 주세요.	Please water the flower/plant.

Lesson 20 Exercises

Exercise 1. Dialogue practice
Practice the dialogue in this lesson with a classmate.

Exercise 2. I can't that day; I can another day
Being a popular person, you have to check your date book to see when you are available. The following is your schedule. Tell your friend what you can do with him/her on which day.

1) can't eat lunch together on Monday
2) can meet on Wednesday
3) can drink beer together on Friday
4) can't watch a movie together on Saturday
5) can make dinner together on Thursday
6) can exercise together on Saturday
7) can make pizza together on Saturday night
8) can't study together next Monday

Exercise 3. That's odd!
Ask your partner about interesting and odd things they can and can't do.

Example: _____ 씨, 엉덩이로 이름 쓸 수 있어요?

엉덩이로 이름쓰기 is a popular penalty in Korea when you don't win a game.

Exercise 4. 뭐 할 수 있어요?
Part I. What can one do when they reach a certain age? Or what can they no longer do?!

Example: 2 살이 되면? 2 살이 되면 말을 잘 할 수 있어요 (one can talk well)

Part II. Soften your assumption with -은/는 것 같아요.

Example: 2 살이 되면? 2 살이 되면 말을 잘 할 수 있는 것 같아요.

1) 1 살이 되면 2) 5 살이 되면

2) 16 살이 되면 4) 18 살이 되면

5) 21 살이 되면 (스물 한 살) 6) 30 살이 되면 (서른 살)

Exercise 5. Translation
Translate the following comparisons.

Example: My feet are smaller than my dad's.
내 발은 아빠 발보다 더 작아요.

1) Korean food is spicier than Japanese food.

2) The older brother is friendlier than the younger brother.

3) 5 is more than 3. (Use 많다)

4) My shoes are prettier than my friend's.

5) Monica's skirt is longer than Jenny's

6) Jessica is busier than Jody.

Exercise 6. Sibling rivalry?
Use any adjectives you know to make comparisions that are true in your life. Work with a partner and have a conversation.

Exercise 7. Best in show.
Ask your partner which is the most ADJECTIVE among the choices given.

Example:
수박, 바나나, 사과 (과일) – 좋아하다
→ 수박하고 바나나하고 사과 중에(서) 어느 과일을 제일 좋아해요?

1) 리바이스, 갭, 켈빈클라인 (청바지) – 멋있다

2) 한국음식, 태국음식, 멕시코 음식 (음식) – 맵다

3) 사우스 파크, 심슨즈, 킹오브더 힐 (만화 cartoons) – 재미있다

4) 매직 잔슨, 샤킬 오닐, 마이클 조던 (운동 선수 athlete) - 키가 크다

5) 포셰, 벤츠, 렉서스 (차) – 비싸다 (expensive)
6) 씨디, 책, 잡지 – 많다 (use 어느게 or 뭐가)
7) 비틀즈, 펄잼, 알이엠 (밴드 band) – 좋아하다
8) 알래니스 모리셋, 시네이드 오카너, 마돈나 (여자 가수 female singer) – 노래를 잘 하다

Exercise 8. Pieces

Translate the following pieces into complete Korean sentences.

1) seem // **정수** // draw // better // than **송희**
2) seem // can't // play basketball // since // don't have // ball (공)
3) where is Tina? // she // seem // drink // beer // bar
4) among // brothers // Charles // seem // smartest
5) teacher // seem // know // everything
6) Mom // seem // feel // tired
7) That girl // always // seem // wear // those same // yellow // sneakers
8) these apples // seem // more // red // those

Exercise 9. Superlative practice

Use the given category (or time frame) and adjective to make a sentence determining what is the most ADJECTIVE in the category. Soften your opinions with *it seems that*...

Example:
한국어 클래스, 짧은 머리
→ 한국어 클래스에서 선생님 머리가 제일 짧은 것 같아요.

1) 요즘 (these days), 재미있는 영화
2) 우리 반, 큰 학생
3) 미국, 멋있는 가수 (singer)
4) 우리 반 (class), 잘생긴 학생
5) 요즘, 웃긴 시트 콤 (funny sitcom)
6) 이번 학기, 어려운 과목(difficult subject)
7) 운동, 쉬운 운동 (easy sport)
8) 워싱턴, 예쁜 곳 (pretty places in Washington)
9) 한국 음식, 매운 음식
10) 과일, 단 과일

Don't forget to use the word "중" if you are talking about a category and not a place or time!

Exercise 10. In your opinion…
Compare the two items, using the adjective provided.

Example: 엄마, 나/아빠, 나 → 내가 엄마보다 (훨씬) 더 큰 것 같아요.

1) 수학, 영어, 재미있다
2) 한국 음식, 태국 음식, 맵다
3) **소크라테스**, **뉴턴**, 머리가 좋다
4) **덴젤 워싱턴**, **이쓴 혹**, 잘 생겼다
5) 사우스 파크, 심슨즈, 재미있다
6) 치토스, 도리토스, 맛있다
7) 워싱턴 대학, 워싱턴 스테이트 대학, 크다

Exercise 11. Survey & Report
You and one partner are in charge of the fashion update for the class. One of you might want to talk about what **will be** in style for fall, and you should give a **summary** of your classmates' clothing preferences (preferences for skirts, pants, shorts, how many T-shirts they own, what their favorite colors are, what they wear to exercise or go to football games, etc.) You will need to interview classmates in order to present some statistics, that is, *4 out of 5 men prefer* …Or, *I interviewed 6 women and 4 of them have…* Don't forget to use -보다 (더), 훨씬, 제일, … 중에, etc.!

Exercise 12. Reading practice

나는 보통 아침 7 시에 일어나서 화장실에 가요. 목욕탕에서 세수를 하고 이를 닦아요. 7 시 반 쯤에 옷을 입어요. 수업이 많은 날에는 청바지를 입어요. 청바지가 치마보다 편하니까요. 청바지를 입으면 신발도 편한 신발로 신을 수 있어요. 그런데, 오늘은 수학 수업이 있는데, 멋있는 중국인 학생이 수학 수업을 같이 듣기 때문에 예쁘게 보이고 싶었어요. 그래서 까만 스웨터를 입고 은목걸이를 껐어요. 그리고 스타일이 비슷한 귀걸이도 껐어요. 시간이 있으면 메니큐어를 칠하고 싶지만 숙제 때문에 시간이 없어요. 아직도 한국어 숙제가 많이 남아 있어요 숙제를 다 하고 시간이 있으면 예쁜색 메니큐어도 칠할 거에요.

수업을 듣기 때문에 because I took the class 예쁘게 보이고 싶다 want to look pretty
숙제 때문에 because of the homework 남아 있어요 remains 메니큐어를 칠하다 paint one's nails

Exercise 13. Reading practice 파란색에 미친[1] 제니

내 이름은 제니에요. 나는 색 중에 파란색하고 초록색을 제일 좋아해요. 하지만 초록색보다 파란색을 더 좋아해요. 그래서 파란색 옷을 제일 많이 입어요. 지금도 파란 반팔 셔츠를 입고 있어요. 백화점에 쇼핑을 가도 항상 파란색 옷을 사고 싶어요. 어디에 가면 항상 파란색 옷을 입고 싶어요.

1. crazy about

어제는 토요일, 내 친구 미샤의 생일이었어요. 미샤는 금요일에 친구들한테 "내 생일에는 여러분 모두[2] 까만색 옷을 입고 오세요. 까만색은 아주 섹시하고 멋있어요! 나는 내 생일에 '블랙 파티'를 하고 싶어요. 까만 모자를 쓰고, 까만 바지를 입고, 까만 셔츠나 까만 스웨터를 입고 오세요. 양말하고 신발도 까만 것으로 신고 오세요." 라고 말했어요[3].

2. all of you

3. said, "..."

나는 혼자 "까만색보다는 파란색이 더 섹시한데!" 하고 생각했어요[4]. 그래서 나는 미샤 한테 오늘 전화를 했어요. "까만색 말고 파란색을 입고 싶은데, 괜찮아요?" 미샤는 "안돼요. 사람들이 모두 까만색을 입고 파티에 올 거에요. 제니 씨도 까만색 옷을 입고 오세요." 하고 말했어요. 나는 기분이 나빴어요. "얘[5]는 내 친구지만 참 답답한 애[6]야. 너무 멋을 몰라!" 하고 생각했어요.

4. thought, "..."

5. *intimate-blunt* form: she (literally, *this child*)

6. child, person

토요일에 나는 미샤 네 집에 파란색 옷을 입고 갔어요. 미샤 는 문 앞에서 말했어요. "어머! 까만색 옷을 안 입었네요! 내 파티에 들어 올 수 없어요. 제니 씨는 이상해요. 오늘은 내 생일인데 왜 파란색 옷을 입고 왔어요? 제니 씨는 똑똑하고 예쁜 친구지만 고집이 너무 세요. 내 파티에 오지 마세요!" 하고 말했어요. 그래서 나는 미샤 파티에 못 가고 집에 그냥 왔어요. 집에 와서 내 파란 의자에 앉아서 파란 책상 위에 파란 공책에 파란색 펜으로 이 일기[7]를 쓰고 있어요.

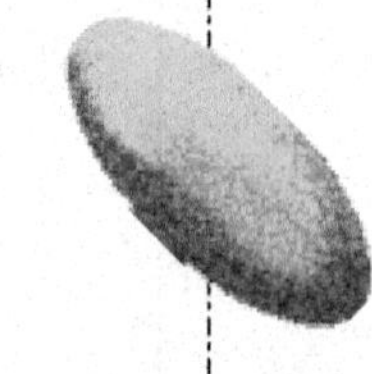

7. diary

Lesson 20 Checkpoint

대화 1 시험 때 걔가 컨닝한 것같아요.

정희: **진주** 씨, 들었어요?

진주: 뭘요?

정희: **칠구**가 시험에서 일등을 했어요.[93]

진주: 믿을 수 없어요[94]. 걔는 수업에도 잘 안 들어오는데 어떻게 일등을 할 수가 있어요?

정희: 그렇지요? 걔는 나보다 중간고사[95]도 잘 못 봤는데 어떻게 갑자기[96] 일등이 돼요?

진주: 시험 때 걔가 컨닝[97]한 것 같아요.

정희: 나도 그렇게 생각해요.

대화 2 안토니오 반데라스보다 한국어를 더 좋아하는 것같아요.

미미: **정인** 씨는 영화 배우[98]중에서 누구를 제일 좋아해요?

정인: 나는 **톰 크루즈**가 제일 좋아요. 연기도 잘 하고 미국 배우 중 제일 잘 생긴 것 같아요. **미미** 씨는요?

미미: 저는 **톰 크루즈**보다 **안토니오 반데라스**를 더 좋아해요. **안토니오 반데라스**는 너무 멋있게 생긴 것 같아요.

정인: 그럼 **안토니오 반데라스**의 **펨파딸** (femme fatale) 봤어요?

미미: 아니오. 요새는 한국어 공부에 너무 바빠서 시간이 없어요.

> ~에 바빠요 means *busy with (something)* or *busy because of (something)*.

정인: **미미** 씨는 항상 공부를 열심히 하는 것 같아요. **안토니오 반데라스**보다 한국어를 더 좋아하는 것 같아요.

미미: 그런가요?[99] 호호호...

---

93 일등을 하다 to get first place
94 믿다 to believe
95 중간고사 midterm
96 suddenly, all of a sudden
97 컨닝하다 to cheat on a test
98 actor
99 You think so?

읽기 1 그런데 이제 남편은…

오늘은 일요일이에요. 남편은 어제 야근을 해서[100] 피곤해해요. 지금 낮 12 시인데 아직도 자고 있어요. 그렇지만 저도 일주일 내내 일해요. 주말에는 남편과 같이 외식도 하고 싶고 영화도 보고 싶어요. 저는 심심해 죽겠어요. 결혼하기 전에는 우리는 주말마다[101] 만나서 즐거운[102] 시간을 보냈어요[103]. 남편은 야근을 해도 그 다음날 나하고 만나서 데이트했어요. 남편은 결혼하고 나서 변했어요.[104] 이제 나를 안 사랑하는 것 같아요. 저보다 잠을 더 좋아하는 것 같아요. 저는 남편이 재미있고 착하고 친절하고 똑똑하고 잘 생겨서 결혼했어요. 그런데 이제[105] 남편은 재미없고 불친절하고 멍청해요!!!

읽기 2 그게 아니라[106]…

오늘 하루종일 아무 것도 안 했어요. 아내는 저랑 외출하고[107] 싶어했지만 어제 야근[108]을 했기 때문에[109] 저는 너무 피곤했어요. 아내는 실망한[110] 것 같았어요. 결혼하고 제가 변했다고 생각하는 것 같아요. 저는 하나도 변하지 않았어요. 아직도 아내를 많이 사랑해요. 크리스마스에 아내에게 멋진 옷을 선물하고 싶어요. 그래서 저는 요즘 일을 더 많이 하고 있어요. 빨리 크리스마스가 돼서 아내의 기뻐하는 모습[111]을 보고 싶어 죽겠어요.

[100] 야근하다 to work on the night shift
[101] …마다 every….
[102] fun, enjoyable
[103] spend (time); send away
[104] 변하다 to change
[105] now (unlike before)
[106] It's not that…
[107] 외출하다 go out
[108] work a night shift
[109] because (of), due to
[110] 실망하다 be disappointed
[111] look, appearance

Culture Point *Scaredy cat!*

One nickname can capture it all – whether you are a braggart, a brain, or a glutton. Here are some nicknames Koreans use daily. Think of people who might be called by these names. Character words can be used as terms of endearment.

겁쟁이: scaredy-cat

깍쟁이: thrifty, self-centered

수다쟁이: chatterbox

잠꾸러기, 잠보 [잠뽀]: sleepy head

먹보: glutton

새침떼기: snotty, snooty; shies away

왕눈이: bug-eyed

빼빼: skinny

박사: brain (Ph.D.)

게으름뱅이: lazy bum

개구쟁이: rascal

멋쟁이: fashion plate

허풍쟁이: braggart, show-off

말썽꾸러기: trouble-maker

칠칠이: clutz

삐쭉이, 삐죽이: pouty face

뚱땡이: fatty

심술쟁이: jealous, crafty

천재: genius

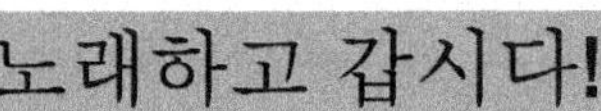

노래하고 갑시다!

옛날 옛날 한 옛날 어떤 마을에

밥만 먹고 잠만 자던 게으름뱅이가

부모 몰래 낮잠자다 물벼락을 맞았다네

봄봄봄

라랄라 닐리리 랄라 봄봄봄

Chapter 5 Review exercise--*You be the teacher*

Fix the errors in each sentence. Each sentence contains at least one error.

1) Miso Soup 는 짠하고 뜨거운 음식이에요.

2) 칠리는 뜨거운, 매운, 맛있는 음식이에요.

3) 나는 한국어 음식을 먹고 싶어요.

4) 떡볶이는 짠하고 단하고 아주 매워요.

5) 나초스는 조금 맵으고 짠 음식이에요.

6) 비빔밥에는 밥하고 채소를 들어가요.

7) 이 사람은 남하고 밤은 코트를 입었어요.

8) 이 사람은 회 스웨터하고 밤 바지를 입었어요.

9) 이 사람은 귀걸이를 꼈어요.

10) 이 사람은 파란색 눈이 있어요. or 이 사람은 파란색 눈이에요.

11) 이 사람은 짧은 머리있어요.

12) 이 사람은 밤색 수염하고 머리가 있어요.

13) 브리트니 스피어즈는 귀엽해요.

14) 할리 베리는 뚱뚱 안 해요.

15) 멜린다 씨는 데이트를 가고 싶어해요.

16) 멜린다 씨는 데이트를 만나고 싶어해요. 나는 남자친구 만나고 안 싶어요.

17) 멜린다 씨는 스키에 가고 싶어해요. or 멜린다 씨는 스키를 가고 싶어해요.

18) 멜린다 씨는 꽃을 받고 싶어해요. 나는 안 꽃을 받고 싶어요.

19) 멜린다 씨는 하와이에 가고 싶어해요. 저도 하와이에 가고 아주 싶어요.

쉬어갑시다!

LET'S TAKE A BREAK!

Irregularities can be handled with fun and ease if you can come up with mnemonic devices… ZZZ…

CHAPTER 5.5 More ㅂ-irregulars

Here are some more ㅂ-irregular predicates that will come in handy in daily conversations.

Adjectives

- 쉽다 – 쉬워요 (easy)
- 어렵다 – 어려워요 (difficult)

Example: 영어는 쉬워요. 그렇지만 한국어는 어려워요!

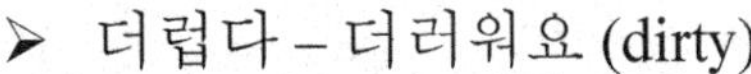

- 더럽다 – 더러워요 (dirty)
- [깨끗하다 – 깨끗해요 (clean)]

Example: 내 방은 더러워도 내 책상은 깨끗해요!

That is, made happy by something. (There's another word for 'content' or ' a happy life' – 행복하다.)

- 즐겁다 – 즐거워요 (happy)
- 괴롭다 – 괴로워요 ('tired of it,' ' it's grueling')

Example: 방학은 즐거워요. 그리고 시험은 괴로워요! (방학: school break)

- 가볍다 – 가벼워요 (light)
- 무겁다 – 무거워요 (heavy)

Example: 종이는 가벼워요. 그렇지만 컴퓨터는 무거워요.

- 덥다 – 더워요 (hot – weather)
- 춥다 – 추워요 (cold – weather)

Example: 여름은 더워요. 그리고 겨울은 추워요. (여름: summer, 겨울: winter)

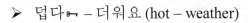

- 곱다 – 고와요 (fine, fair, pretty)

Example: 우리 엄마 얼굴은 아주 고와요.

- 아름답다– 아름다워요 (beautiful)

Example: 장미는 아름다운 꽃이에요. (장미 rose)

- 외롭다 – 외로워요 (lonely)

Example: 여자 친구가 없어서 외로워요.

- 귀엽다 – 귀여워요 (cute)

Example: 고양이가 귀여워요.

- 어둡다– 어두워요 (dark)
- [밝다 – 밝아요 (bright)]

Example: 밖이 어두워요. 그렇지만 내 방은 밝아요. (방: room)

- 가깝다– 가까워요 (close)
- [멀다– 멀어요 (far)]

Example: 학교는 우리 기숙사에서도 가깝고 엄마 집에서도 가까워요.

⊶One-syllable stems like 쉽다 and 곱다 need vowel harmony. Don't forget to use 아요 for words with ㅗ and ㅏ stems. For all other vowels, use 어요.

Verbs

Here are some ㅂ-irregular **verbs** that will come in handy in daily conversations.

- 눕다– 누워요 (lie down)
- [일어나다 – 일어나요]

Example: 밤에는 침대에 누워서 자요. 아침에는 일어나요. (침대: bed)

- 굽다⊶– 구워요 (broil, barbeque)

Example: 돼지 갈비를 구워요.

- 돕다⊶ – 도와요 (help)

Example: 좋은 친구는 서로 도와요. (서로: each other)

Hey, wait! This one has 오 in the 아요 form, instead of 우 like the others!

⊶Verb or adjective, one-syllable stems like 굽다 and 돕다 need vowel harmony. Don't forget to use 아요 for words with ㅗ and ㅏ stems. For all other vowels, use 어요.

A Little Poem

"맛있는 ㅂ restaurant"

맥주는 차갑게, 밥은 뜨겁게,

국은 싱겁게, 김치는 맵게,

갈비는...? 맛있게 구워요!

Here are some sentences to help you remember ㅂ-irregular words.

On a hot day with a light bag, Mimi went to the park. She was happy.
미미는 더운 날 가벼운 가방을 들고 공원에 갔어요. 즐거웠어요.

But, on a cold day with a heavy bag, Sasha went to the dirty park. She was sick of it.
하지만, **싸샤**는 추운 날 무거운 가방을 들고 더러운 공원에 갔어요. 괴로웠어요.

CHAPTER 6 푹 쉬어야 돼요.

You've got to take a good rest.

Preliminary Dialogue

시은: **제프** 씨, 어디 아파요? 얼굴이 안 좋아요.	
제프: 네. 어제 좀 추웠는데 반바지 입고 운동했어요. 그래서 감기에 걸렸어요[1].	[1] caught a cold
시은: 쯧쯧[2]. 안됐네요[3]. 약 먹었어요[4]?	[2] tsk-tsk [3] that's too bad [4] did you take medicine?
제프: 네. 그런데도 아직 많이 아파요.	
시은: 그러면 빨리 병원에 가 보세요[5].	[5] go see a doctor

Exercise 1. Dialogue practice

Practice the preliminary dialogue with a classmate.

LESSON 21

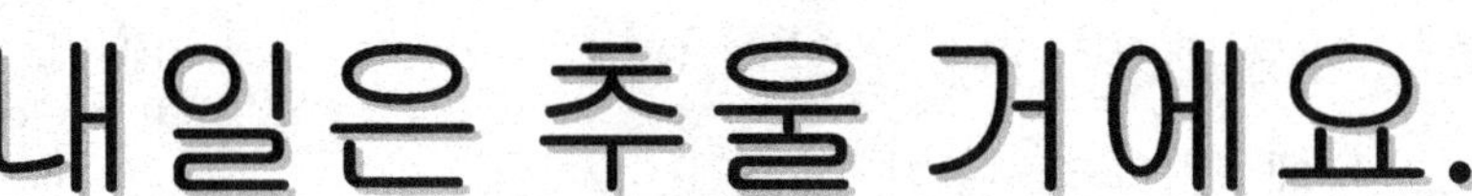

Lesson 21 Vocabulary 날씨

사 계절	four seasons
1. 봄, 여름, 가을, 겨울	spring, summer, autumn, winter
기온	**temperature**
2. 일기 예보를 듣다 (ㄷ irr.)	listen to the weather forecast
3. 덥다 (ㅂ irr.)	hot
4. 춥다 (ㅂ irr.)	cold
5. 따뜻하다	warm
6. 쌀쌀하다	chilly
7. (바람이, 날씨가) 선선하다	(wind, weather) refreshing
8. 기온이 높다; 낮다	temperature is high; low
9. 몇 도에요?	What's the temperature? (What degree is it?)
날씨	**weather**
10. 비가 (많이) 오다	to rain (a lot)
11. 눈이 (많이) 오다	to snow (a lot)
12. 바람이 (많이) 불다	be (very) windy
13. (날씨가 아주) 흐리다	be overcast
14. (날씨가 아주) 맑다	be (very) clear
15. 해가 (많이) 나다	be (very) sunny
16. 구름이 (많이) 끼다 (v.)	be (very) cloudy
17. 해가 뜨다; 지다	the sun rises; sets
18. 닷새	5 days
19. 엿새	6 days
20. 이레	7 days
21. 동안	for the period of
22. 계속	continually, continuously
23. (얼마나 오래) 계속 되다	to continue (for how long)

You can also use 시원하다 for 'refreshing'. 시원하다 is how *you* feel, as opposed to 선선하다, which is how *the weather* or *the wind* is.

구름이 꼈어요 works like the clothing verbs. You will mostly see it being used in the past tense, as for the sky to be overcast, the clouds should have already cluttered around. 해가 나요 is alternately used with 해가 났어요.

Vocabulary Exercise 1. 어느 계절이에요? Which season is it?

1) 이 계절에는 날씨가 따뜻하고 예쁜 꽃을 많이 볼 수 있어요.

2) 이 계절에는 날씨가 쌀쌀하고 바람이 많이 불어요.

3) 이 계절에는 날씨가 선선하고 하늘이 높아요.

4) 이 계절에는 날씨가 춥고 가끔/자주 눈이 와요.

5) 이 계절에는 날씨가 시원한 바람이 불고 해가 별로 안 뜨거워요.

6) 이 계절에는 사람들이 감기에 많이 걸려요. 크리스마스가 있어요.

Vocabulary Exercise 2. 지금 날씨가 어때요? What's the weather like now?
Describe the weather conditions in the pictures.

Vocabulary Exercise 3. 미국의 어느 도시에요? Which U.S. city is it?

1) 겨울에 차가운 바람이 많이 불어요

2) 봄, 가을, 그리고 겨울에 비가 많이 와요

3) 눈이 많이 와요.

4) 항상 비가 오고 흐려요.

5) 항상 더워요.

6) 사계절이 있어요.

Spring in Korea typically begins with 꽃샘추위 and 황사현상. The summer begins with clear, nice and hot days, followed by a month of rainy spell called 장마 and ends up in humid, high-termperatured sultry days. Korean autumn days are famous for their beautiful high, blue skies, often calling for the expression 천고마비의 계절 (High skies, horses fatten). Winters can get quite nippy, sometimes freezing the Han River (한강).

Vocabulary Exercise 4. 어디 기온이 더 높아요?
어느 도시 기온이 제일 낮아요? Which place has the highest temperature? Which city has the lowest temperature?

시애틀: 65 도	런던: 47 도	시카고: 80 도	마이애미: 99 도

Vocabulary Exercise 5. What would you do? 이러면... 어떻게 할 거에요?

1) 아침에 시간이 없어서 일기 예보를 못 들었어요. 날씨가 아주 더운데 긴 팔, 긴 바지를 입었어요. 어떻게 할 거에요?

2) 추워요. 창문을 닫고 싶은데 키가 너무 작아요. 어떻게 할 거에요?

3) 날씨가 좋아요. 공원을 걷고 싶지만 내일 시험이 있어요. 어떻게 할 거에요?

Vocabulary Exercise 6. What would you like to do? 이런 날씨에... 뭐 하고 싶어요?
Complete the sentence with your wishes.

1) 마지막 시험이 끝났는데 첫눈이 와요.
2) 날씨가 맑고 해가 뜨거운데 바람이 하나도 안 불어요.
3) 선선한 바람이 불고, 하늘이 높고 파래요.
4) 바람이 세게 불어서 낙엽이 많이 떨어졌어요. (세게: strongly, 낙엽: fallen leaves, 떨어지다: fall)

Vocabulary Exercise 7. Translation

1) It has rained for 7 continous days. (example: 이레 동안 계속 비가 왔어요.)
2) It snowed for 5 consecutive days.
3) For three hours the wind blew continuously.
4) In the summer, the sun rises at 5:45 A.M.
5) The sun sets at 6:20 P.M. every day.

Lesson 21 Dialogue 내일은 추울 거에요

시은: 와! 춥다, 추워! 바람이 정말 많이 부네요. 문 좀 닫아 주세요!

제프: (closing the door), 그렇게 추워요?

시은: 네. 옷을 얇게[1] 입어서 그래요[2]! 창문도 좀 닫아 줄래요?

제프: 네, 그럴께요. 따뜻한 차 좀 마실래요?

시은: 아니, 됐어요[3]. 오늘 아침에 일기 예보를 들었는데[4], 내일은 아마[5] 더 추워 질 거에요[6]. 비도 오고 바람도 더 불 거에요.

제프: 그래요? 아니[7], 무슨 봄 날씨가 이렇게 추워요?

시은: 하하하! 하느님[8]은 아마 알 거에요[9]. 하느님한테 물어 보세요[10]!

1. "thin-ly" 얇다: thin, light (layer of clothing)
2. It's (so), I am (so) because
3. That's OK
4. heard and… (듣다)
5. possibly ~ probably
6. is going to get colder
7. Whoa! Wait, (an exclamation used with rhetorical Wh-questions)
8. a god, gods (cf. 하나님: God)
9. wil probably know
10. try asking (묻다 + -어 보다)

Lesson 21 Grammar

1. Focus Conjecture

-(으)ㄹ 거에요	**it's probably the case that**

You learned that the ending -(으)ㄹ 거에요 expresses one's future plans and that the closest translation of this ending in English is "*am/are/is going to*".

전 내일 공부하러 도서관에 갈 거에요.	I am going to go to the library tomorrow.
오늘 밤에 일기 예보 들을 거에요?	Are you going to listen to the forecast tonight?

Just like English *will*, -을 거에요 can express your knowledge or strong guess about the world (and someone else). Because -을 거에요 sentences say something about *future* events, they usually accompany time adverbs like 내일, 이따가, 다음 주, 오늘 밤, etc.

내일은 비가 올 거에요.	It is going to rain tomorrow.
내일도 추울 거에요.	It is going to be cold again tomorrow.
이걸 입으면 예쁠 거에요.	You are going to look pretty if you wear this.
전화가 또 올 거에요.	The phone is going to ring again.
은비가 한국에서 올 거에요.	은비 is going to come from Korea.
언니가 L.A.에서 올 거에요.	My sister is going to come from L.A.
내일은 시험이 있을 거에요.	There is going to be a test tomorrow.
다음 주에는 수업이 없을 거에요.	There is going to be no class next week.

 When -(으)ㄹ 거에요 is used to express one's guess, it can be used with a *current* event or an event in the *past*.

그 친구는 지금 바쁠 거에요.	He/she (that friend) is probably busy now.
서울은 지금 추울 거에요.	Seoul is probably cold now.
서울은 어제 추웠을 거에요.	My guess is that Seoul was cold yesterday.

Conjugation

Verbs and adjectives conjugate the way they normally would before the -으 type endings.

	Example sentences
흐리다	내일은 날씨가 흐릴 거에요. It is going to be overcast tomorrow.
쌀쌀하다	오후에는 바람이 쌀쌀할 거에요 The wind is going to be chilly in the afternoon.
높다	내일은 기온이 높을 거에요 The temperature is going to be high tomorrow.
덥다 (hot)	그 옷을 입으면 건물 안에서는 더울 거에요 If you wear those clothes, you are going to be hot inside buildings.
하얗다	눈이 오면 온 세상이 하얄 거에요. When it snows, the whole world is going to be white.
듣다	오늘 저녁 뉴스에서 일기 예보를 들을 거에요. I am going to listen to the weather forecast on this evening's news.

When you use the '-(으)ㄹ 거에요' ending, the sentence is a simple statement/question or a guess. It cannot carry other meanings or nuances like *suggestion* or *confirmation*. Other endings are reserved for these meanings:

내일 또 올 거에요.	I'm going to (i.e., planned to) come back tomorrow.
내일 또 올래요.	I'm gonna come back tomorrow (whether you like it or not).
내일 또 올께요.	I'll come back tomorrow (if it is O.K. with you).
내일 또 올까요?	Shall/should I come back tomorrow (I wonder)?

2. Other Grammar Notes

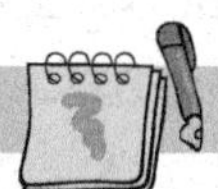

1. ㄷ-irregular verbs

Some verbs that end in ㄷ change the ㄷ to ㄹ before suffixes that begin with a vowel (e.g. -어, -으). These ㄷ~ㄹ alternating verbs are called ㄷ-irregulars. There are four frequently used ㄷ-irregular words: 묻다 (ask), 듣다 (listen to, hear, take a class), 걷다 (walk), and 싣다 (load). Make sure you learn these before moving on!

ㄷ-irregulars	Meaning	어/아 form	으 form	지, 고, 네 form
묻다	ask	물어요	물으세요	묻지요
듣다	hear, listen to, take a class	들어요	들으세요	듣지요
걷다	walk	걸어요	걸으세요	걷지요
싣다	load	실어요	실으세요	싣지요

잘 들으세요. — Listen carefully (please).

이번 학기에 무슨 수업 들어요? — What classes are you taking this quarter?

답을 모르면 물어 보세요. — If you don't know the answer, please ask.

트럭에 이 짐을 실으세요. — Load this luggage onto the truck, please.

우리 여기에서부터 걸어 가요. — Let's walk (and go) from here.

> One point to note about the verb *walk* is that it is most always used with the helping verb 와요 or 가요 in order to express a destination:
>
> 학교에 어떻게 가요? — How do you go to school?
> 걸어 가요. — I walk to school
>
> 걸어요 is used to address the specific act of *walking*.
>
> 매일 어떤 운동 해요? — What kind of exercise do you do daily?
> 집 근처를 그냥 걸어요. — I just walk around the neighborhood.

> There are ㄷ-ending words that conjugate regularly, as you know – 받다 and 닫다, for example. Some ㄷ-words have homophones that sound the same. You can keep them apart by their –어 and -으 conjugation!
> 걷다 – fold, uncover (걷어요, 걷으면)
> 묻다 – bury (묻어요, 묻으면)

You will need to memorize the ㄷ-irregular verbs as you encounter them, just like you did with ㅂ-irregulars. Most ㄷ-irregulars are verbs.

Memorize the ㄷ-irregulars introduced in this lesson in a sentence based on the following sequence of pictures.

How can I improve my Korean? 어떻게 하면 한국어를 더 잘 할 수 있어요?

한국 친구한테 많이 물어 보세요. 그리고 한국어 듣기 테잎을 많이 들으세요
(Ask your Korean friends a lot of questions and listen to Korean listening tapes a lot.)

What should I do with this? 이거 어떻게 해요?

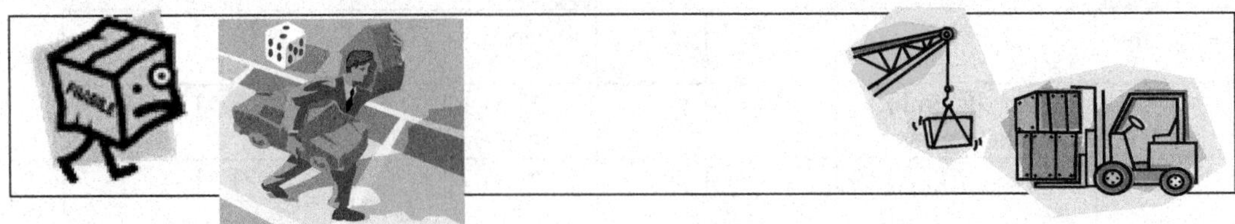

트럭까지 걸어 가세요. 그리고 그걸 트럭에 실으세요
(Walk up to the truck and then load it on the truck)

2. -어/아서 그래요 *it's (so) because*

Answering a question without repeating the question sometimes might sound too curt, even if the politeness marker 요 is added:

A: 오늘 왜 이렇게 더워요? What is it so hot today?
B: 기온이 높아서요. 'Cause the temperature is high. (*matter of factly*)

To avoid sounding curt (and making the person who is asking the question look dumb), you can add 그래요:

A: 오늘 왜 이렇게 더워요? Why is it so hot today?
B: 기온이 높아서 그래요. It is so because the temperature is high (*as I understand it*).

⚠ When you give a noun as an answer, don't forget to use -이라서!

A: 비가 열흘 동안 계속 오네요. It's been raining for 10 coninuous days, huh?
B: 겨울이라서 그래요. 시애틀에는 겨울 내내 비가 와요.
It's because it's winter -- It rains all winter long in Seattle.

3. -어 주세요 *(Do it)… for me?*

There are several auxiliary verbs that are combined with the –어 form of the verb in Korean. One very common auxiliary verb is 주다. When the verb 주다 (to give) is combined with another verb, it means something like *do… for (me)*. It is typically used in a polite request in the -어/아 주세요 form. Try to get the sense of when you might use -어 주세요 from the following examples:

Teacher to a student: 책 19 페이지 읽으세요.
Student to a teacher: 선생님, 책 19 페이지 좀 읽어 주세요.

Because -어 주세요 implies the doer is doing you a favor, this fixed expression has developed:
-어 줘서 고마워요 (Thanks for… for me.)
내 이야기 들어 줘서 고마워요. (Thanks for listening to my story.)

Of course 주세요 can be made negative, but there are two different meanings, depending on where the negation falls:

읽어 주지 마세요 Please don't read it for me (I can do it).
Here, the giving is negated, but the *reading* is positive:
don't do this for me: [*read* it]
i.e., you might read it to youself, but don't read it to/for me.

OR 읽지 말아 주세요 For my sake, please don't read it (it's a secret)
Here, the *reading* is negated, and the giving is positive:
do this for me: [*don't* read it]

4. -어 보세요 *try…ing*

보다 (to see, to look) is another of the most commonly used auxiliary verbs in Korean. When it is combined with the -어/아 form of another verb, it means something like *try* **verb**-*ing and see (how it works).*

이 반찬 맛있어요. 먹어 보세요	This side dish is good. Try (eating) it.
빨간 신발을 신어 보세요	Try these red shoes on.
잘 들어 보세요	Listen carefully (and see what happens).
이 옷 좀 입어 보세요.	Try this outfit on.
이거 식기 전에 먹어 보세요.	Try this before it gets cold.
저 쪽으로 가 보세요.	Go over there (and let me see).
혼자 해 보세요.	Try doing (it) yourself.

In the past tense, -어 보다 can be used to indicate *have* or *have not experienced.*

한국 음식 먹어 봤어요.	I have tried Korean food.
스키 한 번도 안 타 봤어요.	I have never tried skiing.

5. -(으)ㄹ께요 (*review*) Promissory future

The sentence ending -(으)ㄹ께요 corresponds to the English "I will VERB," but has a strong promissory sense to it along with the indication of a future action. For example, 할께요 *I'll do it* indicates a promise or an offer or seeks the listener's approval in some way. Therefore it cannot be used to talk about someone else's actions (you can't promise for them) or about inanimate subjects such as the weather or falling objects!

Here are some illustrative examples of its use:

내일 9 시에 올께요.	I'll be in tomorrow at 9, O.K.?
엄마: 빨리 방 청소 해!	Hurry and clean your room!
아이: 이따 할께요.	I'll do it later, O.K.?

할머니: 슈퍼에가서, 배추 사 와. — Go and get some cabbage at the store.
손자: 지금 갈께요. — I'll go now.

A: 이거 너무 매운데? — This is too spicy!
B: 내가 먹을께. — I'll eat it.

A: 누가 읽을래요? — Who wants to read?
B: 제가 읽을께요. — I will.

A: 

B: 아! 내가 문을 열어 줄께요. — Oh, I'll get the door for you.

Lesson 21 Exercises

Exercise 1. Future practice

Complete the sentences below (in your head) according to the pictures, then write the whole sentence in Korean. Use -(으)ㄹ께요 for promise or offer, -(으)ㄹ 거에요 for either prediction or your plan.

1) If… tomorrow, I'll …

(*You write* "If it's cold tomorrow, I'll wear a sweater" *in Korean*)

2) If …, I'll …

3) If it *doesn't* rain on Friday, I'll … for you.

not 

4) If …this weekend, I'll probably …

5) If … tomorrow morning, I'll probably get up late (늦게).

6) If… this afternoon, I'll…!

Exercise 2. 아마 **…-(으)ㄹ 거에요**

Give a prediction or guess about what will probably be the case.

1) 이 사람들은…

2) 오늘은…

3) 내일은…

4) 여름 방학 때는…(summer vacation)

5) 이렇게 하면, …

6) 러브레터를 받아서, 이 사람은 …

Exercise 3. Try this... 이것 한 번 해 보세요

Your friend has a problem. Tell him or her what to try for each situation.

Example: 열이 나요. (I have a fever.) – 약을 먹어 보세요.

1) 피곤해요.

2) 목이 아파요.

3) 자고 싶지만 내일 시험이 있어요.

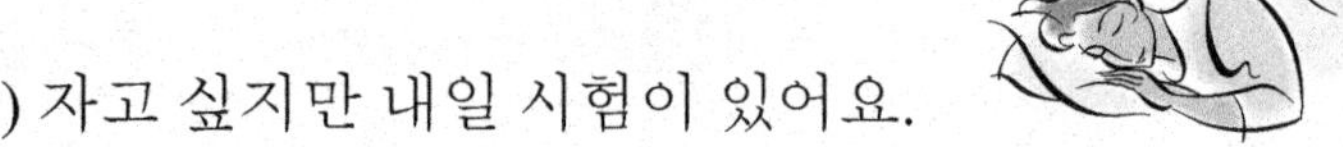

4) 여행* 가고 싶은데 돈이 없어요. *여행: travel

5) 여자 친구가 화가 났어요.

6) 할머니가 보고 싶어요.

7) 동생이 내 사탕을 먹었어요.

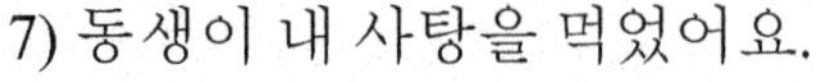

8) 은행에 가야 되는데 시간이 없어요.

9) 놀러 가고 싶은데 날씨가 나빠요.

10) 스노우 보딩 가고 싶은데 눈이 안 오고 비가 와요.

Exercise 4. Always tell your mother where you are going! (promissory, review)

Your mother wants you to be a good son/daughter. Promise her that you will do the right thing and won't do the wrong things.

Example: Mom: 오늘 몇 시에 들어오니? You: 일찍 들어 올께요.
Mom: 담배 피우지 마라! You: 안 피울께요. (담배를 피우다: to smoke)

1) call home
2) study hard
3) eat well
4) drink a lot of 술
5) spend a lot of money
6) do Korean homework
7) make good friends (make friends: 친구를 사귀다)
8) do laundry every week
9) dress warmly
10) eat lots of fruit and vegetables
11) eat spicy and salty food

Exercise 5. Tommy's wild weekend. 뭐 해 봤어요?
What things did Tommy try doing (for the first time)? Complete the sentences for each picture.

1) 산에서

2) 체육관에서

3) 여자 친구 집에서 (eat)

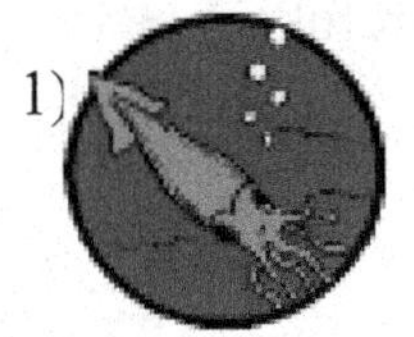

4) 도서관에서

5) 노래방에서

6) 프랑스 파리에서 (eat out)

7) 집에서 다운타운까지…

8) 한국말로 ____를 …

Exercise 6. Could you please… -어/아 주세요…
Ask each person to do something for you and to please *not* do something to you.

Example: 아빠한테: 새 옷 사 주세요! (새: new)

1) 할머니한테:

2) 엄마한테:

3) 직장 상사한테 (your boss at work): (월급: monthly salary, 올리다: raise)

4) 식당의 종업원한테:

5) 선생님한테:

6) 동생한테 (Don't forget to take out 요!):

Exercise 7. -으면, 아마 –을 거에요 chain

Make up a sentence using the pattern **A** –으면, **B** ㄹ 거에요. Your partner then continues the "chain" saying, **B** –으면, **C** ㄹ 거에요. And so on. Make the chain as long as you can!

Example: 비가 오면... 아마 추워질 거에요
→ 추워지면... 아마 감기에 걸릴 거에요.
감기에 걸리면...뜨거운 닭국을 먹고 싶을 거에요...

Exercise 8. Translation

1) Listen to your mother. (Literally, Listen to your mother's words carefully.)
2) My older brother is listening to NPR now.
3) Try asking the teacher that.
4) My mother wants to listen to Korean news.
5) I go to school on foot.
6) Listen carefully and see (what happens next).
7) Dad is listening to music, isn't he?
8) I am going to (I am planning to) take Korean next quarter.
9) Load this bag in the back of the car.
10) It'll probably be cold tomorrow.
11) The whole world will be white when it snows. (the whold world 온세상)
12) A: Why is it so windy?
    B: It's because it's spring. It's always very windy in the spring in Seoul (서울).
13) Take a walk around the block every day. It will be good for you. (Literally, good for your body) (around the block:동네 한 바퀴)

Lesson 21 Checkpoint

대화 1 비는 아마 이번 주 내내 올 거에요.

제리: 어라, 또 비가 와요. 우산 있어요?
영수: 네, 우산 갖고 왔어요. 비는 아마 이번 주 내내 올 거에요.
제리: 어떻게 알아요?
영수: 지금 장마에요. 한국에는 여름에 거의 한 달 동안 비가 계속 와요.
제리: 아, 이게 장마에요? 장마는 얼마나 오래 계속돼요?
영수: 글쎄요. 일기예보를 들어보세요.
제리: 일기예보는 말이 너무 빨라서 잘 못 알아들어요.
영수: 그래요? 그럼 저한테 물어보세요.
제리: 그럴께요. 고마워요.

대화 1 스키 타러 갑시다!

경미: 선배, 내일 스키타러 안 갈래요? **상민**이도 같이 갈 거에요.
영수: 글쎄. 요새 일이 많아서 좀 피곤한데.
경미: 가요. 겨울도 다 끝나가는데. 선배가 많이 피곤하면 제가 운전할께요.
영수: 너 어제 운전면허 땄지[112]? 그 산길[113]을 운전할 수 있어?
경미: 문제없어요. 내가 운전 연습을 얼마나 많이 했는데요.
영수: 너 운전 실력[114] 정말 믿어도 되냐?
경미: 선배, 내 운전 실력을 너무 무시[115]하지 말아요.
영수: 알았어, 알았어. 믿을께.
경미: 그럼 내일 아침 8 시에 선배 집 앞으로 갈께요.
영수: 그래, 내일 보자.

[112] 운전면허 driver's license; 따다 get, obtain
[113] 산길 [산낄, 상낄] mountain path
[114] 실력 ability, capability, competence, proficiency
[115] 무시하다 to ignore, disregard, look down upon

LESSON 22

기분이 좋아질 거에요.

Lesson 22 Vocabulary  기분 & 느낌

형용사	Adjectives
1. 기쁘다	happy, content
2. 즐겁다 (ㅂ-irr.)	happy, excited
3. 슬프다	sad
4. 피곤하다	tired
5. 귀찮다	feel lazy, feel bothered
6. 졸리다	sleepy
7. 불안하다	uneasy, having apprehensive feelings
8. 초조하다	nervous in anticipation, restless, fretful
9. 창피하다 [챙피하다]	ashamed, shy
10. 우울하다	glum, down
11. 외롭다 (ㅂ-irr.)	lonely
12. 답답하다	stir-crazy, feel stifled
13. 무섭다 (ㅂ-irr.)	scary, scared
14. 지겹다 (ㅂ-irr.)	pesky (describes sth. one is sick and tire of)
15. 어색하다	awkward, uncomfortable (situation)
동사	**Verbs**
16. 신나다	excited
17. (-어서) 다행이다	relieved, lucky that…
18. 화가 나다; (-한테) 화를 내다	feel upset with; get angry at
19. 걱정이 되다; 걱정을 하다	worried; worry
20. 놀라다	surprised, startled
21. 스트레스가 쌓이다; 스트레스를 받다	get stressed out; stress out
22. 자존심 상하다	have one's pride hurt
23. 짜증나다; 짜증을 내다	annoyed; get annoyed
24. 기가 막히다	appalled, dumbfound
25. (-에, -한테; -어서) 실망하다	disappointed (at someone; because)
	More days
26. 이레	(for) 7 days
27. 여드레	(for) 8 days
28. 아흐레, 아흘	(for) 9 days
29. 열흘	(for) 10 days
30. 보름	(for) 15 days; half a moon cycle
31. (한) 달	(for one) month
32. (한) 해	(for one) year

-어서/아서 걱정이에요 (instead of 걱정이 돼요) is also very commonly used.

보름달 means *full moon*, what you get after two 보름 (half moon cycles)!

달 means *moon* and 해 means *sun* in Korean!

These words are native Korean vocabulary. You will hear "older folks" using them often. After 3-5 days, the Sino-Korean version of these duration words are also often used:

하루, 이틀, 사흘, 나흘 – 사 일 닷새 – 오 일 엿새 – 육 일 이레 – 칠 일
여드레 – 팔 일 아흐레, 아흘 – 구 일 열흘 – 십 일 한 해– 일 년 [일련]

Vocabulary Exercise 1. Labeling
Label the following emotions (as predicates).

1) ________________ 2) ________________ 3) ________________

4) ________________ 5) ________________ 6) ________________

7) ________________ 8) ________________ 9) ________________

10) ________________ 11) ________________ 12) ________________

13) ________________ 14) ________________ 15) ________________

Vocabulary Exercise 2. Odd one out – pairs game

Make up sets of mood expressions where one expression does not fit with the rest. Ask you partner which one does not fit. Take turns quizzing and being quizzed.

Vocabulary Exercise 3. Label the picture again!

Label each picture with an appropriate mood expression from the box.

기분이 좋다, 기분이 나쁘다, 피곤하다, 심심하다, 졸리다, 화를 내다, 걱정을 하다, 스트레스를 받다, 놀라다, 슬프다

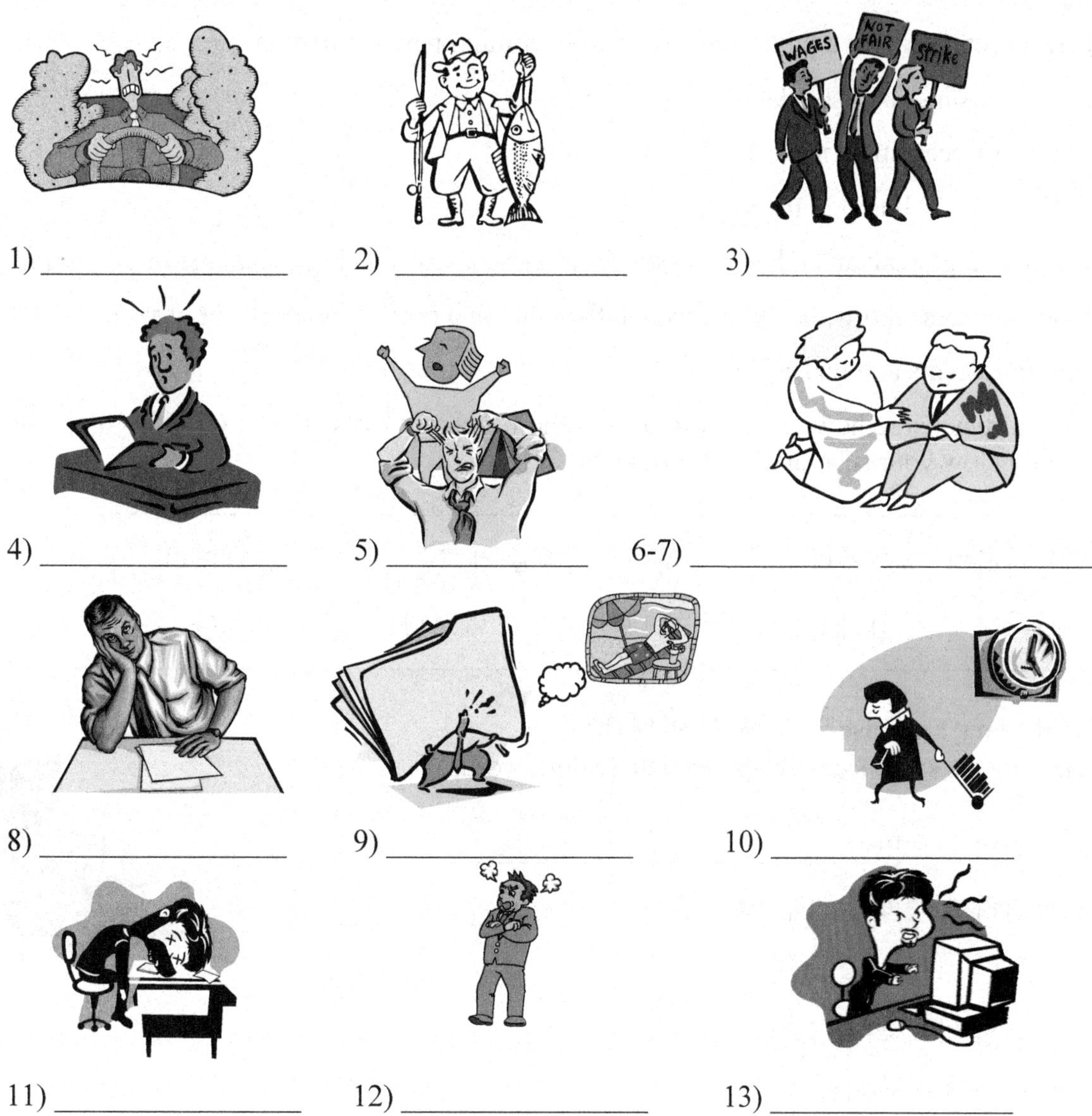

1) ____________ 2) ____________ 3) ____________

4) ____________ 5) ____________ 6-7) ____________ ____________

8) ____________ 9) ____________ 10) ____________

11) ____________ 12) ____________ 13) ____________

14) ________________ 15) ________________ 16) ________________

Vocabulary Exercise 4. How would you feel?
Use the vocabulary to talk to your partner about how you would feel in the following situations. Some suggestions are in the box below.

1) You have an important interview.
2) You know you put your foot in your mouth.
3) It's been rainy for a long time and there is nothing new happening.
4) We're going to Disneyland!
5) You've been stuck in traffic for a long time.
6) You hear a "bump in the night."
7) It's spring break and all your friends have gone away, leaving you alone in the dorm.
8) The waitress threw the chopsticks on the table in a hurry, right in front of your grandparents and guests!
9) You're not sure how you did on the test and if you got worse than a C, your GPA will fall below your scholarship requirements.

불안하다	초조하다	창피하다	우울하다	답답하다
신나다	무섭다	짜증나다	기가 막히다	외롭다

Vocabulary Exercise 5. 기분이 어때요?
Complete the sentence with appropriate feeling words.

1) 애인이 없으면 ____________________.
2) 시험하고 숙제가 너무 많으면____________________.
3) 한국어 시험을 잘 보면____________________.
4) 금요일 밤에 혼자 집에 있으면____________________.
5) 친구들하고 파티하면____________________.
6) 무서운 영화를 혼자 보면 ____________________.

7) 사람들 앞에서 넘어지면 (fall down) ______________________________.

8) 겨울에 계속 비가 오면 ______________________________.

9) 도둑(thief)이 내 지갑을 훔치면 (steal) ______________________________.

10) 코메디 영화를 보면______________________________.

Language Point 1 *Expressing others' feelings*

Do you remember from Chapter 5 (Lesson 19) what needs to happen to adjectives that describe someone else's feelings? Can you complete the following chart according to the "rule"?

왜 그렇게 기분나빠요? → 왜 그렇게 기분나빠해요?

슬퍼요 →

심심해요 →

피곤해요 →

불안해요 →

초조해요 →

All 나다 phrases can have markers before them:
신이 나서...
짜증은 나는데...

Language Point 2 *All about 나다 and 내다*

As you have observed, most "나다" phrases have a 내다 variant. Since 나다 means *come out* and 내다 means *put out* or *cause to go out*, emotion + 내다 implies some intention on the part of the subject, while emotion + 나다 implies the emotion was involuntary. So, to say, "Don't get mad", you would use 내다: 화 내지마. But to describe a person's emotions, you would use 나다 in most cases: 걔 때문에 아주 화가 났어. You could also say, 걔 때문에 화 냈어, which means *I (visibly) got mad at him.*

때문에 means *due to* or *because of*!

Since 화 is the ***subject*** of 나다 ("anger comes out"), it is marked with 이/가. But, since 화 is the ***object*** of 내다 ("I put my anger out"), it is marked with 을/를. Then the person involved is usually marked as a topic using 은/는 (you are talking *about* this person). This patterns is the same for all the 나다-내다 pairs:

내 동생은 컴퓨터 때문에 짜증이 많이 났어. **vs.** 내 동생은 나한테 짜증을 냈어.

Proverbs

Can you guess the meaning of the following proverbs?

낮말은 새가 듣고 밤말은 쥐가 들어요. (쥐: rat, mouse)

아는 길도 물어 가라 (길: road)

천리 길도 한 걸음부터 (천리: 1000 리 , 걸음: step)

The traditional distance measure unit 리 amounts to 0.4 kilometers!

제가 노래할께요!

앞으로

지구는 둥그니까
자꾸 걸어 나가면
온 세상 어린이들
다 만나고 오겠네

온 세상 어린이가
하하하하 웃으면
그 소리 울려 퍼지네
달나라까지
앞으로 앞으로 앞으로 앞으로

Lesson 22 Dialogue 기분이 좋아질 거에요

시은: **제프** 씨, 왜 그래요? 아파 보여요[1].

제프: 피곤해서 그래요.

시은: 피곤하면 좀 쉬거나[2] 공원을 걸어 보세요. 그러면 기분이 좋아질 거에요[3].

제프: 산책이요[4]? 날씨가 이렇게 추운데요? 다 귀찮아요!

시은: 어... 왜 그렇게 화를 내요? 무슨 일 있었어요[5]?

제프: 미안해요. 월요일 수학 시험 때문에[6] 스트레스를 받아서 그래요.

시은: 걱정하지 마세요. **제프** 씨는 시험 잘 볼 거에요[7]. 저녁 식사 전[8]에 같이 산책하러 밖에 나갈래요?

제프: 안돼요[9]. 난 못 나가요. 공부해야 돼요[10].

1. look(s) ill
2. take a rest or
3. your mood will improve (you'll feel better)
4. A walk?!
5. did something happen?
6. because of, due to
7. you are going to do fine on the test
8. before dinner
9. that won't do
10. I have to study

Noun + (이)요 in a statement is used as an answer to a question asking for information. It is almost like giving only a noun as an answer in English, which can be quite blunt:

그게 뭐에요? → 책이에요. (It's a book.)
→ 책이요. (A book.)

When Noun + (이)요 is used in a question, it works like an echo question, with or without a negative nuance.

산책을 해보세요. → 산책이요? (What? A walk?)

The most challenging (thus interesting!) thing about the Korean language is a seemingly random use of markers like -을. In the dialogue, you might have noticed the sentence: 공원을 걸어 보세요.
There is a slight emphasis on the place where you are *walking*, implying *Why don't you walk around in the* ***park*** *(rather than sitting here by yourself)?*

If it is too confusing for you, just keep in mind that some verbs may show up with the object marker –을/를 (usually replacing -에 or -에서). Don't be shocked!
버스를 타세요 vs. 버스에 타세요.
학교를 갔어요. vs. 학교에 갔어요.

Lesson 22 Grammar

1. Focus Change of state

Adjective -어/아져요	becomes (adjective)

-지다 is an auxiliary verb that attaches to the -어 stem of the adjective to mean *become* ADJECTIVE. The -지다 verb turns adjectives into verbs, which conjugate according to tense.

음악을 들으면 기분이 좋아져요.	My mood gets better when I listen to music.
시은 씨가 떠나면 슬퍼질 거에요.	I am going to be(come) sad when you leave.
추워서 입술이 더 파래졌어요.	I was cold so my lips turned blue.
비가 오면 보통 날씨가 추워져요.	When it rains, it usually gets cold.
시험을 못 봐서 기분이 나빠졌어요.	I didn't do well on the test so my mood turned sour.

고춧가루를 너무 많이 넣으면 떡볶이가 매워질 거에요.
떡볶이 will get spicy if you add too much hot pepper.

Sometimes you will see Korean people writing a space before the -지다 auxiliary verb: 바빠 졌어요.

2. Other Grammar Notes

1. Adjective-어 보여요 *looks* Adjective

The verb 보이다, related to 보다 (*see*, *watch*, and *look at*), is an auxiliary verb. When 보이다 is attached to the –어/아 stem form of adjective, it means *appear to be* or *look* ADJ.

짧은 바지를 입으면 다리가 길어 보여요.
Shorts make your legs look long.

좋은 일 있어요? 기분이 좋아 보여요.
Did something nice happen? You look like you are in a good mood.

오늘 바빴어요? 피곤해 보여요.
Have you been busy / Were you busy today? You look tired.

어제 밤에 잠 못잤어요? 졸려 보여요.
Didn't you get good sleep last night? You look sleepy.

2. Noun 때문에 *because of, due to*

때문에 is a full word used after a noun (or noun forms of the verb) that means *because of* (that noun). It is used very often in Korean where English might use a *because* clause.

비 때문에 기온이 낮아졌어요	Because of the rain, the temperature dropped.
날씨 때문에 스키장에 갈 수 없어요.	Due to the bad weather, we can't go skiing.
한국어 시험 때문에 잠을 푹 못 잤어요.	I wasn't able to get enough sleep because of the Korean test.
엄마 때문에 집에 일찍 가야 돼요.	I've got to go home early because of my mom.
너 때문에 다 망쳤어!	Because of you, everything is ruined!
감기 때문에 학교에 못 갔어요.	Because of (my) cold, I couldn't go to school.

때문에 is mostly used in a negative or excuse sense. To express *thanks to* (positive nuance), you can use -덕분에:

선생님의 추천서 덕분에 대학교에 들어갔어요.
Thanks to your recommendation letter, I got into college.

To directly ask for a reason, you can use 뭐 때문에 or 뭣 때문에 (a shortened version of 무엇 때문에):

여기 뭐 때문에 왔어요? What are you here for?

To emphasize the temporal reference point, you can add 이 in front of 전:
주말 이전에
네 시 이전에

3. TIME expression + 전에 *before* TIME; TIME *ago*

전 literally means *before*. It is a noun borrowed from Chinese (前). You can use a combination of "***point*** in time + 전에" to mean *before* that time.

주말 전에	before the weekend
겨울 전에	before the winter (as a season)
여름 방학 전에	before the summer (school) vacation
졸업 전에	before graduation
네 시 전에	before 4 o'clock

As you learned in Chapter 3 (Lesson 10), you can also use the expression -기 전에: 주말이 되기 전에, 졸업을 하기 전에, 네 시가 되기 전에

If the time expression is a specified (usually countable) time ***duration***, 전에 means *ago*.

30 분 전에	30 minutes ago
조금 전에	a little while ago

몇 분 전에	a couple of minutes ago
삼 년 전에	three years ago
네 시간 전에	four hours ago

4. Animate source -한테서 (-에게서) *from* someone

-한테서 means *from* an animate source:

한국의 펜팔한테서 편지가 왔어요.	A letter came from a penpal in Korea.
그 얘기 누구한테서 들었어요?	Who did you hear that (story) from?
그 책 누구한테서 샀어요?	Who did you buy that book from?
할머니한테서 생일 선물을 받았어요.	I got a birthday present from my grandmother.
발렌타인 데이에 여자 친구한테서 초콜렛을 받았어요.	I got chocolate from a girlfriend on Valentine's Day.

Quite comparably to the 한테~에게 pair, 한테서 is replaced with 에게서 in written language.

친구에게서 편지가 왔어요.	A letter arrived from a friend.
선생님에게서 전화를 받았어요.	I got a phone call from the teacher.

⚠ In more colloquial Korean, 한테 can be used to mean 'from'.

그 얘기 누구한테 들었어요?	Who did you hear that (story) from?
할머니한테 생일 선물을 받았어요.	I got a birthday present from my grandmother.
친구한테 편지가 왔어요.	A letter arrived from a friend.

5. Verb-거나 *or*

Remember –(이)나 from Chapter 4 (Lesson 13)? It means *or*, connecting nouns:

A: 얼마나 오랫 동안 거기 있었어요?	How long were you there?
B: 아흘이나 열흘 쯤 있었어요.	I stayed for nine or ten days.

-거나 means the same *or*, but it is used to connect verbs or adjectives:

A: 서울의 겨울 날씨는 어때요?	What's the weather like in Seoul?
B: 항상 춥거나 비가 많이 와요.	It's always either cold or very rainy.

Lesson 22 Exercises

Exercise 1. It has gotten... -어졌어요

Write a sentence for each picture, explaining the new condition (i.e. *It has gotten hot...).*

Exercise 2. She looks like a good girl.

Tell a story about what each person (or dog) has done to look how they look.

Example: 이 여자 아이는 사흘 내내 공부했어요. 토요일에도 파티에도 못 가고 집 에서 공부만 했어요. 오늘 밤에는 아주 피곤해 보여요. 그렇지만 내일 시험은 아주 잘 볼 거에요.

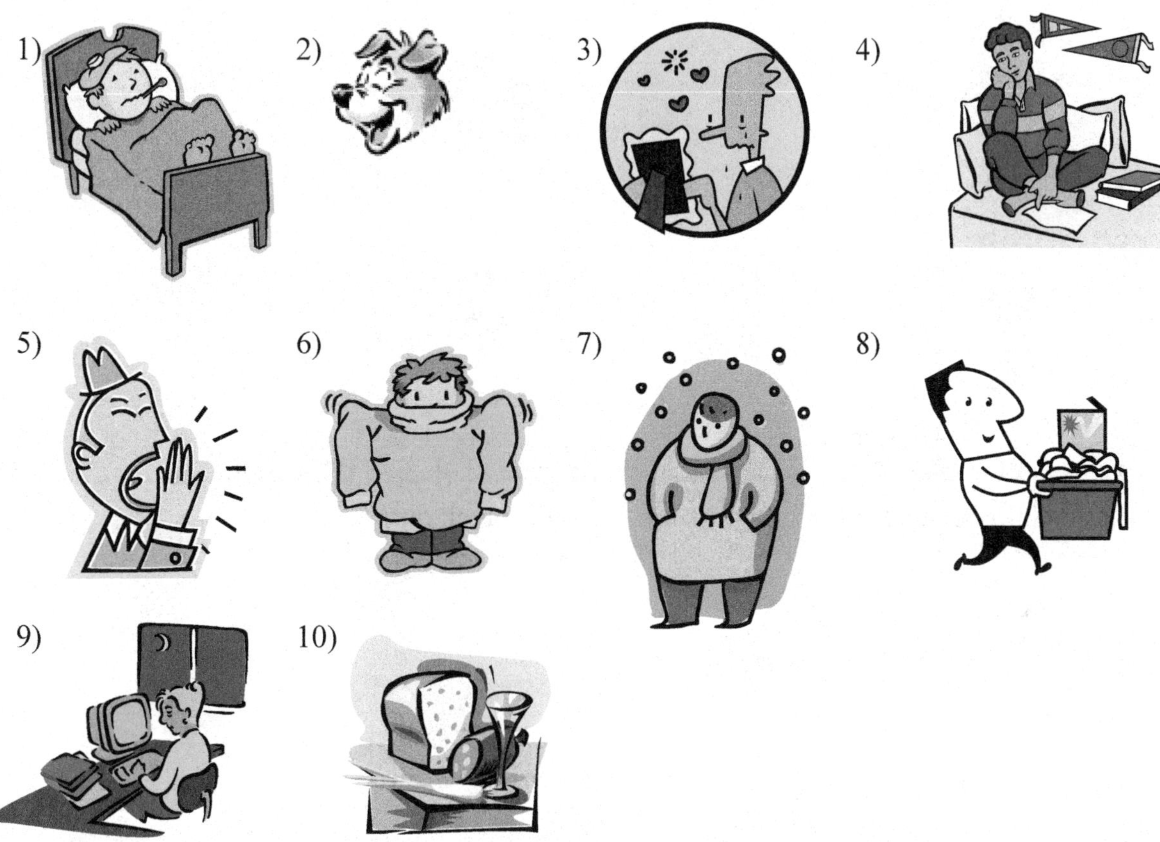

Exercise 3. What is the order?
What is the overall order that the students entered the room, according to the following statements? (Each individual arrived by him/herself.)

진수씨는 보경씨하고 은비씨 전에 왔어요.
아희씨는 보경씨하고 진수씨하고 은비씨 전에 왔어요.

아희씨는 동호씨 전에 안 왔어요.
보경씨는 은비씨 전에 안 왔어요.

"How long ago…?" can be simply asked with "얼마 전에", but Korean speakers like spelling things out, sometimes redundantly. Here are at least two other ways of asking the same question:
지금부터 얼마 전에…
지금으로부터 얼마 전에…

Exercise 4. 지금으로부터 몇 년 전이었어요?
When did the following events take place? *How long ago?*

1492
1) 크리스토퍼 콜럼부스가 아메리카 대륙에… (대륙: continent)

1903
2) 첫번째 (first) 비행기는 … (만들어지다: be made)

1843
3) 오래곤 트레일은…

1927
4) 첫번째 텔레비전은…

60 년대 (60's)
5) 벨 바텀 스타일은… (유행하다: be popular)

6) 미국 시민 전쟁 (U.S. civil war) (나다: break out)

7) 눈이 왔어요.

8) *Make your own*

Exercise 5. Because of what? 뭐 때문에?
Make up a sentence explaining the cause of the problem/situation, using the 'causes' in parentheses.

Example: My cat is scared. (that dog)

→ 저 개때문에 우리 고양이가 놀랐어요. (Because of that dog, my cat got startled.)

1) I can't go to the party. (Mom)
2) I have a headache. (that music)
3) I bombed the test (시험을 잘 못 보다). (a cold 감기)
4) I can't eat. (my teeth)
5) My teeth are blue! (wine)
6) I was late (늦다 *to be late*). (car accident: 차 사고)
7) I caught a cold. (weather)

Exercise 6. From whom? 누구 한테(서)?
Make up a sentence for each picture, explaining from whom you get/got/will get each item (and when).

Example: 크리스마스에 아버지한테(서) 좋은 펜을 받았어요.

1) 2) 3) 4)

5) 6) 7) 8)

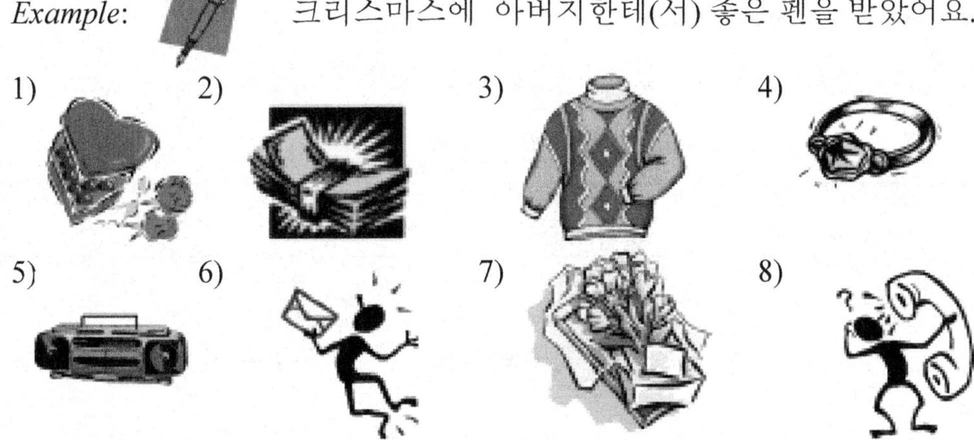

Exercise 7. Translation

1) Finish your homework before 5.
2) Finish your homework by 5.
3) She left 3 hours ago.
4) A: Why are you so nervous?
   B: Because of my math test. I'm waiting for the test result. (result: 결과)
5) Go away! Don't bother me! (Literally, I feel bothered)

6) If my boyfriend/girlfriend leaves me, I will become lonely.

7) If my friend looks prettier than me at the party, I will get stressed out.

8) If you are sleepy, listen to an exciting song. You'll feel better.

9) When did you get here? You scared me. (Literally, I was surprised)

10) (Movie) Friday the 13th was really scary. For the whole 2 hours, I was scared.

11) I bombed the test (literally, I didn't see the test well), so I am worried.

12) Don't worry. You probably did fine.

13) I am appalled! Did you see that car? We are so lucky he didn't come toward us.

Lesson 22 Checkpoint

대화 1 기분이 좋아보여요.

수미: **미미**씨, 무슨 좋은 일 있어요? 기분이 좋아보여요.

미미: 네, 어제 한국어 시험에서 일등을 했어요.

수미: 어머, 축하해요. 지난주 내내 그 시험때문에 잠도 잘 못 자고 공부했지요?

미미: 맞아요. 좀 고생했지요.[116] 다 **수미**씨 덕분이에요. 도와줘서 정말 고마워요.
이번 주말 전에 시간있어요?

수미: 네, 이번 주는 별로 바쁘지 않은데요. 왜요?

미미: 감사의 뜻[117]으로 술 한잔 사고 싶어서요.

대화 2 음악을 들으면 기분이 좋아져요.

수미: **미미**씨는 우울할 때는 뭘 해요?

미미: 저는 기분이 우울하면 음악을 들어요. 음악을 들으면 기분이 좋아져요.
수미씨는요?

수미: 저는 우울하면 영화를 봐요. 영화를 보면서[118] 울고 웃으면 기분이 좋아져요.

미미: **수미**씨 오늘 우울해 보이는데, 우리 영화보러 갈래요?

수미: **미미**씨도 오늘 우울해 보이는데, 우리 영화도 보고 음악회도 가죠.

미미: 좋아요!

---

[116] 고생하다 to have a hard time, suffer
[117] 뜻 meaning, intention
[118] while watching

읽기 섬은 아름다워 보였어요.

내일은 언니가 미국에서 올 거에요. 그런데 한국은 지금 장마라서 비행기가 잘 날[119] 수 없을 것 같아서 걱정이에요. 방금 전[120]에 언니한테서 전화가 왔어요. 언니도 날씨 때문에 좀 걱정하는 것 같았어요. 언니와 나는 사실 장마를 좋아해요. 집에만 있으니까 답답하지만 기온이 높지 않아서 시원하니까요. 장마가 끝나면 무척[121] 더워질 거에요. 사람들은 더우면 쉽게 짜증을 내요. 여름의 유일한[122] 즐거움은 바다에 놀러 가는 거에요. 장마가 끝나면 언니하고 같이 **울릉도**에 놀러 갈 거에요. **울릉도**는 아직 한번도 안 가 봤어요. 사진을 보니까 푸른 바다가 무척 시원해 보이고 섬[123]은 아름다워 보였어요.

Language Puzzle *Some more* BECOMING *words!*

Can you guess the meaning of the following expressions? (You have already seen some of these.)

시은: **제프** 씨, 내일 같이 갈 수 있어요?
제프: 아마 안 될 거에요. (It will probably not work; I probably won't be able to)

제프: 돼요, 안 돼요? (Will it work or not? → May I or not?) (Does it work or not?)
시은: 미안하지만 안돼요. (Sorry, but it won't work; can't do)

시은: 그 일 어떻게 됐어요? (What has become of that business? → How did it turn/work out?)
제프: 잘 안 됐어요. (It didn't work out.)

제프: 그 사람 참 못됐어요. (He doesn't meet the qualifications of a decent human being → He is so mean.)
시은: 사람이 없는데 말하면 안돼요. (If you talk when he is not there, it won't do → You shouldn't.)

시은: 그 사람 참 안 됐어요. (I feel sorry for him. –OR, He is pathetic.)
제프: 왜요?

시은: 어떻게, 안 돼요? (Is there a way to get it to work?)

[119] 날다 to fly
[120] 방금 전 minutes ago, just a few minutes ago
[121] greatly, extremely
[122] 유일한 unique, the only
[123] 섬 an island

LESSON 23

집에서 푹 쉬어야 돼요.

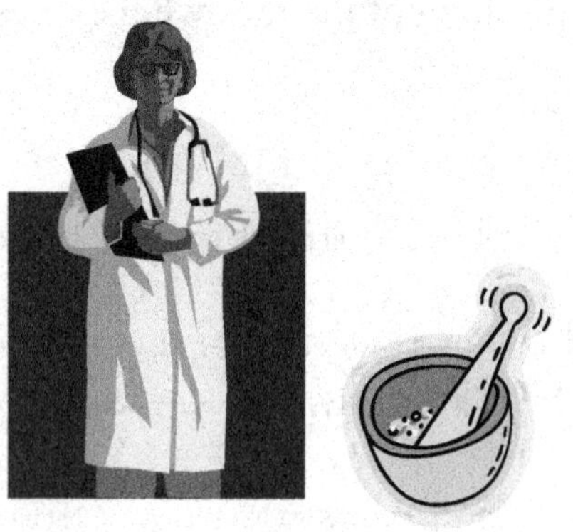

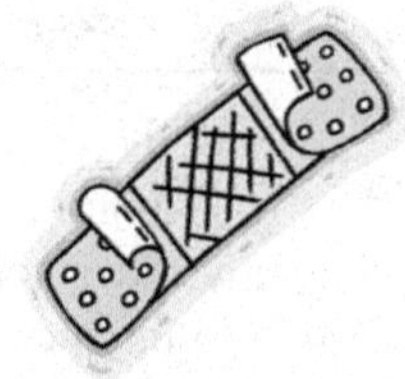

Lesson 23 Vocabulary  병, 그리고 치료

1. 가루약; 알약 [알략]; 물약 [물략]	powder, pill, liquid medicine
2. 약사; 의사; 환자	pharmacist; doctor; patient
3. 병원에 가다	go see a doctor
4. 입원을 하다	be hospitalized, check into the hospital
5. 퇴원을 하다	check out of the hospital
6. 진찰을 받다/ 하다	get/give a (medical) check-up, examination
7. 자리에 눕다 (ㅂ irr.)	lie down in bed
8. 치료를 하다	give a treatment, prognosis
9. 약을 먹다	take medicine
10. 약을 짓다 (지어요 ㅅ irr.)	have a prescription filled
11. 주사를 맞다	to get a shot
12. 몸살; 감기 에 걸리다	have body-aches, be achy; catch a cold
13. 붓다 (부어요 ㅅ irr.)	swell
14. (감기가) 다 낫다 (나아요 ㅅ irr.)	get over (a cold) completely
	sickness
15. 병이 나다	get ill
16. 열이 나다	have a fever
17. 콧물이 나(오)다	have a runny nose
18. 땀이 나(오)다	sweat comes out (to sweat)
19. 기침이 나(오)다 / 기침을 하다	coughs come out (to cough)
20. 재채기가 나(오)다 / 재채기를 하다	sneezes come out (to sneeze)
21. 앨러지가 있다	have an allergy
22. 무리(를) 하다	overextend oneself
23. 밤을 새우다	pull an all-nighter
24. 푹 쉬다	rest sufficiently
25. 심하다; 심하게	severe; severely
26. 쉽다 (ㅂ-irr.)	easy
27. 어렵다 (ㅂ-irr.)	difficult

More often than not, you will use 앨러지에요 with the specific name in front: 피부 앨러지에요. (I have a skin allergy.) Also, be prepared to hear 알레르기 from older folks.

Vocabulary Exercise 1. Matching

Draw a line connecting the phrase at right to the body part that experiences or does it.

- 열이 나다
- 코/콧물이 나오다
- 기침이 나다
- 이가 아프다
- 약을 먹다
- 주사를 맞다

Vocabulary Exercise 2. Label the picture

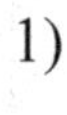

1) 

____

2) 

____

3) 

____

4) 

____

5) 

____

6) 

_______, _______, _______

7) 

____

8) 

____

9) 

____

Vocabulary Exercise 3. What should I do?
What do you do if you have these conditions?

1) 감기가 심하면 ______________________________

2) 몸살에 걸리면 ______________________________

3) 알레르기가 있으면______________________________

4) 열이 나면 ______________________________

5) 머리가 아프면 ______________________________

6) 기침이 나면 ______________________________

7) 콧물이 나오면 ______________________________

Culture Point *Good for what ails you!*

Compare the traditional remedies between the U.S. and Korea. What's common in both cultures and what's different?

problem; illness	US traditional remedy	Korean traditional remedy
touched something hot	put finger in mouth, blow on it	touch your ears
after childbirth	---	미역국
for a cold	chicken soup, lots of liquids	매운 콩나물 국, 생강 차, 목욕을 안 해요; sweat it out
stomach-ache	ginger ale, soda crackers	엄마 손이 약 손 (good 기 through the center of your palm)
stress	herbal tea	술
sore throat	lozenge	honey (꿀)
digestion problem	---	folk-version of acupuncture with a sewing needle

Lesson 23 Dialogue 집에서 푹 쉬어야 돼요

시은: **제프** 씨, 왜 8 신데 벌써 누워 있어요?

제프: 몸이 별로 안 좋네요. 시험 때문에 무리해서 그래요.

시은: 더 아파지기 전에[1] 꼭[2] 병원에 가 보세요.

--------- ** ---------

의사: 열이 많이 나네요. 어디가 아파요?

제프: 팔, 다리, 그리고 허리가 많이 아파요. 그리고 기침이 나요.

의사: 자, 아~ 해 보세요. 목이 좀 부어 있네요[3].

제프: 어떻게 하면 나아요[4]?

의사: 몸살이에요. 푹 쉬어야 돼요[5]. 물을 많이 마시고, 일찍 주무세요[6]. 무리하면 안돼요.[7]

1. before you get sicker
2. definitely, without fail
3. your throat is a little swollen
4. What should I do to get better?
5. should get a good rest
6. sleep (*honorific*)
7. You should not overextend yourself

Lesson 23 Grammar

1. Focus　　Expressing strong necessity

-어/아야 돼요	**have got to**

Through various situations in this chapter, you have been familiarized with the verb 돼요. If you recall the lessons from Chapter 5, 돼요 is the *contracted* –어/아 form of the verb 되다 (the full form, which is used more often in written Korean, is 되어요). 돼요 means *become*, or *be good enough* or *satisfactory*. Let's quickly review the forms and their meanings you have seen.

Preliminary Dialogue
제프: 감기에 걸렸어요.
시은: 쯧쯧… 안 됐네요.　　The need hasn't been met → **That's too bad.**

Lesson 21 dialogue
시은: 이 차 좀 마셔 보세요.
제프: 고맙지만 됐어요. The need has been met → **That's O.K.**

Lesson 22 dialogue
시은: 같이 산책하러 나갈래요?
제프: 안돼요. 저는 못 나가요. The need will not be met → **That won't do.**

-야 is a particle that has the sense of "only if", and it attaches to the -어/아 form of the verb in combination with the auxiliary verb 되다. So the literal meaning of the expression is something like "it will work only if", and the whole phrase has developed an idiomatic meaning of *obligation*. In English, the simple translation is "have got to".

내일 시험이 있어서 공부해야 돼요.	There is a test tomorrow, so I've got to study.
계속 아프면 병원에 가야 돼요.	If you are still sick, you've got to see a doctor.
내일은 일찍 일어나야 돼요.	Tomorrow I've got to get up early.

You will see another form that means *should* or *have to*, found more often in written Korean -- -어/아야 해요

내일 시험이 있어서 공부해야 해요.	There is a test tomorrow, so I've got to study.
계속 아프면 병원에 가야 해요.	If you are still sick, you've got to see a doctor.
내일은 일찍 일어나야 해요.	Tomorrow I've got to get up early.

Be careful with the conjugation of the verb 되다 when you add it to other connectors and endings:

오늘 오후에는 우체국에 가야 **되**고, 슈퍼에 가서 채소도 사야 **돼**요.
I've got to go to the post office, and go to the grocery store to buy vegetables.

내일 일찍 학교에 가야 **되**면, 오늘 저녁에 일찍 자러 가세요.
If you've got to go to school early tomorrow, go to bed early this evening.

Let's make the learning experience a little more interesting by combining endings together. How would you say "I will probably have to go." or "You will have to study for tomorrow's test, of course."? How about "He must have gone there."?

(아마) 가야 될 거예요.
내일 시험 공부 해야지요.
그 사람 거기 갔어야 됐을 거야.

2. Other Grammar Notes

1. -아/어 있다 *is …ing/ed (state)*

The structure "action verb + 아/어 있다" emphasizes that an entity is in such-and-such *resultant state*.

벌써 누워 있어요?	Are you already in bed? (You got in bed at one point and are now *are* in bed)
거기 먼저 가 계세요.	Go there ahead of me and be there.
아픈데 왜 일어나 있어요?	You are sick; how come you are up? (Got up at one point and is up now)

Sometimes 아/어 있다 is best translated in English as an adjective:

목이 부어 있네요	Your throat is swollen. (Started swelling at one point and is swollen now)
이 물고기는 아직도 살아 있어요!	This fish is still alive!

One handy phrase with -어 있다 is X는 Y and Z-(으)로 되어 있다, which means *X consists of Y and Z.* (Auxiliary verbs like 있다 in 되어 있다 may or may not be written with a space before.)

콘크리트는 물이랑, 모래랑, 세멘트로 되어 있다.
Concrete consists of water, sand, and cement.

레모네이드는 레몬주스랑, 물이랑, 설탕으로 되어있다.
Lemonade consists of lemon juice, water, and sugar.

A very similar phrase that you already know "verb stem + 고 있다" emphasizes that an action is *in progress*:

시계가 아직 가고 있어요.	The clock is still ticking.
바람이 불고 있어요.	The wind is blowing.
기침이 많이 나고 있어요.	Coughs are coming out a lot.
그 친구는 아직도 거기 살고 있어요.	He is still living there.

2. Nominalizer -기 *to VERB, VERB-ing; the act of VERB-ing*

The suffix -기 is a nominalizer, which allows verbs and adjectives to function like nouns (very much like the gerund *–ing* in English in *Catching a cold is no fun*).

읽기	reading	쓰기	writing
보기	watching (also *example*)	듣기	listening
뛰기	running	먹기	eating
말하기	speaking	쉬기	resting

Once verbs are changed into -기 forms, just like in English, they can act as the subject or the object of the sentence.

저는 쓰기보다는 읽기를 더 좋아해요. Rather than writing, I like reading better.

Unfortunately, -기 has a restricted usage – You can NOT turn just any verb into a gerund like English. The –기 expressions are typically seen in the following structures:

- ***it's easy to …*** and ***I don't want to ….***

바쁘면 아침을 건너 뛰기가 쉬워요. It's easy to skip breakfast when one is busy.

아~ 너무 귀찮다! 일어나기 싫어요. I feel so lazy! I don't want to get up.

- ***before doing…***

한국어 수업에 오기 전에 숙제를 다 하세요.
Do all your homework before coming to Korean class.

Remember memorizing this as a fixed expression in Lesson 10 (Chapter 3)?

Here are some more examples of "Verb-기 전에". Compare them to "Time 전에":

Noun + -전에	Verb stem + 기 전에	보기
여름 전에	여름이 오기 전에	Before the summer comes
겨울 전에	겨울이 가기 전에	Before the winter goes
시험 전에	시험을 보기 전에	Before taking the test
3 시 전에	3 시가 되기 전에	Before it becomes 3 o'clock

If you want to explicitly say how long before Activity A, activity B took place (e.g., 30 minutes before coming to class), the time expression falls between VERB-기 and 전에 :

수업 오기 30 분 전에 한국어 숙제를 끝냈어요.
Thirty minutes before coming to class, I had finished Korean homework.

This is also the phrasing for *30 minutes ago* when you have no –기 phrase:

30 분 전에 30 minutes ago

 Remember to use 시간 if you want to express duration!

3 시간 전에 three hours ago (cf. 3 시 전에 means *before 3 o'clock*)

 Remember the '-어/아서' clause? You learned **not** to mark the '어/아서' clause with the past tense. The same applies to the '-기 전에' clause. Even if you want to express two events in sequence, you should always use the *verb stem* (present tense) before -기 전에 .

점심 밥 먹기 전에 운동했어요. Before having lunch, I exercised.
(=Before I had lunch, I exercised.)

- ***because***: The –기 gerund can also come in front of the *cause* expression 때문에. In the previous section, you learned that 몸살 때문에 means *because of a bodyache*. ~기 때문에 also means *because,* only this time with verb or a whole clause (*because I have a body-ache*, instead of *because of a body-ache*). Remember! To make a verb or an adjective into a noun, all you have to do is to add ~기 to the stem, then you can use 때문에:

토니 씨가 여기 없기 때문에 because you aren't here, **토니**…

오늘은 날씨가 춥기 때문에 because it is cold today…

얼굴이 노랗기 때문에 because your face is yellow (sickly)…

열이 많이 나기 때문에 because I have high fever…

 If you need to express the reason in the past tense, just conjugate the verb/adjective in the past tense and add ~기 때문에

감기 몸살에 걸렸기 때문에 because I have caught a cold

어제는 추웠기 때문에 because it was cold yesterday

커피가 너무 썼기 때문에 설탕을 더 넣었어요.
Because the coffee was very bitter, I put more sugar in.

Here are some more examples to compare "Noun 때문에" and "Verb-기 때문에":

Noun + -때문에	Verb stem + 때문에	보기
기분 때문에	기분이 나쁘기 때문에	Because I'm in a bad mood
날씨 때문에	날씨가 좋았기 때문에	Because the weather was good
시험 때문에	시험을 봤기 때문에	Because I took a test

You learned in previous lessons that -어/아서 and –으니까 also express a reason. Although the three are somewhat interchangeable, -때문에 has the strongest *cause and effect* connection between the two clauses in a sentence.

시험이 있었기 때문에 못 나갔어요 Because I had a test, I wasn't able to go out.

시험이 있어서 못 나갔어요 (= 시험이 있었어요. 그래서 못 나갔어요.)
There was a test so I couldn't go out.

시험이 있었으니까 못 나갔어요.
It's because I had a test that I couldn't go out. That's why.

To sort out the three:

-(으)니까 provides a justification, as if already asked *why??*: ***it's because/ that's why***

-어서 relates a logical precursor: ***having done x, this being the case,*** ...

-(기) 때문에 best marks the direct *cause:* ***because of x,...***

3. ㅅ-irregular verbs (ㅅ~ 

With some verbs that end in ㅅ, ㅅ disappears before suffixes that begin with a vowel (e.g. -어/아, -으). These verbs are called ㅅ-irregulars. What you need to remember about these ㅅ-irregulars is that although ㅅ disappears before -어/아 and -으 endings, it acts as if it were still there, calling for the empty vowel 으, for example. We will call this ㅅ a ghost segment.

There are three frequently used ㅅ-irregular words you will learn in this lesson:
붓다 (swell), 짓다 (make, build), and 낫다 (get better).

ㅅ-irregulars	Meaning	어/아 form	으 form	기, 지, 고, 네 form
붓다	swell	부어요	부으세요	붓기 쉬워요
짓다	make, build	지어요	지으세요	짓기 때문에
낫다	get better	나아요	나으세요	낫기 어려우니까

목이 부어 있네요. Oh, I see your throat is swollen.

약 좀 지으러 왔는데요. I'm here to get some medicine made/a prescription filled.

약 좀 지어 주세요. Please make me some medicine/fill this prescription.

약을 먹고 감기가 다 나았어요. With the medicine, I have completely recovered.

Memorize these three most frequent ㅅ-irregulars by making a sentence based on the following sequence of pictures.

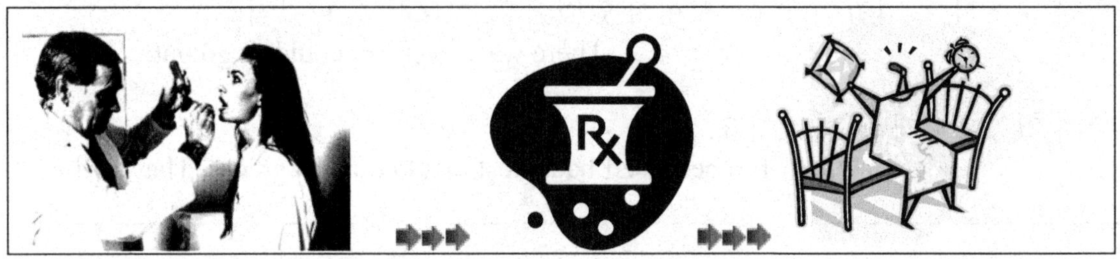

목이 부었어요 → 약을 지었어요 → 다 나았어요.
(My throat was swollen → I got the prescription filled → I took the medicine → I got all better)

Lesson 23 Exercises

Exercise 1. Dialogue practice
Practice the dialogue in this lesson with a classmate.

Exercise 2. -고 있어요 vs -어 있어요?
Write a sentence explaining the state of the person or the action in progress in the picture: provide a reason and try to add in interesting details.

Example: 자니는 늦게까지 공부를 많이해서, 피곤 하기때문에 자고 있어요.

1)  2)  3)  4) 

Translate:
5) I have come to your office, 선생님, because I am stressed out.

6) Because I am sneezing a lot, my nose is swollen.

7) Because I had lots of good soup, my cold is getting better.

Exercise 3. Short composition 쓰기

Make up a short phrase for each ending using the given verb.

	-기 전에	-어야 돼요
먹다	약을 먹기 전에	밥을 먹어야 돼요
가다		
주다		
살다		
쓰다		
닦다		

Exercise 4. 이거 하기 전에 …뭐 해야 돼요?

Ask a classmate what they have got to do before they engage in the following activities.
Example: Sleep

A: 자기 전에 뭐 해야 돼요?
B: 자기 전에 목욕해야 돼요.

1) Exercise
2) Study
3) Put on clothes
4) Put on make-up
5) Buy a Christmas tree
6) Have dinner
7) Do homework
8) Come to class

Exercise 5. Why?

Explain the cause of the problem/situation. Make a sentence where the reason is in the -기 form. Be sure to give the reason in past tense, if necessary! (Part II: Try to make up the corresponding sentences with a *noun* reason.)

1) I can't go to the party.
2) I have a headache.

3) I bombed the test (시험을 망치다).

4) I can't eat.

5) My teeth have become blue! (e.g., because I drank a Slurpy)

6) I was late (늦다 *to be late*)

7) I caught a cold.

Exercise 6. It's easy/difficult to… if you…

Have a conversation with your partner about whether the following are easy or hard given the following conditions in parentheses.

1) (drink a lot of coffee) - teeth get yellow

2) (study really hard) - stay up all night

3) (watch a fun soap opera on TV) - not do homework (soap opera 드라마)

4) (go jogging in the winter) - catch a cold

5) (over-extend oneself) - get a body-ache

6) (cry) - eyes swell

Exercise 7. Translation

1) I don't want to sleep now!

2) Translating Korean is tough! (translate: 번역하다)

3) You've got to call your father before 7 o'clock today.

4) Tell your roommate before you use his computer. Turn it off after you use it. (turn off: 끄다)

5) If you take the pills, you will get better.

6) You look tired.

7) My throat is swollen.

8) My face swells every night. (every night: 매일 밤)

9) It's difficult to learn Korean.

10) It's easy to speak English.

11) Start speaking to your Korean roommates in Korean now!

12) Start using new vocabulary now! (new vocabulary: 새 단어)

13) It's all ruined (망치다) because of you!

14) It's raining outside now – take your umbrella. (take: 가져가다)

15) I was hungry so I ate your pizza.

16) If you smoke a lot, you will cough a lot ("coughs will come out a lot").

Exercise 8. Reading practice 시은에게…

아래의 텍스트를 큰 소리로 읽어 보세요.
다 했어요? 이번에는 눈으로만 빨리 읽어 보세요. 뜻을 guess 해 보세요.

시은 씨에게:

시은 씨, 지난 주에 나한테 "빨리 병원에 가 보세요" 하고 말했지요? 그래서 금요일에 제일 먼저 병원에 갔어요. 의사 선생님이 나한테 "감기가 낫고 싶으면, 약을 먹고 푹 쉬어야 돼요. 아침에 너무 일찍 일어나거나 저녁에 너무 늦게 자면 안돼요. 주스랑 물을 많이 마시고, 일찍 자고 일찍 일어나면, 감기가 빨리 나을 거에요" 하고 말했어요.

진찰 후에 아래층[1]으로 갔어요. 약사가 물약을 한 병 주고 알약도 몇 알 지어 주었어요. 일 주일 동안 밥 먹기 30 분 전에는 물약을 먹고, 밥을 먹고 30 분 후에는[2] 알약을 먹어야 되었어요. 물약은 먹기 쉬웠지만 알약은 먹기가 어려웠어요. 알약을 먹기 전에는 물을 많이 마셔야 됐어요! 처음에는 힘이 들었지만, 계속 물약이랑 알약을 먹고 푹 쉬어서 지금은 감기가 거의 다 나았어요. 하지만 목은 아직도 조금 부어 있어서 말을 작게 해야 돼요. 그래도 전보다는 몸이 훨씬 더 좋아졌어요! 그래서 이제는 **시은** 씨하고 놀 수 있어요. ☺

[1] downstairs

[2] after, later

다음 주에 시간 있으면 우리 집에 한 번 놀러 오세요. 그리고, 내 생각 해 줘서 고마워요!

2004 년 5 월

제프가 (침대에 누워서 썼어요!)

Culture Point 한약, 양약 *Eastern vs. Western medicine*

The way Koreans manage illness is somewhat different from Westerners. When the season changes, mothers who can afford it get 보약 (a restorative, tonic) from a 한약방 (Traditional Korean pharmacy). A more wide-spread affordable home-made summer-time 보약 is called 삼계탕, which has 인삼 (ginseng), 닭 and 대추 (dates) in it. Some folks go to extremes and have 뱀탕 (snake soup), 흑염소 (black goat), or even 보신탕 (dog soup).

Flu shots are common these days, but the folk remedies are still quite widespread. Many people, especially of the older generations, trust 한약방 (traditional Korean pharmacies) where 한의사 practice acupuncture (침을 놓다) and fill his/her own prescriptions. In the olden days, one had to simmer 한약 on low heat under constant vigil, and wring it in a home-devised wringer using cloth and 젓가락. Nowdays 한약 comes in plastic packs and they can handily go in microwave ovens.

Many laypeople have a great knowledge of common drugs in Korea, most of which are easily accessible in drug stores, without prescription. Some of the most common day maladies in Korea are indigestion (소화불량), headache (두통), constipation (변비), and diarrhea (설사). Of course, all these can be psychosomatic (신경성).

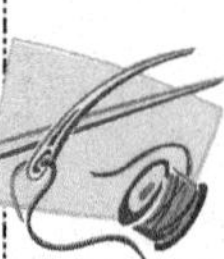

One of the die-hard practices for indigestion that folks use a lot in Korea is quickly pricking just behind the cuticle of the thumb or the big toe with a sewing needle, letting *bad* blood out (손가락을 따다). It works!

Can you guess the meaning of the following ending combinations?

이것도 먹어야 될까요	떠나면 보고 싶을 거에요
거기에 가고 싶었을 거에요	날씬해지고 싶을 거에요
파티에 가도 됐을 거에요	미팅에 가야 됐을 거에요
지금 집에 가야 될 거에요	술 마시면 안 되잖아요!

빨리 병원에 가야 되잖아요

Lesson 23 Checkpoint

대화 1 마지막으로 순이 씨를 언제 만났어요?

형사: **동팔** 씨, 마지막으로 **순이** 씨를 언제 만났어요?
동팔: 어제 학교 가기 전에 **순이** 집에 갔어요.
형사: 그게 언제였지요?
동팔: 아마 7 시 반이었을 거에요.
형사: **순이** 씨 집에는 왜 갔어요?
동팔: **순이**가 감기에 걸려서 제가 약을 좀 주었어요.
형사: **순이**씨가 많이 아팠어요?
동팔: 네, 열이 많이 나고 있었고 기침도 심하게 하고 있었어요.
형사: 그렇게 많이 아팠는데 왜 병원에 안 갔지요?
동팔: **순이**는 병원가기 싫어해요. 게다가[124] 어제 오후에 약속이 있었기 때문에 시간이 없었을 거에요.
형사: 약속? 누구하고 만났어요?
동팔: 저는 잘 모르겠어요. 그렇지만 아주 중요한 약속인 것 같았어요.
형사: **동팔** 씨는 알고 있어요. 그렇죠? **동팔** 씨, 수사[125]에 협조해[126] 주셔야 돼요.
동팔: 저는 정말 몰라요. 이제 가도 돼요? 저는 이제 가야 돼요.

대화 2 봄이 되면 날씨가 따뜻해지기 때문에 졸리지요?

성미: (졸고 있다. 갑자기 재채기를 한다.) 에취! 에취!
경미: **성미** 씨, 감기 걸렸어요?
성미: 잘 모르겠어요. 아닌 것 같아요. 알레르기 때문에 재채기가 나오는 것 같아요.
경미: **성미** 씨 알레르기 있어요?
성미: 네, 봄이 되면 꽃가루[127] 때문에 재채기가 나요.
경미: 또, 봄이 되면 날씨가 따뜻해지기 때문에 졸리지요?
성미: 하하, 어떻게 알았죠? **경미** 씨, 우리 벚꽃[128]이 지기 전에 벚꽃놀이 가요!
경미: **성미** 씨는 꽃가루 알레르기가 있는데 벚꽃놀이 가도 돼요?
성미: 그럼요, 병원에 가서 알레르기 약을 지어 먹으면 금방 나아요.

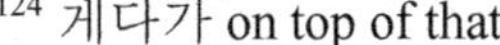

[124] 게다가 on top of that
[125] 수사 a criminal investigation
[126] 협조하다 to cooperate, help, aid
[127] 꽃+가루 [꼬까루], [꼭까루] pollen
[128] 벚꽃 [버꼳], [벅꼳] cherry blossom

LESSON 24
어디로 갈까요?

Lesson 24 Vocabulary 여행, 그리고 자연

1) 싸다	cheap
2) 비싸다	expensive
3) (-에) 가깝다 - 가까워요 (ㅂ irr.)	close
4) (-에서) 멀다	far
5) 신청하다	to apply, make a request
6) 연장하다	to extend
7) 여행하다	to travel
8) 구경하다	to look around, do sight-seeing
9) (사진을) 찍다	to take a picture, imprint
10) 경치	view, scenery
11) 사진	photo, picture
12) 지도	map
13) 여권 [여꿘]	passport
14) 여행사	travel agency
15) 방학	school break, school vacation
16) 휴가; 휴일	vacation; holiday
17) 길	street, road
18) 기차	train
19) 지하철	subway train
20) 배	ship, boat
21) 비행기, 비행기 표	airplane, airplane ticket
22) 자연	nature
23) 바다, 바닷가	sea, beach
24) 강, 강가 [강까]	river, riverside
25) 호수, 호숫가	lake, lakeside
26) 산	mountain
27) 섬	island
28) 언덕	hill
29) 들(판)	open field
30) 하늘	sky
31) 해; 달; 별	sun; moon; star
32) 나무	tree
33) 새	bird
34) 물고기 [물꼬기]	fish (alive)
35) 때	time
36) 데 (dependent noun)	place

Can you guess the meaning of these words? 호텔, 택시, 버스, 보트, 요트, 비자, 카메라…

Vocabulary Exercise 1. Odd one out
Which word does not fit with the others?

1) 여행, 방학, 휴가, 지하철
2) 버스, 택시, 기차, 바다, 지하철, 배, 비행기,
3) 버스, 택시, 기차, 지하철, 비행기
4) 기차, 비행기, 새
5) 새, 나무, 물고기
6) 바다, 강, 호수, 산
7) 바닷가, 하늘, 강가, 호숫가, 섬
8) 해, 달, 별, 나무, 새, 물고기
9) 여행사, 별, 새, 물고기
10) Make your own

Vocabulary Exercise 2. Label the picture
Go through the list in the box below determining whether and where the item is in the picture (label it), and whether and where you might (logically) add the item to the picture.

1) 

2) 

3) 

4) 

싸다	비싸다	가깝다	멀다	버스	택시
기차	지하철	배	비행기	바다	바닷가
강	강가	호수	호숫가	산	섬
하늘	해	달	별	나무	새
물고기	길				

노래하고 싶어요!

달 The Moon

달! 달!	**The moon! The moon!**
무슨 달?	**What moon?**
쟁반같이 둥근 달.	**The round moon like a tray!**
어디 어디 떴나?	**Where? Where did it rise?**
남산 위에 떴지!	**On top of Nam San (South Mountain)!**

바람 부는 날이면 On a windy day

바람 부는 날이면 언덕에 올라	**On a windy day I climb up a hill**
넓은 들을 바라보며	**Looking out over an open field**
그 여인의 마지막 그 말 한 마디	**Her last words**
생각하며 웃음짓네	**Thinking about them, I smile**
랄랄라 라랄랄라 랄랄라라라라	
랄랄라 라랄랄라 랄랄라라라라	

Lesson 24 Dialogue 어디로 갈까요?

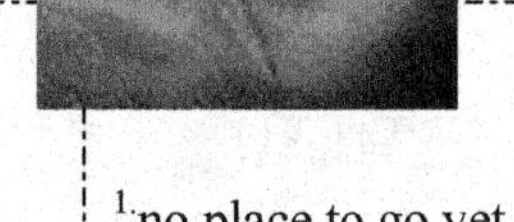

은비: **조디** 씨는 이번 방학 때에 어디에 갈 거에요?	
조디: 나도 아직 갈 데가 없는데[1] 우리 같이 놀러 갈까요[2]?	[1] no place to go yet [2] Shall we?
은비: 그거 좋은 생각이네요. 어디로 갈까요[2]?	
조디: 알래스카가 어때요?	
은비: 거기는 춥지 않을까요[3]? 한국이 어때요?	[3] won't it be cold, I wonder?
조디: 좋은 생각이네요. 그런데, 한국에 볼 데가 많을까요[4]?	[4] will there be many places to see, I wonder?
은비: 네. 한국에는 재미있는 데가 많고 볼 데도 많을 거에요.	
조디: 좋아요. 같이 갑시다. 한국에 가고 싶었는데 잘 됐네요.	
은비: 내일 시간 있을 때[5] 웹에서 싼 비행기 표를 알아 볼께요[6].	[5] when I have time [6] find out about

Dialogue practice
Practice the dialogue in this lesson with a classmate.

It will be helpful to talk about traveling if you review the following duration terms. It may help to note that the number of days have the same beginning consonant as the Korean counting numbers (except for *two* and *two days*):

하나	하루	1 day
둘	이틀	2 days
셋	사흘	3 days
넷	나흘	4 days
다섯	닷새	5 days
여섯	엿새	6 days
일곱	이레	7 days
여덟	여드레	8 days
아홉	아흐레, 아흘	9 days
열	열흘	10 days
	보름	15 days
	한 달	a month

Also get yourself familiarized with the expression 몇박 몇일. It means *How many nights and how many days*.
몇박몇일로 놀러 가세요? =몇일 동안 놀러 가세요?
The typical answers are:
일박이일로 가요. (We are going for one night and two days.)
Or
일박이일이에요. (It's one night and two days.)

Can you guess the meaning of the following phrases?
이박삼일, 삼박사일, 사박오일, 오박육일...

Lesson 24 Grammar

1. Focus I wonder…

-(으)ㄹ까(요)?	**How about…, Shall we? I wonder… Do you think…? Should I/we?**

-(으)ㄹ까 expresses the wondering or **pondering** mindset of the speaker:

점심에 뭐 먹을까?	What should I/we eat for lunch?
이번 여름에 어디 갈까?	I wonder where I should go this summer.

When this kind of thinking-to-oneself mood is expressed to a listener, -(으)ㄹ까 is interpreted as asking for an opinion or **suggestion**, often an **invitation**. If you need to be polite to the listener, you should add -요 to the - (으)ㄹ까 ending. A sentence with an *invitation* sense sometimes has 우리 in it:

방학에 우리 어디 갈까요?	Where shall we go for the break?

When you are asked the "-(으)ㄹ까요 question, you can often ask back with a suggestive question "~ 어때요?" or "~을까요?"

A: 저녁에 뭐 먹을까요?	What shall we have for dinner?
B: 한국 음식은 어때요?	How about Korean food?
B': 한국 음식은 어떨까요?	What do you think of Korean food?
B'': 한국 음식 먹을까요?	Shall we have Korean food?

But if you are talking to your peers you met in a social setting (e.g., work place colleagues, for example), a direct suggestion " -(으)ㅂ시다!" is typically used in response to "-(으)ㄹ까요?"

A: 저녁에 뭐 먹을까요?	What shall we have for dinner?
B: 한국 음식을 먹읍시다!	Let's have Korean food!

If the question is not an invitation, the –(으)ㄹ까요 ending solicits the listener's opinion, having the meaning of "(What) do you think?". You should (still) answer to your best knowledge:

A: 내일 비가 올까요? Do you think it'll rain tomorrow?

B: 아마 올 거에요. It'll probably rain.

B': 글쎄요. 일기예보 안 들었어요. I'm not sure. I didn't listen to the forecast.

Finally, when the answer pertains only to the person who asks the question, the answer should NEVER be -(으)ㅂ시다!

A: 방학에 나, 한국어 연습하러 한국에 갈까요?

B: 그래요. 한국에 가세요.

B': 아니, 한국으로 가지 말고 LA 로 가세요.

B'': 아니, 한국으로 가지 말고 홍콩으로 가면 어때요?

⚠ Like any other -으 ending, "-(으)ㄹ까요" conjugation requires ***irregular*** stems:

어느 게 더 쌀까요?	Which do you think is cheaper?
지하철로 가면 가까울까?	Would it be closer if I take the subway, I wonder?
그 친구가 내일 올까?	I wonder if that friend is coming tomorrow.
이 약 먹으면 감기가 나을까?	If I take this medicine, will my cold get better, I wonder?
심심한데 음악이나 들을까요?	It's quiet and boring. Shall we listen to music or something?
이거 살까 저거 살까?	Which one should I buy, this one or that one?

2. Other Grammar Notes

1. (Prospective marker -(으)ㄹ: -(으)ㄹ Noun *a NOUN to VERB*

You have seen -을 being used as part of future (or uncertainty) verb endings like -을 거에요, -을래요, -을께요 and -을까요. In this lesson, -을 is used as a noun modifier ending indicating a *future* clause (in the sense that something is to happen). Only ***verbs*** can modify nouns this way, and the meaning is *a NOUN to VERB* (usually in the immediate future).

공부할 시간이에요.	It's time to study.
내일은 좀 바빠요. 할 일이 있어요.	I'm busy tomorrow. I've got stuff to do.
읽을 책이 없어요.	I don't have any book to read.
만날 사람이 많아요.	I have a lot of people to meet.

집에 먹을 게 하나도 없어요. We have nothing to eat at home.

너한테 할 얘기가 있어. I have got something to tell you.

When the noun phrase [-(으)ㄹ + Noun] is used as the subject in a sentence embedded in a bigger sentence, the translation is usually *the NOUN who/that will*:

> This kind of sentence usually has a human subject and an existential verb(있어요, 없어요, 많아요) as the predicate.

토요일에 학교에 올 사람이 있어요?
Is there anyone who will come to school on Saturday?

우리하고 같이 영화 구경 갈 사람들은 오늘까지 돈을 내야 돼요!
Those who will go to the movies with us have got to pay the money by today!

2. -(으)ㄹ 때 *when …*

You have already seen the word 때 in noun compounds like 방학 때 (during the vacation), 점심 때 (at the lunch hour). 때 can also be modified by a verb or adjective with the -을 ending. In this case it means *when* VERB/ADJECTIVE *happens*.

시간 있을 때 이거 해 주세요. When you have time, do this (for me).

요즘은 비가 올 때가 더 많아요. There are more times when it rains these days. (It rains more often than not these days.)

머리가 아플 때 이 약을 드세요. When your head hurts, take this medicine.

한국에서 여행할 때는 한국말을 해야지요.
When you are traveling through Korea, you should speak Korean, of course.

퇴원할 때 여기에 싸인하세요. When you check out of the hospital, sign here.

When the action in the 때 clause is completed before the action in the main clause, then it can be put in the "past tense". That is, -(으)ㄹ 때 can be attached to the past tense stem:

숙제 다 했을 때 나가서 놀아라. = 숙제 다 하면 나가서 놀아라.
When you have finished doing homework, go out and play.

밥 다 먹었을 때 나 불러! = 밥 다 먹으면 나 불러!
When you have finished eating, call me.

If the action or state in the 때 clause is not completed before the action in the main clause (for example, if it is an on-going state or background situation for the main clause), then the 때 clause does not use the past tense even if the main clause does:

A: 하와이에 갔을 때 뭐 했어요?
What did you do when you went Hawai'i? (You had arrived in Hawai'i, so "going" is

completed.)

B: 날씨가 좋을 때는 선탠을 했고, 날씨가 나쁠 때는 영화를 보러 갔어요.
When the weather was good, I sunbathed, and when the weather was bad, I went to the movies. (Weather is the background situation, not completed.)

A: 어떻게 여행했어요?
How did you travel?

B: 캘리포니아에 갈 때는 비행기로 갔고, 오레건에 갈 때는 기차로 갔어요.
When I went to California, I flew; when I went to Oregon, I took the train.

Here are some more examples:

캘리포니아에 갔을 때는 날씨가 나빴는데, 오레건에 갔을 때는 좋았어요.
When I got to California, the weather was bad, but when I got to Oregon, it was good.

A: 한국에서 한국말만 했어요?
Did you only speak Korean in Korea?

B: 아니오. 미국 친구하고 말 할 때는 영어를 했어요.
No. When I was talking with American friends, I spoke English.

When -었을 때 describes an action that will be *completed* in the *future*, it can be replaced by –었으면:
숙제 다 했을 때 나가서 놀아라. = 숙제 다 하면 나가서 놀아라.
When you have finished doing homework, go out and play.

밥 다 먹었을 때 나 불러!=밥 다 먹으면 나 불러!
When you have finished eating, call me.

-(으)ㄹ 때 expressions are also very useful to memorize as fixed idioms. Can you guess the meaning of the following phrases?

비행기 여행이 좋을 때도 있고 싫을 때도 있어요.

늦게 일어나면 학교에 못 갈 때도 있어요.

여권을 연장할 때가 되었어요

약 먹을 때가 됐어요

It's time to take the medicine.
It's time to extend my passport.
When I get up late, there are times I can't go to class.
Sometimes I like air travel, and sometimes I don't.

3. –(으)ㄹ데 *a place to...*

데 means *place*, and it can only be used with a modifier just before it. (That's why it is called a "dependent noun."):

어디 갈 데가 있어요?	Is there any place to go?
있을 데가 있어요?	Is there a place to stay?
공부할 데가 없어요.	There is no place to study.

Yes, it's true – 있다 means *to stay* at a hotel, someone's home, etc.

One very important thing to remember is to distinguish the SPELLING of the two words 때 and 데. Although they have the same pronunciation after the modifier –(으)ㄹ, 때 means *the time when* and 데 means *the place where*!

Otherwise, 안 + verb/adjective has the same meaning as verb/adjective + 지 않다 but the latter sounds more formal and educated.

4. -지 않다 *not*

You know the use of –지 as a negative marker in a negative command like 먹지 마세요. -지 is also a used before the negative verb 않다 to negate a sentence.

하와이는 호텔이 비싸지 않아요?	Aren't hotels expensive in Hawai'i?
한국은 L.A.에 가깝지 않아요.	Korea isn't close to L.A.
일본은 한국에서 멀지 않아요.	Japan is not far from Korea.

이 약을 먹으면 콧물이 나오지 않을 거에요.
If you take this medicine, your nose won't run.

푹 쉬지 않으면 몸살에 걸릴 수도 있어요.
If you don't take a good rest, you could have a body-ache.

실망하지는 않았지만 조금 걱정이 되네요.
I am not disappointed, but I am a little worried.

-고 싶어요 is usually negated with -지 않아요, and so are adjectives and multi-syllable verbs.

알래스카는 춥기 때문에 겨울 방학 때 가고 싶지 않아요.
I don't want to go to Alaska during the winter break because (it) is cold.

오늘은 구름이 많이 껴서 사진을 찍고 싶지 않아요.
Today is overcast – I don't want to take pictures.

-지 않아요 has been shortened and made an idiomatic ending -잖아요 which means *you see* or *you should know*:

A: 왜 병원에 환자가 이렇게 많지? Why are there so many patients in the hospital?
B: 감기가 많이 걸릴 때잖아. It's the season for catching colds, isn't it?

A: 재 왜 저렇게 피곤해 보여? Why does she look so tired?
B: 오늘 하루 종일 아르바이트 했잖아. She worked all day, you know.

5. idiomatic -어 보다 constructions

Although the majority of the -어 보다 verbs is transparent in meaning ("try doing…" or "try and see…"), some compound verbs have developed out of the *try and see* and into some other unique meaning.

여행사에 전화해서 알아 봅시다. Let's call the travel agency and *find out*.

머리가 길어서 못 알아 봤어요. Your hair is long so I didn't *recognize* you.

웹에서 싸구려 비행기를 찾아 봤어요. I looked for cheap tickets on the web.

Language Point *About the future…*

We can now wrap up the lessons on future endings. In this textbook, you have seen -어요, -(으)ㄹ 거에요, -(으)ㄹ래요, -(으)ㄹ께요, and -(으)ㄹ까요 used to indicate some kind of future. See if you can get the sense of each ending in the dialogue below.

사촌언니: 와! 설거지가 왜 이렇게 많아?

사촌동생: 내가 도와 줄까요?

사촌언니: 아니, 나 혼자 할래. 혼자 하는 게 더 빠를 거야.

사촌동생: 그래도 내가 도와주면 더 빠르지 않을까요? 도와 줄께요.

사촌언니: 그럼, 조금 도와 줄래? 이따가 아이스크림 사 줄께! ☺

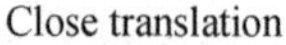

Close translation
cousin (older): Wow! How come so many dishes to do?
cousin (younger): Do you want me to help you? ; Shall I help you?
cousin (older): No, I'll do it myself; I'm gonna do it myself. It'll be faster if I do it by myself.
cousin (younger): But, won't it be faster if I help you? Let me help you; I'll help you, OK?
cousin (older): Then, would you help me a little? I'll treat you to ice cream later! ☺

You can only perfect your *future* skills by practicing. Don't be afraid of making mistakes! (And a friendly reminder to you – as pointed out in the preliminary chapter, your Korean friends might give an instant laugh at your mishap (e.g. when you fall or spill something), but this is very cultural. They are not laughing *at* you. Keep practicing, and don't forget to speak LOUDLY when you speak Korean (or any other foreign language). Clear and loud speech helps reduce miscommunication in many cases!

Lesson 24 Exercises

Exercise 1. Needy roommate

You are the new roommate. You don't have much stuff and you can't find some other things (and places). Ask your partner if he/she has the following items or where they are. As a positive response, your partner can offer to give the item to you or look for them with you (using -(으)ㄹ까요).

Example: slippers to wear → A: 신을 슬리퍼가 (어디) 있어요?
B: 같이 찾아 볼까요?

1) chair to sit on	2) cup to drink (with)
3) sweater to wear	4) spoon to eat (with)
5) magazine to read (잡지)	6) umbrella to use
7) café to go to	8) CD to listen to
9) laundry to do	10) food to eat

Exercise 2. Help your friends out!

Your friend has a problem. Offer to help using "Shall I…?"

Example: 한국어가 어려워요 → 도와 줄까요?

1) 머리가 아파요.
2) 배가 고픈데 돈이 없어요.
3) 추워요.
4) 이 국은 너무 싱거워요.
5) 한국어 숙제가 너무 어려워요.

Exercise 3. What do you think?

Take turns asking what your friend thinks about the following situations.

Example: weather tomorrow, clear → 내일은 날씨가 맑을까요?

1) this Korean food, spicy
2) tomorrow's Korean test, difficult
3) next quarter's Korean teacher, fun (next quarter 다음 학기)
4) get a shot, hurts (주사를 맞다)
5) vacation, long
6) teacher, tired

Exercise 4. NOT!

Make up a statement about the following items or people using the adjectives given. Does your/your partner's opinion of each item or person match the suggested adjective? Answer expressing your disagreement:

Example: your Korean grades (성적): bad
A: ____ 한국어 성적은 나쁘지요?
B: 아니오, 내 성적은 나쁘지 않아요!

1) bananas: bitter
2) your dorm-room/apartment: big
3) basketball: boring
4) Tonya Harding: well-behaved
5) kimchi: sweet
6) Korean: difficult (어렵다: ㅂ-irregular)
7) Alaska: hot
8) Mickey Mouse: scary
9) Mick Jagger: fat
10) tuition (학비): cheap
11) ET's fingers: short
12) your 동생/older sibling: (pick an adjective)

Exercise 5. Want to?

Your friend is suggesting you do the following things together. If you agree, echo the suggestion with an invitation, elaborating on it with a time and/or place.

Example: read the Korean textbook
A: 큰 소리로 한국어 책을 읽을까요? (큰 소리로: out loud)
B: 아니오. 큰 소리로 한국어 책을 읽지 마세요.

1) eat at a Korean restaurant
2) call the teacher late at night (밤 늦게)
3) clean the house
4) go to the hospital
5) play basketball
6) go mountain climbing

Exercise 6. Shall we…?
Give a suggestion of what you and your friend might try doing at each place.

1)

2)

3)

4)

5)

6)

7) 외국에서

8) 가게에서

(map 지도)

Exercise 7. -(으)ㄹ 데가 있어요? Is there a place to…?
Ask your partner about his/her hometown – what kind of places are there to eat, go dancing, etc.? If you are new to the area, ask about the University neighborhood or downtown, etc.

Example: 어디에 살아요 ? … ______에서는 중국 음식을 먹을 데 가 있어요?

How about some other cities? New York? Seattle? Honolulu? Paris? Seoul? Beijing?

Exercise 8.
State when you do/did the following things. Use -(으)ㄹ 때…

1) I will go to Hawai'i
2) I played all day
3) I couldn't eat spinach
4) I watched cartoons
5) I got my first kiss (첫 키스를 하다)
6) *Make your own!*

Exercise 9.
Translate the sentence starter and complete the sentence.

1) When I was in elementary school, I …
2) When I was in junior school, I …
3) When I was in high school, I…
4) During the war… (war: 전쟁)
5) When my mom was in high school
6) *Make your own!*

Exercise 10. There are times when…
Translate the following sentences using the expression -(으)ㄹ 때도 있어요.

1) When I am busy, there are times I can't eat.
2) Sometimes I get sad when it rains.
3) There are times when I travel by myself.
4) When I travel, sometimes I sleep under a tree.
5) I wonder whether there are times he is not hungry.

7) When I am lonely, there are times when I look at the moon.
8) When I go to school, there are times when I take the bus and times when I take the subway.
9) When one travels, it's possible that one gets tired.
10) When you study Korean, do not speak English.
11) When you feel lonely, try finding a good friend.
12) When you travel, look for cheap tickets on the web.
13) When I saw him, because his hair was so long I didn't recognize him.

Exercise 11. 스무 고개 Twenty questions!
Come up with something in your mind that your partner will try to guess. You can only answer with 네 or 아니오 in a complete sentence. When you are answering in a negative sentence, be sure to use -지 않아요, when possible!
Example:

A: 사람이에요?
B: 네, 사람이에요. OR 아니오, 사람이 아니에요.
A: 우리 교실에 있어요?
B: 네, 우리 교실에 있어요. OR 아니오, 우리 교실에 있지 않아요.

Exercise 12. 나하고 여행갑시다! Let's go on a trip!
Invite your friend to go to a place with you for the summer vacation (여름 방학 때에). Discuss candidate places (why you should and shouldn't go there: weather, price, distance)

and the means to get there. Also talk about what you will do once you get to the place. Use a variety of endings such as -이/가 어때요, -이/가 어떨까요, -(으)ㄹ래요, -(으)ㄹ까요, -(으)ㄹ거에요, -(으)ㄹ수 있어요, -(으)ㅂ시다, -지 맙시다, -고 싶어요, -어/아야돼요, -어/아도 돼요, -(으)면 안돼요, etc. Also don't forget to use connectors such as -으(니까), -으(러), -으(면), -은/는데, -어도, -어서, etc.

Exercise 13. 나하고 데이트해 주세요! Ask your friend out!
Ask your friend out to a weekend outing (e.g. movie, concert, dining out, baseball game, etc.). Pick a time and place to meet (after a couple of negotiating turns). Decide on what to wear (trying to match what your friend will be wearing). Use a variety of endings such as -(으)ㄹ래요, -(으)ㄹ까요, -(으)ㄹ거에요, -(으)ㄹ수 있어요, -(으)ㄹ수 없어요, -(으)ㅂ시다, -지 맙시다, -고 싶어요, -어/아야돼요, -어/아도 돼요, -(으)면 안돼요, -은/을/는 것같아요, -어 죽겠어요, etc. Also don't forget to use connectors such as -으(니까), -으(러), -으(면), -은/는데, -어도, -어서, etc.

Language Point *Word Power!*

As you are studying Korean, every bit of what you already know will come in handy. Try to make connections between words if you see similar or identical parts. Analogical sensitivity is more powerful than simple memorization. Based on the words you know, can you deduce the meaning of related words below?

비행기
비행장 주차장, 운동장

지하철
지하실 교실, 사무실, 연구실
지하도

방학
휴가 휴학, 휴게실
학교

바닷가
강가 눈가, 입가(의 미소)
호숫가

Knowledge builds on itself!

Lesson 24 Checkpoint

읽기 1 마지막 시험이 끝나면

이제 이번 학기도 일주일밖에 안 남았어요. 그래서 다음 주는 너무 너무 바쁠 것 같아요. 월요일에는 도서관에서 5 시간 동안 아르바이트를 해야 돼요. 화요일에는 물리학 시험을 봐야 되고 수요일에는 심리학 보고서를 내야 돼요. 목요일은 어머니 생신이에요. 목요일 새벽에 여동생과 만나서 어머니 생신상[129]을 준비할 거에요. 어머니는 영화 보기가 취미[130]이기 때문에 저는 영화티켓을 선물로 준비했어요. 금요일에는 한국어 말하기 시험이 있어요. 시험을 보기 전에 말하기 연습을 많이 해야 돼요. 그런데 너무 바빠서 연습시간이 없기 때문에 걱정이에요. 저한테는 한국어 말하기가 너무 어려워요.

금요일 마지막 시험이 끝나고 친구인 **철수**하고 **종수**와 함께[131] 볼링장에 갈 거에요. 저와 저의 친구들은 만나면 볼링을 자주 쳐요. 우리는 볼링장에서 우연히[132] 만나서 친구가 되었어요. 저는 아직 학생이지만 제 친구들은 사회인[133]들이에요. **철수**는 형사[134]이고 **종수**는 회사원이에요. 직업은 다르지만 우리는 모두 볼링 치기가 취미에요.

읽기 2 오래간만에 식구들이 한 자리에 모였어요.

우리 식구들은 아주 바빠서 일요일에도 같이 식사하기 힘들어요. 오빠는 형사에요. 형사는 일요일도 없어요. 언제나 사건[135]이 생기면[136] 바로 출동해야[137]돼요. 아버지는 무역회사[138]에서 일해요. 일 때문에 자주 출장을 가야[139] 돼서 항상 바빠요. 어머니는 변호사에요. 변호사는 정말 힘든 직업이에요. 매일 늦게까지 사무실에서 일을 해요. 나는 아직 학생인데요. 공부때문에 아주 바쁘지요. 올 해[140]에는 한국어 수업을 듣고 있는데 재미있지만 무척 어려워요.그런데 이번 일요일에는 오래간만에 식구들이 한 자리에 모였어요.[141] 지금은 함께 저녁식사를 준비하고 있어요. 우리는 갈비를 먹을 거에요. 아버지는 마당에서 갈비를 굽고 있고 어머니는 부엌에서 상추를 씻고 있어요. 오빠는 엄마 옆에서 양념장[142]을 만들고 있고 나는 상을 차리고 있어요. 모두 즐거운 얼굴로 식사준비를 하니까 정말 좋아요. 식사 후에는 같이 카드 게임을 할 거에요.

---

129 생신+상 생신 is the honorific form of 생일. 상 means *table*. [생신쌍]
130 hobby, hobbies
131 와 같이 = 하고 같이 together with
132 by chance; 우연히 ~하다 happen to do something
133 a member of society, someone who finishes one's schooling and has a job
134 a detective
135 an incident, accident, case
136 생기다 to happen, come into being
137 출동하다 [출똥아다] mobilize (for an investigation)
138 a trading company
139 출장 [출짱]을 가다 to go on a business trip
140 this year
141 gather in one place
142 sauce

노래할까요?

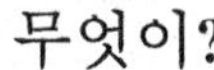

무엇이?

무엇이 무엇이 똑같을까?
젓가락 두 짝이 똑같아요.

무엇이 무엇이 똑같을까?
내 신발 두 짝이 똑같아요.

무엇이 무엇이 똑같을까?
쌍둥이 두 명이 똑같아요.

(Continue the song with your own pairs!)

Chapter 6 Review Exercises

Exercise 1. You be the teacher!
Circle one (or two) error(s) in each sentence and correct it. The error can be spelling, conjugation, or incorrect use of markers or words or expressions.

1) 주말에는 학교에 공부하로 안 가요.
2) 와, 배불러다!
3) 추원 날에는 무슨 옷을 입을까요? (날: day)
4) 우리 언니는 졸업하면 뉴욕에서 살고 싶어요. (졸업하다: graduate)
5) 그 영화는 별로 재미 있어요.
6) 배가 불르면 더 먹지 마세요.
7) 다음 학기에도 한국어를 들어고 싶어요.
8) 내일 세 시에 친구하고 도서관에 마날 거에요.
9) 한국 밥은 숟가락으로, 반찬은 젓가락으로 먹어돼요.
10) 그 한국 친구한테 얼마나 자주 만나요?
11) 우리 오빠가 자주 해는 운동은 야구에요.
12) 재가 제일 좋아하는 선생님은 한국어 선생님이에요!
13) 저는 감기에 걸려면 학교에 오지 안을 거에요.
14) 그 식당에 전화 안 합시다. (Let's not call that restaurant).
15) 점심을 사 먹었기 때문에 배가 고팠어요.
16) 잤기 전에 이빨을 닦았어요.

Exercise 2. Translate the following sentences from Korean to English.

1) 거기는 맛있는 한국 음식을 파는 가게도 많고, 컴퓨터를 쓸 수 있는 PC 방도 있어요.
2) 저는 잘 몰라요. 외국 사람을 많이 만나는 사람한테 물어 보세요.
3) 그 옷 입어 보고 말라 보이면 사세요.
4) 그래도 전보다는 몸이 훨씬 더 좋아졌어요.
5) 일찍 자고 일찍 일어나면 감기 몸살이 곧 나을 거에요.
6) **비타민**을 먹기 전에는 물을 많이 마시세요.

7) 목은 아직도 조금 부어 있지만, 계속 약을 먹어서 감기가 거의 다 나았어요.

8) 아픈데 왜 일어나 있어요?

9) 밖에 나가서 셋이 같이 얘기하면 기분이 좋아질 거에요.

10) 심심하면 공원까지 천천히 걸어 보세요.

11) 청바지에 빨간 물을 들이면 청바지가 빨개질까요 보라색이 될까요?

12) 한국어를 잘 하고 싶으면 매일 한국 사람하고 얘기해 보세요. 한국 텔레비전을 보세요. 한국 노래를 들어보세요...

13) 이 빨간 셔츠는 **로빈** 씨한테 예뻐보일 거에요. 입어 보세요.

14) 저는 매일 집에서 학교까지 걸어(가)요.

15) 스트레스를 받으면, 클래식 음악을 들어 보세요.

16) 저는 여기에서 다섯 시까지 공부할 거에요.

17) 잘 들으세요.

18) 저는 스노콰미에서 스키 타 봤어요. 재미 있었어요.

19) 많이 먹고 운동 안 하면 뚱뚱해질 거에요.

20) 내일 우리 집에 친구들이 올 거에요. 오늘 청소해야 돼요.

21) 한국 음식은 숟가락하고 젓가락으로 먹어야 돼요.

Exercise 3. Translate the following sentences from English to Korean. (Please pay attention to spelling, conjugation, and word choice.)

1) What kind of clothes do you usually wear on days when you go to school?

2) What food can you make best?

3) Let's not sell that brown swimming suit.

4) I have no place to go for this summer vacation.

5) I have something to tell you.

6) Do you wanna go to California by plane or by train?

7) I am going to catch a cold if you don't close that window.

8) Shall we look for a cheap movie ticket in the vicinity of school?

9) Do you want to find a girlfriend? First, try becoming a good friend to your friends.

쉬어갑시다!
LET'S TAKE A BREAK!

What's your sign?
Or should I say,
"What's your *belt*?"

CHAPTER 6.5 무슨 띠에요?

What is your sign?

동물 / 띠	**Animal / zodiac signs**
토끼	**rabbit**
용	**dragon**
뱀	**snake**
말	**horse**
양	**sheep**
원숭이	**monkey**
닭	**chicken**
개	**dog**
돼지	**pig (or boar)**
쥐	**rat (or mouse)**
소	**cow**
호랑이 = 범	**tiger**
고양이	**cat**
곰	**bear**
새끼	**baby (animal)**
강아지	**puppy**
송아지	**calf**
망아지	**foal**
병아리	**chick**

Do you remember 허리띠 from Chapter 5? 띠 basically means *a band* (e.g. 머리띠, 허리띠). In fact, if you ask the question "무슨 띠에요?" of a person who is taking 태권도 lessons, your question means "What belt are you?"

Culture Point What kind of animal are you?

In the Korean culture, animals are often used to describe a person's character.

곰 is thought to be a slow dumb animal, 소 is considered a diligent and hard-working animal. 고양이 is independent but rather selfish, while 호랑이 is fierce and courageous.

개 plays an ambivalent role. It is either a faithful best friend to humans, or sometimes a lowly bastard (개 is thus used as a pejorative prefix to nouns). Here are some expressions involving animals.

토끼 같은 자식들	cute, abundant off-spring
호랑이 같은 마누라	scary and strict wife
여우 같은 여자	attractive but sly woman
늑대 같은 남자	man mainly interested in womanizing

So be careful when you use the term *foxy* in Korean. 여우같은 여자 is definitely **not** a compliment!

Good work this year, kids!
Soon you'll be speaking Korean like a pro!

Are you anticipating a second-year Korean class? How much of the following dialogues and reading can you understand? Pick up a Korean-English dictionary and test it out!

대화 1  **내일 아침 8 시에 선배님 집 앞으로 가겠습니다.**

경미: 선배,[143] 내일 스키 타러 같이 안 가시겠습니까? 상민이도 같이 갈 건데요.

영수: 글쎄. 요새 일이 많아서 좀 피곤한데.

경미: 가십시다! 겨울도 다 끝나가는데. 선배가 많이 피곤하시면 제가 운전하겠습니다.[144]

영수: 너 어제 운전면허[145] 따지 않았니? 그 산길[146]을 운전할 수 있어?

경미: 문제없습니다. 내가 운전 연습을 얼마나 많이 했는데요.

영수: 너 운전 실력[147] 정말 믿어도 되냐?

경미: 선배, 내 운전 실력을 너무 무시하지 마십시오![148]

영수: 알았어, 알았어. 믿을께.[149]

경미: 그럼 내일 아침 8 시에 선배 집 앞으로 가겠습니다.

영수: 그래, 내일 보자.

대화 2  **아홉 시 이후에 전화를 걸면 괜찮을 거에요.**

칼리: 다녀왔어요.[150]

경희: **칼리** 씨, 왔어요? 아까 3 번이나 **동국** 씨한테서 전화왔어요.

칼리: 무슨 일인데요?

경희: 글쎄요. 한 번 전화해 보세요.

칼리: 그래요? 그런데 벌써 11 시가 넘었네요. 지금 전화하면 실례지요?

경희: 그럼요. 남의 집에 너무 늦게 전화하면 안 돼요. 내일 아침 일찍 전화하세요.

칼리: 아침 몇 시 이후에 전화를 걸면 돼요?

경희: 아마 9 시 이후에 전화를 걸면 괜찮을 거에요.

---

143 선배 a senior, an elder
144 운전하다 to drive
145 운전면허 driver's license
146 산길 mountain path
147 실력 ability, capability, competence
148 무시하다 to ignore, disregard
149 믿다 to believe, trust
150 I'm home!

대화 3  **네, 꼭 한 번 먹어 보고 싶어요.**

기원: 떡볶이 너무 맛있죠? 이 집 떡볶이가 이 동네에서는 제일 맛있어요.

앤디: 네, 정말 맛있어요.

기원: 와, 이제 **앤디** 씨 매운 음식 잘 먹네요.

앤디: 네, 저는 이제 매운 음식을 아주 좋아해요. 매운 음식은 처음에는 먹기 힘들지만 자꾸 먹으면 나중에는 익숙해져요.

기원: 그럼 **앤디** 씨, 다음 번에는 매운탕을 먹어 볼래요?

앤디: 네! 꼭 한 번 먹어보고 싶어요.

기원: 정말 자신있어요?[151] 매운탕은 떡볶이보다 훨씬 매운데.

앤디: 네, 정말 자신있어요.

대화 4  **여기서부터 서울역까지 걸어서 얼마나 걸려요?**

상민: 실례합니다. 서울역은 여기서 어떻게 가지요?

행인: 저기 육교[152]가 보이죠? 여기서 저 육교를 향해서 걸어가서 길 모퉁이[153]에서 오른쪽으로 도세요.[154] 그럼 서울역이 보일 거에요.

상민: 길 모퉁이오른쪽에 서울역이 있나요?

행인: 아니오. 길 모퉁이에서 오른쪽으로 돌면 맞으편[155]이 서울역이에요.

상민: 그럼 길건너 편인가요?

행인: 맞아요. 지하도[156]로 건너가면 돼요.

상민: 여기서부터 서울역까지 걸어서 얼마나 걸려요?

행인: 걸어서 한 20분 정도 걸려요.

---

[151] 자신있다 to be confident
[152] 육교 an overpass, an overbridge
[153] 길 모퉁이 a corner of street
[154] 돌다 to turn
[155] 맞은편 the opposite side, the other side
[156] 지하도 an underpass

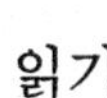  날씨가 맑아질 것같아서 다행이다.

내일은 후배인 **경미**하고 **상민**이와 함께 스키장에 놀러 가기로 했다. 내가 피곤해하니까 **경미**가 자기가 운전한다고 하면서 같이 가자고 했다. **경미**는 어제 운전면허를 따서 아직 운전이 서투를 것 같아서 걱정이다. 스키장에 가는 길은 운전이 쉽지 않다. 게다가 요즘 날씨가 나쁘니까. 내가 불안해하니까 **경미**는 조금 기분 나빠하면서 자기의 운전 실력을 무시하지 말라고 했다. 사실 내일 가는 스키장은 서울에서 제일 가까운 곳이니까 **경미** 혼자 운전할 수 있을 것이다. 날씨를 확인하려고[157] 일기예보를 들어 보았더니 내일은 날씨가 맑아질 것이라고 한다. 정말 다행이다.

You learned "-어하다" as an ending that expresses a third person's feelings. To be more precise,
"-어하다" can be said to *objectify* one's feelings as if you are observing it as a third party. In literary critiques, this is called "God's eye view" or "bird's eye view":
그 사람은 기분 나빠했다.

One can also use it to *objectify* oneself in story-telling. Translating the difference is a bit difficult, but you can probably say *when I acted like… when it was obvious that I was…*

내가 피곤해하니까…
내가 불안해하니까…

The flip-side also works. If you want to express your utter confidence that a third person (not you or your listener) feels such and such, you can say things like:

네가 그러면 걔가 기분 나쁠 거야. If you do that, he'll be ticked off (I can assure you).
걔 지금 심심해. He is bored (I can tell).

[157] in order to check

Cumulative Glossary (volumes I and II)

a little, a little bit 조금/좀 [쪼금/ 쫌] *Ch3 L12 vocab Ch4 L14 vocab*
a lot 많이 (adv.); 많아요 많다 [만타] *Ch3 L11 vocab*
a month ago 한 달 전에 *Ch3 L12 vocab*
A.M. (around 7 A.M. ~ 11 A.M.) 오전 *Ch1.5 B vocab*
about, approximately 쯤 *Ch 2 L8 vocab*
acupuncture 침을 놓아요 놓다 *Ch6 L23 point*
achy (have a body-ache; catch a cold) 몸살에 걸려요 몸살에 걸리다 *Ch6 L23 vocab*
across 건너편, 맞은 편 *Ch1 L4 vocab*
act like one is so great 잘난 척해요, 잘난 체해요 하다 *Ch5 L20 vocab*
adjective 형용사 *bonus*
adult 어른 *Ch5 L18 vocab*
adverb 부사 *bonus*
again 다시 *bonus*
again, what else (adverb) 또 *Ch1 L3 vocab Ch4 L16 vocab*
age, *counter* 살 *Ch3.5 vocab*
ago, before 전에 *Ch6 L22 other*
ago: a little while ago, a few minutes ago 조금 전에 (좀 전에) *Ch 5 L20 vocab*
ago: a long time ago, in the olden days 옛날에, 예전에 *Ch 5 L20 vocab*
ago: a while ago 아까 *Ch 5 L20 vocab*
air-conditioner 에어콘 *Ch 2 L5 point*
airplane 비행기 *Ch6 L24 point*
airplane ticket 비행기 표 *Ch6 L24 vocab*
alcoholic beverages 술 *Ch4 L16 vocab*
all 다 *Ch3 L12 vocab Ch4 L14 vocab*
all together (adv.) 모두 *Ch2.5 vocab*
allergy, have an ... 앨러지가 있어요 앨러지가 있다 *Ch6 L23 vocab*
all-nighter, pull an ... (stay up all night) 밤을 새워요 밤을 새우다 *Ch6 L23 vocab*
almost 거의 *Ch 2 L7 vocab*
almost all 거의 다 *Ch3 L12 vocab*
aloof (reserved) 새침해요 새침하다 *Ch5 L19 vocab*
already 벌써 *Ch3 L12 vocab*
also (noun particle) ~도 *Ch1 L3 vocab*
always 항상 *Ch 2 L7 vocab*
American (person) 미국 사람 *Prelim. I vocab*
among, between, relationship 사이 *Ch5 L20 vocab*
among (in comparison) 중에 *Ch5 L20 vocab*
anchovies 멸치 *Ch4 L14 vocab*
anchovies, salted, fried ... 멸치볶음 *Ch4 L16 point*
and (for Nouns; *spoken*); with ~(이)랑 *Ch4 L15 vocab*
and verb connector ~고 *Ch3 L9 other*
and conjunction 그리고 *Ch 2 L8 other*
and (for Nouns) ~하고 *Ch1 L3 vocab*
and, but...(conjunction)그런데 (shortened form: 근데) *Ch 5 L17 vocab*
and so; so, but, and... ~(으)ㄴ데 (adj.), ~는데 (verbs) *Ch5 L17 other*
and then verb connector ~고 나서 *Ch3 L9 other*
angry (feel angry) 화가 나다 화가 나다 *Ch6 L22 vocab*
angry, get ... at 화를 내요 화를 내다 *Ch6 L22 vocab*
ankle 발목 *Ch 5 L17 vocab*
animal, *counter for* 마리 *Ch3.5 vocab Ch4 L14 vocab*
annoyed, get ... at 짜증을 내다 짜증을 내다 *Ch6 L22 vocab*
annoyed 짜증이 나요 짜증이 나다 *Ch6 L22 vocab*
anybody, anyone 아무나 *Ch 5 L17 point*
anything 아무거나 *Ch 5 L17 point*
apartment 아파트 *Ch2 L5 vocab*
apothecary for traditional medicines 한약 *Ch6 L23 point*
appalled 기가 막혀요 기가 막히다 *Ch6 L22 vocab*
appearance 외모 *Ch5 L19 vocab*
apple 사과 *Ch4 L14 vocab*
applies, makes a request 신청해요 신청하다 *Ch6 L24 vocab*
April 사월 *Prelim. H vocab*
armoire 옷장 *Ch5 L18 vocab*
arms 팔 *Ch5 L17 vocab*
around 주위 *Ch1 L4 vocab*
around your eyes 눈가 *Ch6 L24 point*
around your mouth 입가 *Ch6 L24 point*
arrogant 도도해요 도도하다 *Ch5 L19 point*
art 미학 *Ch 2 L8 point*
Art/painting 미술 *Ch 2 L8 supp*
as many as, up to ~(이)나 *Ch3 L12 vocab*
ashamed 창피해요 창피하다 *Ch6 L22 vocab* [챙피하다]
at (time) ~에 *Ch 2 L7 other*
at first 처음에 *Ch5 L20 vocab*
at the end 마지막에 *Ch5 L20 vocab*
August 팔월 *Prelim. H vocab*
aunt on father's side 고모 *Ch2.5 vocab*
aunt on mother's side 이모 *Ch2.5 vocab*
Auntie (Ma'am) 아주머니, 아줌마 *Ch4 L16 point*
awkward 어색해요 어색하다 *Ch6 L22 vocab*
awkward (for not knowing someone well) 서먹서먹해요 서먹서먹하다 *Ch5 L20 vocab*
baby 아기 [애기] *Ch2.5 vocab*
baby animals 새끼 *Ch6.5*
baby-sits 아기를 봐요 아기를 보다 *Ch2.5 point*
back 등 *Ch5 L17 vocab*
back, lower... ; waist 허리 *Ch5 L17 vocab*
back; behind 뒤 *Ch1 L4 vocab*
back of the hand 손등 *Ch 5 L17 vocab*
bad 나빠요 나쁘다 *Ch3 L11 vocab*
bad mood, in a ... 기분이 나빠요 나쁘다 *Ch5 L19 vocab*
bag 가방 *Ch1 L2 vocab*

bag, counter for 봉지 *Ch3.5 vocab*
ball field 운동장 *Ch2 L5 vocab*
banana 바나나 *Ch4 L14 vocab*
bank 은행 *Ch2 L5 vocab*
barbecue (verb) 구워요 굽다 (ㅂ-irr.) *Ch4 L15 vocab*
barbecued beef 불고기 *Ch4 L15 vocab*
barbecued beef ribs 갈비 *Ch4 L15 vocab*
barber shop 이발소 *Ch5 L17 vocab*
bare handed 맨손으로 *Ch5 L17 point*
bare naked 발가벗었어요 발가벗다 *Ch5 L17 point*
bare-foot 맨발로 *Ch5 L17 point*
barely 별로 *Ch 2 L7 vocab*
barley tea 보리차 *Ch4 L16 vocab*
baseball, plays ... 야구해요 야구하다 *Ch 2 L6 vocab*
basement 지하실 *Ch6 L24 point*
basketball, plays ... 농구해요 농구하다 *Ch 2 L6 vocab*
bathe 목욕해요 목욕하다 [모교카다] *Ch 2 L6 vocab*
bathroom 목욕탕 *Ch5 L18 vocab*
bathtub 욕조 *Ch5 L18 vocab*
be how 어때요 (irregular) 어떻다 *Ch3 L11 vocab*
beach 바닷가 *Ch6 L24 point*
bean sprouts 콩나물 *Ch4 L13 vocab*
bean, black bean 콩 *Ch4 L13 vocab*
bear 곰 *Ch6.5*
beard 수염 *Ch5 L17 vocab*
beautiful 아름다워요 아름답다 (ㅂ-irr.) *Ch5.5*
because ~(으)니까 *Ch4 L14 other*
because, it's so ... ~어서 그래요 그렇다 *Ch6 L21 other*
because it is (for the verb *be*) 이라서 *Ch4 L13 other*
because of 때문에 *Ch6 L21 other*
become (suitable, sufficient) 돼요; 되어요 (written) 되다 *Ch5 L17 other*
becomes ADJECTIVE ~어져요 ~어지다 *Ch6 L21 focus*
before 전에 *Ch 5 L20 vocab*
beef 소고기 *Ch4 L13 vocab*
beef rib soup 갈비탕 *Ch4 L15 vocab*
beef tripe soup 설렁탕 *Ch4 L16 point*
beer 맥주 *Ch4 L16 vocab*
before, ago 전에 *Ch6 L22 other*
before doing ... -기 전에 *Ch3 L10 other*
behind; back 뒤 *Ch1 L4 vocab*
beige 미색 *Ch4.5*
belly 배 *Ch5 L17 vocab*
below 아래 *Ch1 L4 vocab*
belt 벨트, 허리띠 *Ch5 L18 point*
beside; next to 옆 *Ch1 L4 vocab*
best (one) 최고 *Ch5 L20 vocab*
between 사이 *Ch1 L4 vocab Ch5 L20 vocab*
beverages 음료수 *Ch4 L16 vocab* [음뇨수]
bicycle 자전거 *Ch1 L3 vocab*
big 커요 크다 *Ch3 L11 vocab*
bill (in a restaurant) 계산서 *Ch4 L16 vocab*
Biology 생물학 *Ch 2 L8 supp*
bird 새 *Ch6 L24 vocab*
birthday 생일 *Prelim. H vocab*

bitter 써요 쓰다 *Ch4 L15 vocab*
black 까만색 *Ch4.5*
black goat 흑염소 *Ch6 L23 point*
black pepper 후추 *Ch4 L14 vocab*
black pepper powder 후춧가루 *Ch4 L14 vocab*
bland; not salty or spicy 싱거워요 싱겁다 (ㅂ-irr.) *Ch4 L15 vocab*
blond 금발, 금발 머리 *Ch5 L17 vocab*
blue 파란색 *Ch4.5*
blunt (curt, not sociable) 무뚝뚝해요 무뚝뚝하다 *Ch5 L19 point*
boat, ship 배 Ch6 L24 vocab
body 몸 *Ch5 L17 vocab*
body-ache, have a ... (be achy; catch a cold) 몸살에 걸려요 몸살에 걸리다 *Ch6 L23 vocab*
boil (intr) 끓여요 끓이다 *Ch4 L13 vocab*
book 책 *Ch1 L2 vocab*
bookstore 서점 *Ch2 L5 vocab*
boots 부츠 *Ch5 L18 point*
bored 심심해요 심심하다 *Ch5 L19 vocab*
bottle 병 *Ch3.5 vocab Ch4 L16 vocab*
bowl 그릇, 공기 (*counter*) *Ch4 L16 vocab Ch3.5 vocab*
bowl for rice 공기, 밥 그릇 *Ch4 L13 point*
bowl for soup 국그릇 *Ch4 L13 point*
box, *counter* 상자 *Ch3.5 vocab*
braggart, show-off (character nickname) 허풍쟁이 *Ch5 L20 point*
brain (character nickname); PhD 박사 *Ch5 L20 point*
bread 빵 *Ch4 L13 vocab*
break (from school); vacation 방학 *Ch6 L24 vocab*
breaks (e.g., a glass) 깨요 깨다 *Ch3 L10 vocab*
bright (vs. *dark)* 밝아요 밝다 *Ch5.5* [밝다, 박다]
bright blue 새파란 *Ch5 L18 point*
bright red 새빨간 *Ch5 L18 point*
bright, central yellow 샛노란 *Ch5 L18 point*
British (person) 영국 사람 *Prelim. I vocab*
broil 구워요 굽다 (ㅂ-irr.) *Ch4 L15 vocab Ch5.5*
broiled meat or fish 구이 *Ch4 L13 point*
broiled or barbequed over open fire 불~ *Ch4 L13 point*
brother, female's older brother 오빠 *Ch2.5 vocab*
brother, female's older brother who is older than another older brother 큰 오빠 *Ch2.5 vocab*
brother, female's older brother who is younger than another brother 작은 오빠 *Ch2.5 vocab*
brother, male's older brother who is younger than another brother 작은 형 *Ch2.5 vocab*
brother, male's older brother 형 *Ch2.5 vocab*
brother, male's older brother who is older than another older brother 큰형 *Ch2.5 vocab*

brother, younger brother 남동생 *Ch2.5 vocab*
brothers, male siblings 형제 *Ch2.5 vocab*
brown 밤색 *Ch4.5*
bug-eyed (appearance nickname) 왕눈이 *Ch5 L20 point*
building 건물, 빌딩 *Ch1 L4 vocab*
bunches of (flowers) *counter* 다발 *Ch3.5 vocab*
bunches of (vegetables) *counter* 단 *Ch3.5 vocab*
bundle, *counter* 단 *Ch 4 L13 vocab*
bus 버스 *Ch1 L3 vocab*
Business and Administration (study) 경영학 *Ch 2 L8 supp*
busy 바빠요 바쁘다 *Ch3 L11 vocab*
but, and... (conjunction) 그런데 (shortened form: 근데) *Ch 5 L17 vocab*
but; so, but, and... ~(으)ㄴ데 (adj.), ~는데 (verbs) *Ch5 L17 other*
but verb connector ~지만 *Ch3 L9 other*
but conjunction 그렇지만 *Ch 2 L8 other* [그러치만]
butter 버터, 빠다 *Ch4 L14 vocab*
buys, purchases 사요 사다 *Ch3 L10 vocab*
by oneself 혼자 *Ch2 L5 vocab*
cabbage 양배추 *Ch4 L13 vocab*
cafeteria; diner 식당 *Ch2 L5 vocab*
cake 케이크 *Ch4 L14 point*
calf 송아지 *Ch6.5*
calls (out); sings; (stomach) be full 불러요 부르다 (르 irr.) *Ch4 L16 vocab*
camera 카메라 *Ch1 L2 vocab*
can't 못 *Ch3 L9 other*
Canada 캐나다 *Prelim. I vocab*
Canadian (person) 캐나다 사람 *Prelim. I vocab*
candy 사탕 *Ch1 L3 vocab*
care-taking, tending others' comfort well 싹싹해요 싹싹하다 *Ch5 L19 point*
carrot 당근, 홍당무 *Ch4 L13 vocab*
cat 고양이 *Ch2.5 vocab*
catches a bus 잡아요 잡다 *Ch3 L9 vocab*
catches a cold 감기에 걸려요 감기에 걸리다 *Ch6 L23 vocab*
CD (compact disk) 시디 *Ch1 L3 vocab* [씨디]
cellular phone 핸드폰 *Ch1 L3 vocab*
chair 의자 *Ch1 L1 vocab*
chalkboard 칠판 *Ch1 L1 vocab*
change of focus ~은/는 *Ch2 L5 other*
chatterbox (character nickname) 수다쟁이 *Ch5 L20 point*
cheap 싸요 싸다 *Ch6 L24 vocab*
check, bill (in a restaurant) 계산서 *Ch4 L16 vocab*
check into the hospital 입원을 해요 입원을 하다 *Ch6 L23 vocab*
check out of the hospital 퇴원을 해요 퇴원을 하다 *Ch6 L23 vocab*
check-up, get a... ; (get a medical examination) 진찰을 받아요 진찰을 받다 *Ch6 L23 vocab*
check-up, give a ...; give a medical examination 진찰을 해요 진찰을 하다 *Ch6 L23 vocab*
Chemistry 화학 *Ch 2 L8 supp*
chewing gum 껌 *Ch1 L3 vocab*
chewy, tough (of food) 질겨요 질기다 *Ch4 L13 vocab*
chick 병아리 *Ch6.5*
chicken (live animal) 닭 (live); 닭고기 (meat) *Ch6.5*
child (children) 아이, 애 *Ch5 L18 vocab*
children 아이들/애들 *Ch2.5 vocab*
chilly 쌀쌀해요 쌀쌀하다 *Ch6 L21 vocab*
chin (jaws) 턱 *Ch5 L17 vocab*
China 중국 *Prelim. I vocab*
Chinese (language) 중국어 *Prelim. I vocab*
Chinese (person) 중국 사람 *Prelim. I vocab*
chips, crackers, cookies 과자 *Ch4 L14 point*
chocolate 초컬릿, 초컬렛, 초콜렛, 초콜릿 *Ch2 L4 vocab Ch4 L14 point*
chops 썰어요 썰다 *Ch4 L13 vocab*
chopsticks 젓가락, 젓갈 *Ch4 L13 point Ch4 L15 vocab*
class (course) 수업 *Ch 2 L8 vocab*
classroom 교실 *Ch1 L1 vocab Ch6 L24 point*
clean (adjective) 깨끗해요 깨끗하다 *Ch5.5* [깨끄태요]
cleans (house, rooms) 청소해요 청소하다 *Ch 2 L6 vocab*
clear 맑아요 맑다 *Ch6 L21 vocab*
clear noodles 당면 *Ch4 L13 vocab*
clear noodles with seasoned vegetables 잡채 *Ch4 L15 vocab*
clerk, employee 종업원 *Ch 4 L16 supp. vocab*
climbs mountains 등산해요 등산하다 *Ch 2 L6 vocab*
clock, watch 시계 *Ch5 L18 vocab*
clock, watch 시계 *Ch1 L1 vocab* [시게]
close (nearby) 가까워요 가깝다 (ㅂ-irr.) *Ch5.5 Ch6 L24 vocab*
close (be good friends with) 친해요 친하다 *Ch5 L20 vocab*
closes 닫아요 닫다 *Ch3 L9 vocab*
clothes, *counter for* 벌 *Ch3.5 vocab*
clothing 옷 *Ch5 L18 vocab*
cloudy 구름이 꼈어요 구름이 끼다 *Ch6 L21 vocab*
coffee shop 커피숍 *Ch2 L5 vocab*
cold (illness) 감기 *Ch6 L23 vocab*
cold (item) 차가워요 차갑다 (ㅂ-irr.) *Ch4 L15 vocab* [차가워요, 차거워요]
cold (weather, feeling) 추워요 춥다 (ㅂ-irr.) *Ch6 L21 vocab*
cold chewy noodles 냉면 *Ch4 L15 vocab*
cold water 냉수 *Ch4 L16 vocab*
college student 대학생 *Ch 2 L8 vocab*
Come on in! 어서 오세요 오다 *Ch4 L16 vocab*
comes 와요 오다 *Ch3 L10 vocab*
comes home, comes in 들어와요 들어오다 *Ch3 L10 vocab*

comes in order to ~(으)러 와요 오다 *Ch4 L14 other*
comes out(side) 나와요 나오다 *Ch3 L10 vocab*
comfortable 편해요 편하다 *Ch3 L11 vocab*
command (polite command) ~(으)세요 *Ch4 L14 focus*
command (familiar) ~어라 *Ch4 L13 other*
computer 컴퓨터 *Ch1 L1 vocab*
computer lab 컴퓨터 랩 *Ch2 L5 vocab*
Computer Science 컴퓨터 공학 *Ch 2 L8 supp*
computers, cars *counter* 대 *Ch3.5 vocab*
consonant 자음 *Prelim. D vocab*
consonant at end of written syllable 받침 *Prelim. D vocab*
constipation 변비 *Ch6 L23 point*
continually, continuously 계속 *Ch6 L21 vocab*
continues 계속돼요 계속되다 *Ch6 L21 vocab*
convenient 편리해요 편리하다 *Ch3 L11 vocab* [펼리애요]
conversation, start a ... 말을 걸어요 말을 걸다 *Ch5 L20 vocab*
cooked rice (meal) 밥 *Ch4 L13 vocab*
cookies, crackers, chips 과자 *Ch1 L3 vocab Ch4 L14 point*
cooks 요리해요 요리하다 *Ch 2 L6 vocab*
cools down 식어요 식다 *Ch4 L15 vocab*
copier 복사기 *Ch1 L1 supp*
corn tea (often called "물") 옥수수차 *Ch4 L16 vocab*
correct, right 맞아요 맞다 *Ch3 L11 vocab*
coughs (lit. *coughs come out*) 기침이 나와요, 기침이 나요, 기침을 해요 기침이 나오다 *Ch6 L23 vocab*
country 나라 *Prelim. I vocab*
counts 세요 세다 [세다, 시다] *Ch3 L10 vocab* [셔요], [세요]
couple, pair, *counter for* people, animals 쌍 *Ch3.5 vocab*
cousin 사촌 *Ch2.5 vocab*
cow ("ox") 소 *Ch6.5*
cow feet (food) 우족 *Ch4 L16 point*
cow tongue (food) 혀밑구이 *Ch4 L16 point*
crackers, chips, cookies 과자 *Ch1 L3 vocab Ch4 L14 point*
crafty (jealous) 심술쟁이 *Ch5 L20 point*
credit card 신용카드, 크레딧 카드, 크레디트 카드 *Ch1 L3 vocab*
cries 울어요 울다 *Ch3 L9 vocab*
cubed icicle radish Kimchi 깍뚜기 *Ch4 L15 point*
cucumber 오이 *Ch4 L13 vocab*
cucumber Kimchi 오이 소배기 *Ch4 L15 point*
cup 컵 *Ch3.5 vocab Ch4 L16 vocab*
curt, blunt, not sociable 무뚝뚝해요 무뚝뚝하다 *Ch5 L19 point*
customer, guest 손님 *Ch 4 L16 supplementary vocab*
cute 귀여워요 귀엽다 (ㅂ-irr.) *Ch5.5 Ch5 L19 vocab*
cuts 썰어요 썰다 *Ch4 L13 vocab*
cutting board 도마 *Ch4 L14 vocab*
dad 아빠 *Ch2.5 vocab*
dark 어두워요 어둡다 (ㅂ-irr.) *Ch5.5*
dark orange 주홍색 *Ch4.5*
dates (fruit) 대추 *Ch6 L23 point*
daughter 딸 *Ch2.5 vocab*
dawn, early morning (around 3, 4 A.M. ~ 6 A.M.) 새벽 *Ch1.5 B vocab*
day before yesterday 그제, 그제께 *Ch3 L12 vocab*
day time (around 11:30 A.M. ~ 2:30 P.M.) 점심 *Ch1.5 B vocab*
day(s) of the week 요일 *Ch 2 L8 vocab*
December 십 이월 *Prelim. H vocab*
deep 깊어요 깊다 *Ch 5 L17 vocab*
degrees, What's the temperature? How many ... is it?) 몇 도에요? *Ch6 L21 vocab*
department store 백화점 *Ch2 L5 vocab* [배콰점]
desk 책상 *Ch1 L1 vocab* [책쌍]
diarrhea 설사 *Ch6 L23 point*
diet go on a ... 다이어트해요 다이어트하다 *Ch5 L19 vocab*
different, other, another, the other 다른 다르다 (르-irr.) *Ch4 L16 vocab*
different 달라요 다르다 *Ch3 L11 vocab Ch4 L16 vocab*
difficult (of a person), picky (negative implication) 까다로워요 까다롭다 (ㅂ-irr.) *Ch5 L19 vocab*
difficult 어려워요 어렵다 (ㅂ irr.) *Ch5.5 Ch6 L23 vocab*
diligently, (*work*) hard, whole-heartedly 열심히 *Ch3 L12 vocab*
diner; cafeteria 식당 *Ch2 L5 vocab*
direct object (grammar) 목적어 *bonus*
dirty 더러워요 더럽다 (ㅂ-irr.) *Ch5.5*
disappointed (in someone) 실망해요 실망하다 *Ch6 L22 vocab*
dish 접시 *Ch4 L16 vocab*
dishes (does) 설거지해요 설거지하다 *Ch 2 L6 vocab*
disinterested 재미없어요 재미없다 *Ch5 L19 vocab*
disliked 싫어요 싫다 [실타] *Ch3 L11 vocab*
dislikes 싫어해요 싫어하다 *Ch3 L10 vocab*
dissolves (loosens solves, unties) 풀어요 풀다 *Ch5 L18 vocab*
doctor see a ... (lit. *go to the hospital*) 병원에 가요 병원에 가다 *Ch6 L23 vocab*
doctor 의사 *Ch6 L23 vocab*
does 해요 하다 *Ch 2 L6 vocab*
does that 그래요 그러다 *Ch5 L18 other*
does that (distant) 저래요 저러다 *Ch5 L18 other*
does this 이래요 이러다 *Ch5 L18 other*
doesn't talk much (a quiet person) 말이 없어요 (없다) 말이 적어요 (적다) *Ch5 L19 vocab*
doesn't know 몰라요 모르다 (르-irr.) *Ch4 L16 vocab*
dog 개 *Ch2.5 vocab Ch6.5*
dog soup 보신탕 *Ch6 L23 point*
don't (polite command; negative) ~지 마세요 *Ch4 L14 focus*
door 문 *Ch1 L1 vocab*

dormitory 기숙사 *Ch2 L5 vocab*
dragon 용 *Ch6.5*
draws 그려요 그리다 *Ch3 L10 vocab*
dress 원피스 *Ch5 L18 point*
dress shirt (man's) 와이셔츠 *Ch5 L18 vocab*
dress shoes 구두 *Ch5 L18 vocab*
dress suit (woman's) 투피스 *Ch5 L18 point*
dresser 옷장 *Ch5 L18 vocab*
dried baby Pollack 노가리 *Ch4 L16 point*
dried squid 마른 오징어 *Ch4 L16 point*
dried squid (shredded) 마른 오징어채 *Ch4 L16 point*
drinks 마셔요 마시다 *Ch3 L10 vocab*
drug store 약국 *Ch2 L5 vocab*
drunk, get … 취해요 취하다 *Ch4 L16 vocab*
dry 말라요 마르다 (르-irr.) *Ch4 L16 vocab*
dumbfounded 기가 막혀요 기가 막히다 *Ch6 L22 vocab*
during (TIME) (for the period of …) 동안 *Ch5 L18 vocab Ch5 L20 vocab*
during vacation 방학 때(에) *Ch 2 L7 vocab*
dying of ~어 죽겠어요 어 죽겠다 *Ch5 L19 other*
dying to ~고 싶어 죽겠어요 고 싶어 죽겠다 *Ch5 L19 other*
early 일찍 *Ch 5 L20 vocab*
earrings 귀걸이 *Ch5 L18 vocab*
ears 귀 *Ch5 L17 vocab*
ears are thin (idiom: easily swayed) 귀가 얇아요 얇다 *Ch5 L17 point*
easy 쉬워요 쉽다 (ㅂ-irr.) *Ch5.5 Ch6 L23 vocab*
easy-going, not picky 털털해요 털털하다 *Ch5 L19 vocab*
eats 먹어요 먹다 *Ch3 L9 vocab*
eats (honorific) 들어요, 드세요 들다 *Ch4 L13 vocab*
eats out (in restaurant) 외식해요 외식하다 *Ch 2 L6 vocab*
Economics 경제학 *Ch 2 L8 supp*
eggs 계란, 달걀 *Ch4 L13 vocab* [게란]
eight (native Korean vocab.) 여덟 *Prelim. G vocab*
eight (Sino-Korean vocab.) 팔 *Prelim. G vocab*
eight days 여드레 *Ch6 L22 vocab*
eighth 여덟째 *Prelim. G vocab*
eighty (native Korean vocab.) 여든 *Prelim. G vocab*
electric razor 전기 면도기 *Ch5 L18 vocab*
Electrical Engineering 전자 공학 *Ch 2 L8 supp*
email (address) 이메일 *Ch1 L2 vocab*
ends (intransitive) 끝내요 끝나다 *Ch3 L10 vocab* [끈나요]
ends (transitive) 끝내요 끝내다 *Ch3 L10 vocab* [끈내요]
energetic, lively 팔팔해요 팔팔하다 *Ch5 L19 point*
energetic, outgoing, keen 씩씩해요 씩씩하다 *Ch5 L19 point*
English (language) 영어 *Prelim. I vocab*
enough, OK 됐어요 되다 *Ch5 L17 vocab*
eraser 지우개 *Ch1 L2 vocab*
et cetera 기타 *Ch4 L13 vocab*
even ~도 *Ch5 L17 other*
even if, even though ~어도 *Ch5 L18 other*
even so, in spite of that 그런데도 *Ch 5 L19 vocab*
evening (around 5, 6 P.M. ~ 8 P.M.) 저녁 *Ch1.5 B vocab*
every week, each week 매주 *Ch 2 L8 vocab*
everyday, each day 매일 *Ch 2 L7 vocab*
everything 다 *Ch4 L14 vocab*
excited 신나요 신나다 *Ch6 L22 vocab*
excuse me 실례합니다 실례하다 *Prelim. F vocab*
exercise (sports) 운동해요 운동하다 *Ch 2 L6 vocab*
exists; has 있어요 있다 *Ch1 L1 vocab* [이써요]
expensive 비싸요 비싸다 *Ch6 L24 vocab*
expression 표현 *Ch5 L17 vocab*
extend 연장해요 연장하다 *Ch6 L24 vocab*
eyebrows 눈썹 *Ch5 L17 vocab*
eyelashes 속눈썹 *Ch5 L17 vocab*
eyes 눈 *Ch5 L17 vocab*
eyes are high (idiom: have high standards) 눈이 높아요 높다 *Ch5 L17 point*
face 얼굴 *Ch5 L17 vocab*
face is thick (idiom: have no shame) 얼굴이 두꺼워요 두껍다 (ㅂ-irr.) *Ch5 L17 point*
fall 가을 *Ch6 L21 vocab*
family 가족 *Ch2.5 vocab*
far 멀어요 멀다 *Ch5.5 Ch6 L24 vocab*
far (more/less) (in comparatives) 훨씬 *Ch5 L20 vocab*
fashion plate (character nickname) 멋쟁이 *Ch5 L20 point*
fast 빨라요 빠르다 (르-irr.) *Ch4 L16 vocab*
fat thick, plump 굵어요 굵다 *Ch5 L17 vocab*
fat, plump (of a person) 뚱뚱해요 뚱뚱하다 *Ch5 L19 vocab*
fat fingers, have … 손가락이 굵어요 굵다 *Ch5 L17 vocab*
father 아버지 *Ch2.5 vocab*
fatty (character nickname) 뚱땡이 *Ch5 L20 point*
February 이월 *Prelim. H vocab*
feel that (I think, I feel that, it seems to me) ~는 것같아요 는 것같다 *Ch5 L20 focus*
feet 발 *Ch5 L17 vocab*
feet are wide (idiom: know many people) 발이 넓어요 넓다 Ch5 L17 point
fever, have a … 열이 나요 열이 나다 *Ch6 L23 vocab*
few, a little 적어요 적다 *Ch3 L11 vocab*
field (open field; pasture) 들, 들판 *Ch6 L24 vocab*
fifteen days 보름 *Ch 5 L22 vocab*
fifth 다섯째 *Prelim. G vocab*
fifty (native Korean vocab.) 쉰 *Prelim. G vocab*
fights, has an argument 싸워요 싸우다 *Ch3 L10 vocab*
find out about 알아 봐요 알아 보다 *Ch6 L24 other*

find; look for; withdraw (money) 찾아요 찾다 *Ch3 L9 vocab*
fine (refined) 고와요 곱다 (ㅂ-irr.) *Ch5.5*
fingernails 손톱 *Ch5 L17 vocab*
fingers 손가락 *Ch5 L17 vocab*
finishes 끝내요 (transitive) 끝내다 *Ch3 L10 vocab* [끈내요]
first (before other) 먼저 *Ch5 L20 vocab*
first (for the first time) 처음으로 *Ch5 L20 vocab*
first 첫째 *Prelim. G vocab*
first (day of month) 일일 *Prelim. H vocab*
first time 첫번째 *Prelim. G vocab*
fish (live animal) 물고기 *Ch6 L24 vocab* [물꼬기]
fish (meat) 생선 *Ch4 L13 vocab*
five (native Korean vocab.) 다섯 *Prelim. G vocab*
five (Sino-Korean vocab.) 오 *Prelim. G vocab*
five days 닷새 *Ch6 L21 vocab*
flaky person not serious about their studies (character nickname) 날라리 *Ch 2 L8 point*
flat nose, have a low/… 코가 낮아요 낮다 *Ch5 L17 vocab*
flowers, grapes, counter for 송이 *Ch3.5 vocab*
foal 망아지 *Ch6.5*
food 음식 *Ch4 L15 vocab*
foot, top of 발등 *Ch5 L17 vocab*
foot 발 *Ch5 L17 vocab*
footwear, shoes 신 *Ch5 L18 vocab*
for (the period of) 동안 *Ch6 L21 vocab*
for a long time 오랫동안 *Ch3 L12 vocab*
for a short while; just a minute 잠깐 *Ch3 L12 vocab*
for me (VERB for me) ~어 주세요 어 주다 *Ch6 L21 focus*
forehead 이마 *Ch5 L17 vocab*
forty (native Korean vocab.) 마흔 *Prelim. G vocab*
forty (Sino-Korean vocab.) 사 십 *Prelim. G vocab*
four (native Korean vocab.) 넷, 네 *Prelim. G vocab*
four (Sino-Korean vocab.) 사 *Prelim. G vocab*
four days 나흘 *Ch5 L18 vocab*
four seasons 사 계절 *Ch6 L21 vocab*
fourth 넷째 *Prelim. G vocab*
fox 여우 *Ch6.5 point*
France 프랜스, 불란서, 프랑스, 프랑스 *Prelim. I point*
free time, to have … (adj.) 한가해요 한가하다 *Ch3 L11 vocab*
freeze (intr) 얼어요 얼다 *Ch4 L13 vocab*
freezer 냉동실 *Ch4 L14 vocab*
French (language) 프랑스어, 불어 *Prelim. I vocab*
French (person) 프랑스 사람 *Prelim. I vocab*
Friday 금요일 *Ch1.5 A vocab*
fridge 냉장고 *Ch4 L14 vocab*
fried eggs 계란 후라이 *Ch4 L13 vocab*
friend 친구 *Ch1 L2 vocab* [칭구
friendly, kind (kind) 친절해요 친절하다 *Ch5 L19 vocab*
friends, make many … ; (have good social skills) 사교성이 좋아요 좋다 *Ch5 L20 vocab*
friends (be good friends/close with) 친해요 친하다 *Ch5 L20 vocab*
from (a person) (written) ~에게서 *Ch6 L22 other*
from (a person) (spoken) ~한테서 *Ch6 L21 other*
from (a place) ~에서 *Ch4 L14 other*
from (time) ~부터 *Ch3 L10 other*
from now on 앞으로는, 이제부터는 *Ch4 L14 vocab*
front 앞 *Ch1 L4 vocab*
fruit 과일 *Ch4 L14 vocab*
fruit-made liquor 과일주 *Ch4 L16 vocab*
frustrated (stir-crazy, feel trapped, stifled) 답답해요 답답하다 *Ch5 L19 vocab*
full (have eaten enough) 배가 불러요 부르다 (르-irr.) *Ch4 L16 vocab*
fun 재미있어요 재미있다 *Ch3 L11 vocab*
future, in the …; from now on 앞으로는, 이제부터는 *Ch4 L14 vocab*
gain weight 살이 쪄요 살이 찌다 *Ch5 L19 vocab*
garbage can 쓰레기통 *Ch4 L14 vocab*
garlic 마늘 *Ch4 L14 vocab*
gas stove 가스 레인지 *Ch4 L14 vocab*
genius 천재 *Ch5 L20 point*
German (language) 독일어 *Prelim. I vocab*
German (person) 독일 사람 *Prelim. I vocab*
Germany 독일 *Prelim. I vocab*
get along well with (be on good terms) 사이가 좋아요 좋다 *Ch5 L20 vocab*
get over (e.g. a cold); recover 나아요 낫다 (ㅅ-irr.) *Ch6 L23 vocab*
gets up, gets out of bed 일어나요 일어나다 *Ch3 L10 vocab*
ginger 생강 *Ch4 L14 vocab*
ginseng 인삼 *Ch6 L23 point*
ginseng porridge 삼계탕 *Ch6 L23 point*
ginseng-based liquor 인삼주 *Ch4 L16 vocab*
give 줘요, 주어요 주다 *Ch3 L10 vocab*
glass (of drink) 잔 *Ch4 L16 vocab*
glasses 안경 *Ch5 L18 vocab*
glasses, counter for 잔 *Ch3.5 vocab*
gloves 장갑 *Ch5 L18 vocab*
glum 우울해요 우울하다 *Ch6 L22 vocab*
glutton 먹보 *Ch5 L20 point*
go/come and ~어서 *Ch4 L16 other*
goes 가요 가다 *Ch2 L5 focus*
goes home, enters 들어가요 들어가다 *Ch3 L10 vocab*
goes out(side) 나가요 나가다 *Ch3 L10 vocab*
going to (future) ~(으)ㄹ 거에요 (으)ㄹ 것이다, (으)ㄹ 거다 *Ch4 L13 focus*
gold (color) 금색 *Ch4.5*
gonna (wanna/gonna) ~(으)ㄹ래요 *Ch4 L16 other*
good (well-behaved; a good person) 착해요 착하다 *Ch5 L19 vocab*
good mood, in a … 기분이 좋아요 기분이 좋다 *Ch5 L19 vocab*

good; liked 좋아요 좋다 [조타] *Ch3 L11 vocab*
good-looking (man) 잘 생겼어요 잘 생기다 *Ch5 L19 vocab*
grabs, holds (hands) 잡아요 잡다 *Ch3 L9 vocab*
graduate 졸업해요 졸업하다 *Ch5 L17 vocab*
graduate school 대학원 *Ch2 L5 vocab*
graduate student 대학원생 *Ch 2 L8 vocab*
grandchild 손자 *Ch2.5 vocab*
granddaughter 손녀 *Ch2.5 vocab*
grandfather 할아버지 *Ch2.5 vocab*
grandfather maternal grandfather 외할아버지 *Ch2.5 vocab*
grandfather paternal grandfather 친할아버지 *Ch2.5 vocab*
grandmother 할머니 *Ch2.5 vocab*
grandmother maternal grandmother 외할머니 *Ch2.5 vocab*
grandmother paternal grandmother 친할머니 *Ch2.5 vocab*
grandson 손자 *Ch2.5 vocab*
grapes 포도 *Ch4 L14 vocab*
grates 갈아요 갈다 *Ch4 L13 vocab*
gray 회색 *Ch4.5*
gray hair (lit. *white hair*) 흰 머리 *Ch5 L17 vocab*
green 초록색 *Ch4.5*
green onion 파 *Ch4 L13 vocab*
green onion pancake 파전 *Ch4 L15 vocab*
greet (say hello, give regards) 인사해요 인사하다 *Ch5 L17 vocab*
grocery store 슈퍼(마켓) *Ch2 L5 vocab*
ground, field 장 *Ch 2 L5 point*
grueling unbearable 괴로워요 괴롭다 (ㅂ-irr.) *Ch5.5*
guest, customer 손님 *Ch 4 L16 supplementary vocab*
guitar 기타 *Ch1 L3 vocab*
gym 체육관 *Ch2 L5 vocab*
hair, head 머리 *Ch5 L17 vocab*
hair salon 머리방, 미용실, 미장원 *Ch5 L17 vocab*
hair strands 머리카락 *Ch5 L17 vocab*
hall -관 *Ch 2 L5 point*
hand 손 *Ch 5 L17 vocab*
hand, back of the 손등 *Ch 5 L17 vocab*
hand is big (idiom: over-generous, go overboard) 손이 커요 크다 *Ch5 L17 point*
hand is spicy (idiom: have a stinging slap) 손이 매워요 맵다 (ㅂ-irr) *Ch5 L17 point*
hand mirror 손거울 *Ch5 L18 vocab* [송꺼울]
handkerchief 손수건 *Ch5 L18 vocab* [손쑤건]
hands 손 *Ch5 L17 vocab*
hangar 비행장 *Ch6 L24 point*
Han'gul; the Korean alphabet *Prelim. D vocab*
happy (contented) 기뻐요 기쁘다 *Ch6 L22 vocab*
happy (excitedly) 즐거워요 즐겁다 (ㅂ-irr.) *Ch5.5 Ch6 L22 vocab*
hard, as in *work hard* 열심히 *Ch3 L12 vocab*
has 있어요 있다 *Ch1 L3 focus*
has (got) to (must, should) ~어야 돼요 어야 되다 *Ch6 L23 focus*
hat 모자 *Ch5 L18 vocab*
he, him (lit, this/that child; *intimate-blunt*) 얘 (this…), 걔 (that …), 쟤 (distant) *Ch5 L20 other*
head, hair 머리 *Ch5 L17 vocab*
head is good (idiom: smart, intelligent) 머리가 좋아요 좋다 *Ch5 L17 point*
headache 두통 *Ch6 L23 point*
heads (of cabbage), counter for 포기 *Ch3.5 vocab*
heavy 무거워요 무겁다 (ㅂ-irr.) *Ch5.5*
help (out) (for another person) 도와줘요 도와주다 *Ch5 L20 vocab*
helps 도와요 돕다 (ㅂ-irr.) *Ch4 L15 vocab*
her/his *intimate-blunt, possessive* (lit. *that child's*) 얘네 (this…), 걔네 (that …), 쟤네 (distant) *Ch5 L20 other*
here 여기 *Prelim. C vocab*
here; right here 요기 *Ch1 L4 point*
high 높아요 높다 *Ch5 L17 point*
high 높아요 높다 *Ch5 L17 vocab Ch5 L21 vocab*
high nose, have a … 코가 높아요 높다 *Ch5 L17 vocab*
highlighter 마커 *Ch1 L1 supp*
hill 언덕 *Ch6 L24 vocab*
hips, buttocks 엉덩이 *Ch5 L17 vocab*
his/ her *intimate-blunt, possessive* (lit. *that child's*) 얘네 (this…), 걔네 (that …), 쟤네 (distant) *Ch5 L20 other*
History 역사학 *Ch 2 L8 supp*
holds (hands); grab 잡아요 잡다 *Ch3 L9 vocab*
holds (hugs, cradles) 안아요 안다 *Ch3 L9 vocab*
holiday 휴일 *Ch6 L24 vocab*
homework 숙제 *Prelim. C vocab*
homework (does) 숙제해요 숙제하다 *Ch1 L1 vocab* [숙쩨]
horse 말 *Ch6.5*
hospital 병원 *Ch2 L5 vocab*
hospitalized, be (check into the hospital) 입원을 해요 입원을 하다 *Ch6 L23 vocab*
hot (weather, feeling) 더워요 덥다 (ㅂ-irr.) *Ch6 L21 vocab*
hot (item) 뜨거워요 뜨겁다 (ㅂ-irr.) *Ch4 L15 vocab*
hour 시 *Ch1.5 B vocab*
house, home 집 *Ch2 L5 vocab*
houses, buildings, *counter for* 채 *Ch3.5 vocab*
how (much) 얼마나 *Ch 2 L8 vocab*
how about (shall we, I wonder, should I, do you think) ~(으)ㄹ까요 *Ch6 L24 other*
How is it? 어때요? *Ch3 L11 other*
how many 몇 *Ch1.5 B vocab*
how many times 몇 번 *Ch 2 L8 other* [뻔]

how often 얼마나 자주 *Ch 2 L8 other*
hugs, holds (baby) 안아요 안다 *Ch3 L9 vocab*
humble 겸손해요 겸손하다 *Ch5 L20 vocab*
hundred 백 *Prelim. G vocab*
hundred million 억 *Prelim. G vocab*
hundred thousand 십 만 *Prelim. G vocab*
hungry 배가 고파요 *Ch4 L16 vocab*
hurriedly 어서 *Ch4 L16 vocab*
hurt pride (have one's pride hurt) 자존심 상해요 자존심 상하다 *Ch6 L22 vocab*
hurts; sick 아파요 아프다 *Ch3 L11 vocab*
hypochondria 신경성 *Ch6 L23 point*
I will be obliged to you. (greeting) 잘 부탁합니다, 잘 부탁해요 잘 부탁하다 *Prelim. I point*
I, me (humble) 저 *Ch2 L5 vocab*
I, me (familiar form) 나 *Ch 2 L7 vocab*
ice cream 아이스크림 *Ch1 L3 vocab Ch4 L14 point*
iced water 얼음물 *Ch4 L16 vocab*
icicle radish 무, 무우 *Ch4 L13 vocab*
icicle radish Kimchi 총각김치 *Ch4 L15 vocab Ch4 L15 point*
if/when ~(으)면 *Ch4 L13 other*
if/when it is (for the verb *be*) 이라면 *Ch4 L13 other*
ill, get ... 병이 나요 병이 나다 *Ch6 L23 vocab*
important 중요해요 중요하다 *Ch4 L13 vocab*
imprint, take a picture 찍어요, (사진을) 찍다 *Ch6 L24 vocab*
in order to, goes ~(으)러 가요 (으)러 가다 *Ch4 L14 other*
in, at, on -에 *Ch1 L1 vocab*
incorrect, wrong 틀려요 틀리다 *Ch3 L11 vocab*
indigestion 소화불량 *Ch6 L23 point*
inside 안 *Ch1 L4 vocab*
institution -원 *Ch 2 L5 point*
interested 재미있어요 재미있다 *Ch5 L19 vocab*
introduction 소개 *Prelim. C vocab*
introduction of oneself 자기 소개 *Prelim. C vocab*
is ~ing (action in progress) ~고 있어요 고 있다 *Ch5 L19 other*
is...ing/ed (state of being) ~어 있어요 어 있다 *Ch6 L23 other*
island 섬 *Ch6 L24 vocab*
it is (familiar) (familiar) (이)야 *Ch4 L13 other*
Italian (language) 이탈리아어 *Prelim. I vocab*
Italian (person) 이탈리아 사람 *Prelim. I vocab*
Italy 이탈리아, 이태리 *Prelim. I vocab*
items *counter* 개 *Ch3.5 vocab*
jacket 재키트, 자켓, 자킷 *Ch5 L18 point*
jacket with elastic waist 점퍼 ; (잠바 - non-standard spelling) *Ch5 L18 point*
January 일월 *Prelim. H vocab*
Japan 일본 *Prelim. I vocab*
Japanese (language) 일본어 *Prelim. I vocab*
Japanese (person) 일본 사람 *Prelim. I vocab*
jaws (chin) 턱 *Ch5 L17 vocab*
jealous (crafty) 심술쟁이 *Ch5 L20 point*
jeans (blue jeans) 청바지 *Ch5 L18 vocab*
jogging 조깅 *Ch 2 L6 focus*
jogs 조깅해요 조깅하다 *Ch 2 L6 vocab*
juice 주스 or 쥬스 *Ch1 L3 vocab*
July 칠월 *Prelim. H vocab*
June 유월 *Prelim. H vocab*
junior, someone socially 'below' 아랫사람 *Ch1 L4 vocab*
just a minute; for a short while 잠깐 *Ch3 L12 vocab*
just now 방금 *Ch3 L12 vocab*
karaoke room 노래방 *Ch2 L5 vocab*
kettle 주전자 *Ch 4 L16 vocab*
key 열쇠 *Ch1 L3 vocab* [열쐬, 열쎄]
khaki 카키색 *Ch4.5*
Kimchi 김치 *Ch4 L13 point*
Kimchi made from Napa cabbage 배추김치 *Ch4 L15 vocab*
Kimchi stew 김치찌개 *Ch4 L15 vocab*
kind (friendly) 친절해요 친절하다 *Ch5 L19 vocab*
King Sejong, inventor of Han'gul (Korean alphabet) *Prelim. D vocab*
klutz (character nickname) 칠칠이 *Ch5 L20 point*
knife 칼 *Ch1 L1 supp*
know-it-all (be a ...) 아는 체해요, 아는 척해요 아는 체/척하다 *Ch5 L20 vocab*
knows 알아요 알다 *Ch3 L9 vocab*
Korea 한국 *Prelim. I vocab*
Korea Studies 한국학 *Ch 2 L8 supp*
Korea, South Korea 대한민국 *Prelim. I point*
Korean (language) 한국어 *Prelim. I vocab*
Korean (person) 한국 사람 *Prelim. I vocab*
Korean flag 태극기 *Ch4.5 exercises*
Korean stew 찌개 *Ch4 L13 point*
Koreans living in Japan 재일동포 *Prelim. I point*
Koreans living in US 재미동포 *Prelim. I point*
lacks 없어요 없다 *Ch1 L1 vocab* [업써요]
lake 호수 *Ch6 L24 vocab*
lakeside 호숫가 *Ch6 L24 point*
last (for the last one/time) 마지막으로 *Ch5 L20 vocab*
last (final) 마지막 *Prelim. G vocab*
last (Wednesday) 지난 주 (수요일에) *Ch3 L12 vocab*
last night 지난 밤, 어젯밤 *Ch3 L12 vocab*
last semester/quarter 지난 학기에 *Ch3 L12 vocab*
last week 지난 주에 *Ch3 L12 vocab*
last weekend 지난 주말에 *Ch3 L12 vocab*
last year 지난 해에, 작년에 *Ch3 L12 vocab*
last, past 지난 *Ch3 L12 vocab*
late 늦게 *Ch 5 L20 vocab*
later (some time later) 나중에 *Ch 5 L20 vocab*

later (the same day) 이따가 *Ch5 L20 vocab*
laughs, smiles 웃어요 웃다 *Ch3 L9 vocab*
laundry (does) 빨래해요 빨래하다 *Ch 2 L6 vocab*
lazy (feel lazy, feel bothered) 귀찮아요 귀찮다 *Ch6 L22 vocab*
lazy bum (character nickname) 게으름뱅이 *Ch5 L20 point*
learns, studies 배워요 배우다 *Ch3 L10 vocab*
leaves (departs) 떠나요 떠나다 *Ch3 L10*
leaves (for future use) 둬요; 두어요 (*written*) 두다 *Ch4 L14 vocab* [둬요, 도요]
left side 왼쪽 *Ch1 L4 vocab*
legs 다리 *Ch5 L17 vocab*
lemon-lime soda 사이다 *Ch4 L16 vocab*
less 덜 *Ch5 L20 vocab*
let's ~(으)ㅂ시다 *Ch5 L17 other*
let's *(intimate-blunt)* ~자 *Ch4 L13 other*
let's not ~지 맙시다 *Ch5 L17 other*
letter opener 레터 오프너 *Ch1 L3 vocab*
lettuce 상추 *Ch4 L13 vocab*
library 도서관 *Ch2 L5 vocab*
lies down 누워요 눕다 (ㅂ-irr.) *Ch5.5*
lies down in bed 자리에 누워요 자리에 눕다 (ㅂ-irr.) *Ch6 L23 vocab*
light (vs. *heavy)* 가벼워요 가볍다 (ㅂ-irr.) *Ch5.5*
light (color) 연해요 연하다 *Ch4 L13 vocab*
light blue, sky blue 하늘색 *Ch4.5*
light green, spring green 연두색 *Ch4.5*
like, be NOUN-like ~같은 *Ch4 L16 other*
like (something, someone) ~같이 *Ch5 L20 vocab Ch4 L16 other* [가치]
like (something, someone) ~처럼 *Ch5 L20 vocab*
like so 그렇게 *Ch2.5 vocab* [그러케]
liked; good 좋아요 좋다 [조타] *Ch3 L11 vocab*
likes 좋아해요 좋아하다 *Ch3 L10 vocab*
Linguistics 언어학 *Ch 2 L8 supp*
lips 입술 *Ch5 L17 vocab*
liquid medicine 물약 *Ch6 L23 vocab* [물략]
listen 들어요 듣다 (ㄷ-irr.) *Ch6 L21 vocab*
Literature 문학 *Ch 2 L8 supp*
literature studies 문학 *Ch 2 L8 point*
little while ago, few minutes ago 좀 전에 *Ch 5 L20 vocab*
live 살아요 살다 *Ch3 L9 vocab*
loaves, lumps *counter* 덩어리 *Ch3.5 vocab*
Location particle for activities 에서 *Ch 2 L6 other*
lonely 외로워요 외롭다 (ㅂ-irr.) *Ch5.5 Ch6 L22 vocab*
long 길어요 길다 *Ch4 L14 vocab*
long hair, have ... 머리가 길어요 길다 *Ch5 L17 vocab*
long time ago, in the olden days 옛날에, 예전에 *Ch 5 L20 vocab*
long while, for a ...; for a long time 오래 *Ch4 L13 vocab*
look around, sight-see 구경해요 구경하다 *Ch6 L24 vocab*
look for; find; withdraw (money) 찾아요 찾다 *Ch3 L9 vocab*
looks ADJECTIVE ~어 보여요 어 보이다 *Ch6 L22 other*
looks for 찾아 봐요 찾아 보다 *Ch6 L24 other*
loosens (dissolves, solves, unties) 풀어요 풀다 *Ch5 L18 vocab*
lose weight 살을 빼요 살을 빼다 *Ch5 L19 vocab*
lose weight 살이 빠져요 살이 빠지다 *Ch5 L19 vocab*
loudly 큰 소리로 *Prelim. C vocab*
lounge 휴게실 *Ch6 L24 point*
loves 사랑해요 사랑하다 *Ch 2 L6 vocab*
low 낮아요 낮다 *Ch5 L17 vocab*
low 낮다 *Ch5 L21 vocab*
lucky that ~ (relieved) 다행이에요 다행이다 *Ch6 L22 vocab*
lukewarm 미지근해요 미지근하다 *Ch4 L15 vocab*
lumps ***counter*** 모 *Ch3.5 vocab*
ly ~게 *Ch4 L15 other*
ma'am 아줌마, 아주머니 *Ch4 L16 point*
macho (tough guy style) 터프해요 터프하다 *Ch5 L19 vocab*
magazine 잡지 *Ch1 L3 vocab* [잡찌]
magenta 자주색 *Ch4.5*
main side dishes 주 반찬 *Ch4 L15 vocab*
major 전공 *Ch 2 L8 vocab* [전공, 정공]
make friends with, go out with 사귀어요 사귀다 *Ch5 L19 vocab* [사겨요]
makes 만들어요 만들다 *Ch3 L9 vocab*
make-up (puts on) 화장해요 화장하다 *Ch 2 L6 vocab*
male student 남학생 *Ch1 L1 vocab*
man 남자 *Ch5 L18 vocab*
map 지도 *Ch6 L24 vocab*
March 삼월 *Prelim. H vocab*
market 시장 *Ch4 L14 vocab*
Math 수학 *Ch 2 L8 supp*
may (permission) ~어도 돼요 어도 되다 *Ch5 L19 focus*
May 오월 *Prelim. H vocab*
may not, must not ~(으)면 안돼요 (으)면 안 되다 *Ch5 L19 focus*
meal 밥 *Ch4 L13 vocab*
meat 고기 *Ch4 L13 vocab*
Mechanical Engineering 기계 공학 *Ch 2 L8 supp*
medicine 약; 물약 (liquid); 가루약 (powder); 알약 (pill) *Ch6 L23 vocab* [물략]
medicine, to take ... 약을 먹어요 약을 먹다 *Ch6 L23 vocab*
meets 만나요 만나다 *Ch3 L10 vocab*
meticulous (positive implication) 꼼꼼해요 꼼꼼하다 *Ch5 L19 vocab*
Mexico 멕시코 *Prelim. I point*
middle 가운데 *Ch1 L4 vocab*
milk 우유 *Ch4 L16 vocab*
million 백 만 *Prelim. G vocab*
minute 분 *Ch1.5 B vocab*

mirror 거울 *Ch5 L18 vocab*
Mister! (sir, uncle) 아저씨 *Ch4 L16 point*
mom 엄마 *Ch2.5 vocab*
moment; just a moment; for a short while 잠깐, 잠시 *Ch3 L12 vocab Ch4 L16 vocab*
Monday 월요일 *Ch1.5 A vocab*
Monday through Friday 월-화-수-목-금 *Ch1.5 A vocab*
money 돈 *Ch1 L3 vocab*
monkey 원숭이 *Ch6.5*
month, moon 달 *Ch6 L22 vocab*
mood 기분 *Ch5 L19 vocab Ch6 L22 vocab*
moon 달 *Ch6 L22 vocab, Ch6 L24 vocab*
more 더 *Ch3 L12 vocab Ch5 L20 vocab*
more, one ... time 한 번 더 *Prelim. C vocab*
morning (around 7 A.M. ~ 11 A.M.) 아침 *Ch1.5 B vocab*
most, the ... 제일 *Ch5 L20 vocab*
mother 어머니 *Ch2.5 vocab*
motorcycle ("auto-bike") 오토바이 *Ch1 L3 vocab Ch 2 L5 point*
mountain 산 *Ch6 L24 vocab*
mouse 쥐 *Ch6.5*
mouth 입 *Ch5 L17 vocab*
mouth is short (idiom: eat more snacks than meals) 입이 짧아요 짧다 *Ch5 L17 point*
movie theater 극장, 영화관 *Ch2 L5 vocab*
Mr., Ms. 씨 *Ch1 L2 vocab*
munchy (Literally, my mouth is wondering (about snacks). 입이 궁금해요 궁금하다 *Ch4 L16 vocab*
munchy (Literally, my mouth is bored.) 입이 심심해요 심심하다 *Ch4 L16 vocab*
mushroom 버섯 *Ch4 L13 vocab*
Music 음악 *Ch 2 L8 supp*
mustache 콧수염 *Ch5 L17 vocab*
my (familiar) 내 *Ch 2 L7 other*
my, I (humble) 제 *Ch 2 L7 other*
name 이름 *Ch1 L2 vocab*
Napa cabbage 배추 *Ch4 L13 vocab*
Napa cabbage Kimchi 배추 김치 *Ch4 L15 point*
nature 자연 *Ch6 L24 vocab*
navy blue 남색 *Ch4.5*
neck 목 *Ch5 L17 vocab*
necklace, muffler 목걸이 *Ch5 L18 vocab*
necktie 넥타이 *Ch5 L18 vocab*
needed, necessary 필요해요 필요하다 *Ch3 L11 vocab*
nervous in anticipation, restless, fretful 초조해요 초조하다 *Ch6 L22 vocab*
new 새 *Ch4 L16 vocab*
newspaper 신문 *Ch1 L3 vocab*
next month 다음 달에 *Ch 2 L7 vocab*
next week 다음 주에 *Ch 2 L7 vocab*
next weekend 다음 주말에 *Ch 2 L7 vocab*
next year 내년에 *Ch 2 L7 vocab*
Nice to meet you 만나서 반가워요, 반갑습니다 반갑다 *Prelim. I point*
night (around 10, 11 P.M. ~ 2, 3 A.M.) 밤 *Ch1.5 B vocab*
nine (native Korean vocab.) 아홉 *Prelim. G vocab*
nine (Sino-Korean vocab.) 구 *Prelim. G vocab*
nine days 아흐레, 아흘 *Ch6 L22 vocab*
ninety (native Korean vocab.) 아흔 *Prelim. G vocab*
ninth 아홉째 열째 *Prelim. G vocab*
no 아니오 *Prelim. C vocab*
no fun 재미없어요 재미없다 *Ch3 L11 vocab*
nobody, no one 아무도 *Ch5 L17 other*
nominalizer ~기 *Ch6 L23 other*
noodle strands 국수가락 *Ch5 L17 point*
noodles (Sino-Korean) ~면 *Ch4 L13 point*
noodles 국수 *Ch4 L13 vocab*
North Korea 북한 *Prelim. I point*
North Korea (old term) 북조선 *Prelim. I point*
nose 코 *Ch5 L17 vocab*
nose is high (idiom: snobbish) 코가 높아요 높다 *Ch5 L17 point*
nostrils 콧구멍 *Ch5 L17 vocab*
not 안 *Ch 2 L7 focus*
not busy, have a lot of free time 한가해요 한가하다 *Ch3 L11 vocab*
not really, not very, barely 별로 *Ch 2 L7 vocab*
not tasty 맛이 없어요, 맛없어요 맛이 없다 *Ch4 L15 vocab*
notebook 공책 *Ch1 L2 vocab*
nothing 아무것도 *Ch5 L17 other*
noun 명사 *bonus*
November 십 일월 *Prelim. H vocab*
now 지금 *Prelim. H vocab*
number 숫자 *Prelim. G vocab*
O.K. 괜찮아요 괜찮다 *Prelim. F vocab* [괜차나요, 갠차나요]
O.K., enough 됐어요 되다 *Ch5 L17 vocab*
Object marker 을/를 *Ch 2 L6 other*
October 시월 *Prelim. H vocab*
office, professor's; research room 연구실 *Ch6 L24 point*
office 사무실 *Ch1 L1 vocab Ch6 L24 point*
office, official or government department -국 *Ch 2 L5 point*
off-spring (talking about one's own or derogatory) 자식 *Ch6.5 point*
often, very often 자주 *Ch 2 L7 vocab*
often, well 잘 *Ch 3 L8 vocab*
old (and worn out (item)) 헌 *Ch4 L16 vocab*
olden days, in the 옛날에, 예전에 *Ch5 L20 vocab*
oldest child 맏이 *Ch 2 L6 point* [마지]
oldest son 맏아들, 큰 아들 *Ch2.5 vocab*
on leave (by students) 휴학 *Ch 2 L8 point*
on weekdays 평일에 *Ch 2 L7 vocab*
on weekend(s) 주말에 *Ch 2 L7 vocab*

one (native Korean vocab.) 하나, 한 *Prelim. G vocab*
one (Sino-Korean vocab.) 일 *Prelim. G vocab*
oneself 자기 *Ch5 L20 vocab*
onion 양파 *Ch4 L13 vocab*
on-leave (from school) 휴학 *Ch6 L24 point*
only daughter 외동딸 *Ch2.5 vocab*
only son 외아들/독자 *Ch2.5 vocab*
only, just -만 *Ch3 L10 other*
opens 열어요 열다 *Ch3 L9 vocab*
or (for connecting verbs) ~거나 *Ch6 L21 other*
or (for connecting nouns) ~(이)나 *Ch4 L13 other*
or something like that ~(이)나 *Ch5 L17 other*
orange 주황색 *Ch4.5*
order (food) 주문해요, 시켜요 주문하다, 시키다 *Ch4 L16 vocab*
other, the other, another 다른 다르다 (르-irr.) *Ch4 L16 vocab*
other things (et cetera) 기타 *Ch4 L13 vocab*
others (people) 남 *Ch5 L20 vocab*
our (humble) 저희 *Ch 2 L7 other*
outside 밖 *Ch1 L4 vocab*
over there 저기 *Ch1 L3 vocab*
over there; right over there 조기 *Ch1 L4 point*
overcast 흐려요 흐리다 *Ch6 L21 vocab*
overextend oneself 무리를 해요 무리(를) 하다 *Ch6 L23 vocab*
ox (cow) 소 *Ch6.5*
P.M. (around 1 P.M. ~ 5) 오후 *Ch1.5 B vocab*
pairs of shoes, counter for 켤레 *Ch3.5 vocab*
pajamas 파자마 *Ch5 L18 point*
pale (얼굴이) 창백해요 얼굴이 창백하다 *Ch5 L19 vocab*
pan with two short handles 냄비 *Ch4 L16 vocab*
pancakes, thin, savory Korean … 전 *Ch4 L13 point*
pants 바지 *Ch5 L18 vocab*
paper 종이 *Ch1 L2 vocab*
parents 부모님 *Ch2.5 vocab*
park 공원 *Ch2 L5 vocab*
parking lot 주차장 *Ch2 L5 vocab Ch6 L24 point*
partner 짝 *Prelim. C vocab*
part-time work (does) 아르바이트해요 아르바이트하다 *Ch 2 L6 vocab*
passport 여권 *Ch6 L24 vocab*
past tense -ㅆ어요 *Ch3 L12 focus*
past, last 지난 *Ch3 L12 vocab*
patient 환자 *Ch6 L23 vocab*
pear 배 *Ch4 L14 vocab*
pedestrian's underpass 지하도 *Ch6 L24 point*
pen 펜 *Ch1 L2 vocab*
pencil 연필 *Ch1 L2 vocab*
pencil case, holder 필통 *Ch1 L1 supp*
people *counter* 명 *Ch2.5 vocab Ch4 L14 vocab*
people *counter, honorific* 분 *Ch3.5 vocab Ch4 L14 vocab*
per -에 *Ch 2 L8 other*
per day 하루에 *Ch 2 L8 vocab*
per week 일 주일에 *Ch 2 L8 vocab* [일쭈이레]
person 사람 *Prelim. I vocab*
person (honorific) 분 *Ch1 L2 vocab*
personality 성격 *Ch5 L19 vocab*
pharmacist 약사 *Ch6 L23 vocab*
pharmacist (for traditional medicine) 한의사 *Ch6 L23 point*
pharmacy (for traditional medicine) 한약방 *Ch6 L23 point*
PhD 박사 *Ch5 L20 point*
phone number 전화번호 *Ch1 L2 vocab* [저나버노]
phones 전화해요 전화하다 *Ch 2 L6 vocab*
photo, to take a … 사진 (찍다) *Ch6 L24 vocab*
Physics 물리학 *Ch 2 L8 supp*
picks up 들어요 들다 *Ch4 L13 vocab*
picky difficult (negative implication) 깐깐해요 깐깐하다 *Ch5 L19 vocab*
picture, to take a … 사진 (찍다) *Ch6 L24 vocab*
pie 파이 *Ch4 L14 point*
pieces, slices, counter for 조각, 쪽 *Ch3.5 vocab Ch4 L16 vocab* [조각, 쪼각]
pig 돼지 *Ch6.5*
pig feet (food) 돼지족발 *Ch4 L16 point*
pill 알약 *Ch6 L23 vocab* [알략]
pink 분홍색, 핑크색 *Ch4.5*
pitch black 새까만 *Ch5 L18 point*
place, dependent noun 데 *Ch6 L24 vocab*
place to ~(으)ㄹ 데 *Ch6 L24 other*
plate 접시 *Ch4 L16 vocab*
plays 놀아요 놀다 *Ch3 L9 vocab*
plays (tennis/ guitar) 쳐요 치다 *Ch3 L10 vocab*
please do (polite command) ~(으)세요 *Ch4 L14 focus*
plump 통통해요 통통하다 *Ch5 L19 point*
plural marker 들 *Ch2.5 review*
Political Science 정치학 *Ch 2 L8 supp*
popular (many friends/fans) 인기가 좋아요, 인기가 많아요 좋다 *Ch5 L20 vocab*
pork 돼지고기 *Ch4 L13 vocab*
portable CD player 워크맨 *Ch1 L3 vocab*
possessive, (NOUN's) –의 *Ch1 L4 vocab*
possible, is *not* …; can't ~(으)ㄹ 수 없어요 없다 *Ch5 L20 other*
possible, is … ; can ~(으)ㄹ 수 있어요 (으)ㄹ 수 있다 *Ch5 L20 other*
post office 우체국 *Ch2 L5 vocab*
potato 감자 *Ch4 L13 vocab*
pouty face (character nickname) 삐죽이 *Ch5 L20 point*
powder medicine 가루약 *Ch6 L23 vocab*
prescription, have a … filled 약을 지어요 약을 짓다 (ㅅ-irr.) *Ch6 L23 vocab*
pretty 예뻐요 예쁘다 *Ch3 L11 vocab*
pricks your finger (as medical treatment) 손가락을 따요 따다 *Ch6 L23 point*

printer 프린터 *Ch1 L1 vocab*
probably, it's … ~(으)ㄹ 거에요 (으)ㄹ 것이다, (으)ㄹ 거다 *Ch6 L21 focus*
problem 문제 *Prelim. F vocab*
prognosis give a …(treatment) 치료를 해요 치료를 하다 *Ch6 L23 vocab*
Psychology 심리학 *Ch 2 L8 supp* [심니악]
pull an all-nighter 밤을 새워요 밤을 새우다 *Ch6 L23 vocab*
pumpkin, zucchini, squash 호박 *Ch4 L13 vocab*
puppy 강아지 *Ch2.5 vocab Ch6.5*
purple 보라색 *Ch4.5*
puts (something) in 넣어요 넣다 [너타] *Ch3 L9 vocab* [너~요]
puts on, wears (gloves, glasses, rings, something difficult to put on) 껴요 끼다 *Ch5 L18 vocab*
puts on, wears (a necktie), ties 매요 매다 *Ch5 L18 vocab*
puts on, wears (shoes, socks) 신어요 신다 *Ch5 L18 vocab*
puts on, wears (head gear, glasses, umbrella) 써요 쓰다 *Ch5 L18 vocab*
puts on, wears (clothing on the body) 입어요 입다 *Ch5 L18 vocab*
puts on, wears (a watch, belt, something with a band) 차요 차다 *Ch5 L18 vocab*
puts on, wears (accessories) 해요 하다 *Ch5 L18 vocab*
puts, lets go of 놓아요 놓다 [노타] *Ch3 L9 vocab* [놔요]
quarter/semester 학기 *Ch 2 L8 vocab*
question 질문 *Prelim. C vocab*
question ending (familiar) ~니 *Ch4 L13 other*
quickly 빨리 *Prelim. C vocab, Ch5 L20 vocab*
quiet (person) (doesn't talk much) 말이 없어요, 말이 적어요 말이 없다 *Ch5 L19 vocab*
quiet please 조용히 하세요 조용히하다 *Prelim. F vocab*
rabbit 토끼 *Ch6.5*
raincoat 비옷, 레인코트, 우비 *Ch5 L18 point*
rains 비가 와요 비가 오다 *Ch6 L21 vocab*
rascal (character nickname) 개구쟁이 *Ch5 L20 point*
raw fish 생선회 *Ch4 L16 vocab*
raw meat 육회 *Ch4 L16 vocab*
razor 면도기 *Ch5 L18 vocab*
reads 읽어요 읽다 *Ch3 L9 vocab*
really, truly 정말(로) *Ch3 L12 vocab*
Really. That is so. / Let's do. 그래요 *Prelim. F vocab*
Really? Is that so? 그래요? *Prelim. F vocab*
receives, gets 받아요 받다 *Ch3 L9 vocab*
recently 최근에 *Ch5 L20 vocab*
recognize 알아 봐요 알아 보다 *Ch6 L24 other*
red 빨간색 *Ch4.5*
red bean 팥 *Ch4 L13 vocab*
red pepper paste 고추장 *Ch4 L14 vocab*
red pepper powder 고춧가루 *Ch4 L14 vocab*
refined (fine) 고와요 곱다 (ㅂ-irr.) *Ch5.5*
refreshing 시원해요 시원하다 *Ch4 L15 vocab*
refreshing (of wind, weather) 선선해요 선선하다 *Ch6 L21 vocab*
refrigerator 냉장고 *Ch4 L14 vocab*
regular days 평소에 *Ch 2 L7 vocab*
relationship, between, among 사이 *Ch5 L20 vocab*
relieved, lucky that… (lucky that ~) 다행이에요 다행이다 *Ch6 L22 vocab*
remains; is leftover 남아요 남다 [남따] *Ch3 L9 vocab*
repeat (after me), repeats 따라 하세요 따라하다 *Prelim. C vocab*
request, makes a …; applies 신청해요 신청하다 *Ch6 L24 vocab*
reserved, aloof 새침해요 새침하다 *Ch5 L19 vocab*
rest sufficiently 푹 쉬어요 푹 쉬다 *Ch6 L23 vocab* [셔요]
restless, fretful, nervous in anticipation 초조해요 초조하다 *Ch6 L22 vocab*
restroom 화장실 *Prelim. F vocab Ch5 L18 vocab*
rests, rest (takes a) 쉬어요 쉬다 *Ch3 L10 vocab*
rice mixed with vegetables & 고추장 비빔밥 *Ch4 L15 vocab*
rice vodka 소주 *Ch4 L16 vocab*
rice-based dish 밥 *Ch4 L13 point*
rides, gets on 타요 타다 *Ch3 L10 vocab*
right side 오른쪽 *Ch1 L4 vocab*
right?, isn't it so? ~지 *Ch4 L13 other*
right?, isn't it so? 그렇지요 (그죠, 그치 - non-standard spelling) 그렇다 *Ch5 L18 other*
ring 반지 *Ch5 L18 vocab*
rises (of the sun) 해가 떠요 해가 뜨다 *Ch6 L21 vocab*
river 강 *Ch6 L24 vocab*
riverbank, river's edge 강가 *Ch6 L24 point* [강까]
road, street 길 *Ch6 L24 vocab*
room ~실 *Ch 2 L5 point*
room 방 *Ch2 L5 vocab*
rude, unfriendly 불친절해요 불친절하다 *Ch5 L19 vocab*
ruler 자 *Ch1 L1 supp*
runny nose, have a … 콧물이 나요, 콧물이 나와요 콧물이 나다 *Ch6 L23 vocab*
Russia 러시아 *Prelim. I vocab*
Russian (language) 러시아어 *Prelim. I vocab*
Russian (person) 러시아사람 *Prelim. I vocab*
sacks pencils, pens *counter* 자루 *Ch3.5 vocab*
sad 슬퍼요 슬프다 *Ch6 L22 vocab*
salt 소금 *Ch4 L14 vocab*
salty 짜요 짜다 *Ch4 L15 vocab*
same to be (exactly) the .. 똑같아요 똑같다 *Ch4 L16 vocab* [또까타요, 또까태요]
same, alike 같아요 같다 *Ch3 L11 vocab* [가태요]

sandwich 샌드위치 *Ch1 L3 vocab* [쌘드위치]
Saturday 토요일 *Ch1.5 A vocab*
savory 고소해요 고소하다 *Ch4 L15 point Ch4 L16 vocab*
say: How do you say _____ in Korean? _____ 한국말로 뭐에요? *Prelim. F vocab*
scaredy-cat (character nickname) 겁쟁이 *Ch5 L20 point*
scary, scared 무서워요 무섭다 (ㅂ-irr.) *Ch6 L22 vocab*
scenery, view 경치 *Ch6 L24 vocab*
school 학교 *Ch2 L5 vocab Ch6 L24 point*
school vacation 방학 *Ch 2 L8 point*
school year 학년 *Ch 2 L8 point*
scissors 가위 *Ch1 L1 supp*
scrubbing rag 맷수건 *Ch5 L18 vocab* [맨쑤건]
sea 바다 *Ch6 L24 vocab*
seafood 해물 *Ch4 L13 vocab*
seafood green onion pancake 해물 파전 *Ch4 L15 vocab*
seasonings 양념 *Ch4 L14 vocab*
seaweed 김 *Ch4 L13 vocab*
second 둘째 *Prelim. G vocab*
seems that (I think, I feel that, it seems to me) ~(으)ㄴ것같아요 (으)ㄴ 것같다 *Ch5 L20 focus*
sees, *idiomatically* reads (newspaper, book) 봐요 보다 *Ch2.5 point*
selectional marker ~(으)로 *Ch4 L14 other*
self-centered, cold, independent (character nickname) 깍쟁이 *Ch5 L20 point*
selfish 이기적이에요 이기적이다 *Ch5 L19 vocab*
self-study 독학 *Ch 2 L8 point*
sells 팔아요 팔다 *Ch4 L13 vocab*
semester/quarter/ 학기 *Ch 2 L8 vocab*
senior; someone socially 'above' 윗사람 *Ch1 L4 vocab*
sentence 문장 *bonus*
September 구월 *Prelim. H vocab*
sesame oil 참기름 *Ch4 L14 vocab*
sesame salt 깨소금 *Ch4 L14 vocab*
sets (of the sun) 해가 져요 해가 지다 *Ch6 L21 vocab*
sets (the table) 차려요 차리다 *Ch4 L15 vocab*
seven (native Korean vocab.) 일곱 *Prelim. G vocab*
seven (Sino-Korean vocab.) 칠 *Prelim. G vocab*
seven days 이레 *Ch6 L21 vocab*
seventh 일곱째 *Prelim. G vocab*
seventy (native Korean vocab.) 일흔 *Prelim. G vocab*
severe 심해요 심하다 *Ch6 L23 vocab*
severely 심하게 *Ch6 L23 vocab*
sexy 섹시해요 섹시하다 *Ch5 L19 vocab* [쎅씨해요]
shall we (how about, I wonder, should I, do you think) ~(으)ㄹ까요 *Ch6 L24 other*
shallow 얕아요 얕다 *Ch5 L17 vocab*
sharpens (a knife) 갈아요 갈다 *Ch4 L13 vocab*
shave (face) 면도해요 면도하다 *Ch5 L18 vocab*
she, her that child (person, familiar) 얘 (this…), 걔 (that …), 쟤 (distant) *Ch5 L20 other*
sheep (goat, "Aries") 양 *Ch6.5*
sheets, counter 장 *Ch3.5 vocab*
shies away, snooty;새침떼기 *Ch5 L20 point*
ship, boat 배 Ch6 L24 vocab
shirt (man's dress shirt) 와이셔츠 *Ch5 L18 vocab*
shoes 신발 *Ch5 L18 vocab*
shops; goes shopping 쇼핑해요 쇼핑하다 *Ch 2 L6 vocab*
short (item; *not for height*) 짧아요 짧다 *Ch5 L17 point*
short (of a person) 키가 작아요 작다 *Ch5 L17 vocab*
short forehead, have a … 이마가 좁아요 좁다 *Ch5 L17 vocab*
short hair, have … 머리가 짧아요 짧다 *Ch5 L17 vocab*
shot, get a … 주사를 맞아요 주사를 맞다 *Ch6 L23 vocab*
shoulders 어깨 *Ch5 L17 vocab*
shower 목욕해요 목욕하다 [모교카다] *Ch2 L6 vocab* [모교캐요]
shower (takes a) 샤워해요 샤워하다 *Ch2 L6 vocab*
show-off braggart (character nickname) 허풍쟁이 *Ch5 L20 point*
shy 창피해요 창피하다 *Ch6 L22 vocab* [챙피하다]
sibling -- female sibling 자매 *Ch2.5 vocab*
sibling -- male sibling 형제 *Ch2.5 vocab*
sick, hurts 아파요 아프다 *Ch3 L11 vocab*
side (poetic) 곁 *Ch1 L4 vocab*
side dishes 반찬 *Ch4 L13 point*
sight-see, look around 구경해요 구경하다 *Ch6 L24 vocab*
silver (color) 은색 *Ch4.5*
similar 비슷해요 비슷하다 *Ch4 L16 vocab* [비스태요]
similar 비슷해요 비슷하다 *Ch3 L11 vocab* [비스태요]
sings 노래해요 노래하다 *Ch 2 L6 vocab*
sings ; calls (out); (stomach) be full 불러요 부르다 (르- irr.) *Ch4 L16 vocab*
sister, female's older sister who is older than another older sister 큰 언니 *Ch2.5 vocab*
sister, female's older sister who is younger than another sister 언니 *Ch2.5 vocab*
sister, female's older sister who is younger than another sister 작은 언니 *Ch2.5 vocab*
sister, male's older sister 누나 *Ch2.5 vocab*
sister, male's older sister who is older than another older sister 큰 누나 *Ch2.5 vocab*
sister, male's older sister who is younger than another sister 작은 누나 *Ch2.5 vocab*
sister, younger sister 여동생 *Ch2.5 vocab*
sisters, female siblings 자매 *Ch2.5 vocab*
sits 앉아요 앉다 *Ch3 L9 vocab*
six (native Korean vocab.) 여섯 *Prelim. G vocab*
six (Sino-Korean vocab.) 육 *Prelim. G vocab*

six days 엿새 *Ch6 L21 vocab*
sixth 여섯째 *Prelim. G vocab*
sixty (native Korean vocab.) (native Korean vocab.) 예순 *Prelim. G vocab*
skin 피부 *Ch5 L17 vocab*
skin and bones 빼빼 말랐어요 빼빼 마르다 (르- irr.) *Ch5 L19 vocab*
skinny 말랐어요 마르다 (르-irr.) *Ch4 L16 vocab Ch5 L19 vocab Ch5 L20 point*
skirt 치마 *Ch5 L18 vocab*
sky 하늘 *Ch6 L24 vocab*
sky blue, light blue 하늘색 *Ch4.5*
sleeps 자요 자다 *Ch3 L10 vocab*
sleepy 졸려요 졸리다 *Ch6 L22 vocab*
sleepy head, slug-a-bed (character nickname) 잠꾸러기, 잠보 *Ch5 L20 point*
slim 날씬해요 날씬하다 *Ch5 L19 vocab*
sloppy 칠칠맞아요 칠칠맞다 *Ch5 L19 point*
slow 느려요 느리다 *Ch4 L16 vocab*
slowly 천천히 *Prelim. C vocab, Ch5 L20 vocab*
small 작아요 작다 *Ch3 L11 vocab*
smart 똑똑해요 똑똑하다 *Ch5 L19 vocab*
smile 미소 *Ch6 L24 point*
smiles, laughs 웃어요 웃다 *Ch3 L9 vocab*
snack for beer and alcoholic beverages 안주 *Ch4 L16 vocab*
snake 뱀 *Ch6.5*
snake soup 뱀탕 *Ch6 L23 point*
sneakers (sports shoes) 운동화 *Ch5 L18 vocab*
sneezes (lit. … come out); to sneeze 재채기가 나와요, 재채기를 해요, 재채기가 나요 재채기를 하다 *Ch6 L23 vocab*
snooty ; snooty; shies away 새침떼기 *Ch5 L20 point*
snow white 새하얀 *Ch5 L18 point*
snows 눈이 와요 눈이 오다 *Ch6 L21 vocab*
so, for that reason (conjunction) 그러니까 *Ch4 L14 vocab*
so ; so, but, and… ~(으)ㄴ데 (adj.), ~는데 (verbs) *Ch5 L17 focus*
so (conjunction) 그래서 *Ch 2 L8 other*
so (verb connector) -어서 *Ch3 L11 other*
soap 비누 *Ch5 L18 vocab*
soccer, play … 축구해요 축구하다 *Ch 2 L6 vocab*
sociable (make many friends ; have good social skills) 사교성이 좋아요 좋다 *Ch5 L20 vocab*
Sociology 사회학 *Ch 2 L8 supp*
socks 양말 *Ch5 L18 vocab*
solves, loosens, dissolves, unties 풀어요 풀다 *Ch5 L18 vocab*
somehow 어떻게 *Ch3 L9 other* [어떠케]
someone 누가, 누구 *Ch3 L9 other*
something 뭐 *Ch3 L9 other*
sometime 언제 *Ch3 L9 other*
sometimes, rarely 가끔 *Ch 2 L7 vocab*
somewhere 어디 *Ch3 L9 other*
son 아들 *Ch2.5 vocab*
sorry -- I am sorry 미안합니다 미안하다 *Prelim. F vocab*
soup (clear) 국 *Ch4 L15 vocab*
soup based on meat broth ~ 탕 *Ch4 L13 point*
sour 셔요 시다 *Ch4 L15 vocab*
South Korea 남한 *Prelim. I point*
South Korea (old term) 남조선 *Prelim. I point*
soy bean paste (Korean miso) 된장 *Ch4 L15 vocab*
soy bean paste (Korean *miso*) stew 된장찌개 *Ch4 L15 vocab*
soy sauce 간장 *Ch4 L14 vocab*
Spain 스페인 *Prelim. I vocab*
Spanish (language) 서반아어, 스페인어 *Prelim. I point*
Spanish (person); Spaniard 스페인사람 *Prelim. I vocab*
specialty 전문 *Ch4 L16 vocab*
spicy 매워요 맵다 (ㅂ-irr.) *Ch4 L15 vocab*
spinach 시금치 *Ch4 L13 vocab*
spoon 숟가락, 숟갈 *Ch4 L13 point Ch4 L15 vocab*
sports complex; gym 체육관 *Ch2 L5 vocab*
sports field 운동장 *Ch6 L24 point*
spring 봄 *Ch6 L21 vocab*
squash, zucchini, pumpkin 호박 *Ch4 L13 vocab*
squid, shredded dried ... snack 마른 오징어 채 *Ch4 L16 vocab*
squid 오징어 *Ch4 L13 vocab*
stands, stops 서요 서다 *Ch3 L10 vocab*
star 별 *Ch6 L24 vocab*
Stars and Stripes 성조기 *Ch4.5 exercises*
startled, surprised 놀라다 놀라다 *Ch6 L22 vocab*
stay up all night, pull an all-nighter 밤을 새워요 밤을 새우다 *Ch6 L23 vocab*
stew, salty Korean stew 찌개 *Ch4 L13 point , Ch4 L15 vocab*
stifled (frustrated, stir-crazy, trapped) 답답해요 답답하다 *Ch5 L19 vocab*
stir-crazy (frustrated, trapped, stifled) 답답해요 답답하다 *Ch5 L19 vocab Ch6 L22 vocab*
stir-fried dish 볶음; 볶이; 볶기 (widely used spelling, non-standard) *Ch4 L13 vocab*
store 가게 *Ch4 L14 vocab*
store ~점 *Ch 2 L5 point*
strands 가락 *Ch5 L17 point*
strawberry 딸기 *Ch4 L14 vocab*
street, road 길 *Ch6 L24 vocab*
stress out 스트레스를 받아요 스트레스를 받다 *Ch6 L22 vocab*
stressed out, (get…) 스트레스가 쌓여요 스트레스가 쌓이다 *Ch6 L22 vocab*
strong (e.g., coffee, tea) 진해요 진하다 *Ch4 L13 vocab*
strong, sturdy, healthy 튼튼해요 튼튼하다 *Ch5 L19 point*

stubborn 고집이 세요 고집이 세다 *Ch5 L19 vocab*
student 학생 *Ch1 L1 vocab* [학쌩]
student center 학생회관 *Ch2 L5 vocab*
student ID card 학생증 *Ch1 L3 vocab* [학쌩쯩]
student ID number 학번 *Ch 2 L8 point*
student, female 여학생 *Ch1 L1 vocab*
student, male 남학생 *Ch1 L1 vocab*
studies 공부해요 공부하다 *Ch 2 L6 vocab*
study 공부 *Ch 2 L6 focus*
stupid 멍청해요 멍청하다 *Ch5 L19 vocab*
stylish, 'cool' 멋있어요 멋있다 *Ch5 L19 vocab*
subject (grammatical) 주어 *bonus*
subject marker (after a noun ending in a consonant) -이 *Ch1 L1 vocab*
subject marker (after a noun ending in a vowel) -가 *Ch1 L1 vocab*
subway 지하철 *Ch6 L24 point*
suddenly 갑자기 *Ch3 L12 vocab*
sugar 설탕 *Ch4 L14 vocab*
summer 여름 *Ch6 L21 vocab*
sun 해 *Ch6 L24 vocab*
sun, year 해 *Ch6 L22 vocab, Ch6 L24 vocab*
Sunday 일요일 *Ch1.5 A vocab*
sunglasses 썬글라스, 썬글래스 *Ch5 L18 point*
sunny 해가 나요, 해가 났어요 해가 나다 *Ch6 L21 vocab*
surprise ending, unexpectedness ~네 *Ch4 L15 other*
surprised, startled 놀라다 놀라다 *Ch6 L22 vocab*
sweat comes out (to sweat) 땀이 나와요 땀이 나오다 *Ch6 L23 vocab*
sweater 스웨터 (세타, 셰타 non-standard) *Ch5 L18 point*
sweet 달아요 달다 *Ch4 L14 vocab*
sweet potato 고구마 *Ch4 L13 vocab*
sweetened Kimchi made of cubed icicle radish 깍두기 *Ch4 L15 vocab*
swell 부어요 붓다 (ㅅ-irr.) *Ch6 L23 vocab*
swims 수영해요 수영하다 *Ch 2 L6 vocab*
T.V. 텔레비전, 테레비 *Ch1 L1 vocab*
table, low, traditional eating ... 상 *Ch4 L15 vocab*
table (for eating) 식탁 *Ch4 L15 vocab*
table 탁자 *Ch1 L1 vocab* [탁짜]
tactful, tending others' comfort well 싹싹해요 싹싹하다 *Ch5 L19 point*
tail 꼬리 *Ch5 L17 vocab*
take medicine 약을 먹어요 약을 먹다 *Ch6 L23 vocab*
takes (a class); hears, listens 들어요 (irregular) 듣다 *Ch 2 L8 vocab*
takes (a picture), imprints 찍어요, (사진을) 찍다 *Ch6 L24 vocab*
takes off (clothing, shoes) 벗어요 벗다 *Ch5 L18 vocab*
takes off (a ring, glasses, gloves, something difficult to take off) 빼요 빼다 *Ch5 L18 vocab*
takes out of container 꺼내요 꺼내다 *Ch4 L14 vocab*
talk (start a conversation) 말을 걸어요 말을 걸다 *Ch5 L20 vocab*
talkative 말이 많아요 말이 많다 *Ch5 L19 vocab*
talks 이야기해요, 얘기해요 이야기하다, 얘기하다 *Ch 2 L6 vocab*
tall 키가 커요 크다 *Ch5 L17 vocab*
taste 맛 *Ch4 L15 vocab*
tasty 맛이 있어요, 맛있어요 맛있다 *Ch4 L15 vocab*
taxi 택시 *Ch1 L3 vocab*
teacher 선생님 *Prelim. C vocab*
teaches 가르쳐요 가르치다 *Ch3 L10 vocab*
telephone 전화 *Ch1 L1 vocab* [저놔, 저나]
temperature, What's the ... ? How many degrees is it?) 몇 도에요? *Ch6 L21 vocab*
temperature 온도; 기온 (air temp) *Ch4 L15 vocab*
ten (Sino-Korean) 십 *Prelim. G vocab*
ten days 열흘 *Ch6 L22 vocab*
ten million 천 만 *Prelim. G vocab*
ten thousand 만 *Prelim. G vocab*
tender 연해요 연하다 *Ch4 L13 vocab*
tenth 열째 *Prelim. G vocab*
test 시험 *Ch1 L1 vocab* [시험, 시엄]
than 보다 *Ch5 L20 vocab*
thanks (Thank you!) 감사합니다 감사하다 *Prelim. F vocab*
that (adj.) 그 *Ch1 L2 vocab*
that/it 그거 *Ch1 L2 vocab*
that/it (contrast, topic) 그건 *Ch1 L2 vocab*
that/it as (subject, focus) 그게 *Ch1 L2 vocab*
that little/exact thing 고거 *Ch1 L4 point*
that little/exact thing over there 조거 *Ch1 L4 point*
that over there (adj.) 저 *Ch1 L2 vocab*
that thing over there (noun) 저거 *Ch1 L2 vocab*
that thing over there (topic, contrast) 저건 *Ch1 L2 vocab*
that thing over there (subject, focus) 저게 *Ch1 L2 vocab*
that way 그리 *Ch4 L14 vocab*
that (distant) way 저리 *Ch4 L14 vocab*
the day after tomorrow 모레 *Ch 2 L7 vocab*
there 거기 *Ch1 L3 vocab*
there is no 없어요 없다 *Ch1 L1 vocab* [업써요]
there is; exists; has 있어요 있다 *Ch1 L1 vocab* [이써요]
there; right there 고기 *Ch1 L4 point*
thick (of flat items) 두꺼워요 두껍다 (ㅂ-irr.) *Ch5 L17 vocab*
thin (of flat items) 얇아요 얇다 *Ch5 L17 vocab*
thin, narrow 가늘어요 가늘다 *Ch5 L17 vocab*
thing 것 *Ch1 L2 vocab*
thing (cf. written form 것) 거 *Ch1 L2 vocab*
things (that can be held in the hand), *counter* 개 *Ch4 L14 vocab*
think that (I think, I feel that, it seems to me) ~(으)ㄴ 것같아요 (으)ㄴ 것같다 *Ch5 L20 focus*

third 셋째 *Prelim. G vocab*
thirsty (Literally, My throat is dry.) 목이 말라요 마르다 (르-irr.) *Ch4 L16 vocab*
thirty (native Korean vocab.) 서른 *Prelim. G vocab*
thirty (Sino-Korean vocab.) 삼 십 *Prelim. G vocab*
this (adj.) 이 *Ch1 L2 vocab*
this (noun) 이거 *Ch1 L2 vocab*
this (topic, contrast) 이건 *Ch1 L2 vocab*
this (subject, fosuc) 이게 *Ch1 L2 vocab*
this little/exact thing 요거 *Ch1 L4 point*
this month 이번 달에 *Ch 2 L7 vocab*
this morning 오늘 아침 *Ch1.5 B vocab*
this way 이리 *Ch4 L14 vocab*
this week 이번 주에 *Ch 2 L7 vocab*
this weekend 이번 주말에 *Ch 2 L7 vocab*
this year 금년, 올해 *Ch 2 L7 vocab*
thousand 천 *Prelim. G vocab*
three (native Korean vocab.) 셋, 세 *Prelim. G vocab*
three (Sino-Korean vocab.) 삼 *Prelim. G vocab*
three days 사흘 *Ch5 L18 vocab*
three to four days 사나흘 *Ch5 L18 vocab*
Thursday 목요일 *Ch1.5 A vocab*
ties, wears, puts on (a necktie) 매요 매다 *Ch5 L18 vocab*
tiger 범, 호랑이 *Ch6.5*
time 시간 *Ch 2 L7 vocab*
time (at the time of NOUN) 때 *Ch4 L15 vocab*
tired 피곤해요 피곤하다 *Ch3 L11 vocab Ch6 L22 vocab*
to; a NOUN ... VERB ~(으)ㄹ NOUN *Ch6 L24 other*
to (a person) 한테 (spoken), 에게 (written) *Ch3 L11 other Ch5 L20 other*
to (a place) -에 *Ch2 L5 other*
today 오늘 *Prelim. H vocab*
toenails 발톱 *Ch5 L17 vocab*
toes 발가락 *Ch5 L17 vocab*
tofu 두부 *Ch4 L13 vocab*
together 같이 *Ch 2 L6 vocab* [가치]
toilet 변기 *Ch5 L18 vocab*
tomato 토마토 *Ch4 L13 vocab*
tomorrow 내일 *Ch1 L1 vocab*
tongue 혀 *Ch5 L17 vocab*
tongue, top of 혓바닥 *Ch5 L17 vocab*
tonic 보약 *Ch6 L23 point*
tonight 오늘 밤 *Ch1.5 B vocab*
toothbrush 칫솔 *Ch5 L18 vocab*
toothpaste 치약 *Ch5 L18 vocab*
top; above (n.) 위 *Ch1 L4 vocab*
top of the foot 발등 *Ch5 L17 vocab*
topic marker -은/는 *Ch1 L2 vocab*
tough, chewy (of food) 질겨요 질기다 *Ch4 L13 vocab*
towel 수건 *Ch5 L18 vocab*
train 기차 *Ch6 L24 vocab*
transfer (schools) 전학 *Ch 2 L8 point*
trapped (frustrated, stir-crazy, stifled) 답답해요 답답하다 *Ch5 L19 vocab*
trash can 휴지통 *Ch4 L14 vocab*
travel 여행해요 여행하다 *Ch6 L24 vocab*
travel agency 여행사 *Ch6 L24 vocab*
Treat us. (pay for meal) 한 턱 내세요 ... 내다 *Ch4 L16 vocab* [한텅 내세요]
treatment give a medical ... (prognosis) 치료를 해요 치료를 하다 *Ch6 L23 vocab*
tree 나무 *Ch6 L24 vocab*
trees *counter* 그루 *Ch3.5 vocab* [구루]
trouble-maker (character nickname) 말썽꾸러기 *Ch5 L20 point*
truly 정말(로), 진짜(로) *Ch3 L12 vocab*
try ~ing ~어 보세요 어 보다 *Ch6 L21 other*
t-shirt 티셔츠 *Ch5 L18 vocab*
Tuesday 화요일 *Ch1.5 A vocab*
turns in (work); put out 내요 내다 *Ch3 L10 vocab*
twenty (native Korean vocab.) 스물, 스무 *Prelim. G vocab*
twenty (Sino-Korean vocab.) 이 십 *Prelim. G vocab*
twins 쌍둥이 *Ch2.5 vocab*
two (native Korean vocab.) 둘, 두 *Prelim. G vocab*
two (Sino-Korean vocab.) 이 *Prelim. G vocab*
two days 이틀 *Ch5 L18 vocab*
two weeks ago 이 주일 전에 *Ch3 L12 vocab*
ugly 못 생겼어요 못 생기다 *Ch5 L19 vocab*
umbrella 우산 *Ch5 L18 vocab*
uncle 삼촌 *Ch2.5 vocab*
uncomfortable; inconvenient 불편해요 불편하다 *Ch3 L11 vocab*
uncooked rice 쌀 *Ch4 L13 vocab*
underneath 밑 *Ch1 L4 vocab*
uneasy, apprehensive 불안해요 불안하다 *Ch6 L22 vocab*
unfriendly, rude 불친절해요 불친절하다 *Ch5 L19 vocab*
uniform (clothing) 유니폼 *Ch5 L18 point*
United Kingdom 영국 *Prelim. I vocab*
United States of America 미국 *Prelim. I vocab*
university, college 대학교 *Ch2 L5 vocab*
unnecessary; not needed 필요없어요 필요없다 *Ch3 L11 vocab*
unrefined rice wine 막걸리 *Ch4 L16 vocab*
unties (loosens, dissolves, solves) 풀어요 풀다 *Ch5 L18 vocab*
until (time); up to (place) -까지 *Ch3 L10 other*
usually, on regular days 보통 *Ch 2 L7 vocab*
vacation (from school) 방학 *Ch6 L24 vocab*
vacation (days off work) 휴가 *Ch6 L24 point*
VCR 비디오 *Ch1 L1 vocab*
vegetables (cooked) 나물 *Ch4 L13 point*
vegetables 채소, 야채 *Ch4 L13 vocab*
verb 동사 *Ch6 L22 vocab*
very 아주 *Ch3 L12 vocab*

very (slang) 굉장히, 되게 *Ch3 L12 vocab* [굉장이, 갱장이]
very; too 너무 *Ch3 L12 vocab*
Vietnam 월남, 베트남 *Prelim. I vocab*
Vietnamese (language) 베트남어 *Prelim. I vocab*
Vietnamese (person) 베트남 사람 *Prelim. I vocab*
view, scenery 경치 *Ch6 L24 vocab*
vinegar 식초 *Ch4 L14 vocab*
vocabulary, word 단어 *Ch5 L17 vocab*
volleyball, plays … 배구해요 배구하다 *Ch 2 L6 vocab*
volumes, books *counter* 권 *Ch3.5 vocab*
vowel 모음 *Prelim. D vocab*
waist, lower back 허리 *Ch5 L17 vocab*
waits 기다려요 기다리다 *Ch3 L10 vocab*
wakes up 깨요 깨다 *Ch3 L10 vocab*
walk (takes a) 산책해요 산책하다 *Ch 2 L6 vocab* [산채캐요]
wall 벽 *Ch1 L1 vocab*
wallet 지갑 *Ch1 L3 vocab*
wanna (wanna/gonna) ~(으)ㄹ래요 *Ch4 L16 other*
want to ~고 싶어요, ~고 싶어해요 (third person) 고 싶다, 고 싶어하다 *Ch5 L18 other*
warm 따뜻해요 따뜻하다 *Ch4 L15 vocab* [따뜨태요, 따드태요]
wash 씻어요 씻다 *Ch3 L9 vocab*
wash face 세수해요 세수하다 *Ch 2 L6 vocab*
watch, clock 시계 *Ch5 L18 vocab*
watches (TV, movie) 봐요 보다 *Ch2.5 point*
water 물 *Ch4 L16 vocab*
watermelon 수박 *Ch4 L14 vocab*
watery, French-cut icicle radish Kimchi 동치미 *Ch4 L15 point*
watery, thinly-sliced icicle radish Kimchi 나박 김치 *Ch4 L15 point*
we, our (familiar form) 우리 *Ch 2 L7 vocab*
weak (coffee, tea, color) 연해요 연하다 *Ch4 L13 vocab*
wears, puts on (gloves, glasses, rings, something difficult to put on) 껴요 끼다 *Ch5 L18 vocab*
wears, puts on (head gear, glasses, umbrella) 써요 쓰다 *Ch5 L18 vocab*
wears, puts on (clothing on the body) 입어요 입다 *Ch3 L9 vocab Ch5 L18 vocab*
wears, puts on (a watch, belt, something with a band) 차요 차다 *Ch5 L18 vocab*
wears, puts on (accessories) 해요 하다 *Ch5 L18 vocab*
wears, puts on, ties (a necktie) 매요 매다 *Ch5 L18 vocab*
weather 날씨 *Ch6 L21 vocab*
weather forecast, hear … 일기 예보 *Ch6 L21 vocab*
wedding dress 웨딩드레스 *Ch5 L18 point*
Wednesday 수요일 *Ch1.5 A vocab*
weird, strange 이상해요 이상하다 *Ch3 L11 vocab*
Welcome! (in a store, restaurant) 어서 오세요 오다 *Ch4 L16 vocab*
what (adjective); what kind of 무슨 *Ch 2 L8 vocab*
what 무엇, 뭐 *Ch1 L1 vocab Ch3 L9 other*
what date 며칠 *Prelim. H vocab*
what day(s) of the week 무슨 요일 *Ch1.5 A vocab* [무슨뇨일]
what month 몇월 *Prelim. H vocab* [며뒬]
when 언제 *Ch3 L9 other*
when ~ ~(으)ㄹ 때 *Ch6 L24 other*
when there is a test 시험 때(에) *Ch 2 L7 vocab*
where 어디 *Ch3 L9 other*
which 어느 *Prelim. I vocab*
while, for a long … 오랫동안 *Ch6 L24 vocab* [오래똥안, 오랟똥안]
while, for a short … 잠깐 *Ch4 L16 vocab*
white 하얀색 *Ch4.5*
white hands (idiom: people who are jobless after college graduation) 백수 *Ch 2 L8 point*
white-out 화이트 *Ch1 L1 supp*
who 누구 *Ch1 L2 vocab Ch2 L5 other*
who (as subject) 누가 *Ch2 L5 other*
whole TIME, all + TIME 내내 *Ch5 L19 other*
whose 누구 거 *Ch3 L9 other* [누구 꺼]
why 왜 *Ch3 L9 other*
wide 넓어요 넓다 Ch5 L17 point
wide forehead, have a … 이마가 넓어요 넓다 *Ch5 L17 vocab*
wife (talking about one's own or derogatory) 마누라 *Ch6.5 point*
will (simple future plan) ~(으)ㄹ거에요 (으)ㄹ 것이다, (으)ㄹ 거다 *Ch4 L13 focus*
will, OK? (promissory, seeking OK) ~(으)ㄹ께요 *Ch5 L18 focus*
window 창문 *Ch1 L1 vocab*
windy 바람이 불어요 바람이 불다 *Ch6 L21 vocab*
winter 겨울 *Ch6 L21 vocab*
wipes, cleans 닦아요 닦다 *Ch3 L9 vocab*
with, and *(spoken)* ~(이)랑 *Ch4 L15 vocab*
with -하고 *Ch2 L5 vocab*
with, and 이랑 *Ch4 L15 vocab*
with/by (instrument, tool) –으로 *Ch3 L9 other*
withdraw (money from the bank); look for; find 찾아요 찾다 *Ch3 L9 vocab*
within (noun) 속 *Ch1 L4 vocab*
wolf 늑대 *Ch6.5 point*
woman 여자 *Ch5 L18 vocab*
Women Studies 여성학 *Ch 2 L8 supp*
wonder, I … (shall we, how about, should I, do you think) ~(으)ㄹ까요 *Ch6 L24 other*
word, vocabulary 단어 *Ch5 L17 vocab*
works 일해요 일하다 *Ch 2 L6 vocab*
worry 걱정을 해요 걱정을 하다 *Ch6 L22 vocab*
wrist 손목 *Ch5 L17 vocab*
write; use 써요 쓰다 *Ch3 L10 vocab*
written syllable 글자 *Prelim. D vocab* [글짜]
year (in school) 학년 *Ch 2 L8 vocab* [항년]
year, sun 해 *Ch6 L22 vocab, Ch6 L24 vocab*
yellow 노란색 *Ch4.5*

yes 네, 예 *Ch1 L1 vocab*
yesterday 어제 = 어저께 *Ch3 L12 vocab*
yet; not yet 아직 *Ch3 L12 vocab*
you all (respectful) 여러분 *Ch 2 L8 vocab*
younger sibling 동생 *Ch2.5 vocab*
youngest child 막내 *Ch2.5 vocab* [망내]
zucchini, pumpkin, squash 호박 *Ch4 L13 vocab*

_____ **한국말로 뭐에요?** say: How do you say _____ in Korean? *Prelim. F vocab*
~가 *subject marker (after a noun ending in a vowel) Ch1 L1 vocab*
가게 store(s) *Ch4 L14 vocab*
가까워요 가깝다 (ㅂ-irr.) close *Ch5.5 Ch6 L24 vocab*
가끔 sometimes, rarely *Ch 2 L7 vocab*
가늘어요 가늘다 thin, narrow (e.g. neck, fingers) *Ch5 L17 vocab*
가락 strands *Ch5 L17 point*
가루약 powder medicine *Ch6 L23 vocab*
가르쳐요 가르치다 teaches *Ch3 L10 vocab*
가방 bag *Ch1 L2 vocab*
가벼워요 가볍다 (ㅂ-irr.) light *Ch5.5*
가스 레인지 gas stove *Ch4 L14 vocab*
가요 가다 goes *Ch2 L5 focus*
가운데 middle *Ch1 L4 vocab*
가위 scissors *Ch1 L1 supp*
가을 fall *Ch6 L21 vocab*
가족 family *Ch2.5 vocab*
간장 soy sauce *Ch4 L14 vocab*
갈비 barbecued beef ribs *Ch4 L15 vocab*
갈비탕 beef rib soup *Ch4 L15 vocab*
갈아요 갈다 sharpens (a knife); grates (onions) *Ch4 L13 vocab*
감기 cold *Ch6 L23 vocab*
감기에 걸려요 감기에 걸리다 catches a cold *Ch6 L23 vocab*
감사합니다 감사하다 thanks (Thank you!) *Prelim. F vocab*
감자 potato *Ch4 L13 vocab*
갑자기 suddenly *Ch3 L12 vocab*
강 river *Ch6 L24 vocab*
강가 riverbank, river's edge, riverside *Ch6 L24 vocab* [강까] *Ch6 L24 point*
강아지 puppy *Ch2.5 vocab Ch6.5*
같아요 같다 same; alike *Ch3 L11 vocab* [가태요]
~같은 A like B *Ch4 L16 other*
같이 together *Ch 2 L6 vocab* [가치]
~같이 like a NOUN *Ch4 L16 other* [가치] *Ch5 L20 vocab*
개 things (that can be held in the hand), counter *Ch4 L14 vocab*
개 dog *Ch2.5 vocab Ch6.5*
개 items *counter Ch3.5 vocab*
개구쟁이 rascal *Ch5 L20 point*
걔 he, she (familiar; literally, *that child*) *Ch5 L20 other*
걔네 his, her; they, their (familiar; literally, *that child's*) *Ch5 L20 other*
거 thing (cf. written form 것) *Ch1 L2 vocab*
거기 there *Ch1 L3 vocab*
~거나 or (for connecting verbs) *Ch6 L21 other*
거울 mirror *Ch5 L18 vocab*
거의 almost *Ch 2 L7 vocab*
거의 다 almost all *Ch3 L12 vocab*
걱정을 해요 걱정을 하다 worry *Ch6 L22 vocab*
걱정이 돼요 걱정이 되다 worried *Ch6 L22 vocab*
건너편 across *Ch1 L4 vocab*
건물 building *Ch1 L4 vocab*
걸려요 걸리다 catches (illness), gets caught *Ch6 L23 vocab*
걸어요 걸다 hangs (on a hook) *Ch5 L20 vocab*
검은색 black *bonus*
검정색 black *bonus*
겁쟁이 scaredy-cat *Ch5 L20 point*
것, 거 thing *Ch1 L2 vocab*
~게 ~ly *Ch4 L15 other*
게으름뱅이 lazy bum *Ch5 L20 point*
겨울 winter *Ch6 L21 vocab*
겸손해요 겸손하다 be humble *Ch5 L20 vocab*
경영학 Business and Administration *Ch 2 L8 supp*
경제학 Economics *Ch 2 L8 supp*
경치 view, scenery *Ch6 L24 vocab*
곁 side (poetic) *Ch1 L4 vocab*
계란 eggs *Ch4 L13 vocab* [게란]
계란 후라이 fried eggs *Ch4 L13 vocab*
계산서 bill, check (restaurant) *Ch4 L16 vocab*
계속 continually, continuously *Ch6 L21 vocab*
계속돼요 계속되다 continues *Ch6 L21 vocab*
~고 and *Ch3 L9 other*
~고 나서 and then *Ch3 L9 other*
~고 싶어 죽겠어요 ~고 싶어 죽겠다 dying to *Ch5 L19 other*
~고 싶어요 ~고 싶다 want to *Ch5 L18 other*
~고 싶어해요 ~고 싶어하다 wants to *Ch5 L18 other*
~고 있어요 ~고 있다 is doing *Ch5 L19 other*
고거 that little/exact thing *Ch1 L4 point*
고구마 sweet potato *Ch4 L13 vocab*
고기 meat *Ch4 L13 vocab*
고기 there; right there *Ch1 L4 point*
고모 aunt on father's side *Ch2.5 vocab*
고모부 paternal aunt's husband *Ch2.5 vocab*
고소해요 고소하다 savory *Ch4 L15 point Ch4 L16 vocab*
고양이 cat *Ch2.5 vocab Ch6.5*
고와요 곱다 (ㅂ-irr.) fine, refined *Ch5.5*
고집이 세요 고집이 세다 stubborn *Ch5 L19 vocab*
고추장 red pepper paste *Ch4 L14 vocab*
고춧가루 red pepper powder *Ch4 L14 vocab*
곰 bear *Ch6.5*
공기 bowl for rice *Ch4 L13 point*
공부 study *Ch 2 L6 focus*
공부해요 공부하다 studies *Ch 2 L6 vocab*

공원 park *Ch2 L5 vocab*
공책 notebook (blank book that you will fill in!) *Ch1 L2 vocab*
과일 fruit *Ch4 L14 vocab*
과일주 fruit-made liquor *Ch4 L16 vocab*
과자 cookies, crackers, chips *Ch1 L3 vocab Ch4 L14 point*
~관 a large hall *Ch 2 L5 point*
괜찮아요 괜찮다 O.K. *Prelim. F vocab* [괜차나요, 갠차나요]
괴로워요 괴롭다 (ㅂ-irr.) unbearable *Ch5.5*
굉장히 very (slang) *Ch3 L12 vocab* [굉장이, 갱장이]
교실 classroom *Ch6 L24 point*
교실 classroom *Ch1 L1 vocab*
구 nine (Sino-Korean vocab.) *Prelim. G vocab*
구경해요 구경하다 to look around, do sight-seeing *Ch6 L24 vocab*
구두 dress shoes *Ch5 L18 vocab*
구름이 꼈어요 구름이 끼다 cloudy *Ch6 L21 vocab*
구워요 굽다 (ㅂ-irr.) broils, barbecues *Ch4 L15 vocab Ch5.5*
구월 September *Prelim. H vocab*
구이 broiled meat or fish *Ch4 L13 point*
~국 office, official or government department *Ch 2 L5 point*
국 (clear) soup *Ch4 L13 point*
국그릇 bowl for soup *Ch4 L13 point*
국수 noodles *Ch4 L13 vocab*
국수가락 noodle strands *Ch5 L17 point*
굵어요 굵다 thick (in diameter) *Ch5 L17 vocab*
권 volumes, books *counter Ch3.5 vocab*
귀 ears *Ch5 L17 vocab*
귀가 얇아요 귀가 얇다 easily swayed (Literally, *ears are thin.*) *Ch5 L17 point*
귀걸이 earrings *Ch5 L18 vocab*
귀여워요 귀엽다 (ㅂ-irr.) cute *Ch5 L19 vocab Ch5.5*
귀찮아요 귀찮다 feel lazy, feel bothered *Ch6 L22 vocab*
그 that (adj.) *Ch1 L2 vocab*
그거 that/it *Ch1 L2 vocab*
그건 that thing/it (topic, contrast) *Ch1 L2 vocab*
그게 that thing/it (as subject, focus) *Ch1 L2 vocab*
그래서 so *Ch 2 L8 other*
그래요 그렇다 be that way *Ch5 L18 other*
그래요 그러다 does that, is so *Ch5 L18 other*
그러니까 so, for that reason *Ch4 L14 vocab*
그런데 근데 and, but… *Ch5 L17 vocab*
그런데도 even so, in spite of that *Ch5 L19 vocab*
그렇게 like so *Ch2.5 vocab* [그러케]
그렇지만 but *Ch 2 L8 other* [그러치만]
그려요 그리다 draws *Ch3 L10 vocab*
그루 trees *counter Ch3.5 vocab* [구루]
그릇, 공기 bowls *counter Ch3.5 vocab Ch4 L16 vocab*
그리 that way *Ch4 L14 vocab*
그리고 and *Ch 2 L8 other*
그제 day before yesterday *Ch3 L12 vocab*
그제께 day before yesterday *Ch4 L13 vocab*
그쵸 그렇다 right?, isn't it so?, non-standard spelling *Ch5 L18 other*
그치 그렇다 right?, isn't it so? non-standard spelling *Ch5 L18 other*
극장 movie theater *Ch2 L5 vocab*
근데 그런데 and, but… *Ch5 L17 vocab*
글자 written syllable *Prelim. D vocab* [글짜]
금년에 this year *Ch 2 L7 vocab*
금발 blond *Ch5 L17 vocab*
금발 머리 blond *Ch5 L17 vocab*
금색 gold (color) *Ch4.5*
금요일 Friday *Ch1.5 A vocab*
~기 *nominalizer Ch6 L23 other*
~기 전에 before doing … *Ch3 L10 other*
기가 막혀요 기가 막히다 appalled, dumbfounded (Literally, *Chi is getting blocked*) *Ch6 L22 vocab*
기계 공학 Mechanical Engineering *Ch 2 L8 supp*
기다려요 기다리다 waits *Ch3 L10 vocab*
기분 mood, moods *Ch5 L19 vocab Ch6 L22 vocab*
기분이 나빠요 기분이 나쁘다 in a bad mood *Ch5 L19 vocab*
기분이 좋아요 기분이 좋다 in a good mood *Ch5 L19 vocab*
기뻐요 기쁘다 happy, content *Ch6 L22 vocab*
기숙사 dormitory *Ch2 L5 vocab*
기온이 낮아요 기온이 낮다 temperature is low *Ch6 L21 vocab*
기온이 높아요 기온이 높다 temperature is high *Ch6 L21 vocab*
기차 train *Ch6 L24 vocab*
기침을 해요 기침을 하다 coughs *Ch6 L23 vocab*
기침이 나와요 기침이 나오다 has a cough *Ch6 L23 vocab*
기침이 나요 기침이 나다 has a cough *Ch6 L23 vocab*
기타 others; etc. *Ch4 L13 vocab*
기타 guitar *Ch1 L3 vocab*
길 street, road *Ch6 L24 vocab*
길어요 길다 long *Ch4 L14 vocab*
김 seaweed *Ch4 L13 vocab*
김치 Kimchi *Ch4 L13 point*
김치찌개 Kimchi stew *Ch4 L15 vocab*
깊어요 깊다 deep *Ch5 L17 vocab*
까다로워요 까다롭다 (ㅂ-irr.) picky, difficult (negative implication) *Ch5 L19 vocab* [까다로워요, 까다로와요]
까만색 black *Ch4.5*
~까지 until (time); up to (place) *Ch3 L10 other*
깍뚜기 sweetened Kimchi made of cubed icicle radish *Ch4 L15 vocab Ch4 L15 point*
깐깐해요 깐깐하다 picky, difficult (negative implication) *Ch5 L19 vocab*
깨끗해요 깨끗하다 clean *Ch5.5* [깨끄태요]
깨소금 sesame salt *Ch4 L14 vocab*
깨요 깨다 wakes up; breaks (e.g., a cup) *Ch3 L10 vocab*
꺼내요 꺼내다 takes out *Ch4 L14 vocab*
껌 chewing gum *Ch1 L3 vocab*

껴요 끼다 puts on (gloves, glasses, rings, something difficult to put on) *Ch5 L18 vocab*
꼬리 tail *Ch5 L17 vocab*
꼼꼼해요 꼼꼼하다 meticulous (positive implication) *Ch5 L19 vocab*
끓여요 끓이다 (something) boils *Ch4 L13 vocab*
끝나요 끝나다 ends (intransitive) *Ch3 L10 vocab* [끈나요]
끝내요 끝내다 ends, finishes (something) *Ch3 L10 vocab* [끈내요]
~ㄴ/은 것같아요 ~ㄴ/은 것같다 I think, I feel that, it seems to me *Ch5 L20 focus*
~ㄴ/은 것같아요 ~은 것같다 I think, I feel that, it seems to me *Ch5 L20 focus*
~ㄴ/은데 so, but, and… *Ch5 L17 other*
~ㄴ/은데 so, but, and… *Ch5 L17 focus*
~나 as many as *Ch3 L12 vocab*
~나 or something like that *Ch5 L17 other*
~나 or (for connecting verbs) *Ch4 L13 other*
나 I (familiar form) *Ch 2 L7 vocab*
나가요 나가다 goes out(side) *Ch3 L10 vocab*
나라 country *Prelim. I vocab*
나무 tree *Ch6 L24 vocab*
나물 cooked vegetables *Ch4 L13 point*
나박 김치 watery, thinly-sliced icicle radish Kimchi *Ch4 L15 point*
나빠요 나쁘다 bad *Ch3 L11 vocab*
나아요 낫다 (ㅅ-irr.) gets over (a cold) completely *Ch6 L23 vocab*
나와요 나오다 comes out(side) *Ch3 L10 vocab*
나중에 later *Ch5 L20 vocab*
나흘 four days *Ch5 L18 vocab*
날라리 someone who is flaky and not serious about their studies *Ch 2 L8 point*
날씨 weather *Ch6 L21 vocab*
날씬해요 날씬하다 slim *Ch5 L19 vocab*
남 others *Ch5 L20 vocab*
남동생 male younger sibling *Ch2.5 vocab*
남색 navy blue *Ch4.5*
남아요 남다 [남따] remains; is leftover *Ch3 L9 vocab*
남자 man *Ch5 L18 vocab*
남조선 South Korea (North Korean term) *Prelim. I point*
남학생 male student *Ch1 L1 vocab*
남한 South Korea *Prelim. I point*
낮아요 낮다 low *Ch6 L21 vocab*
내 my (familiar form) *Ch 2 L7 other*
내내 the whole TIME, all TIME *Ch5 L19 other*
내년에 next year *Ch 2 L7 vocab*
내요 내다 turns in (work); put out *Ch3 L10 vocab*
내일 tomorrow *Ch1 L1 vocab*
냄비 pan with two short handles *Ch4 L16 vocab*
냉동실 freezer *Ch4 L14 vocab*
냉면 cold chewy noodles *Ch4 L15 vocab*
냉수 cold water *Ch4 L16 vocab*
냉장고 fridge *Ch4 L14 vocab*
너무 very; too *Ch3 L12 vocab*
넓어요 넓다 wide *Ch5 L17 point*
넣어요 넣다 [너타] puts (something) in *Ch3 L9 vocab* [너~요]
~네 *unexpectedness Ch4 L15 other*
네 four (native Korean vocab.) *Prelim. G vocab*
네, 예 yes *Ch1 L2 vocab*
넥타이 necktie *Ch5 L18 vocab*
넷 four (native Korean vocab.) *Prelim. G vocab*
넷째 fourth *Prelim. G vocab*
노가리 dried baby Pollack *Ch4 L16 point*
노란색 yellow *Ch4.5*
노래방 karaoke room *Ch2 L5 vocab*
노래해요 노래하다 sings *Ch 2 L6 vocab*
놀라요 놀라다 surprised, startled *Ch6 L22 vocab*
놀아요 놀다 plays *Ch3 L9 vocab*
농구해요 농구하다 plays basketball *Ch 2 L6 vocab*
높아요 높다 high *Ch6 L21 vocab*
놓아요 놓다 [노타] puts, lets go of *Ch3 L9 vocab* [놔요]
누가 who (as subject), someone *Ch2 L5 other Ch3 L9 other*
누구 who (other than subject), someone *Ch1 L2 vocab Ch3 L9 other*
누구 거 whose *Ch3 L9 other* [누구 꺼]
누나 male's older sister *Ch2.5 vocab*
누워요 눕다 (ㅂ-irr.) lies down *Ch5.5*
눈 eyes *Ch5 L17 vocab*
눈가 around your eyes *Ch6 L24 point*
눈썹 eyebrows *Ch5 L17 vocab*
눈이 높아요 높다 have high standards (Literally, *eyes are high.*) *Ch5 L17 point*
눈이 와요 눈이 오다 snows *Ch6 L21 vocab*
느려요 느리다 slow *Ch4 L16 vocab*
늑대 wolf *Ch6.5 point*
~는 것같아요 ~는 것같다 I think, I feel that, it seems to me *Ch5 L20 focus*
~는데 so, but, and… *Ch5 L17 other*
늦게 late *Ch5 L20 vocab*
~니? *question ending (intimate-blunt) Ch4 L13 other*
다 all, everything *Ch3 L12 vocab Ch4 L14 vocab*
다른 다르다 (르-irr.) other, different *Ch4 L16 vocab* [다른, 따른]
다리 legs *Ch5 L17 vocab*
다발 bunches of (flowers) counter *Ch3.5 vocab*
다섯 five (native Korean vocab.) *Prelim. G vocab*
다섯째 fifth *Prelim. G vocab*
다음 달에 next month *Ch 2 L7 vocab* 다음따레]
다음 주말에 next weekend *Ch 2 L7 vocab* [다음쭈마레]
다음 주에 next week *Ch 2 L7 vocab* [다음쭈에]
다이어트해요 다이어트하다 goes on a diet (to lose weight) *Ch5 L19 vocab*

다행이에요 다행이다 relieved, lucky that... *Ch6 L22 vocab*
닦아요 닦다 wipes, cleans *Ch3 L9 vocab*
단 bunches of (vegetables); bundles *counter Ch3.5 vocab, Ch4 L13 vocab*
단어 vocabulary, word *Ch5 L17 vocab*
닫아요 닫다 closes *Ch3 L9 vocab*
달 moon, month *Ch6 L22 vocab, Ch6 L24 vocab*
달걀 eggs *Ch4 L13 vocab*
달라요 다르다 (르-irr.) different *Ch3 L11 vocab Ch4 L16 vocab*
달아요 달다 sweet *Ch4 L14 vocab*
닭 chicken (live animal) *Ch6.5*
닭고기 chicken (meat) *Ch4 L13 vocab* [닥꼬기]
답답해요 답답하다 frustrated, stir-crazy, trapped *Ch5 L19 vocab Ch6 L22 vocab*
닷새 5 days *Ch6 L21 vocab*
당근 carrot *Ch4 L13 vocab*
당면 clear noodles *Ch4 L13 vocab*
대 computers, cars, *counter Ch3.5 vocab*
대추 dates (fruit) *Ch6 L23 point*
대학교 university, college *Ch2 L5 vocab*
대학생 college student *Ch 2 L8 vocab*
대학원 graduate school *Ch2 L5 vocab*
대학원생 graduate student *Ch 2 L8 vocab*
대한민국 Korea, South Korea *Prelim. I point*
더 more *Ch3 L12 vocab Ch5 L20 vocab*
더러워요 더럽다 (ㅂ-irr.) dirty *Ch5.5*
더워요 덥다 (ㅂ-irr.) hot *Ch6 L21 vocab*
덜 less *Ch5 L20 vocab*
덩어리 loaves, lumps, *counter Ch3.5 vocab*
데 place (*dependent noun*) *Ch6 L24 vocab*
~도 also *Ch1 L3 vocab*
도 even *Ch5 L17 other*
도도해요 도도하다 arrogant *Ch5 L19 point*
도마 cutting board *Ch4 L14 vocab*
도서관 library *Ch2 L5 vocab*
도와요 돕다 (ㅂ-irr.) helps *Ch4 L15 vocab*
도와줘요 도와주다 help out (another person) *Ch5 L20 vocab*
독일 Germany *Prelim. I vocab*
독일 사람 German (person) *Prelim. I vocab* [도길싸람]
독일어 German (language) *Prelim. I vocab*
독자 only son *Ch2.5 vocab*
독학 self-study *Ch 2 L8 point*
돈 money *Ch1 L3 vocab*
동사 verbs *Ch6 L22 vocab*
동생 younger sibling *Ch2.5 vocab*
동안 during (TIME), for the period of (TIME) *Ch5 L18 vocab Ch5 L20 vocab Ch6 L21 vocab*
동치미 watery, French-cut icicle radish Kimchi *Ch4 L15 point*
돼요 되다 becomes, suitable, sufficient *Ch5 L17 other*
돼지 pig *Ch6.5*
돼지고기 pork *Ch4 L13 vocab*
돼지족발 pig feet *Ch4 L16 point*
됐어요 되다 that's enough; that's O.K. *Ch5 L17 vocab*
되게 very (slang) *Ch3 L12 vocab* [되게, 데게, 디게]
되어요 되다 becomes, suitable, sufficient *Ch5 L17 other*
된장 soy bean paste (Korean miso) *Ch4 L15 vocab*
된장찌개 soy bean paste (Korean *miso*) stew *Ch4 L15 vocab*
두 two (native Korean vocab.) *Prelim. G vocab*
두꺼워요 두껍다 (ㅂ-irr.) thick *Ch5 L17 point*
두부 tofu *Ch4 L13 vocab*
두어요 두다 leaves (for future use), written *Ch4 L14 vocab*
두통 headache *Ch6 L23 point*
둘 two (native Korean vocab.) *Prelim. G vocab*
둘째 second *Prelim. G vocab*
둬요 두다 leaves (for future use) *Ch4 L14 vocab* [둬요, 도요]
뒤 back; behind *Ch1 L4 vocab*
~들 *plural marker Ch2.5 review*
들 open field *Ch6 L24 vocab*
들어가요 들어가다 goes home, enters *Ch3 L10 vocab*
들어와요 들어오다 comes home, comes in *Ch3 L10 vocab*
들어요 들다 picks up; eats *Ch4 L13 vocab*
들어요 듣다 (ㄷ-irr.) takes (a class); hears, listens *Ch 2 L8 vocab Ch6 L21 vocab*
들판 open field *Ch6 L24 vocab*
등 back *Ch5 L17 vocab*
등산해요 등산하다 climbs mountains *Ch 2 L6 vocab*
따뜻해요 따뜻하다 warm *Ch4 L15 vocab* [따뜨태요, 따드태요] *Ch6 L21 vocab*
따라 하세요 따라하다 repeat (after me), repeats *Prelim. C vocab*
따요 따다 picks (flowers), pricks *Ch6 L23 point*
딸 daughter *Ch2.5 vocab*
딸기 strawberry *Ch4 L14 vocab*
땀이 나와요 땀이 나오다 sweat comes out (to sweat) *Ch6 L23 vocab*
땀이 나요 땀이 나다 sweat (verb) *Ch6 L23 vocab*
때 (at the) time (of Noun) *Ch4 L15 vocab Ch4 L15 other Ch6 L24 vocab*
때문에 because of *Ch6 L21 other*
땟수건 scrubbing rag *Ch5 L18 vocab* [때쑤건, 땐쑤건]
떠나요 떠나다 leaves *Ch3 L10 vocab*
떠요 뜨다 rises, floats *Ch6 L21 vocab*
또 again *Ch4 L16 vocab*
또 again; what else (adverb) *Ch1 L3 vocab*
똑같아요 똑같다 (exactly) the same *Ch4 L16 vocab* [또까타요, 또까태요]
똑똑해요 똑똑하다 smart *Ch5 L19 vocab*
뚱땡이 fatty *Ch5 L20 point*
뚱뚱해요 뚱뚱하다 fat, plump *Ch5 L19 vocab*

뜨거워요 뜨겁다 (ㅂ-irr.) hot *Ch4 L15 vocab*
~ㄹ 거에요 ~ㄹ 것이다, ~ㄹ 거다 it's probably *Ch6 L21 focus* [ㄹ꺼에요]
~ㄹ 데 place to *Ch6 L24 other* [ㄹ떼]
~ㄹ 때 when... *Ch6 L24 other*
~ㄹ 수 없어요 ~ㄹ 수 없다 isn't possible *Ch5 L20 other* [ㄹ쑤업써요]
~ㄹ 수 있어요 ~ㄹ 수 있다 is possible *Ch5 L20 other* [ㄹ쑤이써요]
~ㄹ께요 will, OK? *Ch5 L18 focus*
~ㄹ까요 shall we, how about, I wonder, should I, do you think *Ch6 L24 other*
~ㄹ래요 I'm gonna, I wanna *Ch4 L16 other*
~랑 and (spoken) *Ch4 L15 vocab*
~랑 with (spoken) *Ch4 L15 vocab Ch4 L15 other*
러시아 Russia *Prelim. I vocab*
러시아 사람 Russian (person) *Prelim. I vocab* [러시아싸람]
러시아어 Russian (language) *Prelim. I vocab*
레인코트 raincoat *Ch5 L18 point*
레터 오프너 letter opener *Ch1 L3 vocab*
~를, ~을 *Object marker Ch 2 L6 other*
마누라 wife (talking about one's own or derogatory) *Ch6.5 point*
마늘 garlic *Ch4 L14 vocab*
마른 오징어 dried squid *Ch4 L16 point*
마른 오징어 채 shredded dried squid *Ch4 L16 vocab Ch4 L16 point*
마리 counter for animals *Ch2.5 vocab*
마리 animal, counter *Ch4 L14 vocab*
마셔요 마시다 drinks *Ch3 L10 vocab*
마지막 last *Prelim. G vocab*
마지막에 at the end *Ch5 L20 vocab*
마지막으로 for the last time *Ch5 L20 vocab*
마커 highlighter *Ch1 L1 supp*
마흔 forty (native Korean vocab.) *Prelim. G vocab*
막걸리 unrefined rice wine *Ch4 L16 vocab*
막내 youngest child *Ch2.5 vocab* [망내]
막혔어요 막히다 blocked, clogged, congested *Ch6 L22 vocab* [마켜써요]
~만 only, just *Ch3 L10 other*
만 ten thousand *Prelim. G vocab*
만나서 반가워요, 반갑습니다 만나서 반갑다 Nice to meet you *Prelim. I point* [방가워요, 방갑씀니다]
만나요 만나다 meets *Ch3 L10 vocab*
만들어요 만들다 makes *Ch3 L9 vocab*
많아요 많다 [만타] abundant, be a lot *Ch3 L11 vocab*
많이 a lot *Ch3 L12 vocab*
맏아들 oldest son *Ch2.5 vocab*
맏이 oldest child *Ch 2 L6 point* [마지]
말 horse *Ch6.5*
말라요 마르다 (르-irr.) dry *Ch4 L16 vocab*
말랐어요 마르다 (르-irr.) skinny *Ch4 L16 vocab Ch5 L19 vocab*
말썽꾸러기 trouble-maker *Ch5 L20 point*
말을 걸어요 말을 걸다 starts a conversation (Literally, *hooks a word*) *Ch5 L20 vocab*
말이 많아요 말이 많다 talkative *Ch5 L19 vocab*
말이 없어요 말이 없다 doesn't talk much, quiet *Ch5 L19 vocab*
말이 적어요 말이 적다 doesn't talk much, quiet *Ch5 L19 vocab*
맑아요 맑다 clear *Ch6 L21 vocab*
맛 taste *Ch4 L15 vocab* [맏]
맛없어요 맛없다 not tasty *Ch4 L15 vocab*
맛이 없어요 맛이 없다 not tasty *Ch4 L15 vocab*
맛이 있어요 맛이 있다 tasty *Ch4 L15 vocab*
맛있어요 맛있다 tasty *Ch4 L15 vocab*
망아지 foal *Ch6.5*
맞아요 맞다 correct, right *Ch3 L11 vocab*
맞은 편 across *Ch1 L4 vocab*
매요 매다 puts on (ties), ties *Ch5 L18 vocab*
매워요 맵다 (ㅂ-irr.) spicy *Ch4 L15 vocab*
매일 everyday, each day *Ch 2 L7 vocab*
매주 every week, each week *Ch 2 L8 vocab*
맥주 beer *Ch4 L16 vocab*
맨발로 bare-foot *Ch5 L17 point*
맨손으로 bare handed *Ch5 L17 point*
머리 head, hair *Ch5 L17 vocab*
머리가 길어요 머리가 길다 has long hair *Ch5 L17 vocab*
머리가 짧아요 머리가 짧다 has short hair *Ch5 L17 vocab*
머리가 좋아요 머리가 좋다 smart (Literally, *head is good.*) *Ch5 L17 point*
머리방 hair salon *Ch5 L17 vocab*
머리카락 hair strands *Ch5 L17 vocab*
먹보 glutton *Ch5 L20 point*
먹어요 먹다 eat *Ch3 L9 vocab*
먼저 first *Ch5 L20 vocab*
멀어요 멀다 far *Ch5.5 Ch6 L24 vocab*
멋있어요 멋있다 stylish, be cool *Ch5 L19 vocab*
멋쟁이 fashion plate *Ch5 L20 point*
멍청해요 멍청하다 not so sharp, dumb *Ch5 L19 vocab*
멕시코 Mexico *Prelim. I point*
며칠 what date *Prelim. H vocab*
~면 noodles *Ch4 L13 point*
~면 if/when *Ch4 L13 other*
~면 안돼요 ~면 안 되다 you may not, you can't *Ch5 L19 focus*
면도기 razor *Ch5 L18 vocab*
면도해요 면도하다 shaves (one's face) *Ch5 L18 vocab*
멸치 anchovies *Ch4 L14 vocab*
멸치볶음 salted, fried anchovies *Ch4 L16 point*
명 people *counter Ch2.5 vocab*
명 people, counter *Ch4 L14 vocab*
명사 noun *bonus*
몇 how many *Ch1.5 B vocab*

몇 도에요? What's the temperature? (What degree is it?) *Ch6 L21 vocab*
몇 번 how many times *Ch 2 L8 other* [뻔]
몇월 what month *Prelim. H vocab* [며뒬]
모 lumps *counter Ch3.5 vocab*
모두 all together (adv.) *Ch2.5 vocab*
모레 the day after tomorrow *Ch 2 L7 vocab*
모음 vowel *Prelim. D vocab*
모자 hat *Ch5 L18 vocab*
목 neck *Ch5 L17 vocab*
목걸이 necklace *Ch5 L18 vocab*
목요일 Thursday *Ch1.5 A vocab*
목욕탕 bathroom *Ch5 L18 vocab*
목욕해요 목욕하다 [모교카다] bathes, take a shower *Ch 2 L6 vocab* [모교캐요]
목이 가늘어요 목이 가늘다 has a thin neck *Ch5 L17 vocab*
목이 굵어요 목이 굵다 has a thick neck *Ch5 L17 vocab*
목이 말라요 마르다 (르-irr.) I am thirsty. (Literally, *My throat is dry*) *Ch4 L16 vocab*
목적어 direct object (grammar) *bonus bonus bonus*
몰라요 모르다 (르- irr.) doesn't know *Ch4 L16 vocab*
몸 Body *Ch5 L17 vocab*
몸살 body-ache *Ch6 L23 vocab*
몸살이 걸려요 몸살이 걸리다 has a body-ache, be achy; catch a cold *Ch6 L23 vocab*
못 can't *Ch3 L9 other*
못 생겼어요 못 생기다 ugly *Ch5 L19 vocab*
무 icicle radish *Ch4 L13 vocab*
무거워요 무겁다 (ㅂ-irr.) heavy *Ch5.5*
무뚝뚝해요 무뚝뚝하다 blunt, curt, not sociable *Ch5 L19 point*
무리를 해요 무리(를) 하다 overextend oneself *Ch6 L23 vocab*
무서워요 무섭다 (ㅂ-irr.) scary, scared *Ch6 L22 vocab*
무슨 what (adj.) *Ch 2 L8 vocab*
무슨 요일 what day(s) of the week *Ch1.5 A vocab* [무슨뇨일]
무엇 what (written) *Ch3 L9 other*
무우 icicle radish *Ch4 L13 vocab*
문 door *Ch1 L1 vocab*
문장 sentence *bonus bonus bonus*
문제 problem *Prelim. F vocab*
문학 literature studies *Ch 2 L8 point*
물 water *Ch4 L16 vocab*
물고기 fish (alive) *Ch6 L24 vocab* [물꼬기]
물리학 Physics *Ch 2 L8 supp*
물약 liquid medicine *Ch6 L23 vocab* [물략]
뭐 something *Ch3 L9 other*
뭐 what (무엇) *Ch1 L1 vocab*
미국 United States of America *Prelim. I vocab*
미국 사람 American (person) *Prelim. I vocab*
미색 beige *Ch4.5*
미소 smile *Ch6 L24 point*
미술 Art/painting *Ch 2 L8 supp*
미안합니다 미안하다 I am sorry, sorry *Prelim. F vocab*
미용실 hair salon *Ch5 L17 vocab*
미장원 hair salon *Ch5 L17 vocab*
미지근해요 미지근하다 lukewarm *Ch4 L15 vocab*
미학 art *Ch 2 L8 point*
밑 underneath *Ch1 L4 vocab*
~ㅂ시다 let's *Ch5 L17 other*
바나나 banana *Ch4 L14 vocab*
바다 sea *Ch6 L24 vocab*
바닷가 beach *Ch6 L24 vocab Ch6 L24 point*
바람이 불어요 바람이 불다 windy *Ch6 L21 vocab*
바빠요 바쁘다 busy *Ch3 L11 vocab*
바지 pants *Ch5 L18 vocab*
박사 brain (Ph.D.) *Ch5 L20 point*
밖 outside *Ch1 L4 vocab*
반지 ring *Ch5 L18 vocab*
반찬 side dishes *Ch4 L13 point*
받아요 받다 receives, gets *Ch3 L9 vocab*
받침 consonant at end of written syllable *Prelim.D vocab*
발 foot, feet *Ch5 L17 vocab*
발가락 toes *Ch5 L17 vocab*
발가벗었어요 발가벗다 bare naked *Ch5 L17 point*
발등 top of the foot *Ch5 L17 vocab*
발목 ankle *Ch5 L17 vocab*
발이 넓어요 발이 넓다 feet are wide
발이 넓어요 발이 넓다 know many people (Literally, *feet are wide*) *Ch5 L20 vocab Ch5 L17 point*
발톱 toenails *Ch5 L17 vocab*
밝아요 밝다 light *Ch5.5* [밝다]
밤 night (around 10, 11 P.M. ~ 2, 3 A.M.) *Ch1.5 B vocab*
밤색 brown *Ch4.5*
밤을 새워요 밤을 새우다 pull an all-nighter *Ch6 L23 vocab*
~밥 rice-based dish *Ch4 L13 point*
밥 meal; cooked rice *Ch4 L13 vocab*
밥 그릇 bowl for rice *Ch4 L13 point*
방 room *Ch2 L5 vocab*
방금 just now *Ch3 L12 vocab*
방학 vacation (from school) *Ch6 L24 vocab Ch6 L24 point*
방학 school vacation *Ch 2 L8 point*
방학 때(에) during vacation *Ch 2 L7 vocab*
배 pear *Ch4 L14 vocab*
배 belly *Ch5 L17 vocab*
배 ship, boat *Ch6 L24 vocab*
배가 고파요 배가 고프다 I am hungry. *Ch4 L16 vocab*
배가 불러요 배가 부르다 (르-irr.) I am full. *Ch4 L16 vocab*
배구해요 배구하다 plays volleyball *Ch 2 L6 vocab*
배워요 배우다 learns, studies *Ch3 L10 vocab*
배추 Napa cabbage *Ch4 L13 vocab*

배추김치 Kimchi made from Napa cabbage *Ch4 L15 vocab Ch4 L15 point*
백 hundred *Prelim. G vocab*
백 만 million *Prelim. G vocab* [뱅만]
백수 unemployed person (*Literally, white hands*) *Ch 2 L8 point*
백화점 department store *Ch2 L5 vocab* [배콰점]
뱀 snake *Ch6.5*
뱀탕 snake soup *Ch6 L23 point*
버섯 mushroom *Ch4 L13 vocab*
버스 bus *Ch1 L3 vocab*
버터 butter *Ch4 L14 vocab*
벌 clothes, *counter for Ch3.5 vocab*
벌써 already *Ch3 L12 vocab*
범 tiger *Ch6.5*
벗어요 벗다 takes off (clothing) *Ch5 L18 vocab*
베트남 Vietnam *Prelim. I vocab*
베트남 사람 Vietnamese (person) *Prelim. I vocab* [베트남싸람]
베트남어 Vietnamese (language) *Prelim. I vocab*
벨트 belt *Ch5 L18 point*
벽 wall *Ch1 L1 vocab*
변기 toilet *Ch5 L18 vocab*
변비 constipation *Ch6 L23 point*
별 star *Ch6 L24 vocab*
별로 not really, not very, barely *Ch 2 L7 vocab*
병 bottle *Ch4 L16 vocab*
병 bottle *Ch3.5 vocab*
병아리 chick *Ch6.5*
병원 hospital *Ch2 L5 vocab*
병원에 가요 병원에 가다 goes to see a doctor *Ch6 L23 vocab*
병이 나요 병이 나다 gets ill *Ch6 L23 vocab*
~보다 (rather) than *Ch5 L20 vocab Ch5 L20 other*
보라색 deep purple *Ch4.5*
보름 15 days *Ch6 L22 vocab*
보리차 barley tea *Ch4 L16 vocab*
보신탕 dog soup *Ch6 L23 point*
보약 tonic *Ch6 L23 point*
보통 usually, on regular days *Ch 2 L7 vocab*
복사기 copier *Ch1 L1 supp*
볶기 lightly stir-fried dish (widely used spelling, non-standard) *Ch4 L13 vocab*
볶음 lightly stir-fried dish *Ch4 L13 vocab*
볶이 lightly stir-fried dish *Ch4 L13 vocab*
봄 spring *Ch6 L21 vocab*
봉지 bag, *counter for Ch3.5 vocab*
봐요 보다 sees, watches, *idiomatically* reads (newspaper, book) *Ch2.5 point*
부모님 parents *Ch2.5 vocab*
부사 adverb *bonus*
부어요 붓다 (ㅅ-irr.) swells, pours *Ch6 L23 vocab*
부츠 boots *Ch5 L18 point*
~부터 from (time) *Ch3 L10 other*
북조선 North Korea (North Korean term) *Prelim. I point*
북한 North Korea *Prelim. I point*
분 people, counter, honorific *Ch4 L14 vocab*
분 minute *Ch1.5 B vocab*
분 people, (honorific) *counter for Ch3.5 vocab*
분홍색 pink *Ch4.5*
불~ broiled or barbequed over open fire *Ch4 L13 point*
불고기 barbecued beef *Ch4 L15 vocab*
불란서 France *Prelim. I point*
불러요 부르다 (르 -irr.) sings call (out); (stomach) be full *Ch4 L16 vocab*
불안해요 불안하다 uneasy, having apprehensive feelings *Ch6 L22 vocab*
불어 French *Prelim. I point*
불어요 불다 blows (e.g. wind, musical instruments) *Ch6 L21 vocab*
불친절해요 불친절하다 unfriendly, rude *Ch5 L19 vocab*
불편해요 불편하다 uncomfortable; inconvenient *Ch3 L11 vocab*
비가 와요 비가 오다 rains *Ch6 L21 vocab*
비누 soap *Ch5 L18 vocab*
비디오 VCR *Ch1 L1 vocab*
비빔밥 rice mixed with vegetables & 고추장 *Ch4 L15 vocab*
비슷해요 비슷하다 similar *Ch3 L11 vocab* [비스태요] *Ch4 L16 vocab*
비싸요 비싸다 expensive *Ch6 L24 vocab*
비옷 raincoat *Ch5 L18 point*
비행기 airplane *Ch6 L24 vocab Ch6 L24 point*
비행기 표 airplane ticket *Ch6 L24 vocab*
비행장 hangar *Ch6 L24 point*
빌딩 building *Ch1 L4 vocab* [삘딩, 빌딩]
빠져요 빠지다 falls into (a hole, love), fall out (of a group) *Ch5 L19 vocab*
빨간색 red *Ch4.5*
빨라요 빠르다 (르-irr.) fast *Ch4 L16 vocab*
빨래해요 빨래하다 laundry (does) *Ch 2 L6 vocab*
빨리 quickly *Prelim. C vocab, Ch5 L20 vocab*
빵 bread *Ch4 L13 vocab*
빼빼 skinny *Ch5 L20 point*
빼빼 말랐어요 빼빼 마르다 (르-irr.) skin and bones *Ch5 L19 vocab*
빼요 빼다 takes off (a ring, glasses, gloves, something difficult to take off) *Ch5 L18 vocab*
삐쭉이 (삐죽이) pouty face *Ch5 L20 point*
사 four (Sino-Korean vocab.) *Prelim. G vocab*
사 십 forty (Sino-Korean vocab.) *Prelim. G vocab*
사계절 four seasons *Ch6 L21 vocab*
사과 apple *Ch4 L14 vocab*
사교성 ability to make friends; social skills *Ch5 L20 vocab* [사교썽]
사교성이 좋아요 사교성이 좋다 has good social skills, make many friends *Ch5 L20 vocab*

사귀어요 사귀다 makes friends with, go out with *Ch5 L19 vocab* [사겨요]
사나흘 three to four days *Ch5 L18 vocab*
사람 person *Prelim. I vocab*
사랑해요 사랑하다 loves *Ch 2 L6 vocab*
사무실 office (teacher, worker) *Ch1 L1 vocab Ch6 L24 point*
사요 사다 buys, purchases *Ch3 L10 vocab*
사월 April *Prelim. H vocab*
사이 relationship; between, among *Ch1 L4 vocab Ch5 L20 vocab*
사이가 좋아요 사이가 좋다 gets along well with, be on good terms *Ch5 L20 vocab*
사이다 lemon-lime soda *Ch4 L16 vocab*
사진 (찍다) photo, picture, to take *Ch6 L24 vocab*
사촌 cousin *Ch2.5 vocab*
사탕 candy *Ch1 L3 vocab*
사회학 Sociology *Ch 2 L8 supp*
사흘 three days *Ch5 L18 vocab*
산 mountain *Ch6 L24 vocab*
산책해요 산책하다 walk (takes a) *Ch 2 L6 vocab* [산채캐요]
살 fat (of human body); flesh (of meat)
살 age, *counter Ch3.5 vocab*
살아요 살다 live *Ch3 L9 vocab*
살을 빼요 살을 빼다 (tries to) lose weight (Literally, *subtracts fat*) *Ch5 L19 vocab*
살이 빠져요 살이 빠지다 has lost weight (lose weight) *Ch5 L19 vocab*
살이 쪄요 살이 찌다 fat (gain weight) *Ch5 L19 vocab*
삼 three (Sino-Korean vocab.) *Prelim. G vocab*
삼 십 thirty (Sino-Korean vocab.) *Prelim. G vocab*
삼계탕 ginseng porridge *Ch6 L23 point*
삼월 March *Prelim. H vocab*
삼촌 uncle (by blood) *Ch2.5 vocab*
상 low, traditional eating table *Ch4 L15 vocab*
상자 box, *counter Ch3.5 vocab*
상추 lettuce *Ch4 L13 vocab*
새 new *Ch4 L16 vocab*
새 bird *Ch6 L24 vocab*
새까만 pitch black *Ch5 L18 point*
새끼 baby animals *Ch6.5*
새벽 dawn, early morning (around 3, 4 A.M. ~ 6 A.M.) *Ch1.5 B vocab*
새빨간 bright red *Ch5 L18 point* [새빨간, 쌔빨간]
새침떼기 snotty, snooty; shies away *Ch5 L20 point*
새침해요 새침하다 aloof and reserved *Ch5 L19 vocab*
새파란 bright blue *Ch5 L18 point* [새파란, 쌔파란]
새하얀 snow white *Ch5 L18 point* [새하얀, 쌔하얀]
샌드위치 sandwich *Ch1 L3 vocab* [쌘드위치]
샛노란 bright, central yellow *Ch5 L18 point* [샌노란, 쌘노란]
생강 ginger *Ch4 L14 vocab*
생겼어요 = 났어요 생기다 appeared, came into existence *Ch5 L19 vocab*
생물학 Biology *Ch 2 L8 supp*
생선 fish *Ch4 L13 vocab*
생선회 raw fish *Ch4 L16 vocab*
생일 birthday *Prelim. H vocab*
샤워해요 샤워하다 shower (takes a) *Ch 2 L6 vocab*
서른 thirty (native Korean vocab.) *Prelim. G vocab*
서먹서먹해요 서먹서먹하다 be awkward (for not knowing someone well) *Ch5 L20 vocab*
서반아어 Spanish (language) *Prelim. I point*
서요 서다 stands, stops *Ch3 L10 vocab*
서점 bookstore *Ch2 L5 vocab*
선생님 teacher *Prelim. C vocab*
선선해요 선선하다 (wind, weather) refreshing *Ch6 L21 vocab*
설거지해요 설거지하다 dishes (does) *Ch 2 L6 vocab*
설렁탕 beef tripe soup *Ch4 L16 point*
설사 diarrhea *Ch6 L23 point*
설탕 sugar *Ch4 L14 vocab*
섬 island *Ch6 L24 vocab*
성격 personality *Ch5 L19 vocab*
성조기 Stars and Stripes *Ch4.5 exercises*
세 three (native Korean vocab.) *Prelim. G vocab*
세수해요 세수하다 wash face *Ch 2 L6 vocab*
~세요 셔요 (less frequently) please do *Ch4 L14 focus*
세요 세다 [세다, 시다] counts *Ch3 L10 vocab* [셔요, 세요]
세종 King Sejong, inventor of Han'gul (Korean alphabet) *Prelim. D vocab*
세타 sweater, non-standard *Ch5 L18 point*
섹시해요 섹시하다 sexy *Ch5 L19 vocab* [쌕씨해요]
셋 three (native Korean vocab.) *Prelim. G vocab*
셋째 third *Prelim. G vocab*
셔요 시다 sour *Ch4 L15 vocab*
셰타 sweater, non-standard *Ch5 L18 point*
소 cow ("ox") *Ch6.5*
소개 introduction *Prelim. C vocab*
소고기 beef *Ch4 L13 vocab*
소금 salt *Ch4 L14 vocab*
소주 rice vodka *Ch4 L16 vocab*
소화불량 indigestion *Ch6 L23 point*
속 within *Ch1 L4 vocab*
속눈썹 eyelashes *Ch5 L17 vocab*
손 hands *Ch5 L17 vocab*
손가락 fingers *Ch5 L17 vocab*
손가락을 따요 손가락을 따다 pricks your finger *Ch6 L23 point*
손가락이 가늘어요 손가락이 가늘다 has thin fingers *Ch5 L17 vocab*
손가락이 굵어요 손가락이 굵다 has fat fingers *Ch5 L17 vocab*
손거울 hand mirror *Ch5 L18 vocab* [송꺼울]
손녀 granddaughter *Ch2.5 vocab*

손님 customer, guest *Ch4 L16 supplementary vocab*
손등 back of the hand *Ch5 L17 vocab*
손목 wrist *Ch5 L17 vocab*
손수건 handkerchief *Ch5 L18 vocab* [손쑤건]
손이 매워요 손이 맵다 (ㅂ-irr) has a stinging slap (*Literally, hand is spicy*) *Ch5 L17 point*
손이 커요 손이 크다 overly generous (*Literally, hand is big*) *Ch5 L17 point*
손자 grandson; grandchildren *Ch2.5 vocab*
손톱 fingernails *Ch5 L17 vocab*
송아지 calf *Ch6.5*
송이 flowers, grapes, *counter for Ch3.5 vocab*
쇼핑해요 쇼핑하다 shops; goes shopping *Ch 2 L6 vocab*
수건 towel *Ch5 L18 vocab*
수다쟁이 chatterbox *Ch5 L20 point*
수박 watermelon *Ch4 L14 vocab*
수업 class (course) *Ch 2 L8 vocab*
수염 beard *Ch5 L17 vocab*
수영해요 수영하다 swims *Ch 2 L6 vocab*
수요일 Wednesday *Ch1.5 A vocab*
수학 Math *Ch 2 L8 supp*
숙제 homework *Prelim. C vocab*
숙제해요 숙제하다 homework (does) *Ch1 L1 vocab*
숟가락 spoon *Ch4 L15 vocab Ch4 L13 point*
숟갈 spoon *Ch4 L15 vocab* [숟깔, 수깔]
술 alcoholic beverages *Ch4 L16 vocab*
숫자 number *Prelim. G vocab*
쉬어요 쉬다 rests, rest (takes a) *Ch3 L10 vocab Ch6 L23 vocab*
쉬워요 쉽다 (ㅂ-irr.) easy *Ch5.5 Ch6 L23 vocab*
쉰 fifty (native Korean vocab.) *Prelim. G vocab*
슈퍼(마켓) grocery store *Ch2 L5 vocab*
스무 twenty (native Korean vocab.) (adj.) *Prelim. G vocab*
스물 twenty (native Korean vocab.) *Prelim. G vocab*
스웨터 sweater *Ch5 L18 point*
스트레스가 쌓여요 스트레스가 쌓이다 gets stressed out *Ch6 L22 vocab*
스트레스를 받아요 스트레스를 받다 stresses out *Ch6 L22 vocab*
스페인 Spain *Prelim. I vocab*
스페인사람 Spanish (person); Spaniard *Prelim. I vocab* [스페인싸람]
스페인어 Spanish (language) *Prelim. I vocab*
슬퍼요 슬프다 sad *Ch6 L22 vocab*
시 hour *Ch1.5 B vocab*
시간 time *Ch 2 L7 vocab*
시계 clock, watch *Ch1 L1 vocab Ch5 L18 vocab*
시금치 spinach *Ch4 L13 vocab*
시디, 씨디 CD (compact disk) *Ch1 L3 vocab* [씨디]
시원해요 시원하다 refreshing *Ch4 L15 vocab*
시월 October *Prelim. H vocab*
시장 market *Ch4 L14 vocab*
시켜요 시키다 orders (food) *Ch4 L16 vocab*
시험 test *Ch1 L1 vocab* [시험, 시엄]
시험 때(에) when there is a test *Ch 2 L7 vocab*
식당 cafeteria; diner *Ch2 L5 vocab*
식어요 식다 cools down *Ch4 L15 vocab*
식초 vinegar *Ch4 L14 vocab*
식탁 eating table *Ch4 L15 vocab*
신 shoes, foot wear *Ch5 L18 vocab*
신경성 hypochondria *Ch6 L23 point*
신나요 신나다 excited *Ch6 L22 vocab*
신문 newspaper *Ch1 L3 vocab*
신발 shoes, foot wear *Ch5 L18 vocab*
신어요 신다 puts on (shoes, socks) *Ch5 L18 vocab*
신용카드 credit card *Ch1 L3 vocab*
신청해요 신청하다 applies, makes a request *Ch6 L24 vocab*
실 a single room *Ch 2 L5 point*
실례합니다 실례하다 excuse me *Prelim. F vocab*
실망해요 실망하다 disappointed (at someone; because) *Ch6 L22 vocab*
싫어요 싫다 [실타] disliked *Ch3 L11 vocab*
싫어해요 싫어하다 dislikes *Ch3 L10 vocab*
심리학 Psychology *Ch 2 L8 supp* [심니악]
심술쟁이 jealous, crafty *Ch5 L20 point*
심심해요 심심하다 bored *Ch5 L19 vocab*
심하게 severely *Ch6 L23 vocab*
심해요 심하다 severe *Ch6 L23 vocab*
십 ten (Sino-Korean vocab.) *Prelim. G vocab*
십 만 hundred thousand *Prelim. G vocab* [심만]
십 이월 December *Prelim. H vocab*
십 일월 November *Prelim. H vocab* [시비뤌]
싱거워요 싱겁다 (ㅂ-irr.) bland; not salty or spicy *Ch4 L15 vocab*
~ㅆ어요 *past tense Ch3 L12 focus*
싸요 싸다 cheap *Ch6 L24 vocab*
싸워요 싸우다 fights, has an argument *Ch3 L10 vocab*
싹싹해요 싹싹하다 tactful, tending others' comfort well *Ch5 L19 point*
쌀 uncooked rice *Ch4 L13 vocab*
쌀쌀해요 쌀쌀하다 chilly *Ch6 L21 vocab*
쌍 couple, pair, *counter for* people, animals *Ch3.5 vocab*
쌍둥이 twins *Ch2.5 vocab*
쌓여요 쌓이다 gets accumulated, get stacked *Ch6 L22 vocab*
써요 쓰다 puts on (head gear, glasses, umbrella) *Ch5 L18 vocab*
써요 쓰다 write; use *Ch3 L10 vocab*
써요 쓰다 bitter *Ch4 L15 vocab*
썬글래스 sunglasses *Ch5 L18 point*
썰어요 썰다 cuts, chops *Ch4 L13 vocab* [써러요, 쓰러요]
쓰레기통 garbage can *Ch4 L14 vocab*
씨 Mr., Ms. *Ch1 L2 vocab*
씩씩해요 씩씩하다 energetic, outgoing, keen *Ch5 L19 point*
씻어요 씻다 wash *Ch3 L9 vocab*

아기 baby *Ch2.5 vocab* [아기, 애기]
아기를 봐요 아기를 보다 baby-sits *Ch2.5 point*
아까 a while ago *Ch5 L20 vocab*
아는 척해요 아는 척하다 acts like a know-it-all *Ch5 L20 vocab*
아는 체해요 아는 체하다 acts like a know-it-all *Ch5 L20 vocab*
아니오 no *Prelim. C vocab*
아들 son *Ch2.5 vocab*
아래 below *Ch1 L4 vocab*
아랫사람 junior, someone socially 'below' *Ch1 L4 vocab*
아르바이트해요 아르바이트하다 does part-time work *Ch2 L6 vocab*
아름다워요 아름답다 (ㅂ-irr.) beautiful *Ch5.5*
아무거나 anything *Ch5 L17 point*
아무것도 nothing *Ch5 L17 point*
아무나 anybody, anyone *Ch5 L17 point*
아버지 father *Ch2.5 vocab*
아빠 father (dad) *Ch2.5 vocab*
아이 child(ren) *Ch5 L18 vocab*
아이들, 애들 children *Ch2.5 vocab*
아이스크림 ice cream *Ch1 L3 vocab Ch4 L14 point*
아저씨 uncle; Mr.! Sir! *Ch4 L16 point*
아주 very *Ch3 L12 vocab*
아주머니 ma'am, Auntie *Ch4 L16 point*
아줌마 ma'am, Auntie *Ch4 L16 point*
아직 yet; not yet *Ch3 L12 vocab*
아침 morning (around 7 A.M. ~ 11 A.M.) *Ch1.5 B vocab*
아파요 아프다 sick, hurts *Ch3 L11 vocab*
아파트 apartment *Ch2 L5 vocab*
아홉 nine (native Korean vocab.) *Prelim. G vocab*
아홉째 열째 ninth *Prelim. G vocab*
아흐레 9 days *Ch6 L22 vocab*
아흔 ninety (native Korean vocab.) *Prelim. G vocab*
안 not *Ch 2 L7 focus*
안 inside *Ch1 L4 vocab*
안경 glasses *Ch5 L18 vocab*
안아요 안다 holds (hugs, cradles) *Ch3 L9 vocab*
안주 snack for beer and alcoholic beverages *Ch4 L16 vocab*
앉아요 앉다 sits *Ch3 L9 vocab*
알아 봐요 알아 보다 finds out about; recognizes *Ch6 L24 other*
알아요 알다 knows *Ch3 L9 vocab*
알약 pill *Ch6 L23 vocab* [알략]
앞 front *Ch1 L4 vocab*
앞으로는 in the future, from now on *Ch4 L14 vocab*
애 child(ren) *Ch5 L18 vocab*
앨러지가 있어요 앨러지가 있다 has an allergy *Ch6 L23 vocab*
야 it is (familiar) *Ch4 L13 other*
야구해요 야구하다 plays baseball *Ch 2 L6 vocab*
야채 vegetables *Ch4 L13 vocab*
약국 drug store *Ch2 L5 vocab*
약사 pharmacist *Ch6 L23 vocab*
약을 먹어요 약을 먹다 takes medicine *Ch6 L23 vocab*
약을 지어요 약을 짓다 (ㅅ-irr.) has a prescription filled *Ch6 L23 vocab*
얇아요 얇다 thin (of of flat items, e.g. paper, clothing, books) *Ch5 L17 vocab*
양 sheep, goat, "Aries" *Ch6.5*
양념 seasonings *Ch4 L14 vocab*
양말 socks *Ch5 L18 vocab*
양배추 cabbage *Ch4 L13 vocab*
양파 onion *Ch4 L13 vocab*
얕아요 얕다 shallow *Ch5 L17 vocab*
얘 he, she (familiar; literally, *this child*) *Ch5 L20 other*
얘기해요 얘기하다 talks *Ch 2 L6 vocab*
얘네 his, her; they, their (familiar; literally, *this child's*) *Ch5 L20 other*
~어 보세요 ~어 보다 try... ing *Ch6 L21 other*
~어 보여요 ~어 보이다 looks ADJECTIVE *Ch6 L22 other*
~어 있어요 ~어 있다 is...ing/ed (state) *Ch6 L23 other*
~어 주세요 ~어 주다 (do it) for me *Ch6 L21 focus*
~어 죽겠어요 ~어 죽겠다 dying of *Ch5 L19 other*
어깨 shoulders *Ch5 L17 vocab*
어느 which *Prelim. I vocab*
~어도 even if, even though *Ch5 L18 other*
~어도 돼요 ~어도 되다 you may, may I *Ch5 L19 focus*
어두워요 어둡다 (ㅂ-irr.) dark *Ch5.5*
어디 where; somewhere *Ch3 L9 other Ch3 L9 other*
어때요? 어떻다 (ㅎ-irr.) How is it? *Ch3 L11 other*
어떤 somehow *Ch3 L9 other* [어떠케]
어떻게 somehow *Ch3 L9 other* [어떠케]
~어라 do! (familiar) *Ch4 L13 other*
어려워요 어렵다 (ㅂ-irr.) difficult *Ch5.5 Ch6 L23 vocab*
어른 adult *Ch5 L18 vocab*
어머니 mother *Ch1 L2 vocab*
어색해요 어색하다 awkward *Ch6 L22 vocab*
~어서 goes/comes and *Ch4 L16 other*
~어서 so *Ch3 L11 other*
어서 hurriedly *Ch4 L16 vocab*
~어서 그래요 ~어서 그렇다 it's so because *Ch6 L21 other*
어서 오세요 오다 Welcome! Come on in! *Ch4 L16 vocab*
~어야 돼요 ~어야 되다 has (got) to *Ch6 L23 focus*
어제 = 어저께 yesterday *Ch3 L12 vocab*
어젯밤 last night *Ch3 L12 vocab*
~어져요 ~어지다 becomes ADJECTIVE *Ch6 L21 focus*
억 hundred million *Prelim. G vocab*
언니 female's older sister who is younger than another sister *Ch2.5 vocab*
언덕 hill *Ch6 L24 vocab*

언어학 Linguistics *Ch 2 L8 supp*
언제 when, sometime *Ch3 L9 other*
얼굴 face *Ch5 L17 vocab*
얼굴이 두꺼워요 두껍다 (ㅂ-irr.) has no shame (Literally, *face is thick*) *Ch5 L17 point*
얼굴이 창백해요 얼굴이 창백하다 pale *Ch5 L19 vocab*
얼마나 how *Ch 2 L8 vocab*
얼마나 자주 how often *Ch 2 L8 other*
얼어요 얼다 (something) freezes *Ch4 L13 vocab*
얼음물 iced water *Ch4 L16 vocab*
엄마 mom *Ch2.5 vocab*
없어요 없다 there is no; is lacking *Ch1 L1 vocab* [업써요]
엉덩이 hips, buttocks *Ch5 L17 vocab*
~에 at (time) *Ch 2 L7 other*
~에 to (a place) *Ch2 L5 other*
~에 per *Ch 2 L8 other*
~에 in, at, on *Ch1 L1 vocab*
~에게 to (a person), (written) *Ch5 L20 other*
~에게서 from (a person), (written) *Ch6 L22 other*
~에서 from (a place); *location particle for activities Ch 2 L6 other Ch4 L14 other*
에어콘 air-conditioner *Ch 2 L5 point*
여권 passport *Ch6 L24 vocab* [여꿘]
여기 here *Prelim. C vocab*
여덟 eight (native Korean vocab.) *Prelim. G vocab*
여덟째 eighth *Prelim. G vocab*
여동생 female younger sibling *Ch2.5 vocab*
여드레 8 days *Ch6 L22 vocab*
여든 eighty (native Korean vocab.) *Prelim. G vocab*
여러분 you all (respect) *Ch 2 L8 vocab*
여름 summer *Ch6 L21 vocab*
여섯 six (native Korean vocab.) *Prelim. G vocab*
여섯째 sixth *Prelim. G vocab*
여성학 Women Studies *Ch 2 L8 supp*
여우 fox *Ch6.5 point*
여자 woman *Ch5 L18 vocab*
여학생 female student *Ch1 L1 vocab*
여행사 travel agency *Ch6 L24 vocab*
여행해요 여행하다 to travel *Ch6 L24 vocab*
역사학 History *Ch 2 L8 supp*
연구실 professor's office *Ch6 L24 point*
연두색 light green *Ch4.5*
연장해요 연장하다 extends (deadline, e.g. passport) *Ch6 L24 vocab*
연필 pencil *Ch1 L2 vocab*
연해요 연하다 weak (coffee, tea); light (color); tender *Ch4 L13 vocab*
열쇠 key *Ch1 L3 vocab* [열쐬, 열쎄]
열심히 diligently, (*work*) hard, whole-heartedly *Ch3 L12 vocab*
열어요 열다 opens *Ch3 L9 vocab*
열이 나요 열이 나다 has a fever *Ch6 L23 vocab*
열째 tenth *Prelim. G vocab*
열흘 10 days *Ch6 L22 vocab*
엿새 6 days *Ch6 L21 vocab*
영국 United Kingdom *Prelim. I vocab*
영국 사람 British (person) *Prelim. I vocab*
영어 English (language) *Prelim. I vocab*
영화관 movie theater *Ch2 L5 vocab*
옆 beside; next to *Ch1 L4 vocab*
예, 네 yes *Ch1 L1 vocab*
예뻐요 예쁘다 pretty *Ch3 L11 vocab*
예순 sixty (native Korean vocab.) *Prelim. G vocab*
예전에 long time ago, in the olden days *Ch5 L20 vocab*
옛날에 long time ago, in the olden days *Ch 5 L20 vocab*
오 five (Sino-Korean vocab.) *Prelim. G vocab*
오늘 today *Prelim. H vocab*
오늘 밤 tonight *Ch1.5 B vocab* [오늘빰]
오늘 아침 this morning *Ch1.5 B vocab*
오래 a long while *Ch4 L13 vocab*
오랫동안 for a long time *Ch3 L12 vocab* [오랜똥안] *Ch6 L24 vocab*
오른쪽 right side *Ch1 L4 vocab*
오빠 female's older brother *Ch2.5 vocab*
오월 May *Prelim. H vocab*
오이 cucumber *Ch4 L13 vocab*
오이 소배기 cucumber Kimchi *Ch4 L15 point*
오전 A.M. (around 7 A.M. ~ 11 A.M.) *Ch1.5 B vocab*
오징어 squid *Ch4 L13 vocab*
오토바이 motorcycle ("auto-bike") *Ch1 L3 vocab*
오후 P.M. (around 1 A.M. ~ 5) *Ch1.5 B vocab*
옥수수차 corn tea (often called "물") *Ch4 L16 vocab*
온도 temperature *Ch4 L15 vocab*
올해에 this year *Ch 3 L8 vocab* [오래에]
옷 clothing *Ch5 L18 vocab*
옷장 dresser, armoire *Ch5 L18 vocab*
와요 오다 comes *Ch3 L10 vocab*
와이셔츠 man's dress shirt *Ch5 L18 vocab*
왕눈이 bug-eyed *Ch5 L20 point*
왜 why *Ch3 L9 other*
외동딸 only daughter *Ch2.5 vocab*
외로워요 외롭다 (ㅂ-irr.) lonely *Ch5.5 Ch6 L22 vocab*
외모 appearance *Ch5 L19 vocab*
외식해요 외식하다 eats out *Ch 2 L6 vocab*
외아들 only son *Ch2.5 vocab*
외할머니 maternal grandmother *Ch2.5 vocab*
외할아버지 maternal grandfather *Ch2.5 vocab*
왼쪽 left side *Ch1 L4 vocab*
요거 this little/exact thing *Ch1 L4 point*
요기 here; right here *Ch1 L4 point*
요리해요 요리하다 cooks *Ch 2 L6 vocab*
요일 day(s) of the week *Ch 2 L8 vocab*
욕조 bathtub *Ch5 L18 vocab*
용 dragon *Ch6.5*
우리 we, our (familiar form) *Ch 2 L7 vocab*

우비 raincoat *Ch5 L18 point*
우산 umbrella *Ch5 L18 vocab*
우울해요 우울하다 glum *Ch6 L22 vocab*
우유 milk *Ch4 L16 vocab*
우족 cow feet *Ch4 L16 point*
우체국 post office *Ch2 L5 vocab*
운동장 ball field, sports field *Ch2 L5 vocab Ch6 L24 point*
운동해요 운동하다 exercise (sports) *Ch 2 L6 vocab*
운동화 sneakers *Ch5 L18 vocab*
울어요 울다 cries *Ch3 L9 vocab*
웃어요 웃다 laughs, smiles *Ch3 L9 vocab*
웃어요 웃다 smiles, laughs *Ch3 L9 vocab*
워크맨 portable CD player *Ch1 L3 vocab*
~원 an institution *Ch 2 L5 point*
원숭이 monkey *Ch6.5*
원피스 women's dress *Ch5 L18 point*
월남 Vietnam *Prelim. I point*
월요일 Monday *Ch1.5 A vocab*
월-화-수-목-금 Monday through Friday *Ch1.5 A vocab*
웨딩드레스 wedding dress *Ch5 L18 point*
위 top; above (n.) *Ch1 L4 vocab*
윗사람 senior; someone socially 'above' *Ch1 L4 vocab*
유니폼 uniform *Ch5 L18 point*
유월 June *Prelim. H vocab*
육 six (Sino-Korean vocab.) *Prelim. G vocab*
육회 raw meat *Ch4 L16 vocab* [유쾨]
~으니까 because *Ch4 L14 other*
~으러 가요 ~으러 가다 goes in order to *Ch4 L14 other*
~으러 와요 ~으러 오다 comes in order to *Ch4 L14 other*
~으로 *selectional marker Ch4 L14 other*
~으로 with/by *Ch3 L9 other*
~으면 if/when *Ch4 L13 other*
~으면 안돼요 ~으면 안 되다 you may not, you can't *Ch5 L19 focus*
~으세요 please do *Ch4 L14 focus*
~은/~는 *change of focus, topic marker Ch1 L2 vocab Ch2 L5 other*
은색 silver (color) *Ch4.5*
은행 bank *Ch2 L5 vocab*
~을 거에요 ~을 것이다, ~을 거다 it's probably *Ch6 L21 focus*
~을 거에요 ~을 것이다, ~을 거다 be going to, will *Ch4 L13 focus*
~을 데 place to *Ch6 L24 other*
~을 때 when... *Ch6 L24 other*
~을 수 없어요 ~을 수 없다 isn't possible *Ch5 L20 other*
~을 수 있어요 ~을 수 있다 is possible *Ch5 L20 other*
~을, ~를 *Object marker Ch 2 L6 other*
~을께요 will, OK? *Ch5 L18 focus*
~을까요 shall we, how about, I wonder, should I, do you think *Ch6 L24 focus*
~을래요 I'm gonna, I wanna *Ch4 L16 focus*
음료수 beverages *Ch4 L16 vocab* [음뇨수]
음식 food *Ch4 L15 vocab*
음악 Music *Ch 2 L8 supp*
~읍시다 let's *Ch5 L17 other*

~의 *possessive (NOUN's) Ch1 L4 vocab*
의사 doctor *Ch6 L23 vocab*
의자 chair *Ch1 L1 vocab*
~이 *subject marker (after a noun ending in a consonant) Ch1 L1 vocab*
이 two (Sino-Korean vocab.) *Prelim. G vocab*
이 this (adj.) *Ch1 L2 vocab*
이 십 twenty (Sino-Korean vocab.) *Prelim. G vocab*
이 주일 전에 two weeks ago *Ch3 L12 vocab*
이거 this (noun) *Ch1 L2 vocab*
이건 this (topic, contrast) *Ch1 L2 vocab*
이게 this (as subject, focus) *Ch1 L2 vocab*
이기적이에요 이기적이다 selfish *Ch5 L19 vocab*
~이나 as many as *Ch3 L12 vocab*
~이나 or something like that *Ch5 L17 other*
~이나 or (for connecting nouns) *Ch4 L13 other*
~이나 as many as *Ch3 L12 other*
이따가 later today *Ch5 L20 vocab*
~이라도 even if, even though *Ch5 L18 other*
~이라면 if/when (for the verb *be*) *Ch4 L13 other*
~이라서 because (for the verb *be*) *Ch4 L13 other*
~이랑 with (spoken); and *Ch4 L15 other Ch4 L15 vocab*
이래요 이러다 does this *Ch5 L18 other*
이래요 이렇다 is like this *Ch5 L18 other*
이레 7 days *Ch6 L21 vocab Ch6 L22 vocab*
이름 name *Ch1 L2 vocab*
이리 this way *Ch4 L14 vocab*
이마 forehead *Ch5 L17 vocab*
이마가 넓어요 이마가 넓어요 has a wide forehead *Ch5 L17 vocab*
이마가 좁아요 이마가 좁아요 has a short forehead (Literally, *narrow*) *Ch5 L17 vocab*
이메일 email (address) *Ch1 L2 vocab*
이모 aunt on mother's side *Ch2.5 vocab*
이모부 maternal aunt's husband *Ch2.5 vocab*
이발소 barber's *Ch5 L17 vocab* [이발쏘]
이번 달에 this month *Ch 2 L7 vocab* [이번따레]
이번 주말에 this weekend *Ch 2 L7 vocab* [이번쭈마레]
이번 주에 this week *Ch 2 L7 vocab* [이번쭈에]
이상해요 이상하다 weird, strange *Ch3 L11 vocab*
~이야 it is (familiar) *Ch4 L13 other*
이야기해요 이야기하다 talks *Ch 2 L6 vocab*
이월 February *Prelim. H vocab*
이제부터는 in the future, from now on *Ch4 L14 vocab*
이탈리아 Italy *Prelim. I vocab*
이탈리아 사람 Italian (person) *Prelim. I vocab* [이탈리아싸람]
이탈리아어 Italian (language) *Prelim. I vocab*
이태리 Italy *Prelim. I point*
이틀 two days *Ch5 L18 vocab*
인기 popularity *Ch5 L20 vocab* [잉끼]

인기가 많아요 인기가 많다 popular (among friends) *Ch5 L20 vocab*
인기가 좋아요 인기가 좋다 popular (among friends) *Ch5 L20 vocab*
인사해요 인사하다 greets, says hello *Ch5 L17 vocab*
인삼 ginseng *Ch6 L23 point*
인삼주 ginseng-based liquor *Ch4 L16 vocab*
일 one (Sino-Korean vocab.) *Prelim. G vocab*
일 주일에 per week *Ch 2 L8 vocab* [일쭈이레]
일곱 seven (native Korean vocab.) *Prelim. G vocab*
일곱째 seventh *Prelim. G vocab*
일기 예보 weather forecast, hear *Ch6 L21 vocab*
일본 Japan *Prelim. I vocab*
일본 사람 Japanese (person) *Prelim. I vocab*
일본어 Japanese (language) *Prelim. I vocab*
일어나요 일어나다 gets up, gets out of bed *Ch3 L10 vocab*
일요일 Sunday *Ch1.5 A vocab* [이료일]
일월 January *Prelim. H vocab* [이뤌]
일일 first (day of month) *Prelim. H vocab* [이릴]
일찍 early *Ch5 L20 vocab*
일해요 일하다 works *Ch 2 L6 vocab*
일흔 seventy (native Korean vocab.) *Prelim. G vocab*
읽어요 읽다 reads *Ch3 L9 vocab*
입 mouth *Ch5 L17 vocab*
입가 around your mouth *Ch6 L24 point*
입술 lips *Ch5 L17 vocab*
입어요 입다 puts on (clothing on the body) *Ch5 L18 vocab*
입어요 입다 wears, puts on (clothes) *Ch3 L9 vocab*
입원을 해요 입원을 하다 be hospitalized, check into the hospital *Ch6 L23 vocab*
입이 궁금해요 입이 궁금하다 I feel munchy. (Literally, *my mouth is wondering*) *Ch4 L16 vocab*
입이 심심해요 입이 심심하다 I feel munchy. (Literally, *my mouth is bored*) *Ch4 L16 vocab*
입이 짧아요 입이 짧다 doesn't like main meals (Literally, *mouth is short*) *Ch5 L17 point*
있어요 있다 there is; exists; has *Ch1 L1 vocab* [이써요]
~자 let's (familiar) *Ch4 L13 other*
자 here, take this; here it is; here you go (*intimae-blunt*) *bonus*
자 ruler *Ch1 L1 supp*
자기 oneself *Ch5 L20 vocab*
자기 소개 introduction of oneself *Prelim. C vocab*
자루 *counter for* sacks pencils, pens *Ch3.5 vocab*
자리에 누워요 자리에 눕다 (ㅂ-irr.) lie down in bed *Ch6 L23 vocab*
자매 female sibling *Ch2.5 vocab*
자요 자다 sleeps *Ch3 L10 vocab*
자식 off-spring (talking about one's own or derogatory) *Ch6.5 point*
자연 nature *Ch6 L24 vocab*
자음 consonant *Prelim. D vocab*
자전거 bicycle *Ch1 L3 vocab*
자존심 상해요 자존심 상하다 has one's pride hurt *Ch6 L22 vocab*
자주 often, very often *Ch 2 L7 vocab*
자주색 magenta *Ch4.5*
자켓, 자케트, 쟈케트 jacket *Ch5 L18 point*
작년에 last year *Ch3 L12 vocab*
작아요 작다 small *Ch3 L11 vocab*
작은 누나 male's older sister who is younger than another sister *Ch2.5 vocab*
작은 언니 female's older sister who is younger than another sister *Ch2.5 vocab*
작은 오빠 female's older brother who is younger than another brother *Ch2.5 vocab*
작은 형 male's older brother who is younger than another brother *Ch2.5 vocab*
잔 glasses, *counter for Ch3.5 vocab Ch4 L16 vocab*
잘 often, very often *Ch 3 L8 vocab*
잘 부탁합니다, 잘 부탁해요 잘 부탁하다 I will be obliged to you. (greeting) *Prelim. I point* [잘 부탁함니다]
잘 생겼어요 잘 생기다 good-looking (man) *Ch5 L19 vocab*
잘난 척해요 잘난 척하다 acts like one is so great *Ch5 L20 vocab*
잘난 체해요 잘난 체하다 acts like one is so great *Ch5 L20 vocab*
잠깐, 잠시 (just) a minute; (for) a short while *Ch3 L12 vocab Ch4 L16 vocab*
잠꾸러기 sleepy head *Ch5 L20 point*
잠바 jacket with elastic waist, non-standard spelling *Ch5 L18 point*
잠보 sleepy head *Ch5 L20 point* [잠뽀]
잠시, 잠깐 (just) a minute; (for) a short while *Ch3 L12 vocab Ch4 L16 vocab*
잡아요 잡다 grabs, holds (hands); catches (a bus) *Ch3 L9 vocab*
잡지 magazine *Ch1 L3 vocab* [잡찌]
잡채 clear noodles with seasoned vegetables *Ch4 L15 vocab*
~장 ground, field *Ch 2 L5 point*
장 sheets, *counter for Ch3.5 vocab*
장갑 gloves *Ch5 L18 vocab*
재미동포, 재미교포 Koreans living in US *Prelim. I point*
재미없어요 재미없다 no fun *Ch3 L11 vocab Ch5 L19 vocab*
재미있어요 재미있다 fun, interesting *Ch3 L11 vocab Ch5 L19 vocab*
재일동포 Koreans living in Japan *Prelim. I point*
재채기 sneeze *Ch6 L23 vocab*
재채기가 나와요 재채기가 나오다 sneezes come out (to sneeze) *Ch6 L23 vocab*
재채기가 나요 재채기가 나다 sneezes come out (to sneeze) *Ch6 L23 vocab*
재채기를 해요 재채기를 하다 sneezes come out (to sneeze) *Ch6 L23 vocab*
재키트 (쟈케트) jacket *Ch5 L18 point*
쟤 he, she (familiar; literally, that child) over there *Ch5 L20 other*

걔네 his, her; they, their (familiar; literally, that child's) over there *Ch5 L20 other*
저 I, me (humble) *Ch2 L5 vocab*
저 that over there (adj.) *Ch1 L2 vocab*
저거 that thing over there (noun) *Ch1 L2 vocab*
저건 that thing over there (topic, contrast) *Ch1 L2 vocab*
저게 that thing over there as subject/focus *Ch1 L2 vocab*
저기 over there *Ch1 L3 vocab*
저녁 evening (around 5, 6 P.M. ~ 8 P.M.) *Ch1.5 B vocab*
저래요 저러다 does that (distant) *Ch5 L18 other*
저리 that (distant) way *Ch4 L14 vocab*
저희 our (humble) *Ch 2 L7 other*
적어요 적다 be only a little *Ch3 L11 vocab*
전 thin, savory Korean pancakes *Ch4 L13 point*
전공 major *Ch 2 L8 vocab* [전공, 정공]
전기 면도기 electric razor *Ch5 L18 vocab*
전문 specialty *Ch4 L16 vocab*
전에 before, ago *Ch6 L22, vocab, other*
전자 공학 Electrical Engineering *Ch 2 L8 supp*
전학 transfer to another school *Ch 2 L8 point*
전화 telephone *Ch1 L1 vocab* [저놔, 저나]
전화번호 phone number *Ch1 L2 vocab* [저나버노]
전화해요 전화하다 phones *Ch 2 L6 vocab*
점 a store *Ch 2 L5 point*
점심 day time (around 11:30 A.M. ~ 2:30 P.M.) *Ch1.5 B vocab*
점퍼 jacket with elastic waist *Ch5 L18 point*
접시 dish, plate *Ch4 L16 vocab*
젓가락 (젓가락) chopsticks *Ch4 L13 point Ch4 L15 vocab*
젓갈 chopsticks *Ch4 L15 vocab*
정말(로) really, truly *Ch3 L12 vocab*
정치학 Political Science *Ch 2 L8 supp*
제 my (humble), I (humble) *Ch 2 L7 other*
제일 best, most *Ch5 L20 vocab*
조각, 쪽 piece *Ch4 L16 vocab* [조각, 쪼각]
조거 that little/exact thing over there *Ch1 L4 point*
조금, 좀 a little, a little bit *Ch3 L12 vocab* [조금, 쪼금 / 좀, 쫌] *Ch4 L14 vocab*
조금 전에 a little while ago, few minutes ago *Ch5 L20 vocab*
조기 over there; right over there *Ch1 L4 point*
조용히 하세요 조용히하다 quiet *Prelim. F vocab*
졸려요 졸리다 sleepy *Ch6 L22 vocab*
졸업해요 졸업하다 graduate *Ch5 L17 vocab*
좀, 조금 a little, a little bit *Ch4 L14 vocab* [좀, 조금 / 쫌, 쪼금]
좀 전에 a little while ago, few minutes ago *Ch5 L20 vocab*
좁아요 좁아요 narrow, crowded *Ch5 L17 vocab*
종업원 clerk, employee *Ch4 L16 supplementary vocab* 종이 paper *Ch1 L2 vocab*
좋아요 좋다 [조타] good; liked *Ch3 L11 vocab*
좋아해요 좋아하다 likes *Ch3 L10 vocab*
죠깅, 조깅 jogging *Ch 2 L6 focus*
죠깅해요, 조깅해요 죠깅하다, 조깅하다 jogs *Ch 2 L6 vocab*
주 반찬 main side dishes *Ch4 L15 vocab*
주말에 on weekend(s) *Ch 2 L7 vocab*
주문해요 주문하다 to order (food) *Ch4 L16 vocab*
주사 (to get) a shot *Ch6 L23 vocab*
주스 juice *Ch1 L3 vocab*
주어 subject *bonus*
주어요, 줘요 주다 give *Ch3 L10 vocab*
주위 around *Ch1 L4 vocab*
주전자 kettle *Ch4 L16 vocab*
주차장 parking lot *Ch2 L5 vocab Ch6 L24 point*
주홍색 dark orange *Ch4.5*
주황색 orange *Ch4.5*
중국 China *Prelim. I vocab*
중국 사람 Chinese (person) *Prelim. I vocab*
중국어 Chinese (language) *Prelim. I vocab*
중에 among (in comparison) *Ch5 L20 vocab*
중요해요 중요하다 important *Ch4 L13 vocab*
줘요, 주어요 주다 give *Ch3 L10 vocab*
쥐 mouse *Ch6.5*
즐거워요 즐겁다 (ㅂ-irr.) happy, excited *Ch5.5 Ch6 L22 vocab*
~지 right?, isn't it so? *Ch4 L13 other*
~지 마세요 ~지 말다 please don't *Ch4 L14 focus*
~지 맙시다 ~지 말다 let's not *Ch5 L17 other*
지갑 wallet *Ch1 L3 vocab*
지금 now *Prelim. H vocab*
지난 last, past *Ch3 L12 vocab*
지난 밤 last night *Ch3 L12 vocab*
지난 주 (수요일에) last (Wednesday) *Ch3 L12 vocab*
지난 주말에 last weekend *Ch3 L12 vocab*
지난 주에 last week *Ch3 L12 vocab*
지난 학기에 last semester, quarter *Ch3 L12 vocab*
지난 해에 last year *Ch3 L12 vocab*
지난 해에, 작년에 last year *Ch3 L12 vocab*
지도 map *Ch6 L24 vocab*
~지만 but *Ch3 L9 other*
지우개 eraser *Ch1 L2 vocab*
지하도 pedestrian's underpass *Ch6 L24 point*
지하실 basement *Ch6 L24 point*
지하철 subway train *Ch6 L24 vocab Ch6 L24 point*
진짜(로) truly *Ch3 L12 vocab*
진찰 medical check-up *Ch6 L23 vocab*
진찰을 받아요 진찰을 받다 gets a (medical) check-up, examination *Ch6 L23 vocab*
진찰을 해요 진찰을 하다 gives a (medical) check-up, examination *Ch6 L23 vocab*
진해요 진하다 strong (e.g., coffee, tea) *Ch4 L13 vocab*
질겨요 질기다 tough, chewy *Ch4 L13 vocab*
질문 question *Prelim. C vocab*
집 house, home *Ch2 L5 vocab*
짜요 짜다 salty *Ch4 L15 vocab*
짜증을 내요 짜증을 내다 gets annoyed *Ch6 L22 vocab*
짜증이 나요 짜증이 나다 annoyed *Ch6 L22 vocab*

짝 partner *Prelim. C vocab*
짧아요 짧다 short *Ch5 L17 vocab*
쪽 side *Ch1 L4 vocab*
쪽, 조각 pieces, slices, *counter for Ch3.5 vocab*
~쯤 about, approximately *Ch 2 L8 vocab*
찌개 salty Korean stew *Ch4 L13 point Ch4 L15 vocab*
찍어요, (사진을) 찍다 takes a picture, imprints *Ch6 L24 vocab*
차가워요 차갑다 (ㅂ-irr.) cold *Ch4 L15 vocab* [차가워요, 차거워요]
차려요 차리다 sets (the table) *Ch4 L15 vocab*
차요 차다 puts on (a watch, belt, something with a band) *Ch5 L18 vocab*
착해요 착하다 good (well-behaved; a good person) *Ch5 L19 vocab*
참기름 sesame oil *Ch4 L14 vocab*
창문 window *Ch1 L1 vocab*
창백해요 창백하다 pale *Ch5 L19 vocab*
창피해요 창피하다 ashamed, shy *Ch6 L22 vocab* [챙피하다]
찾아 봐요 찾아 보다 look for *Ch6 L24 other*
찾아요 찾다 look for ; find; withdraw (money) *Ch3 L9 vocab*
채 houses, buildings, *counter for Ch3.5 vocab*
채소 vegetables *Ch4 L13 vocab*
책 book *Ch1 L2 vocab*
책상 desk *Ch1 L1 vocab* [책쌍]
~처럼 like (something, someone) *Ch5 L20 vocab*
처음에 at first *Ch5 L20 vocab*
처음으로 for the first time *Ch5 L20 vocab*
천 thousand *Prelim. G vocab*
천 만 ten million *Prelim. G vocab*
천재 genius *Ch5 L20 point*
천천히 slowly *Prelim. C vocab, Ch5 L20 vocab*
첫번째 first time *Prelim. G vocab*
첫째 first *Prelim. G vocab*
청바지 (blue) jeans *Ch5 L18 vocab*
청소해요 청소하다 cleans (house, rooms) *Ch 2 L6 vocab*
체육관 sports complex; gym *Ch2 L5 vocab*
쳐요 치다 play (tennis/ guitar) *Ch3 L10 vocab*
초록색 green *Ch4.5*
초조해요 초조하다 nervous in anticipation, restless, fretful *Ch6 L22 vocab*
초컬릿, 초콜렛, 쵸컬렛, 초코렛 chocolate *Ch1 L3 vocab Ch4 L14 point*
총각김치 icicle radish Kimchi *Ch4 L15 vocab Ch4 L15 point*
최고 the best (one) *Ch5 L20 vocab*
최근에 recently *Ch5 L20 vocab*
추워요 춥다 (ㅂ-irr.) cold *Ch6 L21 vocab*
축구해요 축구하다 play soccer *Ch 2 L6 vocab*
취해요 취하다 gets drunk *Ch4 L16 vocab*
치료 treament (of a disease) *Ch6 L23 vocab*
치료를 해요 치료를 하다 gives a treatment, prognosis *Ch6 L23 vocab*
치마 skirt *Ch5 L18 vocab*
치약 toothpaste *Ch5 L18 vocab*
친구 friend *Ch1 L2 vocab* [칭구]
친절해요 친절하다 friendly, kind *Ch5 L19 vocab*
친할머니 paternal grandmother *Ch2.5 vocab*
친할아버지 paternal grandfather *Ch2.5 vocab*
친해요 친하다 be good friends with *Ch5 L20 vocab*
칠 seven (Sino-Korean vocab.) *Prelim. G vocab*
칠월 July *Prelim. H vocab* [치뤌]
칠칠맞아요 칠칠맞다 sloppy *Ch5 L19 point*
칠칠이 klutz *Ch5 L20 point*
칠판 chalkboard *Ch1 L1 vocab*
침 acupuncture needle(s) *Ch6 L23 point*
침을 놓아요 놓다 acupuncture *Ch6 L23 point*
칫솔 toothbrush *Ch5 L18 vocab*
카메라 camera *Ch1 L2 vocab*
카키색 khaki *Ch4.5*
칼 knife *Ch1 L1 supp*
캐나다 사람 Canadian (person) *Prelim. I vocab* [캐나다싸람]
캐나다, 카나다 Canada *Prelim. I vocab*
커요 크다 big *Ch3 L11 vocab*
커피숍 coffee shop *Ch2 L5 vocab*
컴퓨터 computer *Ch1 L1 vocab*
컴퓨터 공학 Computer Science *Ch 2 L8 supp*
컴퓨터 랩 computer lab *Ch2 L5 vocab*
컵 cup *Ch3.5 vocab Ch4 L16 vocab*
케이크 cake *Ch4 L14 point*
켤레 pairs of shoes, *counter for Ch3.5 vocab*
코 nose *Ch5 L17 vocab*
코가 낮아요 코가 낮다 has a flat nose *Ch5 L17 vocab*
코가 높아요 코가 높다 has a big, high nose; haughty, snobbish *Ch5 L17 vocab Ch5 L17 point*
콧구멍 nostrils *Ch5 L17 vocab*
콧물이 나와요 콧물이 나오다 have a runny nose *Ch6 L23 vocab*
콧물이 나요 콧물이 나다 have a runny nose *Ch6 L23 vocab*
콧수염 mustache *Ch5 L17 vocab*
콩 (black) bean *Ch4 L13 vocab*
콩나물 bean sprouts *Ch4 L13 vocab*
크레디트 카드, 크레딧 카드 credit card *Ch1 L3 vocab*
큰 누나 male's older sister who is older than another older sister *Ch2.5 vocab*
큰 소리로 loudly *Prelim. C vocab*
큰 아들 oldest child *Ch2.5 vocab*
큰 언니 female's older sister who is older than another older sister *Ch2.5 vocab*
큰 오빠 female's older brother who is older than another older brother *Ch2.5 vocab*
큰형 male's older brother who is older than another older brother *Ch2.5 vocab*
키가 작아요 키가 작다 short *Ch5 L17 vocab*
키가 커요 키가 크다 tall *Ch5 L17 vocab*
타요 타다 rides, gets on *Ch3 L10 vocab*
탁자 table *Ch1 L1 vocab* [탁짜]

~탕 soup based on meat broth *Ch4 L13 point*
태극기 Korean flag *Ch4.5 exercises*
택시 taxi *Ch1 L3 vocab*
터프해요 터프하다 macho *Ch5 L19 vocab*
턱 chin, jaws *Ch5 L17 vocab*
털털해요 털털하다 not picky, easy-going *Ch5 L19 vocab*
테레비, 텔레비전, 텔레비젼 T.V. *Ch1 L1 vocab*
토끼 rabbit *Ch6.5*
토마토 tomato *Ch4 L13 vocab*
토요일 Saturday *Ch1.5 A vocab*
통통해요 통통하다 plump *Ch5 L19 point*
퇴원을 해요 퇴원을 하다 check out of the hospital *Ch6 L23 vocab*
투피스 women's dress suit *Ch5 L18 point*
튼튼해요 튼튼하다 strong, sturdy, healthy *Ch5 L19 point*
틀려요 틀리다 incorrect, wrong *Ch3 L11 vocab*
티셔츠 t-shirt *Ch5 L18 vocab*
파 green onion *Ch4 L13 vocab*
파란색 blue *Ch4.5*
파이 pie *Ch4 L14 point*
파자마 pajamas *Ch5 L18 point*
파전 green onion pancake *Ch4 L15 vocab*
팔 eight (Sino-Korean vocab.) *Prelim. G vocab*
팔 arms *Ch5 L17 vocab*
팔아요 팔다 sells *Ch4 L13 vocab*
팔월 August *Prelim. H vocab* [파뤌]
팔팔해요 팔팔하다 energetic *Ch5 L19 point*
팥 red bean *Ch4 L13 vocab*
펜 pen *Ch1 L2 vocab*
편, 쪽 side *Ch1 L4 vocab*
편리해요 편리하다 convenient *Ch3 L11 vocab*
편해요 편하다 comfortable *Ch3 L11 vocab*
평소에 usually, on regular days *Ch 2 L7 vocab*
평일에 on week days *Ch 2 L7 vocab*
포기 heads (of cabbage), *counter for Ch3.5 vocab*
포도 grapes *Ch4 L14 vocab*
표현 expression *Ch5 L17 vocab*
푹 sufficiently, deeply *Ch6 L23 vocab* [셔요]-with lip rounding
풀어요 풀다 loosens, dissolves, solves, unties *Ch5 L18 vocab*
프랑스 France *Prelim. I vocab*
프랑스 사람 French (person) *Prelim. I vocab* [프랑쓰싸람]
프랑스어 French (language) *Prelim. I vocab*
프랜스 France *Prelim. I point*
프린터 printer *Ch1 L1 vocab*
피곤해요 피곤하다 tired *Ch3 L11 vocab Ch6 L22 vocab*
피부 skin *Ch5 L17 vocab*
필요없어요 필요없다 unnecessary; not needed *Ch3 L11 vocab*
필요해요 필요하다 needed, necessary *Ch3 L11 vocab*
필통 pencil case *Ch1 L1 supp*
핑크색 pink *Ch4.5*
~하고 with *Ch2 L5 vocab*
~하고 and (*noun particle*) *Ch1 L3 vocab*
하나, 한 one (*native Korean vocab.*) *Prelim. G vocab*
하늘 sky *Ch6 L24 vocab*
하늘색 sky blue, light blue *Ch4.5*
하루에 per day *Ch 2 L8 vocab*
하얀색, 흰색 white *Ch4.5*
학교 school *Ch2 L5 vocab Ch6 L24 point*
학기 quarter/semester *Ch 2 L8 vocab*
학년 year (in school) *Ch 2 L8 vocab* [항년]
학번 student number; year of entry to college *Ch 2 L8 point*
학생 student *Ch1 L1 vocab* [학쌩]
학생증 student ID card *Ch1 L3 vocab* [학쌩쯩]
학생회관 student center *Ch2 L5 vocab*
한 달 전에 a month ago *Ch3 L12 vocab*
한 번 더 more, one more time *Prelim. C vocab*
한 턱 내세요 내다 Treat us. *Ch4 L16 vocab* [한텅 내세요]
한가해요 한가하다 not busy, have a lot of free time *Ch3 L11 vocab*
한국 Korea *Prelim. I vocab*
한국 사람 Korean (person) *Prelim. I vocab*
한국어 Korean (language) *Prelim. I vocab*
한국학 Korea Studies *Ch 2 L8 supp*
한글 Han'gul; the Korean alphabet *Prelim. D vocab*
한약방 pharmacy for traditional medicines *Ch6 L23 point*
한의사 pharmacist (for traditional medicine) *Ch6 L23 point*
~한테 to (a person) (*spoken*) *Ch3 L11 other Ch5 L20 other*
~한테서 from (a person), (spoken) *Ch6 L21 other*
할머니 grandmother *Ch2.5 vocab*
할아버지 grandfather *Ch2.5 vocab*
항상 always *Ch 2 L7 vocab*
해 year, sun *Ch6 L22 vocab, Ch6 L24 vocab*
해가 나요, 해가 났어요 해가 나다 sunny *Ch6 L21 vocab*
해가 떠요 해가 뜨다 the sun rises *Ch6 L21 vocab*
해가 져요 해가 지다 the sun sets *Ch6 L21 vocab*
해물 seafood *Ch4 L13 vocab*
해물 파전 seafood green onion pancake *Ch4 L15 vocab*
해요 하다 puts on (accessories) *Ch5 L18 vocab*
해요 하다 does *Ch 2 L6 vocab*
핸드폰 cellular phone *Ch1 L3 vocab*
허리 waist, lower back *Ch5 L17 vocab*
허리띠 belt *Ch5 L18 vocab*
허풍쟁이 braggart, show-off *Ch5 L20 point*
헌 old and worn out *Ch4 L16 vocab*
혀 tongue *Ch5 L17 vocab*
혀밑구이 cow tongue *Ch4 L16 point*
혓바닥 tongue *Ch5 L17 vocab*
형 male's older brother *Ch2.5 vocab*

형용사 adjectives *Ch4 L16 vocab*
형제 siblings; male sibling *Ch2.5 vocab*
호랑이 tiger *Ch6.5*
호박 pumpkin, zucchini, squash *Ch4 L13 vocab*
호수 lake *Ch6 L24 vocab*
호숫가 lakeside *Ch6 L24 point* [호순까, 호숙까]
혼자 by oneself *Ch2 L5 vocab*
홍당무 carrot *Ch4 L13 vocab*
화가 나요 화가 나다 feels angry with *Ch6 L22 vocab*
화를 내요 화를 내다 gets angry at *Ch6 L22 vocab*
화요일 Tuesday *Ch1.5 A vocab*
화이트 white-out *Ch1 L1 supp*
화장실 restroom *Prelim. F vocab Ch5 L18 vocab*
화장해요 화장하다 make-up (puts on) *Ch 2 L6 vocab*
화학 Chemistry *Ch 2 L8 supp*
환자 patient *Ch6 L23 vocab*
회색 gray *Ch4.5*
후추 black pepper *Ch4 L14 vocab*
후춧가루 black pepper powder *Ch4 L14 vocab*
훨씬 far, much, way (more, better, etc.) *Ch5 L20 vocab*
휴가 vacation (days off work) *Ch6 L24 vocab Ch6 L24 point*
휴게실 lounge *Ch6 L24 point*
휴일 holiday *Ch6 L24 vocab*
휴지통 trash can *Ch4 L14 vocab*
휴학 on leave (by students) *Ch 2 L8 point Ch6 L24 point*
흐려요 흐리다 overcast *Ch6 L21 vocab*
흑염소 black goat *Ch6 L23 point*
흰 머리, 하얀 머리 gray hair *Ch5 L17 vocab*
흰, 하얀 white *Ch4.5*

Overview of Grammar Volume I

예비장 Preliminary Chapter	A. 인사 Greetings	B. 문화 Culture C. 교실에서는 In the Classroom	D. 한글 Hangul	E. 발음 길잡이 Pronunciation Guide	F. 유용 표현 Useful Expressions	G. 숫자 Numbers	H. 날짜 Days and Months	I. 국적 묻기 Nationalities
	Classroom Nouns		**Other Basic Nouns**		**More Nouns and Markers**		**Location Nouns**	
	제 1 과 Lesson 1 내일은 시험이 있어요?		**제 2 과 Lesson 2** 그게 뭐예요?		**제 3 과 Lesson 3** 사탕도 있어요?		**제 4 과 Lesson 4** 선생님의 사무실	
	Focus	Other	Focus	Other	Focus	Other	Focus	Other
제 1 장 그 게 뭐예요? **Chapter 1** **What is it?**	• A 이/가 있어요 There is A • A 이/가 없어요 There is no A	• 뭐, 무엇 what • -에 in, on, at	• A 은/는 B(이)에요 A is B • A 은/는 B 이/가 아니에요 A is not B	• -이, -그, -저 this, that, that over there • 거, 것 thing • 제, 저의, …씨 my (humble) • *compounds* • 네/아니오 yes/no	• A 은/는 B 이/가 있어요 A has B • A 은/는 B 이/가 없어요 A doesn't have B	• -도 also • A 하고 B A and B • 여기, 거기, 저기 here, there, way over there	__(의) 앞에 __이/가 있어요 location words & construction	• -의 's • 어디 where • -은/는 contrast • contracted pronouns
제 1.5 장 **Chapter 1.5**	요일 **Days of the week** 시간 **Telling time**							
	Place Nouns		**해요-Verbs**		**Time Adverbs**		**Connectors and Time Words**	
	제 5 과 Lesson 5 어디 가요?		**제 6 과 Lesson 6** 지금 뭐 해요?		**제 7 과 Lesson 7** 평일에 별로 공부 안 해요.		**제 8 과 Lesson 8** 동호의 하루	
	Focus	Other	Focus	Other	Focus	Other	Focus	Other
제 2 장 뭐 해요? **Chapter 2** **What are you doing?**	"가요" **The Verb "Go"**	• -에 to • -요 politeness • -은/는 change of focus • -하고 with • 누구/누가 who, whom	"해요" 동사 **The Verb "Do"**	• -을/를 *Object Marker* • 같이 together • -에서 at (location of an activity)	안 **not**	• 나, 내, 우리, 저, 제,저희 1st person PN • Use of markers, frequency adv, position of time adverbs • -에 in, on at (time)	-에도, -에서도 -에는, -에서는 stacking of markers	• 그리고, 그래서, 그렇지만 **and, so, but** • -에 per • 몇 how many • 얼마나 자주, 몇 번 how often
제 2.5 장 **Chapter 2.5**	가족 **Family**							
	Daily Activity Verbs A		**Daily Activity Verbs B**		**Adjectival Verbs**		**Adverbs**	
	제 9 과 Lesson 9 미안해요. 파티에 못 가요.		**제 10 과 Lesson 10** 친구를 만나요.		**제 11 과 Lesson 11** 일요일이 어때요?		**제 12 과 Lesson 12** 제인 씨가 없어서 재미없었어요!	
	Focus	Other	Focus	Other	Focus	Other	Focus	Other
제 3 장 일요일은 괜찮아요. **Chapter 3** **Sunday is O.K.**	자음으로 끝나는 동사 현재형 Consonant-ending Verbs **(*Present Tense*)**	• 못 • -고 and -지만 but • -고 나서 and then • -(으)로 with, by • 뭐 something	모음으로 끝나는 동사 현재형 Vowel-ending Verbs **(*Present Tense*)**	• -기 전에 before doing • -만 only, just • 와요 vs. 가요 come vs. go • -부터…-까지 from until, up to	형용사 현재형 Adjectives **(*Present Tense*)**	• -어서 so… • -(으) irregular predicates • 우리 같이..어요 Let's • 어때요? How is it • 어디, 거기+에, 에서 • -한테 to a person • 좋아하다, 좋다 to like, to be good	과거형 ***Past Tense***	• -었고, -었지만 vs. -어서/-아서 • -은/는 vs. -이/가 (Review) • -도 (usage) • -(이)나 as many as
제 3.5 장 **Chapter 3.5**	Counters							

Overview of Grammar Volume II

Chapter								
	Ingredients		Seasonings and Fruit		Food, Taste & Temperature		Food Expressions	
	제 13 과 갈비에는 뭐가 들어가요?		제 14 과 시장에서		제 15 과 잘 먹겠습니다!		제 16 과 뭐 먹을래요?	
	문법 촛점	Other	문법 촛점	Other	문법 촛점	Other	문법 촛점	Other
제 4 장 뭐 먹을래요? Chapter 4 What do you wanna eat?	-(으)ㄹ 거예요 going to, will	• -지 right? Isn't it? • 반말체 -어/니/어라/자/니 *intimate-blunt* speech form • -이야 it is (*intimate-blunt*) • -(으)면 if/when • -(이)나 or	• -(으)세요 Please do • -지 마세요 Please don't	• -(으)로 (choice) • -(으)러 가요/와요 go/come (in order) to • -(으)니까 because • Counters 명, 마리, 개 • -에서 (from)	ㅂ-불규칙 형용사, 동사 ㅂ-irregular predicates	• -네 *unexpectedness* • -게 -ly • -씩 each, one by one • 때 at the time of • -(이)랑 and, with	-(으)ㄹ래요 gonna, wanna	• 관형어미 -은/는 Noun-modifier ending • …가서/와서… go/come and then and there • More counters 병, 잔, 그릇… • 르-불규칙 동사, 형용사 르- irregular words • N 같다 like N
제 4.5 장 Chapter 4.5	색(깔)							
	The Body		Clothing & Toiletries		Mood, Personality & Appearance		Important Miscellany	
	제 17 과 코가 높은 남자		제 18 과 엄마 스타킹 신을께.		제 19 과 두 얼굴의 사나이		제 20 과 까만 머리가 더 좋아요.	
제 5 장 추운데…문을 닫아도 돼요? Chapter 5 I'm cold… May I close the door?	-은데/는데 and, so, but…	• 돼요 become, suitable • -(으)ㅂ시다! Let's! -지 맙시다! Let's not! • -이나 or something like that • -도 even • 아무 것도/ 아무도 nothing, no body • ㄹ-Type Conjugation Review	-(으)ㄹ께요 will, O.K.?	• -고 싶어요/-고 싶어해요 wish to, want to • ㅎ 불규칙 형용사 ㅎ-irregular predicates • -어도 even if, even though • -그쵸, 그치(요)? Isn't it so? • -었 (usage)	• -어도 돼요? May I? • -(으)면 안돼요! You may not! You should not!	• -고 있어요 am/is -ing • 내내 All Time • adj -다 form (self talk) • -어 죽겠어요 dying of -고 싶어 죽겠어요 dying to • ADJ-어 해요 (describing others' feelings)	-은/는 것 같아(요) it seems like, it seems that	• -을 수 있어요/없어요 is/isn't possible • 애, 개, 재(네) he, she, they • -보다 더/덜 more/less than • …중에 제일 the most among/in… • -한테 to/for (a person)
제 5.5 장 Chapter 5.5	ㅂ 불규칙 형용사, 동사							
	Weather		Moods		Illnesses & Treatments		Travel & Nature	
	제 21 과 내일은 추울 거예요.		제 22 과 기분이 좋아질 거예요.		제 23 과 집에서 푹 쉬어야 돼요.		제 24 과 어디로 갈까요?	
제 6 장 푹 쉬어야 돼요. Chapter 6 You've got to take a good rest.	-을 거예요 it's probably	• -ㄷ 불규칙 동사 ㄷ-irregular verbs • -어/아서 그래요 it's so because • -어 줘요 (Do it) for me? • -어 보세요 try -ing, -어봤어요 have ever -ed • -(으)ㄹ께요 (*review*)	ADJ-어져요 becomes ADJ	• ADJ-어 보여요 looks ADJ • N 때문에 because of N • Time 전에 before Time • -한테서 /-에게서 from (a person) • Verb-거나 or	-어야 돼요 have got to	• -어 있어요 is ing/ed (state) • -기 명사형 to verb, verb-ing • ㅅ 불규칙 동사, 형용사 ㅅ-irregular predicates	-(으)ㄹ까요 I wonder… Shall we? Should I?	• -을 Noun Noun to verb… • -을 때 when… • -을 데 place to… • -지 않아요 not • idiomatic -어 봐요
제 6.5 장 Chapter 6.5	동물과 띠							

CPSIA information can be obtained
at www.ICGtesting.com
Printed in the USA
FSOW04n0438090916
24737FS

9 780972 835656